CONVENTION
1500–1750

CONVENTION

1500–1750

Lawrence Manley

HARVARD UNIVERSITY PRESS
*Cambridge, Massachusetts
and London, England*
1980

Library of Congress Cataloging in Publication Data

Manley, Lawrence, 1949–
    Convention, 1500–1750.

    Includes bibliographical references and index.
    1. Literature—Philosophy.   2.   Criticism—History.
I.   Title.
PN45.M343   801'.95   79-27773
ISBN 0-674-17015-6

Publication of this volume
has been aided by a grant from
the Hyder Edward Rollins Fund

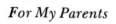

For My Parents

Acknowledgments

I am indebted to the two extraordinary teachers who directed the dissertation out of which this book has grown. Professor Craig La Drière first led me to the problem of convention at its source in antiquity. He was an exacting but charitable critic whose life enriched the early stages of this book and whose death has left it finally impoverished. From beginning to end Professor Herschel Baker has been a steady source of criticism, enlightenment, and encouragement. His exemplary work in many of the disciplines and developments touched on in this book helped me to believe it could be attempted; his patience and many sacrifices have made it easier to finish.

Ronald Bush, Gwynne Evans, and Joseph Biancalana were friendly adversaries who helped me to define the inarticulate at an early stage. A. Bartlett Giamatti, W. Speed Hill, and John M. Wands offered encouragement on portions of the manuscript when it was later sorely needed. Bernard Saint-Donat and Heinrich von Staden have tried to save me from errors in matters scientific and classical, respectively; errors that remain are mine alone. The cost of typing was defrayed by a grant from the A. Whitney Griswold Research Fund at Yale. My typists, Alberta Guise and Marianne Pearsall, best know how much they have lightened a great burden.

My greatest debts are to my parents, to whom this book is dedicated with my love, and to Ruth Handlin, whose help has been unfailing through it all.

Contents

Introduction   1

I. Art, Nature, and Convention

1. Art, Nature, and Convention   15
2. Art and Nature in Antiquity   25
3. Art and Convention in Antiquity   36
4. The Medieval Redefinition   54

II. Convention in the Sixteenth Century

1. The "Duble Name" of Custom: The Reformation Attack on
   Convention   67
2. "Use Becomes Another Nature": Custom in Sixteenth-Century
   Politics and Law   90
3. A World on Wheels: Convention in Sixteenth-Century Moral
   Philosophy   106
4. Neo-Stoic and Baconian Nature: Seventeenth-Century Prospects   133

III. Convention and the Sixteenth-Century
Arts of Speech

1. The Possibilities of Discourse: Renaissance Logic, Rhetoric,
   and Poetics   137
2. "Conveniency to Nature" and the "Secretes of Privitie": Nature and
   Convention in Defense of Poetry   158
3. The Artlessness of Art: Convention in Renaissance Poetics   175
4. "The Separation of Opinions": The Role of Convention in Criticism
   and Controversy   188

IV. Contextualism and the Role of Convention in Historiography

1. Historical Rhetoric and Historical Explanation   203
2. The Emergence of Historical Consciousness   215
3. "A Genius of Times": The Contexts of Historical Periods   226
4. "A Passable Contexture": Convention and the Practice of
   Contextualism   231

V. The Triumph of Convention

1. "A Latitude of Sense": Testing for Truth   241
2. Real and Mental Theater: The Complex of Classicism   264
3. "Betwixt Two Ages Cast": Dryden's Criticism   290
4. "These Broken Ends": Ancients, Moderns, and Modernity   321

   Index   349

The circumstances of life are only the bases or instruments of life: the fruition of life is not in retrospect, not in description of the instruments, but in expression of the spirit itself, to which those instruments may prove useful; as music is not criticism of violins, but a playing upon them.

—Santayana

NOTE ON CITATIONS

Subdivisions of original works are given in arabic numerals. References to multivolume editions are given by roman numeral for the volume and arabic numeral for the page. References to works frequently cited are incorporated in the text after a complete citation has been given in the notes. Unless otherwise indicated, quotations of classical texts are from the editions in the Loeb Classical Library, published in the United States by Harvard University Press. The following abbreviations are used in the notes:

CL	Comparative Literature	MLQ	Modern Language Quarterly
CLS	Comparative Literature Studies	MLR	Modern Language Review
		MP	Modern Philology
ES	English Studies	NLH	New Literary History
HLQ	Huntington Library Quarterly	N&Q	Notes and Queries
		PLL	Papers on Language and Literature
JAAC	Journal of Aesthetics and Art Criticism		
		PQ	Philological Quarterly
JEGP	Journal of English and Germanic Philosophy	RES	Review of English Studies
		SEL	Studies in English Literature, 1500–1900
JHI	Journal of the History of Ideas		
		SP	Studies in Philology
JWCI	Journal of the Warburg and Courtauld Institutes	SRen	Studies in the Renaissance
		UTQ	University of Toronto Quarterly
MLN	Modern Language Notes		

Introduction

The concept of convention so pervades modern thinking as to seem coeval with modernity itself. In logic, mathematics, and the natural sciences, convention has come to play a prominent role in the procedures of valid reasoning and scientific explanation. The various forms of logical and legal positivism have brought convention toward the center stage in moral and civic philosophy as well. Sometimes in tandem, sometimes at odds with what these fields have proposed for themselves, modern anthropology and social science have given special scrutiny to the irreducibly social element in virtually every human endeavor.[1] In modern literary scholarship, to which the term "conven-

1. For conventionalism in scientific logic, see W. V. Quine, "Truth by Convention," in *Philosophical Essays for Alfred North Whitehead* (London: Longman's, Green, and Co., 1936), p. 90; Quine, "Two Dogmas of Empiricism," in *From a Logical Point of View* (1961; rpt., Cambridge: Harvard University Press, 1971), pp. 20–46; Henri Poincaré, *Science and Hypothesis* (New York: Dover Publications, 1952), pp. 35–110; Pierre Duhem, *The Aim and Structure of Physical Theory*, trans. Philip Wiener (New York: Atheneum, 1962), 1.2–3 and Appendix; Karl Popper, *The Logic of Scientific Discovery* (New York: Science Editions, 1961), secs. 8, 10–11, 19–20; Popper, *Conjectures and Refutations* (1963; rpt., New York: Harper Torchbooks, 1968), ch. 3; Moritz Schlick, "Are Natural Laws Conventions?" in *Readings in the Philosophy of Science*, ed. Herbert Feigl and May Brodbeck (New York: Appleton-Century-Crofts, 1953), pp. 181–188. For morals and law, see Shia Moser, *Absolutism and Relativism in Ethics* (Springfield, Ill.: Charles C. Thomas, 1968); Helmut Schoeck and James Wiggins, ed., *Relativism and the Study of Man* (Princeton: Van Nostrand, 1961); and Carl J. Friedrich, *The Philosophy of Law in Historical Perspective* (Chicago: University of Chicago Press, 1963), ch. 18. For the social sciences, see Clifford Geertz, "The Impact of the Concept of Culture on the Concept of Man," in *The Interpretation of Cultures* (New York: Basic Books, 1973); Peter Berger and Thomas Luckmann, Introduction to *The Social Construction of Reality*

1

tion" has become nearly indispensable, the successful claims of historicism have made it less revolutionary than routine to argue that the understanding of literature requires a sense of its "context," the historical "ideals, values, commonplaces or conventions" that shape literary expression.[2] Both the variety of these developments and the complex range of issues with which convention is involved in each suggest that in our time the concept of convention has become pervasive because it is versatile.

The conceptual versatility of convention derives from the two opposing faces of conventions themselves, their tendency to behave as both timeless forms of objective order and temporal expressions of changing social values. Every sphere of human activity involves conventions to the extent that it defines and constitutes itself with reference to a patterned order of objective rules and norms at whose core lies a tacit social dimension. Such behavior has come to be called "intersubjective"; in contrast to purely natural phenomena, conventions derive their quasi-objective status and whatever normative force they have from a dynamic social dimension underlying them.[3] Not surprisingly, language has become for other forms of "intersubjectivity" the model par excellence, for language has its roots on the one hand in the nature of formal order itself, and on the other in that common consent that underlies the possibility of all communication whatsoever.[4]

The concept of convention, then, is animated by the generic tensions and interplay between the "objective" and "social" dimensions it encompasses. Historically, however, convention has emerged as a distinctive concept only where such tensions are most extreme, where the "objective" and "social" elements of order have tended to precipitate toward polar opposition, so that convention finds itself contrasted as a social phenomenon to what is more objectively either universal or unique. In fact, the universal and the unique are the two conceptual

(New York: Doubleday, 1966); and James E. Curtis and John W. Petras, Introduction to *The Sociology of Knowledge* (New York: Praeger, 1970).

2. See, e.g., Hallett Smith, *Elizabethan Poetry: A Study in Convention, Meaning, and Expression* (Cambridge: Harvard University Press, 1952), p. v.

3. The classic definition of convention as an "intersubjective" phenomenon is in Ferdinand de Saussure, *Course in General Linguistics,* trans. Wade Baskin (1959; rpt., New York: McGraw-Hill, 1966), esp. pp. 71–74. The definitive application of "intersubjectivity" in the Anglo-American critical tradition remains that of René Wellek and Austin Warren, *Theory of Literature* (New York: Harcourt Brace & World, 1956), ch. 12.

4. I here adapt to language a statement made about poetry by John Livingston Lowes, in *Convention and Revolt in Poetry* (Boston: Houghton Mifflin, 1919), p. 27.

means by which the peculiarly social character of "convention" has been distinguished from "nature." On the one hand, the universal contrasts with the conventional in a way that involves an interplay between the timeless and the temporal, the natural and the cultural bases of normative order in collective life. On the other hand, the unique contrasts with the conventional in a way that usually assumes or presupposes the cultural relativity of normative order and seeks to transcend the historicity of such order through the concrete particular or the individual.

In the linguistic arts, which are the central but not exclusive focus of this book, both of these contrasts are in some ways timeless. Each exerts a lively influence in the present through engagement with the other, but nevertheless the logical order that obtains among them is a function of the historical order in which they developed. The first is a *classical* opposition between universal nature and convention as the basis for collective order. The second, inasmuch as it assumes the failure of collective order to transcend its own historicity, may be described as a *romantic* opposition between convention and the individual.

These terms are justified by history, for the individual came to critical prominence in the Romantic period partly through the failure of classical nature to uphold collective order, or through the dissolution of this order into cultural relativity. The most important critical implication of Romantic individualism, M. H. Abrams has observed, is that "the poet has moved into the center of the critical system and taken over many of the prerogatives which had once been exercised by his readers, the nature of the world in which he found himself, and the inherited precepts and examples of his poetic art."[5] One of the main reasons for this development was a disintegration of the essentially harmonious relationships among readers, nature, and precedents that constituted the "timeless whole"[6] of classical theory. The identity between social and natural order, which prompted Pope's assertion that "Nature and Homer were . . . the same,"[7] was constantly challenged and eventually undermined by the encroachment of convention on the natural order. By divorcing both cultural values and poetic precedents

5. M. H. Abrams, *The Mirror and the Lamp: Romantic Theory and the Critical Tradition* (New York: Oxford University Press, 1953), p. 29.

6. Claudio Guillén, *Literature as System: Essays toward the Theory of Literary History* (Princeton: Princeton University Press, 1971), p. 5.

7. Pope, *An Essay on Criticism,* l. 135, in *The Poems of Alexander Pope,* ed. John Butt (New Haven: Yale University Press, 1963), p. 148. See also Northrop Frye, "Nature and Homer," in *Fables of Identity: Studies in Poetic Mythology* (New York: Harcourt Brace & World, 1963), pp. 39–51.

from the fixity of nature, convention eventually slipped between Homer and his prime authority, and engendered Thomas Blackwell's counterclaim that Homer, like other poets, "talks masterly but in his own language and proper idiom, nor mimics truly other manners than those whose originals he has practised and known."[8] It was largely in response to its exile from cultural order that nature reasserted itself dialectically against this order in the individual and the "concrete universal."

Just as the classical opposition between nature and convention in collective order historically preceded the Romantic contrast between convention and the individual, so in our own time emphasis on the "concrete universal" has generally presupposed the failure of formalism to transcend historicity and to account for the truly constitutive and determinate features of aesthetic experience. Furthermore, just as formalist attempts to isolate the universal elements of collective order from their historically plural manifestations have turned to the classical precedent of Aristotle,[9] so the critical assertion of the "concrete universal" against the historicity of convention has found its romantic impetus in Coleridge and Croce.[10]

Each of these positions has largely defined itself through opposition to the notions of social relativity and historical limitation implicit in the concept of convention. R. S. Crane, for example, proposed as the basis for a formalist account of literary order a study of the "qualities which can truly be said to be timeless . . . in the sense that they can be adequately discerned and evaluated in the light of general principles quite apart from any knowledge of their origin or historical filiation."[11] Such "natural" qualities were to be distinguished from the merely "conventional" on the grounds that

8. Thomas Blackwell, *An Inquiry into the Life and Writings of Homer,* quoted in *Eighteenth-Century Critical Essays,* ed. Scott Elledge (Ithaca: Cornell University Press, 1961), I, 563.

9. See, e.g., Northrop Frye, *Anatomy of Criticism* (1957; rpt., New York: Atheneum, 1969), p. 14; R. S. Crane, Introduction to *Critics and Criticism, Ancient and Modern* (Chicago: University of Chicago Press, 1952), pp. 12–24; and Elder Olson, "The Poetic Method of Aristotle: Its Powers and Limitations," in *Aristotle's Poetics and English Literature* (Toronto: University of Toronto Press, 1965), pp. 175–191.

10. See, e.g., W. K. Wimsatt, "Battering the Object," in *Day of the Leopards: Essays in Defense of Poems* (New Haven: Yale University Press, 1976), pp. 184, 202. See also Wimsatt, "The Chicago Critics," in *The Verbal Icon: Studies in the Meaning of Poetry* (Lexington: University of Kentucky Press, 1954), p. 49, and "The Concrete Universal," in *The Verbal Icon,* pp. 81–83.

11. R. S. Crane, "History versus Criticism in the Study of Literature" (1935), in *The Idea of the Humanities and Other Essays Critical and Historical* (Chicago: University of Chicago Press, 1967), I, 18.

"convention" denotes any characteristic of the matter or technique of a poem the reason for the presence of which cannot be inferred from the necessities of the form envisaged but must be sought in the historical circumstances of its composition—that is to say, in the habitual practice of other writers or in a prevailing opinion as to what ought to be done . . . In relation to the nature and inherent necessities of any kind of poetry a convention is thus an accidental attribute, however long-lived or influential it may be.[12]

Such attempts to elevate the ordered patterns of literature to the status of universals by excluding purely social norms presuppose some sure means of distinguishing between the social and natural, the historical and universal, the accidental and essential factors of literary order. As an intersubjective phenomenon, however, convention has tended to resist distinctions between such characteristics, because it wears the masks of both. Historically as well as logically, formalist systems have found themselves in "a continual oscillation between the description of phenomena and abstract theory."[13] The incursion of convention and historicity into system thus continues to provoke the objection that every formalist "system remains . . . an historical one" in which "conventions and genres play the role of premature ultimates."[14]

With this objection, the tensions between nature and convention within the system of literature give way to opposition between conventional literary order and the individual work. Like the various formalist systems, the individual work has been defined by opposition to the historicity of convention, and evaluated on the basis of a distinction between the social relativity of artistic conventions and the timelessness of aesthetic value, "between the contingent and what is in any

12. Crane, *The Languages of Criticism and the Structure of Poetry* (Toronto: University of Toronto Press, 1953), p. 198, n. 62.

13. Tzvetan Todorov, *The Fantastic: A Structural Approach to a Literary Genre*, trans. Richard Howard (Cleveland: Case Western Reserve University Press, 1973), pp. 13–14; see also Wellek and Warren, p. 234; and J. Craig La Drière, "Classification, Literary," in Joseph T. Shipley, *Dictionary of World Literature* (Totowa, N.J.: Littlefield, Adams, 1972), p. 64.

14. Wimsatt, "The Chicago Critics," in *The Verbal Icon*, pp. 55–56; and "Northrop Frye: Criticism as Myth," in *Day of the Leopards*, p. 93. H. P. H. Teesing similarly observes of the Chicago School that "alle zeigen ein gründliches, historisch Wissen," "The Chicago School," *Orbis Litterarum*, suppl. 2 (1958), 199. Charles McLaughlin also points to the historical basis of the neo-Aristotelian systems in "Two Views of Poetic Unity," *The University of Kansas City Review*, 22 (1956), 316.

sense necessary, probable, or ideal, between what merely *was* and what in any way *is*."[15] Though each work uses and depends upon the common formal patterns and assumptions of its time, culture, and tradition, it transcends them through its unique interpretive synthesis.

This view combines a conservative respect for the collective order with a Crocean insistence on the uniqueness of each work and a Coleridgean insistence on the work's self-contained organic character. Thus critical interrogation of the particular work always asks whether "conventional 'materials' remain conventional, or are . . . somehow rendered dramatic and moving."[16] The true poem, Allen Tate observes, like "the living person is . . . the convention plus the individual experience; the clothes in the attic are the convention alone."[17] Accordingly, as Cleanth Brooks has proposed, there must be "a distinction between the kind of understanding with which literary history usually concerns itself and the special understanding of poetic structure . . . which is vital to real appreciation."[18] What is most essential to poetic structure is "not so much determined by size, title, and genre definitions as by the value principle of variety in unity or the reconciliation of opposites."[19] The prime importance of the "concrete universal" is thus in part, at least, a product of a contrast between convention and the truly transcendent character of aesthetic experience.

Significantly, the most recent attempts to reconcile convention with natural order have come from structuralists whose "sciences of man" would deny the primacy of individual consciousness and intentionality. Their effort hinges first of all upon a frank recognition of the conventionality of cultural norms and systems, but then transcends this "chaos of discontinuity"[20] by analyzing conventions in relational rather than substantive terms. In using this method Lévi-Strauss has sought "to overcome the false opposition between . . . objectivism and the conventionalism of modern theorists."[21] His analyses have challenged the validity of this opposition by showing that while systems of cultural

15. Wimsatt, "History and Criticism," in *The Verbal Icon*, p. 253.

16. Cleanth Brooks, *The Well-Wrought Urn: Studies in the Structures of Poetry* (New York: Harcourt Brace & World, 1947), p. 98.

17. Allen Tate, "Modern Poets and Convention," in *The Forlorn Demon* (Chicago: Regnery, 1953), p. 169.

18. Brooks, "Criticism, History, and Critical Relativism," in *The Well-Wrought Urn*, p. 208.

19. Wimsatt, "The Chicago Critics," in *The Verbal Icon*, p. 51.

20. Claude Lévi-Strauss, "Structural Analysis in Linguistics and in Anthropology," in *Structural Anthropology*, trans. Claire Jacobson and Brooke Grundfest Schoepf (New York: Basic Books, 1963), p. 35.

21. Lévi-Strauss, *The Raw and the Cooked*, trans. John and Doreen Weightman (New York: Harper & Row, 1969), p. 21.

norms exhibit diversity and apparently arbitrary characteristics at an empirical level, they are universal and apparently natural at the level of relational structure.

This has produced what Lévi-Strauss has called "a *scandal,* that is to say, something which no longer tolerates the nature/culture opposition . . . and which seems to require *at one and the same time* the predicates of nature and those of culture."[22] Historically, there have always been efforts to soften the nature/convention distinction by explaining convention as an ideally "conscious or unconscious adjustment to and interpretation of nature."[23] Nevertheless, none has so fully challenged the distinction between nature and convention as the structuralist project of reintegrating "culture in nature and finally . . . life within the whole of its physico-chemical conditions."[24] From the point of view of this project, the nature/convention opposition is not so much a distinction which describes a real difference as an antinomy which conceals a contradiction.[25] This contradiction is the identity of the state of human nature with the system of social coordinates which at once determine and express it. Accordingly, the structuralist effort to "rediscover the 'natural Man' in his relation to the social state outside of which our human condition cannot be imagined"[26] seems to provide a new perspective on the conceptual history of nature and convention; it suggests that the pervasiveness of debate over convention is "congenital to philosophy,"[27] and reflects a basic embarrassment over the condition of humanity and an effort to disguise it metaphysically.

Ultimately this embarrassment falls upon the individual. The structuralist view maintains that the distinction between artificial man and natural man, or the view that the state of society succeeds a prior state of nature, "is absurd. Whoever says 'Man' says 'Language,' and whoever says 'Language' says 'Society.' "[28] The elevation of social codes

22. Lévi-Strauss, *Les structures élémentaires de la parenté,* p. 9, quoted in Jacques Derrida, "Structure, Sign, and Play in the Discourse of the Human Sciences," in *The Languages of Criticism and the Sciences of Man: The Structuralist Controversy,* ed. Richard Macksey and Eugenio Donato (Baltimore: The Johns Hopkins Press, 1970), p. 253.

23. J. Craig La Drière, "Rule," in Shipley, p. 354.

24. Lévi-Strauss, *The Savage Mind* (Chicago: University of Chicago Press, 1966), p. 247.

25. See Frederic Jameson, *The Prison-House of Language: A Critical Account of Structuralism and Russian Formalism* (Princeton: Princeton University Press, 1972), pp. 170, 213.

26. Lévi-Strauss, *Tristes tropiques,* trans. John Russell (New York: Criterion Books, 1961), p. 391.

27. Derrida, "Structure, Sign, and Play," p. 252.

28. Lévi-Strauss, *Tristes tropiques,* p. 391.

and systems to the level of universals suggests that within these codes the present and consciousness are "toujours-déjà-donnée."[29] The absorption of consciousness into the organizing structures of codes thus entails the abolition of the distinction between self and world, and hence implies a radical critique of the Cartesian *cogito*. The self "comes to appear more and more as a construct, the result of systems of convention."[30] Thus, Lévi-Strauss observes, "the goal of the human sciences is not to constitute man but to dissolve him."[31]

THE CONFRONTATION of the individual with a world of predetermined codes and values is part of our post-Romantic heritage. Although this confrontation was in certain ways anticipated in antiquity,[32] the utter incompatibility of collective order with the individual was not then seriously at issue. Rather, within the framework of an order-centered and collectively minded world, the principal concern was with the difference between natural patterns and social ones, between those which were universal or permanent and those which were merely arbitrary or temporary. Collective patterns and norms, in other words, were valued for their conformity to permanent principles of rectitude and fitness. Accordingly, the task of critics and philosophers alike consisted in the separation of arbitrary values from natural ones within the context of a code-centered natural world, a logocentric or divine text.

If it seems impossible for us to imagine such a world, or to understand it as more than the temporary domination of a specific social code over the minds of individuals, we should remember that neither are we conscious of ourselves as individuals except through opposition to collective order. We are not likely to imagine our collective life as a preexisting order into which we are born in order to reach the fullness of our being; rather, we will be disposed to see collective life as a constellation of conventions created to protect our individual rights and aspirations, which both ideally and historically precede it.

Our opposition to convention is in this respect a post-Romantic issue. Harry Levin, for example, has argued that in the Romantic period "the recognition of convention . . . historically coincided with its re-

---

29. Jameson, quoting Louis Althusser and Derrida, in *The Prison-House of Language*, p. 184.

30. Jonathan Culler, *Structuralist Poetics* (Ithaca: Cornell University Press, 1975), p. 29; see also Jameson, *The Prison-House of Language*, pp. 134–135, 139–140.

31. Lévi-Strauss, quoted in Culler, *Structuralist Poetics*, p. 28.

32. See, e.g., Thomas McFarland, "The Originality Paradox," *NLH*, 5 (1974), 447–476.

pudiation."[33] Levin and others have traced this repudiation to the growth of individualism and to the corresponding aesthetic ideals of sensibility and creative originality. The success of these ideals, however, was in part prepared by the collapse of an older order that preceded them. The emergence of the individual, in other words, was prompted by a critique to which the classical order had always subjected its own conventional elements, but which was now beginning to undermine the normative authority of that very order.

This is why Romantic individuation so frequently expressed itself as a necessary alienation from collective order: the Romantic individual depended for his existence upon a conceptual opposition between convention and the true, ideal, or universal. This conceptual dependency reflected a real and verbal dependency arising from the painful quest for poetic originality; the poet could be conscious of his individuality only through oppositional relation to others. What Coleridge called the task of "awakening the mind's attention from the lethargy of custom"[34] entailed a hateful dependency upon what Shelley called "the code of custom's lawless law"[35] and required a struggle against "the intertexture of conventional expressions."[36] The poet's search for authenticity, in other words, assumed the failure of collective or traditional order to embody the ideal. The conscious possibility of such a failure, however, preceded modern consciousness of the individual, and expressed itself in a major classical dialectic—a normative conflict between nature and convention as the test of fitness in the arts.

This conflict took place within the framework of what we may call the "technical" tradition. From the time of their formal inception in classical antiquity, and through the later Renaissance, the various practical and productive arts were governed by the abstract concept of art (Gr. *techne;* Lat. *ars*) as an intellectual habit that guides all proper human action and production. This concept involved two assumptions: first, that intellectual acts and products differed from works of chance by observing and embodying certain basic relations of fitness—of matter to form, means to ends, parts to wholes; and second, that the means to fitness could be specified as artistic principles or precepts. Taken together, these two assumptions produced the prescriptive outlook of the

33. Harry Levin, "Notes on Convention," in *Perspectives of Criticism* (Cambridge: Harvard University Press, 1950), p. 67.

34. Coleridge, *Biographia Literaria*, ed. John Shawcross (Oxford: Clarendon Press, 1907), II, 6.

35. Shelley, *The Witch of Atlas*, 62.5.

36. Shelley, *A Defense of Poetry*, in *The Complete Works*, ed. Roger Ingpen and Walter E. Peck (1926–1930); rpt., New York: Gordian Press, 1965), VII, 136.

"technical" tradition and implied that each field of human endeavor was distinguished by and describable in terms of its own constituent aims, rules, and procedures. Manifesting itself in the form of technical handbooks on politics, morals, law, and the fine arts, this outlook dominated both the philosophy and pedagogy of human activity until the later Renaissance.

At the same time, however, this basic outlook encompassed considerable diversity in approaches taken toward the arts, largely because of a conflict over the principles at its normative center. The very possibility of artistic prescription assumed not only that a general and abstract test or principle of fitness could generate and organize the norms of a particular art, but also that this principle could stand in abstract justification of the whole normative approach. This assumption, however, frequently produced uncertainty, and sometimes open dispute. Because the technical aim of shaping human activity on the basis of universal norms was balanced by a need to adapt activity to its temporal and intersubjective setting, the competition between these needs expressed itself in principle as a conflict between nature and convention as alternative tests of fitness.

On the one hand, each of these alternatives derived its force and meaning through a continual dialectic with the other, and together they provoked and animated discussions of the function and value of civilization itself. Until the later Renaissance, the various philosophic oppositions of nature and culture, or of nature and art, tended to hinge upon a deeper distinction between nature and convention, and ultimately between rational and voluntary human powers (I.1).[37] Human arts and practices tended to be valued, in other words, not as conscious and deliberate efforts opposed to what man does without forethought, but as the product of human right reason in conformity with natural law and opposed to what man does merely willfully, arbitrarily, and habitually. From within the technical tradition itself, the value, necessity, and power of human artifice was assumed, so that the debate between nature and culture was not a debate between the preconscious and the conscious, or between the nonhuman and the human, but between the universal and the conventional in the matrix of a fully humanized world. The opportunities for balance and interplay between these principles produced in the mature forms of classicism a highly complex aggregate capable of a variety of emphases. In part, therefore, the history of thought about the arts until the later Renaissance is the

37. Roman numerals in parentheses in the following summary refer to chapters and sections in this book.

history of a continuous dialectical relationship between nature and convention, in which each was repeatedly opposed, adjusted, and re-adjusted in changing configurations with the other.

On the other hand, the continuous dialectic between these concepts resulted in a major change in their relationship, so that convention gradually displaced nature from the normative center of the technical tradition. The threat of this displacement had long preoccupied the technical tradition, beginning with the conventionalist antagonism of the Sophists. Their derivation of the concept of convention from a nominalist linguistic model, and their systematic application of it to the fields of politics and law, first demonstrated the philosophic threat convention posed to the technical tradition as a whole (I.2). Plato's response to this threat contrasted nature and convention in terms that subsequently defined the rival claims of the ancient rhetorical and philosophical schools.[38] The focus of the one upon the plurality of changing social values, and hence upon prudence and the multiple precedents of history, and the focus of the other upon the integrity of universal principles, and hence upon wisdom and the unity of philoso-phy, helped to delineate the alternative technical emphases available to the Middle Ages and the Renaissance (I.3–4). Given these alterna-tives, the Renaissance witnessed a gradual displacement of the philo-sophic bias by a rhetorical one, and an increasingly frequent substitu-tion of convention for nature as an adequate test of rectitude and fit-ness. The result of this transition was a major redefinition of man's right life within the sphere of culture, and a corresponding revision of the order and techniques for the study of human things.

In morals, politics, and law, this revision eventually took shape as a growing skepticism toward the value of the normative approach itself, and as a corresponding development of historical and comparative techniques designed to reinterpret human activity in the empirical and relativistic context of different social settings. Civic and rhetorical hu-manists sought to rehabilitate the human will in such a way as to le-gitimize the collective social will as well. As a result, legal philosophy developed increasingly empirical and historical habits of "presumptive" and retrospective reasoning; laws were increasingly interpreted as con-ventional projections of the collective will, and were increasingly justi-fied in terms of their merely relative "convenience" to social circum-stances (II.1–2). Reinforced by a developing strain of epistemological skepticism and an increasingly pervasive sense of mutability, these legal

38. See Richard Lanham, *The Motives of Eloquence: Literary Rhetoric in the Renaissance* (New Haven: Yale University Press, 1976), ch. 1.

and moral developments helped to undermine the technical tradition by confronting the presumed universality of prescribed norms with the variety and mutability of social values (II.3–4).

In keeping with the isomorphic structure of the technical tradition, a similar transformation occurred in the verbal arts. Tensions between nature and convention were embedded in the very structure of the Renaissance technical legacy and were exacerbated by difficulties in adapting the supposedly natural norms of classical technique to the special rhetorical demands of the European setting (III.1–2). Through the prominence of rhetorical thinking, these difficulties resulted in an increased emphasis upon the social and relative character of poetic norms (III.3), and in the first anticipations of comparative and historical criticism (III.4).

These new approaches challenged the normative framework by subjecting it to the contingencies of experience. The tensions between reason and experience implicit in this challenge resulted in the elevation of historical thinking from a position where, as ancillary to philosophy, it had merely provided examples in support of philosophic norms, to a point where, as rival to philosophy, it demonstrated that the values by which men live are largely conventional (IV.1). The concept of convention figured with increasing prominence as both a datum and an instrument of historical thinking (IV.2); and by emphasizing the conventional basis of civilized life, the reciprocal influence of historical theory and techniques (IV.3–4) helped to supplant the philosophic contemplation of man's natural ends with a scientific scrutiny of his social beginnings.

This retrospective turn to origins formed the counterpart of an inward turn to mind itself. The preoccupation of the later Renaissance with epistemology, like its growing interest in historiography, was prompted by normative debate and was intended to resolve conflicting claims on novel scientific grounds. In seventeenth-century England, the new "endeavor to find out truth"[39] was inspired by the practical aims of political moderates and religious latitudinarians, who sought to legitimize differences in norms and opinions by attributing the test of truth to the subjective assent of the individual mind. Accordingly, they distinguished between the greater certainty established by universal assent, and the merely relative, provisional, and lesser certainty upheld by the limited consensus of differing societies or groups (V.1). While the theory of assent was thus in part an objective theory of natural law that reaffirmed the older technical ideal of collective order, it was also

---

39. Jeremy Taylor, *A Discourse of the Liberty of Prophesying*, in *The Whole Works* (London, 1822), VII, 440.

a subjectivist theory that contrasted social consensus to the individual. In its later stages, then, the normative conflict between nature and convention was coextensive with a novel debate about the origins of knowledge.

This overlap accounts for the ambiguous and complex character of European classicism in its mature phase (V.2). Mature classicism encompassed at one threshold the ancient language of legalism, and at the other a novel dialectic in which a rationalist insistence on the noumenal grounds of fitness, certainty, and rectitude was balanced by empirical claims for their changing social, historical, and psychological contexts. Thus while the legalism of the classical complex was framed by ancient technical alternatives, it was increasingly animated by a new insistence on the powers of the human mind. In other words, classicism as a whole continued to embrace differing normative emphases, but these were increasingly polarized by a developing conflict between scientifically alternative views of mind—views archetypally represented by Hobbes and Descartes. These new alternatives helped to undermine the normative tradition altogether, and to furnish some of the argumentative bases for Romanticism. But while the new content of these alternatives was decisive, their purpose was representative, and they are rightly understood as extensions of the technical crises they sought to resolve.

The transitional character of mature classicism, as exemplified perhaps best by Dryden's criticism, was thus a product of the novel tensions and impulses that its ancient terms embraced. The growing prominence of convention as a test of technical fitness had turned the contemplation of natural ends toward a critical analysis of their social origins and specifications in time, and Dryden's efforts to relate artistic norms to their human setting was based in part upon the novel methods being developed in all the human sciences as a result of challenges to their normative framework (V.3). Since they insisted on the relativity of nonscientific knowledge, these methods marked a decisive turning point between the ancient and modern views of man (V.4). By subjecting human acts and products to their changing historical and social contexts, they not only denied the ancient claims of the normative tradition, but also subjected the arts to the critical scrutiny of scientific method. This scrutiny was a necessary corollary to the exhaustion of normative order by the concept of convention. Not surprisingly, the opposition of Romantic individualism to convention was coeval with its fears that scientific method threatened man himself. The sundering of nature from social order, and the growing split between historical priority and normative authority, helped to provide a space for the individual's communion with nature. As absolutes surrendered to convention and historicity, an ancient dialectic opened onto the threshold of another.

To study the concept of convention between 1500 and 1750 is therefore to study at once not only the end of one tradition in the human sciences and the beginning of another, but also an enduring conflict between alternative views of man, his works, and his setting. As Harry Levin has said, to look beyond the term "convention" is "to pursue an idea so comprehensive and so ubiquitous that, in full justice to it, the history of criticism ought some day to be rewritten."[40] While necessarily falling short of full justice, I have chosen to examine the period 1500–1750 because I believe it is the most decisive period in this larger history. In part, therefore, this study is a general survey of the beginnings of literary criticism in England, but its particular point of view is designed to demonstrate a major change in ways of thinking about man's work in general. I have tried to show that this change was neither a minor shift between basically compatible "perspectives" nor an inevitable "progress" toward an enlightened or correct model, but one outcome of a vital dialectic between philosophical alternatives whose claims are not yet fully resolved.

Accordingly, I have tried to set literary developments within the context of a much larger debate over the function and value of convention in the life of man. In so doing, I have meant to demonstrate how this debate affected the shape of intellectual history, and to show how one aspect of Romantic thought was an outcome of a self-inflicted critique within the mature forms of classicism. Consequently, this study is also in part an essay on the end of classicism, and it interprets this end as a transition between ancient and modern views of man's relation to his civilized setting.

40. Levin, "Notes on Convention," p. 72.

I. Art, Nature,
and Convention

1. Art, Nature, and Convention

From antiquity through the later Renaissance, the concept of convention was part of a technical complex whose most comprehensive terms were Art and Nature. Every sphere of human activity was in part a "technical" sphere whose constituent aims, rules, and procedures drew prescriptive force and vitality from a creative interplay between the powers of nature and artifice. Thus, in keeping with traditional demands imposed by the very title of his *Arte of English Poesie* (1589), George Puttenham concluded his treatise by asking "how arte should be used in all respects . . . in what cases the artificiall is more commended than the natural, and contrariwise."[1] In the course of his inquiry, Puttenham compares the several ways in which the powers and functions of human artifice relate to the forms and processes of external nature. In its various capacities as ancilla, mime, midwife, and rival to nature, artifice gives shape to a wide range of human activities, from gardening and carpentry to dancing and smithery. Nature, as the source and environment of man, and art, as the source of his productions and practices, form a basic conceptual framework so broad as to include not only the arts proper, but also the different ways in which men live. Puttenham's inquiry is in this respect representative of his age, for as parts of a basic framework the concepts of nature and art, as Edward Tayler points out, "encompass the totality of specifically human experience as it was understood by Renaissance thinkers."[2]

What most distinguishes this pervasive framework is its complexity. Like many of his contemporaries, Puttenham entertains on the subject of art a variety of views that in other circumstances might seem con-

1. George Puttenham, *The Arte of English Poesie,* ed. Gladys Doidge Willcock and Alice Walker (Cambridge: Cambridge University Press, 1936), p. 298.
2. Edward Tayler, *Nature and Art in Renaissance Literature* (New York: Columbia University Press, 1964), p. 21.

15

tradictory. All the differing capacities of artifice, some of which taken alone appear to contradict nature, unite in the poet's art to form the perfect complement and servant to nature (pp. 306–307). Art and nature thus define a conceptual field of play that Puttenham shares with Perdita and Polixenes, whose remarkable dialogue in *The Winter's Tale* hinges upon a similarly complex interplay between elaborate artifice and the sustaining power of nature. In answer to Perdita's reluctance to cultivate the "gillyvor," which in its pied beauty rivals great creating nature, Polixenes offers the more than witty solution that even such rival art harmonizes with nature:

> over that art
> Which you say adds to nature, is an art
> That nature makes. You see, sweet maid, we marry
> A gentler scion to the wildest stock,
> To make conceive a bark of baser kind
> By bud of nobler race. This is an art
> Which does mend nature—change it rather—but
> The art itself is nature.
>
> (4.4.92–99)

The key to such paradoxes, of course, is the conception of nature itself as both producer and product of art: "By an order the whole worke of Nature, and the perfite state of all the Elements have their appointed course," Thomas Wilson explains in *The Arte of Rhetorique;* "By an order wee devise, wee learne and frame our doings to good purpose."[3] The logocentric universe of the Renaissance assumed a firm analogy between cosmic order and artistic principle, and came to bear with special force upon the verbal arts through the virtual identity of ordered principle, reason, and speech. "The order of God's creatures in themselves is not only admirable and glorious," says John Hoskins, "but eloquent; then he that could apprehend the consequence of things in their truth and utter his apprehensions as truly were a right orator."[4] Accordingly, as Ben Jonson observes, the arts of speech "accommodate all they invent to the use, and service of nature."[5]

Puttenham's questions about external nature and human artifice, however, are equally questions about the habit of art within man him-

---

3. Thomas Wilson, *The Arte of Rhetorique,* ed. G. H. Mair (Oxford: Clarendon Press, 1909), p. 157.

4. John Hoskins, *Directions for Speech and Style,* ed. Hoyt T. Hudson, Princeton University Studies in English, 12 (Princeton: Princeton University Press, 1935), p. 2.

5. Ben Jonson, *Timber, Or Discoveries,* in *Works,* ed. C. H. Hereford and Percy and Evelyn Simpson (Oxford: Clarendon Press, 1947), VIII, 609–610.

self, for man is the creature of both nature and artifice. The capacity for language, Puttenham remarks, "is given by nature to man," but "speeche it selfe is artificiall and made by man" (p. 8). That is, within "the habite, or the Art,"[6] and quite apart from the powers of external nature, there remains the important question of whether man's artistic efforts are subject to his own rational and deliberate control, or governed only by the inarticulate power of innate ability. In addition to the *natura* that constitutes the external sphere in which man works artistically, there is the *ingenium* that moves him, as individual, to work.

The relation of *ingenium* to *ars* is a common topic in Renaissance literary criticism, and whatever the extent to which individual thinkers endorse the "poeticall Rapture," there is a consensus that "no doctrine will doe good, where nature is wanting."[7] Nonetheless, as in the comparison of external nature with artifice, the relation of artistic control to inspiration or talent within the purely human habit of art is almost unanimously characterized as a complementary one. Renaissance critics "always write on the basis of an unquestioned assumption of the value of controlled form."[8] Thus Puttenham's aim in writing a technical "art," as Gregory Smith points out, "is to bring order into the literary chaos . . . Poetry cannot be good unless it show the discipline of Art. This admitted, it was the function of criticism to teach that discipline."[9] The precepts of art therefore serve to "helpe our neede, such as by Nature have not such plentiful gifts."[10] Jonson neatly summarizes this view when he observes that "without Art, Nature can ne'er bee perfect; &, without Nature, Art can clayme no being" (*Works,* VIII, 639).

It is usually in such complementary relationships as these that the conceptual pair, art and nature, make their frequent appearances in Renaissance literary criticism. But while together they account for the relations drawn between natural process and human artifice, and between inspiration and formal technique within human artifice, they leave unresolved a major question about the essence of formal control designated as "art." The terms "nature" and "art" cannot themselves account fully for the difference between a habit of *ars* whose norms

6. Jonson, VIII, 636.

7. Jonson, VIII, 637, 584.

8. Madeleine Doran, *Endeavors of Art* (Madison: University of Wisconsin Press, 1954), p. 16; see also Hiram Haydn, *The Counter-Renaissance* (New York: Scribner's, 1950), ch. 8, "The Counter-Renaissance and the Nature of Nature."

9. G. Gregory Smith, *Elizabethan Critical Essays* (1904; rpt., Oxford University Press, 1967), I, xxxiv.

10. Thomas Wilson, p. 159.

derive from nature and one whose norms do not. The concept of convention can. Polixenes' comparison of nature and art should therefore be understood in the light of Shakespeare's introduction of a third concept in the prologue to Act 4—the concept of convention. The pastoral scene that frames the discussion of nature and art is itself framed, not only by the artifice of the Bohemian court, but by the artifice of drama as well. This last fact is emphasized when the allegorical persona of Time appears to announce the violation of a dramatic unity:

> it is in my pow'r
> To o'erthrow law, and in one self-born hour
> To plant, and o'erwhelm custom.
>
> (4.1.7–9)

Implicitly, this interlude poses an important distinction between the art that produces "gillyvors" and the art that produces drama. Ideally, of course, both are compatible with nature and natural process; but in fact, it would seem, some dramas are more purely governed by conventions that come to live or die with an afternoon's fare. Through the power of time, "custom" is linked decisively with its social setting.

The addition of this third term to the framework accounts in large measure for the many and complex views of art and nature in the Renaissance. Edward Tayler has maintained that although the fundamental distinction between nature and art "crops up in many other and related terms—usually in controversies opposing the natural and universal to the customary and conventional . . . —the two categories are most often subsumed by the terms Nature and Art" (p. 25). It would be more accurate to say, however, that the concept of convention represents a third and distinct term in Renaissance speculation about nature and art, because it frequently appears as such. In attempting to define the status of the poetic art, both Minturno and Jonson use not two but three basic terms:

> If the Art of Poetry handed down to us by Aristotle and Horace according to the example of poetry is true, I do not see how another art, different from that, can be legitimate; for truth is one, and what is true at one time must necessarily be true in every age, nor does time have power to change it, as it changes our lives and customs.[11]

11. Minturno, *L'arte poetica* (1564), p. 33, trans. Harold S. Wilson, in "Some Meanings of 'Nature' in Renaissance Literary Theory," *JHI*, 2 (1941), 432. Cf. A. O. Lovejoy, " 'Nature' as Aesthetic Norm," *MLN*, 42 (1927), 444–450.

> Whatsoever Nature at any time dictated to the most happy
> or long exercise to the most laborious; that the Wisdom and
> Learning of Aristotle hath brought into an Art; because,
> he understood the Causes of things; and what other men did
> by chance or custom, he doth by reason.[12]

In these instances, the concept of convention is not being "sub-sumed" under the categories of nature and art; rather, the concept of "art" is itself being measured on the one hand against values perceived to be natural and rational and on the other hand against values that are merely conventional or arbitrary. Puttenham clearly has such a distinction in mind when he observes that "all artes grew firste by observation of nature's proceeding and custom" (p. 128). This distinction between nature and convention greatly complicates the concept of art and the character of its formal control. Without some further theoretical specification, it remains unclear whether art owes more to nature or convention, reason or experience; whether its principles are to be derived through theoretical or historical investigation; and whether the application of such principles is universally binding and valid or relative only to particular social or historical circumstances. Many of the major differences in Renaissance views of art hinge upon this important distinction between norms rationally derived from nature and norms conventionally received from tradition or prudentially derived from historical and contemporary circumstance.

Such a distinction, for instance, pervades Tasso's discussion of artistic unity in his *Discorsi*. Some artistic techniques are "in their nature neither good nor bad, since they depend on custom," while others are "either good or bad in themselves, and custom has no rule or authority over them." These latter are dictated by nature, whose "mode of working is always the same." Following the precedent of Cicero's *Topics*, Tasso enumerates "nature and art among the causes that are unchangeable, for their effects are invariable." While he qualifies this assertion by admitting the influence of convention upon *ars* through diction and "things that depend on custom, as the manner of jousting, the customs of sacrifices and banquets, ceremonies, and the dignity and decorum of persons," he excludes from the "tyranny of convention" such "constant causes" as the unity of plot. His justification for so doing is the identity of art with nature: "Aristotle professes to teach only those things that fall within the realm of art; and since art is fixed and determined, nothing can be comprehended within its rules which, being dependent on the instability of custom, is mutable and uncertain

---

12. Jonson, VIII, 641.

. . . he would not have discussed unity of plot if he had not thought it necessary in every age. But while some wish to found a new art on new custom, they destroy the nature of art and show that they do not know that of custom."[13]

This distinction between natural and conventional norms within the formal and technical discipline of *ars* is paralleled by the sometimes conflicting claims of rational precept and personal experience upon the artist himself. The commonplace prerequisites of the artist—genius, art, exercise, imitation, and study—appear to follow the nature/art dichotomy because they distinguish between the innate and the acquired aspects in the agent's habit of art. At the same time, however, the addition of "exercise" and "imitation" to "art" expresses a tension between theory and practice. Richard Mulcaster, for example, maintains that an *ars* weds reason with custom, the natural with the conventional, the rational with the practical.[14] Roger Ascham similarly suspends *ars* in a continuum whose extremes are rational nature and practice.[15] These same extremes characterize Jonson's analysis of different kinds of artists into those who follow nature ("whatsoever Nature dictated to the most happy") and those who follow convention ("whatsoever long exercise dictated to the most laborious . . . what other men did by custom"). *Ars* is a comprehensive term, which must somehow take account of both sources of norms; it is to be derived not only from the rational order of nature, but also from the traditional demands set by practice and imitation.

The combination of these demands helps to explain the varied emphases of Renaissance literary criticism. On the one hand, art aims for the abiding integrity of nature. There is, as Sidney claims, "no art delivered to mankind that hath not the works of Nature for his principal object, without which they could not consist, and on which they depend, as they become actors and players, as it were, of what Nature will have set forth."[16] On the other hand, art is practical; as such, it must yield to the particular, diverse, and therefore less reliable aspects of human experience. "There are some things," says Castelvetro, "that reason shows to be of great efficacy in the art, but which experience shows of little efficacy." In such cases, reason must give place to ex-

13. Tasso, *Discorsi*, trans. Allan H. Gilbert, *Literary Criticism, Plato to Dryden* (New York: American Book Co., 1940), pp. 496–498.

14. Richard Mulcaster, *The First Part of the Elementarie* (Menston, Eng.: Scolar Press, 1970), p. 74.

15. Roger Ascham, *The Scolemaster*, ed. Edward Arber (London: Constable, 1923), p. 155.

16. Sir Philip Sidney, *An Apology for Poetry*, ed. Geoffrey Shepherd (London: Nelson's Medieval Renaissance Library, 1965), pp. 99–100.

perience, "which is the strongest proof that can be brought forward in the arts and the one to which in dealing with the arts we should alone give heed; we ought not to doubt at all, *even though reason induces us to believe otherwise.*"[17]

Accordingly, it is a frequent commonplace of Renaissance criticism that the practice of art precedes its theoretical formulation, that "eloquence it selfe came not firste by the arte, but the arte was gathered upon eloquence."[18] Thus, while art is conscious, systematized, and characterized by a "step up" from practice to principle, it retains its attachment to experience: "as there was no art in the world till by experience found out: so if Poesie be now an Art & of al antiquitie hath bene among the Greekes and Latines, & yet were none, until by studious persons fashioned and reduced into a method of rules & precepts, then no doubt there may be the like with us."[19] So powerful is the exemplary effect of practice itself that William Webbe, for example, doubts whether any formal *ars* is needed: "Surely it is to be thought that if any one . . . should put foorth some famous worke, contayning dyvers forms of true verses . . . it would of it selfe be sufficient authority, without any prescription of rules, to the most part of Poets for them to follow and by custome to ratify."[20] The power of "custome to ratify" poetic norms thus implies potential skepticism toward the rational "prescription of rules." There are, says Jonson, "many diverse opinions of an Art," so that "rules are ever of lesse force, and valew, then experiments" (*Works,* VIII, 617). Jonson's untiring insistence upon practice, his demand that the writer "bring all to the forge" (VIII, 637), suggests that the achievements of art are not to be discovered in the cool light of reason, but wrought in the fires of experience. This skeptical outlook not only reinforces the power of experiment, but enhances the claims of collective experience and tradition to sovereignty over the habit of *ars.* As the gradual articulation of long and arduous practice, the collective norms of custom and tradition represent an immense fund of practical wisdom. For this reason Samuel Daniel not only rejects the rationalistic speculation "of these great Schollers" whose "hie knowledges doe but give them more eyes to looke out into uncertaintie and confusion," but also follows Montaigne in walking "the plaine tract I finde beaten by Custome and the Time, contenting me with what I see in use."[21]

---

17. Ludovico Castelvetro, *Poetria,* in Allan H. Gilbert, pp. 349–350; my italics.
18. Thomas Wilson, p. 5.
19. Puttenham, p. 5.
20. William Webbe, *A Discourse of English Poetry,* in G. Gregory Smith, I, 279.
21. Samuel Daniel, *A Defense of Rhyme,* in G. Gregory Smith, II, 374.

Acquiescence in "use," or in the ways of tradition, was by no means always incompatible with the view that the arts derive ultimately from universal nature. Indeed, the commonplace that "to follow Virgil is to follow nature" demonstrates the ease with which adherence to tradition could be identified with adherence to nature and the extent to which the collective social order could be virtually synonymous with the natural order. In such cases, the difficulty of direct intellectual access to natural principle formed no impediment to ultimate adherence to nature through tradition and trial. "Nature hath not stirred some," Wilson remarks, "yet through the experience that man hath, concerning his commoditie: many have turned the lawe of nature into an ordinarie custome, and followed the same as though they were bound to it by a lawe" (p. 32). In this manner norms dictated by tradition and convention are brought into harmony with the demands of reason: "that is right by custome, which long time hath confirmed, being partly grounded upon nature, & partly upon reason" (p. 34).

This last point, however, marks a major source of controversy in Renaissance thought. Despite the inclination to identify nature with collective social norms, both individual experience and the collective experience of tradition are characterized by diversity and complexity. How can the variety of opinion and practice be reconciled with nature, which is one and unchanging? What assurance does one have that convention is not merely arbitrary and changeful, a mere reflection of "the times"? "Do you not know," asks Castiglione, "that figures of speech . . . are all the abuse of Grammer rules, and yet are received and confirmed by use, because men are *able to make no other reason* than that they delite?"[22] Given the sometimes arbitrary character of convention, there arises the danger of "turning nature's lyght, into blinde custome."[23] Chaucer, Surrey, and Wyatt, says Roger Ascham, fell short of excellence, having been "caryed by tyme and custome, to content themselves with the barbarous and rude Rhyming."[24]

In such cases, convention seems to stand opposed to nature in principle and by definition. Arbitrary, mutable, and socially contagious, convention can differ radically from the rational and abiding integrity of nature as a measure of artistic fitness. This difference is implicit in a number of literary issues and controversies in the Renaissance, and indeed to some degree in the terminology of Renaissance criticism it-

---

22. Baldassare Castiglione, *The Book of the Courtier,* trans. Sir Thomas Hoby (1561), ed. W. H. D. Rouse (New York: Everyman's Library, 1928), p. 60; my italics.

23. Thomas Wilson, pp. 33–34.

24. Ascham, *Scolemaster,* p. 145.

self. When Gabriel Harvey, for example, introduced the Ramist "method" of literary imitation to England in his *Ciceronianus* (1577), he clearly had in mind the claims of reason as against the inarticulate counterclaims of use, experience, and tradition. Unlike the copy and commonplace technique of such humanists as Erasmus, Sturm, and Ascham, the Ramist alternative possesses what Harvey calls the "resplendant glory of Method."[25] Instead of merely following the social precedent of linguistic and rhetorical tradition, this rational method observes the "fundamental principle of tracing causes and not merely effects" (p. 73), and thus resolves rhetorical conventions into universal principles of discourse.

The deeper implications of Harvey's claims on behalf of "method" fully emerge, however, only when Harvey's printer, William Lewin, subjects the term to scrutiny in his prefatory letter. He draws upon the etymology of Harvey's catchword in order to turn its meaning to different account: "just as there usually may be found many ways to climb the same hill and various paths to the same city, likewise there are diverse routes and many roads leading to eloquence. Crassus did not take the same road as Antinous, nor does Harvey go, I believe, the same way as others" (p. 39). Against the power of reason to cut a direct route to achievement, Lewin more tolerantly poses the multiplicity of well-worn and conventional paths. His metaphor aptly seizes upon a point of difference between the normative claims of universal nature and those of collective experience and conventional practice. By confronting Harvey's use of "method" with its semantic origins (Gr. *hodos* = "way"), Lewin also confronts the rigid rationalism of the Ramist short cut with its pluralistic alternative—the gradual and inarticulate establishment of a path through use and repetition. Far from being an ad hoc invention of the Renaissance, this conceptual contrast reflects a fundamental difference—at times a fundamental opposition—between two modes of thought that pose alternative views of man, his setting, and the source and value of his activities and productions. One of these views places the source of order and regularity in universal, natural principles, and the other places it in established social usages and customs. One source articulates its principles through discursive reason; the other articulates them through tradition.

25. Gabriel Harvey, *Ciceronianus* (1577), ed. Harold S. Wilson, trans. Clarence A. Forbes, University of Nebraska Studies in the Humanities, 4 (1945), p. 90. For explanation of the Ramist procedure of imitation, see Walter J. Ong, *Ramus, Method, and the Decay of Dialogue* (Cambridge: Harvard University Press, 1958), p. 264.

In certain respects these alternatives are timeless, and might be said to mark one difference between the civilizations of Jerusalem and Athens. The Old Testament lacks a word for "nature," the closest equivalents being words which mean "way" or "custom."[26] "Prior to the discovery of nature, men knew that each kind of thing had its 'way' or 'custom'—its form of regular behavior."[27] The equivalent for adherence to nature is thus adherence to the ancient or ancestral "way."[28] The guidance for man's right life is not to be found by reason, but by obedience to revealed and received practices. Coincident with this attitude is a strong sense of national identity and an appeal to national tradition and covenants.[29] In such identification of nature with tradition, suffering and natural disaster appear as the consequences of violating ancestral "ways." Even God's knowledge of his creation is not a knowledge of its "nature," but of its "ways."[30]

In contradistinction to this tradition stands the Greek "discovery of nature"—the discovery that "the whole of the surrounding world of which our senses give us any knowledge is natural."[31] Unlike the Old Testament concept of the "way," however, the Greek concept of nature seems to depend for its existence upon a dialectical contrast with some concept of social or traditional norms. Indeed, it seems proper to regard these two intellectual traditions as "alternatives" only within the framework of Greco-Roman thought itself, where, despite various attempts at combination and resolution, the natural and the social have always tended to presuppose each other as opposites. In Parmenides, for example, the discovery of nature involves a distinction between what is known veridically and what is known by report, tradition, opinion, or

26. See Leo Strauss, *Natural Right and History* (Chicago: University of Chicago Press, 1950), ch. 3; *The Jerome Biblical Commentary*, ed. R. E. Brown, J. A. Fitzmeyer, and R. E. Murphy (Englewood Cliffs: Prentice-Hall, 1968), 77:47–49; and *The New Bible Dictionary*, ed. J. D. Douglas (Grand Rapids: Eerdmans, 1962), pp. 869–870.

27. Strauss, *The History of Political Philosophy* (Chicago: Rand McNally, 1963), p. 3.

28. See, e.g., Jeremiah 6:16, Isaiah 43:16, and the commentary on Jeremiah of Stanley Romaine Hopper in *The Interpreter's Bible*, ed. George A. Buttrick (New York: Abingdon Press, 1962), V, 862–865.

29. Karl Popper, *The Open Society and Its Enemies* (1945; rpt., London: George Routledge and Sons, 1947), I, 7, 50–52.

30. Job 28:23, 26; see E. J. Bicknell, "Introduction to the Wisdom Literature," in *A New Commentary on Holy Scripture*, ed. Charles Gore, H. L. Goudge, and A. Guillaume (New York: Macmillan, 1928), pp. 307–311.

31. Francis M. Cornford, *Before and after Socrates* (1932; rpt., Cambridge: Cambridge University Press, 1965), p. 8.

belief.[32] This view presupposes that what *is* truly and always differs from traditional and purely practical ways. "Nature," says Heraclitus, "is wont to hide herself" (frag. 10). Nature's favorite hiding place, according to Parmenides, is in the differing beliefs, practices, and experiences of men. It is the task of science to penetrate the veils of the Way of Seeming, and to reveal the first principles beneath changing phenomena in the Way of Truth. Yet to the mind of Parmenides, these two sources of knowledge have not been fully distinguished. Substituting a mythopoetic vocabulary for a technical one, Parmenides speaks of the Way of Truth in terms of revelation. The key to knowledge of the truth is neither an art nor a science, but a "way [*hodos*]" revealed by the goddess Ananke" (*Proem,* ll. 2, 5, 27).[33]

While Parmenides does not distinguish between these kinds of knowledge in a technical sense, his distinction between the two on the grounds of veracity anticipates the test that will later be brought to bear upon the concept of *ars.* This test is implicit in the two principal perspectives—the rhetorical and the philosophic—from which the Renaissance draws its concept of art. The often fruitful coexistence of these perspectives within the ancient technical tradition, and their further confusion in the eclectic approach of Renaissance interpretation, should not obscure their difference in principle. Indeed, it is precisely the difference in principle between the appeal to prudence, history, practice, and convention, on the one hand, and the appeal to virtue, philosophy, reason, and nature, on the other, that contributes to the two-sided character of Renaissance definitions of art.

2. ART AND NATURE IN ANTIQUITY

Although the conceptual importance of nature probably originated in the early researches of the Milesian cosmologists, and although it is contrasted with the flux of opinion by Parmenides and Heraclitus, the habit of consistently opposing it to convention begins with the Sophists. The purpose of this opposition varies from one Sophist to

32. See the various translations and commentary on frag. 8.50-53 in John Burnet, *Early Greek Philosophy* (1892; rpt., New York: Meridian Books, 1958); G. S. Kirk and J. E. Raven, *The Pre-Socratic Philosophers* (Cambridge: Cambridge University Press, 1957); and Philip Wheelright, *The Pre-Socratics* (New York: Odyssey Press, 1966). Despite differences of interpretation, it is at least clear that Parmenides here distinguishes between truth (*aletheies*) and opinion (*doxas*) (l.51), and that Plato understood him to have done so, *Theaetetus,* 152E.

33. See Neal H. Gilbert, *Renaissance Concepts of Method* (New York: Columbia University Press, 1960), pp. 39–40.

another, but "none of them would hold that human laws, customs, and religious beliefs were unshakeable because rooted in an unchanging natural order."[1] Along with the growing conception of nature as a stable order accessible to reason, fifth-century Athens was heir to both political turmoil, which underscored the lack of abiding political principles, and a growing awareness, through historical and geographical inquiry, that laws and customs vary from people to people. "If one were to offer to men to choose out of all the customs [*nomous*] in the world such as seemed to them the best," Herodotus observes, "they would examine the whole number, and end by preferring their own; so convinced are they that their own usages [*nomous*] far surpass those of all others" (3.38). Such observations are implicit in the formula of Protagoras, which declares that "man is the measure of all things."[2] Plato explicitly connects this anthropocentrism with the views of Antiphon and Prodicus, who maintained that the governing principle of language is anomaly or convention (*Cratylus,* 384B, 386A). He devotes his most intense examination, however, to the more important substitution of convention for nature in the moral philosophies of Archelaus and Hippias.[3]

The threat of this substitution is posed most forcefully by Plato in the arguments of Socrates' two most shameless interlocutors, Thrasymachus and Callicles. The state and its laws, they argue, are mere conventions, contracts made by the naturally inferior to protect themselves against the stronger.[4] As such, they are subject to change, and have no foundation in the nature of things. In fact, they contradict the law of nature by allowing the weaker to rule the stronger. At the same time that they exalt the natural law of might, however, these men attribute to convention a radical power that virtually commands conformity without regard for what by nature constitutes man's right life. They inculcate "nothing else than the opinions of the multitude . . . knowing nothing in reality about which of these opinions and desires is honorable or base, good or evil, just or unjust, but applying all these judgements to the great beast, calling the things that pleased it good, and the things that vexed it bad, having no other account to render of them" (*Republic,* 493B-C). Adherence to established convention is a matter of convenience (*Republic,* 359A-D). The just is identified with popular opinion, so that the success or failure of Thrasy-

---

1. W. K. C. Guthrie, *The Sophists* (Cambridge: Cambridge University Press, 1971), p. 48.

2. See, e.g., *Theaetetus,* 151E–152A and *Cratylus,* 386C.

3. See *Protagoras,* 337D; Diogenes Laertius, 2.17; and Xenophon, *Memorabilia,* 4.4.6–25.

4. *Republic,* 338C, 339A, 347E, 345D, 385C; *Gorgias,* 483A–D, 492B, 484B.

machus and Gorgias as rhetoricians stands or falls by their exploitation of it. Given this identification of law with opinion, there can be no higher appeal for guidance of man's right life than convention; by nature "licentiousness and injustice are pleasant and easy to win and are only in opinion and by convention disgraceful" (*Republic,* 364A).

Against the views of such men of action, Plato poses the views of those who are rightly called philosophers (*Republic,* 476A). Philosophers derive their knowledge not from opinion but from science (*episteme*) (*Republic,* 477B). The philosopher apprehends what is "eternal and unchanging," that which is always; such knowledge, Socrates explains, is a coming "into touch with the nature (*tes physeos*) of each thing in itself" (*Republic,* 454B). The many conventions of the many are relegated to the realm of opinion (*Republic,* 479D). The true political art will be a *techne* like medicine, taking account of, and serving, the nature of its object (*Republic,* 409E). Justice belongs to the class of highest goods that are operative by their very nature and not by opinion (*Republic,* 367D). By virtue of the identity of justice with nature, "a city established on principles of nature (*kata physin*) would be wise as a whole" (*Republic,* 428E).

Such a city is, by Sophist standards, decidedly nonpractical. The *Republic* proceeds from a discussion of the practical arts and politics to a presentation of the theoretical life as the best life for man. In the *Statesman,* however, Plato turns from the theoretical life to that which is practical and commanding, and so from philosophy to the practical arts (260B). It is the task of kingship, as presented in the *Statesman,* "not to act itself, but to rule over the arts that have the power of action" (305D). Like the art of weaving, the art of statesmanship must distinguish the good materials from the bad, and out of disparate elements produce a whole. Thus, by virtue of their subordination to the commanding part of intellectual science, the practical arts take on a paramount importance in the fabric of the state. But given the alliance between kingship and philosophy, between the commanding part and the judging or speculative part of intellectual life, the fitness of these arts for the state will be judged according to the standard of nature. The same principles applied to justice in the state therefore apply to the practice of the arts.

In accordance with this philosophical task, Plato repudiates in the tenth book of the *Laws* the sophistical view that the foundation of the arts is merely conventional. The sophistical argument involves three terms: nature (*physis*), art (*techne*), and convention (*nomos*). These terms, however, are aligned by the Sophists in binary fashion, to distinguish between those things that exist by nature and chance and those that are of mortal birth (889B-C). Art is included with convention in the latter category, since neither has any basis in nature. Both art and convention vary arbitrarily, and so give rise to debate about the norms that they engender: "men are continually in dispute about them, and continually altering them, and whatever alteration they make at any time is at that time authoritative, though it owes its existence to art and the laws [*technei kai tois nomois*], and not in any way to nature" (890A). Against this view Plato maintains that proper arts and laws are "things which exist by nature, or by a cause not inferior to nature, since according to right reason they are the offspring of mind" (890D). True art, that is, is linked to nature by means of reason. As such, it is "no less a product of nature than the nonrational elements in man's constitution."[5]

In this instance, Plato is not merely offering a counter-assertion to the sophistical view that arts and laws are constituted by opinion: he would never assume that any practice bearing the name of art or law automatically follows the standard of nature. Rather, he asserts against the implicit relativism of the Sophists the more theoretical proposition that there is an abiding principle by which arts and laws can be judged. This principle is elaborated and applied to specific arts in the *Ion, Phaedrus,* and *Gorgias.*

The *Ion* explicitly and almost exclusively concentrates upon the philosophic status of the rhapsode's art. If Ion plied his trade with either art or science, Socrates observes, he would discourse equally well on all poets, and not just on Homer, because "when one has acquired a whole art the principle of inquiry is the same" (532C-E). The significance of the link between *techne* and *episteme* is that *techne* possesses a principle that makes the art a whole (532C-D).[6] Here, as elsewhere, *techne* is "the practice of a vocation or profession based not merely on routine experience but on general rules and fixed knowledge; and so it is never very far from theory."[7] In addition, the rational character of *techne* depends upon the presence of orderly structure in its object. The *poietike techne* referred to at 532C is the rhapsode's art, the art of discoursing about poetry rather than the art of producing poems,[8] but the impossibility of such an art of commentary or criticism hinges upon the lack of rational principle in the art of production. If the production of poetry consisted in the intellectual understanding and deployment of some potential in nature, then this productive *techne*

5. A. O. Lovejoy and F. S. Boas, *Primitivism and Related Ideas in Antiquity* (1935; rpt., New York: Octagon Books, 1965), p. 166.

6. *Techne* is also used interchangeably with *episteme* at *Theaetetus,* 146C.

7. Werner Jaeger, *Paideia: The Ideals of Greek Culture* (1945; rpt., New York: Oxford University Press, 1965), II, 129–130.

8. J. Craig Drière, "The Problem of Plato's *Ion,*" *JAAC,* 10 (1951), 32.

would presumably be susceptible to analysis by a second *techne* of critical discourse.

The link between *techne* and *physis* is more explicit in the *Phaedrus*, in which Socrates subjects the art of making speeches to more extended scrutiny. The point of departure is the criterion reached in *Ion,* that there must be "a method [*tropos*] of writing well or badly" (*Phaedrus,* 258D). This need for principle is advanced against the sophistical concept of rhetoric, which dictates that "persuasion comes from what seems to be true and not from the truth" (260A). According to this concept, the "art" of rhetoric is founded not upon unchanging principles, but merely upon opinion and convention: Socrates connects it with the names of Gorgias, Lysis, and Thrasymachus. The meaning of *tropos* was left ambiguous in *Ion*—it can mean simply "way" or "habit," as does the *hodos* of Parmenides. But this ambiguity is immediately resolved in the *Phaedrus,* where "all great arts demand discussion and high speculation about nature" (269E). This speculative bias effectively excludes any connotations of inarticulate habit. The best rhetoric accordingly shares with dialectic a knowledge of the truth of its subject; it exercises the intellectual powers of division and synthesis (259E). Instead of addressing itself to popular opinion and convention, the art of rhetoric looks to "the real nature of things" (262B). As so often in Plato, the test of a *techne* is its resemblance to medicine (268A);[9] in both cases one must "analyze a nature" (270B). This procedure requires resolution of the object into its constituent elements and analysis of its powers and capacities both as a whole and in its parts. In accord with the biological analogy, the product of rhetorical art will have the fitness of a healthy natural object; it will be "a living being" with "a middle and members, composed in fitting relation to each other and to the whole" (264C). This is a natural rather than a conventional fitness and as such contrasts with the sophistical "craft devoid of art" (260E). Although practical experience is required in both the medical and rhetorical arts, it represents the lower end of a spectrum in which rational principle is the highest and controlling factor (269D). The intellectual discipline of art lies suspended between these two extremes, but always relies upon the guidance of *episteme* if the artist "is to proceed in a scientific manner and not merely by practice and routine" (270B).

This contrast is further elaborated in the *Gorgias,* which returns the discussion of *techne* to the larger framework of the conflict between nature and convention in the moral life of man. In order to refute the analogy between verbal art and medicine, Polus advances the view that

9. See Jaeger, II, 33.

the rhetoric of Gorgias is "discovered experimentally, as the result of experience" (448D). Gorgias further defines this practical foundation when he asserts that the orator need not know the truth of actual matters, but need know only the means of persuading an audience, because rhetoric provides belief without knowledge in place of certain knowledge (459C, 454E).

Such activity fails the Platonic test. It is mere experience devoid of theory, a practice that in its adherence to convention rather than rational principle forms a mere resemblance to the branch of politics labeled justice.[10] Rhetoric compares to justice as cookery to medicine, cosmetic to gymnastic, and sophistry to legislation: it is a practical but inferior substitute for knowledge based on principle. Like all inferior practices, it aims at what will please popular opinion, and not at what is best by nature. It does not deserve the name of art (*techne*) because "it has no account to give of the real nature [*physin*] of the things it applies, and so cannot tell the cause of any of them" (465A). Mere experience falls short of *techne* because it is *alogon*, lacking in rational principle (465A, 501A).

This technical emphasis on nature is linked conceptually to Socrates' ethical debate with Callicles. Like Thrasymachus, Callicles holds that nature's law declares that "might makes right." To act unjustly in the eyes of other men is merely to violate convention (483A). Justice and temperance are polite embellishments, the unnatural covenants of mankind, mere stuff and nonsense (491C). Such ethical relativism accords with the sophistical view of rhetoric, which exploits convention without regard for principle (482C). The chief path that the prudent Sophist takes is to accustom himself from his earliest youth to conform with the opinions and conventions in ascendancy, "to be delighted and annoyed with the same things as his master, and to continue to be as like the other as possible" (510D).

In Plato's view, however, this pragmatism, relying on routine and habit (*tribe kai empeiria*) for prudential memory of what will produce successful results, resembles the practice of swimming in order to save one's own life, as compared with the science (*episteme*) of piloting, which saves the lives of many. In this most dramatic of Plato's examinations of *techne*, conventional practice compares with rational art as the fashion of rhetoric compares with the life of philosophy (500C). The Platonic arts are the children of this life, and the chief assurance of its continuity.

Despite the Platonic alignment of the arts with nature and reason, their simultaneous source and sphere of operation in experience pre-

10. *Gorgias,* 462C–463C, 463E, 500E.

vents a full resolution of the conflicting claims of principle and practice in Plato's thought. It is never fully clear in Plato how the norm of
nature, as the test of rectitude and fitness, is actually to be realized in
any but the most theoretical of arts. The clarification of this problem was one of the main achievements of Aristotle, and one of the
main foundations for the later technical tradition. By articulating a
coherent system in which the arts could be examined from a variety
of perspectives, and by referring various characteristics of the arts to
separate perspectives or principles, Aristotle preserved the basis of the
arts in nature while accounting more fully for their practical character.

Aristotle's emphasis on practice begins in a difference with Plato.
In the *Nichomachean Ethics,* Aristotle observes that Socrates "was mistaken in thinking that all the virtues are forms of prudence," not because knowledge is unnecessary, but because the view that "knowledge
is virtue" overlooks the fact that virtue is realized in practice. Virtue
is a habitual disposition (*hexis*) not merely conforming to right principle, but cooperating with right principle (1141b4–28). Virtues and
arts, which are a form of virtue, are different from natural powers, not
only because they are external rather than internal causes of change,[11]
but also because they originate in practice. While nature provides potential, men acquire arts and virtues "by first having practiced them
. . . we learn an art or craft by doing the things we shall have to do
when we have learnt it" (*Ethics,* 1130a30–35). It is through experience
(*empeiria*) that men acquire art and science (*techne kai episteme*)
(*Metaphysics,* 981a3).

Because they are so closely connected with the practical life of man,
the arts take on the character of habitual dispositions (*hexeis*) (*Ethics,*
1098a3–4). These dispositions occupy a middle position between powers
and acts in that they direct power but are not themselves acts, and between activity and passivity in that they are the product of accumulated
practices that in turn direct activity.[12] They also lie midway between
principles and practice, because they are governed by the calculative intellect rather than by the scientific intellect. Unlike the scientific intellect, which contemplates those things whose first principles are invariable, the calculative intellect contemplates those things "which
admit of variation" (*Ethics,* 1139a10). As such, it includes in its pur-
view both things made and things done, administered respectively by
the virtues of art (*techne*) and prudence (*phronesis*) (*Ethics,* 1140a1–5).

11. See *Metaphysics,* 1070a7–10; cf. *Ethics,* 1140a14–16.
12. See Richard McKeon, "Rhetoric and Poetic in Aristotle," in *Aristotle's Poetics and English Literature,* ed. Elder Olson (Chicago: University of Chicago Press,
1965), p. 226 and n. 43.

It follows that art is a rational disposition concerned with making that reasons truly, or, as the scholastic commentators expressed it, *recta ratio factibilium* (*Ethics*, 1140a10–11).[13]

On this basis the productive arts are at once distinguished from the theoretical sciences and from the practical arts. But despite the difference between the productive and practical arts, between art and prudence (*Ethics*, 1140b3–26), they are alike in their concern with things susceptible to change. Prudence therefore presides over all of the calculative faculty, including art, just as wisdom presides over the scientific faculty (*Ethics*, 1144a1–4). This enables Aristotle to account for the relation between *techne* and practice. Prudence accounts for particular facts because action is concerned with particular things (*Ethics*, 1141b14–17).

Despite its relation to practical experience, however, *techne* depends as well upon nature and rational principle. Although it differs from nature in its mode of existence as a disposition, art resembles nature in its mode of operation. Not only does it resemble nature as an efficient cause of coming-to-be, but it also resembles nature because it differs from chance; it operates in accord with a final rational principle. "That cause seems to be first which we call final, for it is the reason [*logos*] and the reason is the principle alike in works of art and in works of nature."[14] Both art and nature are characterized by purposeful operation; in art, as in nature, the relation of consequent to antecedent is identical. Thus "the arts either, on the basis of nature, carry things farther than nature can, or they imitate nature" (*Physics*, 199a16–17). This does not mean that the product of art resembles the product of nature, but that the process of art is analogically the same as that of nature in bringing things into existence in accord with principle or purpose.

This analogy qualifies the relation of *techne* to experience. Although the arts arise from experience, they do not fully exist until "a single universal judgment [*katholon*] is formed with regard to like objects. To have a judgment that when Callias was suffering from this or that disease that this or that benefitted him, and similarly with Socrates and various other individuals, is a matter of experience; but to judge that it benefits all persons of a certain type, considered as a class, who suffer this or that disease, is a matter of art" (*Metaphysics*, 981a24–b7). In some individual instances, simple appeal to experience can be more

13. See Jacques Maritain, *Art and Scholasticism*, trans. J. F. Scanlon (New York: Scribner's, 1946), p. 7.

14. *De Partibus Animalium*, 639b14, quoted by McKeon, in Olson, p. 217n25. Cf. *Physics*, 194a33, b8; and *Metaphysics*, 1065a26–28.

successful than art, because experience is a knowledge of particulars, while art is knowledge of universals *(Metaphysics, 981a16–17)*. But on the whole, artists are superior to men of experience because they possess a theory and know the causes of things *(Metaphysics, 981a24–67)*. In this sense art is more closely aligned with nature and scientific accounts of nature than with experience.

This alignment pervades Aristotle's analysis of the poetic art, which more than any other represents as well as shapes the future position of nature as a technical norm in the verbal arts. Aristotle's bias toward the norm of nature is borne out from the very opening paragraph of the *Poetics:*

> Concerning the poetic art as a whole and its species, the particular capacities of each; how the plots should be constructed / if the poetic process is to be artistically satisfactory, and further how many and what kind of parts it has; and all the other questions that belong to the same branch of study—let us discuss all this, beginning in the natural order with first principles.
>
> Now the writing of epic and tragedy, also [of] comedy, and the art of composing dithyrambs, and most of the / art of flute and lyre—all these are in point of fact forms of imitation, by and large. They differ from one another in three respects: viz. in the fact that the imitating has (1) different media, (2) different objects, or (3) different modes or methods.[15]

Peri poietikes ("Concerning the poetic art")—the form of the substantive *poietike* indicates that Aristotle is here dealing with a *techne;* its grammatical form is the same as that of other *technai: dialektike, mathematike, politike.* Moreover, that the subject under discussion is the "art of poetry," and not "poetry" generally, is born out in the second paragraph; the species of poetic art are not epic, tragedy, and dithyramb, but the construction of epic *(epopoiia)*, the construction of tragedy *(tragodias poiesis)*, and the construction of dithyramb *(dithyrambopoietike).*[16] These constructive arts are further differentiated from

15. Translation by Gerald F. Else, *Aristotle's Poetics: The Argument* (Cambridge: Harvard University Press, 1967); unless otherwise indicated, however, all further references to the *Poetics* are to the text and translation of W. Hamilton Fyfe, Loeb Classical Library (Cambridge: Harvard University Press, 1927).

16. "Naturally [Aristotle] does not drag these cumbrous phrases into further discussion; but whenever he writes *tragodia* in the *Poetics,* unless the context demands another meaning, we are to read it as 'tragic art,'" Else, p. 6. Else does not

mere practice in their contrast with the visual and vocal modes of
representation, only some of which proceed through a technical knowledge, while others simply rely upon routine or convention (1447a20).
Those activities that proceed merely through experience or convention
are differentiated from those directed by the rational control of
techne.[17]

The poetic art is therefore subjected to analysis in its character as
techne. All arts involve principle, or a true course of reasoning. In all
productive arts, this course of reasoning forms the first part of a two-
part process: "In generations and motions, part of the process is called
cogitation [*noesis*], and part production [*poiesis*]—that which proceeds
from the starting-point and the form is cogitation, and that which
proceeds from the conclusion of the cogitation is production."[18] This
explains what Gerald Else has called the "Platonic-Aristotelian intel-
lectualist bias" of the opening paragraph.[19] The *Poetics* begins "in
the natural order with first principles." Aristotle announces that the
analysis will proceed from the first principle or essence of the art itself
to its species, the powers, functions, or capacities of each, and to their
constituent elements. This analysis follows the procedure dictated in
the *Physics:* "for we conceive ourselves to know about a thing when we
are acquainted with its ultimate causes and first principles, and have
got down to its elements" (184a10–15). Because of the relation of
techne to *physis,* the art of poetry will receive the same analysis as any
natural process.[20]

Accordingly, the second paragraph of the *Poetics* begins with a
statement of the first principle of the art of poetry in itself, *mimesis*.
Because the poetic arts include such nonverbal arts as music and
painting, the principle of *mimesis* generically includes the imitation
of character and feeling or experience as well as the imitation of actions (1447a10). But in Aristotle's conception of poetry proper, character and feeling or experience are subordinated to action, for "while

---

remark, however, that the word standing for "art of comedy" in this second paragraph is simply *commodia*. Cf. C. W. Lucas, *Aristotle's Poetics* (Oxford: Clarendon
Press, 1968), p. 64.

17. See Ingram Bywater, *Aristotle on the Art of Poetry* (Oxford: Clarendon Press,
1909), p. 102. Cf. Else, p. 20, and Lucas, p. 56. See also O. B. Hardison, *"Poetics,
Chapter I: The Way of Nature," Yearbook of Comparative and General Literature,*
16 (1967), 5–15.

18. *Metaphysics,* 1032b15–18; see also Elder Olson, "The Poetic Method of
Aristotle," in *Aristotle's Poetics and English Literature,* pp. 180–181.

19. Else, pp. 9–10.

20. See J. H. Randall, *Aristotle* (New York: Columbia University Press, 1960),
p. 280, and McKeon, in Olson, p. 212.

character makes men what they are, it is their actions and experiences that make them happy or the opposite" (1450a15). Character and feeling or experience come under the larger head of action, so that the end aimed at in *mimesis* is representation of action (1450a13). The opening sentence of Chapter 2, summarizing the conclusions of the first chapter, observes that imitations are of "men doing or acting" (1448a1). The poetic art therefore has as its essence or first principle the imitation of action (1449b26; 1451b26).

This explains the otherwise mysterious appearance of the constituent element of plot, or *mythos,* in the opening paragraph. If the poetic art has as its essence the imitation of action, then it follows that its most important function is the construction of plots, or *mythoi.* The proper constructing of plot enables the *poiesis* to "have itself well," because the *poiesis* essentially is, as Else points out, the mak-ing, the construct-ing, the composi-tion.[21] The poetic art imitates nature in the sense that it is the purposeful completion of a process on the basis of principle. For this reason the poetic art "does not tell what actually happened, but what could happen potentially according to either probability or necessity" (1451a32); it is more philosophic and noble than history. History deals only with particulars, while the poetic art deals with universals, which are explicitly the principles of probability or necessity (1451b8). Because it is not bound to experience, the poetic art excludes mere possibility, what has happened or might happen according to chance. As all arts considered generically resemble nature rather than chance, so the specific art of poetry excludes all elements that are inexplicable, or *alogon* (1454b5).

The abstract structure of differentiae proceeds from the same assumptions. While Aristotle begins the second paragraph with a simple ad hoc enumeration of forms that may be said generically to be imitations, in the next sentence he quickly establishes the criteria by which the generic category may be divided according to the objects, manner, and means of imitation, and then devotes a chapter to each. The fourth and fifth chapters provide a kind of "history," and taken together with the preceding chapters enable him to "gather up" a definition of the tragic art in its nature.[22] Its constituent elements are then distinguished and related to the whole just defined. At the same time, they are arranged and aligned according to the first principle of definition in the opening paragraphs. Because *mythos* is the first principle and the soul of the tragic art, character is subordinated to it. Thought is then subordinated to character, and in referring the reader to the *Rhetoric* for

21. Else, p. 9.
22. See Olson, pp. 183–184.

further discussion of thought and diction, Aristotle effectively indicates, in accordance with the central principle of that other *techne,*
the further subordination of style to meaning.

As a result, the product of the poetic art resembles the product of
natural process in having a beginning, middle, and end (1450b30). Like
any living creature, or act, or thing possessed of beauty, the product
of the poetic art is beautiful by virtue of its having an orderly arrangement and a certain magnitude of its own (1450b33). These structural qualities are dictated by neither opinion, practice, nor convention, but by internal principles analogous to natural process and
accessible and pleasing to reason.

The requirement that art imitate nature is thus fulfilled specifically
by the poetic art, whose essential function is the *mimesis* of action
through the purposeful construction of *mythos* and its subordinate
elements on the basis of principle. The constant references to nature
and principle in the *Poetics* emphasize the rational character of *techne*.
Because the poetic art embodies principles (1450a32), it falls under the
generic definition of art as a rational power that reasons truly about
making.

Thus, while Aristotle's conception of *techne* partially resolves the
conflicting claims of experience and reason that pervade Plato's ideal-
ist analysis, it supports Plato's philosophic demand that art derive its
principles from, and exercise them in harmony with, the structured
norms of nature. This philosophic bias toward natural rectitude and
fitness lies at the foundation of the technical tradition; it lends prescriptive force to normative thinking, and constitutes one pole of emphasis throughout its later history. It is the basis for such later claims
as Sidney's, that "there is no art delivered to mankind that hath not
the works of Nature for his principal object."

3. Art and Convention in Antiquity

As an alternative to nature, convention represents the second pole
of emphasis in the ancient technical tradition. While the technical
ideals of Plato and Aristotle were largely defined in opposition to sophistical appeals to convention, the concept of convention entered the
technical tradition itself through the ongoing conflict of rhetorical
and philosophical ideals. From within the tradition, the concept of
convention exercised a powerful influence upon the framework and
content of technical thought.

This influence and its implications are graphically exemplified in
Horace's epistle to the Pisos. Compared with Aristotle's *Poetics,*
Horace's account of the poetic art appears deceptively nontechnical,

leading one Renaissance commentator to remark that "while he teacheth the art, he goeth unartificially to work."[1] Nevertheless, Quintilian was justified in giving to the epistle its subsequently traditional name: *ars poetica,* or *liber de arte poetica* (*Praefatio,* 2, and 8.3.60). Though Horace frequently balances the claims of inspiration against those of technique (ll. 295, 408), he opens and closes the epistle by satirically sketching the dubious fruits of artistic production in the absence of controlled form. In the opening lines (32–37), he couples the demand for control with a contrast between the articulate knowledge of art and the lesser skill of a mere craftsman,[2] and his exposition of the art of poetry follows a specifically technical framework. The subject of the epistle is therefore not merely the controlled form of a skilled craftsman, but control on the basis of articulate principle and definition.[3]

For Horace, the chief expression of formal control lies in the central principle of decorous unity (l.23), and its introduction through the portrait of a failed *mimesis*—the feathered horse—would seem at first to suggest an Aristotelian concept of *techne* as a *mimesis* of nature. The function of poetic art, it would seem, is the achievement, through *mimesis,* of a decorous whole, *simplex et unum,* on the basis of principle rather than skilled craftsmanship. But the principle of decorous unity is referred here, as it is throughout the epistle, to a consideration lacking in Aristotle's *Poetics*—the presence of the Roman audience. Though the *Ars* opens and closes with the demand for controlled form, this demand is created by the audience, the ultimate arbiter of the artistically proper. The consequence of lacking art is not merely failure to produce the desired product, but failure to elicit the desired response of the audience, resulting in public ridicule or banishment.

1. Henry Peacham, *Of Poetry,* from *The Compleat Gentleman,* in *Critical Essays of the Seventeenth Century,* ed. J. E. Spingarn (1908; rpt., Bloomington: Indiana University Press, 1957), I, 127.

2. C. O. Brink, *Horace on Poetry,* vol. II, *The "Ars Poetica"* (Cambridge: Cambridge University Press, 1971), p. 83; hereafter cited as *Ars Poetica.* Vol. I, *Prolegomena to the Literary Epistles* (Cambridge: Cambridge University Press, 1963), is hereafter cited as *Prolegomena.* George C. Fiske maintains that *nil scribens* (306) signifies that Horace is not writing a *techne,* Cicero's *"De Oratore"* and Horace's *"Ars Poetica",* University of Wisconsin Studies in Language and Literature, 27 (1929), 12n5. If anything, however, this phrase strengthens the claim that Horace in fact is writing a *techne* by raising the question whether the epistle is to be understood as being a *poem;* cf. *Satires,* 1.4.38–63.

3. "The subject of this eccentric didactic poem . . . is not poetry, but poetics: the body of theory formulated, largely out of earlier insights, by Aristotle and his successors, and current in Hellenistic times," D. A. Russell, "Ars Poetica," in *Horace,* ed. C. D. N. Costa (London: Routledge and Kegan Paul, 1973), pp. 113–114.

The criterion for artistic unity is to be derived not merely from internal probability or necessity—for poets are "licensed" to hazard anything (ll. 9–11)—but from the public expectations and demands as to what that internal coherence should entail. Not only must an art formulate its principles in view of the thing to be produced; it must derive them in view of the particular *kind* of thing to be produced—is this case a verbal construct whose very existence hinges upon the intercourse of men.

This raises an important question, for Horace himself seems to wonder whether the norms of art are derived from nature or convention, and whether the central principle of decorum is to be referred to what is universally natural or to what is relatively and conventionally proper. To be sure, these alternatives are never far removed from each other in Horace's mind; the whole aim in adhering to convention lies in securing a natural effect.[4] But the alliance between these concepts is achieved not, as in the Platonic instance, by attempting to subordinate the conventional to the natural or universal, but by the very nearly opposite procedure of identifying the natural with the relativity of convention. The extraordinary comparison (ll. 60–72) of changes in linguistic usage with natural mutability establishes an important principle that runs throughout the *Ars Poetica*. Not only does language change with the passage of the seasons, the lives of men, and all mortal things, but the very nature presiding over these changes resembles the guiding principle of convention. Nature is not without principle, but, as in the case of human convention, its principle is adaptation. Given the relativity of nature and "the difficulty of determining the absolutely natural in a relative world," Craig La Drière explains, it is easy to confuse the natural with the conventional, and sometimes to substitute convention for nature "as a satisfactory alternative criterion of fitness."[5]

Consequently, consideration of the audience pervades Horace's presentation of guidelines for poetic production, but in such a way as to acknowledge the formal and institutional integrity of convention, its mediate character. Thus, as R. S. Crane observes, Horace does not strictly posit "an equivalence between what is 'natural' or according to decorum in the poem and what will give pleasure to the highly selected Roman audience, the applause of which is to measure the poet's

4. See, e.g., Archibald Y. Campbell, *Horace: A New Interpretation* (London: Methuen, 1924), p. 241.

5. J. Craig La Drière, review of Wolf Steidle, *Studien zur Ars poetica des Horaz*, in *American Journal of Philology*, 63 (1942), 238–243.

success."[6] In the first place, not only is the imagined audience "highly select," but it serves as a device to which the diffident Horace can attribute his own highly sophisticated judgment.[7] Moreover, the influence of public opinion upon the poet is exercised through a conventional but nonetheless technical medium. If the poet's task were merely to please the audience, he would do better to throw them acorns. In fact, however, the poet constructs a harmonious and decorous whole from the conventional elements currently available; public opinion and tradition alike are formalized in such conventions as the five-act structure, the *nuntio,* the chorus, and the medium of language itself. Far from simply identifying poetic decorum with public taste, Horace defines the poetic art as a continuing and dynamic interchange between the integrity of formal control and its simultaneous reliance in practice upon means and materials that are for the most part conventional.

In the degree of emphasis his *Ars* places on this second phenomenon, Horace shares with the rhetorical tradition a displacement of the philosophic principle of universal nature by its rival principle, the relativity of convention. Ancient literary criticism was for the most part practiced as a branch of the study of rhetoric, and therefore concerned itself with the relations between poetry and its effect upon an audience. In dealing primarily with the drama, Horace chooses a poetic form that since the fifth century in Athens had best exemplified that relationship.[8] The resulting dual concept of form as conventional medium as well as principle of rational control in the *Ars Poetica* therefore reflects the larger conflict in antiquity between philosophic and more purely rhetorical aims.

Explicitly, and often aggressively, the major figures of the rhetorical tradition pose this conflict as a central and definitive issue for rhetoric itself. Even Cicero, with his strong philosophic bias, finds that the ideally natural integrity of art is compromised by its intersubjective setting. On the one hand, his efforts to portray the perfect orator are founded on the supposition of the *virtus,* the natural perfection of a thing, its *arete* or *telos.*[9] In search of a rhetoric worthy of coexistence with philosophy, Cicero derives the perfect orator not from the work-

6. R. S. Crane, review of P. F. Santoigne, L. G. Burgevin, and Helen Griffith, *Horace: Three Phases of His Influence,* in *PQ,* 16 (1937), 163.

7. George C. Fiske, "Cicero's *Orator* and Horace's *Ars Poetica,*" *Harvard Studies in Classical Philology,* 35 (1924), 58–59.

8. Gordon Williams, *Tradition and Originality in Roman Poetry* (Oxford: Clarendon Press, 1968), p. 350.

9. See Cicero, *Orator,* 39.101; *De Oratore,* 1.24.118; and Brink, *Ars Poetica,* p. 359.

shops of the rhetoricians, but from the spacious groves of the Academy (*Orator*, 3.12). In the *Orator*, the art of rhetoric receives the same idealistic and philosophic treatment as the orator himself.[10] Like Phidias sculpting Jupiter or Minerva, the rhetorician looks not to practical models but to universal ideas for the outlines of his art. Cicero's enumeration of the functions and styles of rhetoric presumably partakes of these ideas on the assumption that "whatever is to be discussed rationally and methodically, must be reduced to the ultimate form and type of its class" (*Orator*, 3.10).

On the other hand, these ideal forms, like the type of the orator himself, are subject to the practical demands of oratory. The eloquence of orators, Cicero observes, has always been controlled by the good sense of the audience, because all who desire to win approval have regard to the good will of their auditors, and shape and adapt themselves completely to their opinion and approval (*Orator*, 3.24). This complicates the task of depicting the form of the "best," because different people have different notions of what is best (*Orator*, 9.36–7); varying preferences in habits of speech and style displace ideals under the pressure of practice (*Brutus*, 21.83). The skeptical Antonius reminds Crassus in the *De Oratore* of the inherent conflict between philosophic and rhetorical aims; in seeking dialectical certainty in art "there is the danger of our being led away from our traditional practice of speaking in a style acceptable to the populace" (1.18.81). Because in Antonius' view rhetoric is founded upon practical experience, the orator will do well to relegate philosophy to holiday entertainment; in addressing the court or assembly, the orator should part with Plato, who, "when he thought fit to put these things into writing, depicted in his pages an unknown sort of republic, so completely in contrast with everyday life and the customs [*vitae consuetudine*] of human communities were his considered statements concerning justice" (1.3.224).

The need to accommodate discourse to its social setting—to the "everyday life and the customs of human communities"—therefore marks a point of crisis and debate for the technical tradition. The conflict between nature and convention, so clearly at issue in Plato's opposition to the Sophists, is accordingly reflected in the divided ideals of discourse that become the technical concerns of rhetoric, beginning with Aristotle's distinction between the sophistical or Isocratean rhetoric aimed only at persuading the dicast and his own proposed rhetoric, which was to concern itself only with the matter at hand (*Rhetoric*, 1354a16). Logical integrity and rhetorical accommodation reappear as

10. See Fiske, "Cicero's *De Oratore* and Horace's *Ars Poetica*," p. 25.

alternative ideals in the Theophrastean distinction between a speech composed with a view to the nature of a case and a speech composed with a view to its audience,[11] as well as in the Stoic contrast of the closed fist of logic with the open palm of rhetoric.[12] The impact of these alternatives upon the concept of art itself, however, is most vivid in the surviving books of the *Rhetorica* of Philodemus. Refuting the claim that rhetoric shares with philosophy the task of making men virtuous, Philodemus points to the philosophic identification of justice with universal nature, in contrast to the rhetorical identification of justice with convention.[13] He then applies this contrast to the claim that rhetoric is a *techne*. While there may be "a transmission of knowledge which is acquired by experience and observation" (p. 272), such knowledge "lacks the distinctive characteristic of an art, which is its method and general principles applying to the individual cases" (p. 275). Epicurus, he points out, "makes a hard and fast distinction between *episteme* [science] and *tribe* [mere practice], and considers that all rhetoric, not merely the forensic and deliberative branches, depends entirely upon experience" (p. 282). Because it addresses itself to a social setting, the normative basis of rhetoric is conventional rather than natural. In consequence, rhetoric falls short of the name of art: "sciences [*episteme*] are the same in different localities, but . . . rhetoric differs in different countries and cities . . . art [*techne*] does not vary with locality, and does not adapt itself to different peoples" (p. 288).

Like most ancient rhetoricians, Philodemus speaks of convention in terms that are essentially sophistic and skeptical. Both the critical skepticism of the New Academy and the practical skepticism of Pyrrho and his revivers accepted the Platonic-Aristotelian ideal of art as rational, uniform, and stable; but they subsequently denied the possibility that such an ideal could exist by reasserting the sophistical claim that man's life is ruled by convention. Moreover, they obliterated the sophistical opposition of nature to convention by taking from Atomism the view that even nature exists by convention: "the qualities of

11. The distinction is found in a fragment quoted by Ammonius in his commentary on the *De Interpretatione* of Aristotle. For a text and discussion of this fragment, see G. M. A. Grube, "Theophrastus as a Literary Critic," *Transactions and Proceedings of the American Philological Association,* 83 (1952), 172–183.

12. See, e.g., Cicero, *Orator,* 32.113; Quintilian, 2.20.7; and Sextus Empiricus, *Mathematicos,* 2.7.

13. *The Rhetorica of Philodemus,* trans. Harry M. Hubbell, *Transactions and Proceedings of the Connecticut Academy of Arts and Sciences,* 23 (1920), 315–317; I quote also from the Greek text of Siegfried Sudhaus (Leipzig: Teubner, 1892).

things exist merely by convention; in nature there is nothing but the atoms and the void."[14] The famous speech on justice delivered at Rome by the skeptic Carneades thus differs in an essential point from the brutal naturalism of the Sophists Thrasymachus and Callicles: convention rules men not simply for the most part, but always.[15] By delivering contradictory speeches on successive days, Carneades carried the sophistical view of convention beyond mere opposition to nature, substituting it for nature itself. According to the skeptical view, there can be no appeal even to biological nature, for, as Pyrrho is said to have maintained, "there is nothing really existant but custom and convention to govern human action; for no single thing is in itself any more this than that."[16]

So profound was the importance of convention in the skeptical view that it was generally accorded a central place in skeptical epistemologies. Aenesidemus, a younger contemporary of Cicero, for example, erected a system of ten Modes, or means, of refutation, which accounted for conflicting points of view. Nine of these categories enumerate the various psychological sources of perplexity, but the category of convention accounts for the entire range of difficulties that beset man's normative life. Convention is the source of confusion and argument in "customs, laws, beliefs in myths, compacts between nations, and dogmatic assumptions": as a source of conflict it encompasses "consideration with regard to things beautiful and ugly, true and false, good and bad, with regard to the gods, and with regard to the coming into being and passing away of the world of phenomena."[17] Later elevated to the place of highest distinction by Sextus Empiricus, the Mode of Convention shows so much "divergency to exist in objects, we shall not be able to state what character belongs to the object in respect of this particular rule of conduct, or law, or habit, and so on with the rest. It is because of this Mode that we are compelled to suspend judgment regarding the real nature of external objects."[18]

This same argument extends through Sextus' refutation of the arts and sciences, and applies with special relevance to the verbal arts. Adhering to an extreme form of anomalism, Sextus wields the conventional character of language as a weapon to demolish the possibility

14. Attributed to Democritus by Diogenes Laertius, 9.45. For the connection between Democritus and Pyrrho, see 9.58, 61, 67, 71–72, and Cicero, *Academica*, 1.2.6–8.

15. See Cicero, *De Republica*, 3.8.13–11.18.

16. Diogenes Laertius, 9.61.

17. Diogenes Laertius, 9.83.

18. Sextus Empiricus, *Outlines of Pyrrhonism*, 1.63.

of rational control in the verbal arts. Grammar possesses "no criterion which is of itself reliable for deciding that one ought to speak in this way rather than that way, unless indeed it be each man's practice, and this is neither technical nor natural."[19] In the case of rhetoric, the additional application of an already conventional medium to a world of manifold particulars constitutes a further obstacle to rational control. "Since every art has an end which is fixed and stable, like philosophy or grammar, rhetoric too, if it is an art, will have to profess one or the other of these. But it has not an end which is always stable . . . and therefore is not an art."[20] By virtue of its connection with legal and political contingencies rhetoric is pragmatic in character; connected with the temporary and circumstantial, it is incapable of rational analysis.

Philodemus shares much of this skeptical bias, but where his account of rhetoric potentially enhances the claims of the philosophic life and adherence to the norm of nature, the more extreme position of skepticism, by undermining the concept of universal nature, and therefore the very possibility of philosophy, leaves convention as the only reliable guide in life. Unhappy is the man, says Sextus, "who recks not aught of custom."[21] While the critical skepticism of the New Academy had in the face of uncertainty offered "the reasonable" or "the probable" as alternatives to a life of utter uncertainty, the disciples of Pyrrho offered conformity with convention as the only means of making life tolerable. Thus Timon, a student of Pyrrho, was proud to say that he had never stepped beyond what convention demanded.[22] According to the skeptical view, the very thing that makes life unreasonable at the same time renders life possible. With this in mind Sextus formulates what he significantly labels the *agoge,* the "way" or "custom," the beaten path, of skeptical life: "the sceptic does not conduct his life according to philosophical theory, but as regards the non-philosophic regulation of life . . . he will perchance choose one course and avoid the other owing to the preconception formed from ancestral laws and customs."[23] It is therefore significant that the skeptical mind more often than not finds itself embracing the conventional life of man, the manifold life of precedent, practice, and tradition. In one of Lucian's dialogues, for example, a skeptic consoles an ardent

19. Sextus Empiricus, *Against the Professors,* 1.187–196.

20. *Against the Professors,* 2.13–15.

21. *Against the Ethicists,* 1.156.

22. Diogenes Laertius, 9.104–105, 9.108.

23. Sextus Empiricus, *Against the Ethicists,* 1.165–166. Cf. 1.23–24, 137, 226, 231, and *Outlines of Pyrrhonism,* 3.21.235 ff.

Stoic, whose rational certainty he has just demolished, by urging him to "make up your mind to join in the common life. Share in the everyday life of the city."[24]

Through the engagement of rhetoric with skepticism and the panorama of practical life, the Theophrastean distinction between a speech composed with a view to the nature of a case and a speech composed with a view to its audience came to be expressed in conceptual contrasts between uniformity and variety, the transcendent and the immanent, between nature and convention. Thus Cicero observes that while other arts derive as a rule

> from hidden and remote sources, the whole of oratory lies open to the view, and is concerned in some measure with the common practice, custom, and speech of mankind so that, whereas in all the other arts that is most excellent which is furthest removed from the understanding and mental capacity of the untrained, in oratory the very cardinal sin is to depart from the language of everyday life, and the usage approved by the sense of community. (*De Oratore*, 1.3.12)

Thus the distinction between speech composed with a view to the nature of a case and speech composed with a view to its audience was brought to bear on the concept of perfect oratory in terms of the concrete and immanent particularity of convention. In Cicero's view, the ideal oration unites, under the principle of propriety, careful consideration of the subject of discourse with attention to the contingencies of speaker and audience (*Orator*, 21.71). The fitting of words to things is therefore made contingent upon the context of place, time, and audience; the foundation of eloquence is wisdom, but the form this wisdom takes is the ability to adapt to time and occasion (*Orator*, 21.70, 35.23). As such, this wisdom differs essentially from the wisdom of philosophers, who discuss absolute perfection, which is one and unchanging (*Orator*, 21.72). The difference between speech with a view to its subject and speech with a view to its audience therefore gives rise to the alternative types of fitness that Philodemus called *to prepon kata sophian* and *to prepon kath' hekaston prosopon kai pragma*, propriety in the most unchanging and philosophic sense and adaptation to persons and topics in the practical sense.[25] "It is wholly another ques-

24. Lucian, *Hermotimus*, sec. 84; see also Cicero, *De Natura Deorum*, 3.5; and Minucius Felix, *Octavius*, 6.1–2.

25. "As concerns the further demand, which requires that the poet be capable of observing what is in keeping with every kind of poetry, one must urge against them that the poet must bring with him much more besides; and that if by speak-

tion," Cicero maintains, "whether you should say 'appropriate [*de-cere*]' or 'right [*oportere*]'—for by 'right' we indicate the perfect line of duty which everyone must follow everywhere, but 'propriety' is what is fitting and agreeable to an occasion or person" (*Orator*, 22.74).

The difference between these two kinds of fitness or decorum qualifies the idea of rhetorical perfection and therefore the kind of artistic control applicable to the practice of rhetoric. If art consists of intellectual principles that are thoroughly examined and clearly apprehended, and that are outside the control of mere opinion, then by this definition there seems to be no such thing as an art of oratory, for the kinds of language "we ourselves use in public speaking are changeable matter, and adapted to the general understanding of the crowd" (*De Oratore*, 1.23.108). Reason alone cannot arrive at rhetorical perfection, Quintilian remarks, because no universal criterion of fitness exists, "a fact which is due in part to conditions of time and place, and in part to the tastes and ideals of individuals" (12.10.2). Contingencies demand a wise adaptability; it is one thing to grasp a particular subject or art, but another to be "no dullard or raw hand in social life and the general practices of mankind" (*De Oratore*, 1.68.248). Because the decorous relation of part to whole demanded by formal control is itself a function of the dynamic relation of means to ends, the orator simultaneously observes the complementary principles of decorum and expediency (Quintilian, 2.13.8); knowledge of what is appropriate to particular circumstances is a matter of practical sagacity, which subjects the formal principles of art to the "social intercourse, precedent, tradition, and manners of the citizenry" (*De Oratore*, 3.55.212, 2.30.131).

Out of such engagement with collective will emerges the view that art is a "child of expediency" (Quintilian, 2.13.6); "eloquence is not the offspring of art, but the art of eloquence" (*De Oratore*, 1.22.136). While certain rules of thumb derived from practice may be gathered together to form something like an art, these are actually the product of a long and arduous course of trial, precedent, and practice (*De Oratore*, 1.23. 109). The result is not so much a universally valid *techne* as a varied

---

ing of decorum they mean something in the universal or philosophic sense [*kata sophian*], then they signify a virtue that is remote and nearly impossible to attain. But if they mean what is proper for each single person and in each single matter [*kata hekaston prosopon kai pragma*], then it follows, because it is possible in particular cases, that the poet can observe decorum; but in such particular cases, he neither knows nor follows it (in the universal or philosophical sense)." My translation, based on the text of Christian Jensen, *Philodemus Über die Gedichte, Fünftes Buch* (Berlin: Weidmannsche Buchhandlung, 1923), p. 77.

body of precepts that reflect tradition and convention (Quintilian, 2.13.15). Such precepts indicate the *diversas vias* (Quintilian, 3.1.5–7) demanded by the concrete and resistant texture of social contingency.

A similarly rhetorical outlook colors the Horatian concept of *ars* and its bias toward convention. At the very beginning of Horace's discussion of the poet (ll. 306–309), the ideal excellence or *virtus* of the poet is linked decisively with the perfection of art itself. The wisdom of the poet is the source and fount of good writing, of formal control on the basis of principle. This wisdom seems at first to resemble the *sapientia* of Cicero's *Orator,* or the philosophic wisdom recommended by Crassus in *De Oratore,* because it derives from the "Socratic pages" (l. 310). But in the subsequent elaboration of this wisdom (ll. 310–316), Horace turns from philosophic principle to the bewildering variety of particulars in contemporary Roman life.[26] It is knowledge of these particulars that enables the poet to give to each character his fitting part (l. 316).

This view of decorum represents a significant departure from the Aristotelian concept in two related ways. In the first place, *ethos* replaces *mythos* in importance as the central artistic concern. In the second place, and as a corollary of this, variety is substituted for unity, for Horace refers to decorum of character not to a single principle, such as Aristotelian *mythos,* but to the myriad variety of familiar life. Just as the principle of decorous unity was earlier referred in part to the external criterion of public opinion, so now the poet is directed to life and manners (*vitae morumque*) (l. 317), not to nature, for the model of decorum. In the terms of Philodemus, therefore, good writing consists not so much in deriving particulars from universal forms as in imposing formal control upon particular contingencies; its goal is not propriety in the philosophic sense but the practical decorum that adapts to particular persons and topics.

That the rational control governing artistic production should be of this particular kind is a corollary of Horace's understanding of the poet's duty, which is not merely the habit of right reasoning about making, but the exercise of this habit within a particular social and political context. In order to emphasize this second point, Horace follows the sophistical and rhetorical tradition of reciting a mythography of poetry (ll. 391–407), which asserts the claim that from Orpheus and Amphion to Homer the true quality of poetry has been coeval with its social function.[27] Set in the context of man's civil and conventional life, poetry reflects that life: the formal and mimetic dimensions of

26. Brink, *Ars Poetica,* p. 341.

27. Brink, *Ars Poetica,* p. 385; cf. Cicero, *Pro Archia,* 8.19–12.32. See also Williams, chs. 2 and 6; and for Horace, Campbell, pp. 61–63.

poetic art are understood as a function of its social or communicative dimension. It is therefore in the light of the social and communicative powers of Orphic *psychagogia* that Horace demands that poetry should be sweet (*dulce*) as well as formally beautiful (*pulchra*) (ll. 99). Not only are these poetic qualities complementary, but they represent the two dimensions that together constitute the poetic art. The formal unity that is the principle of beauty completes the civilizing function initiated by rhetorical sweetness: men are not only drawn out of primitive existence, but are brought together in the formal unity of institutions. The formal principle of beauty requires that the poet literally draw together in a formal sense the myriad elements addressed by the dynamic dimension of art. It is in just this way that the poet serves the state:

> os tenerum pueri balbumque poeta figurat,
> torquet ab obscenis iam nunc sermonibus aurem,
> mox etiam pectus praeceptis format amicis,
> asperitatis et invidiae corrector et irae,
> recte facta refert, orientia tempora notis
> instruit exemplis, inopem solatur et aegrum.
> castis cum pueris ignara puella mariti
> disceret unde preces, vatem ni Musa dedisset?
>
> (*Epistles,* 1.1.126–133)

The poet fashions the tender, lisping lips of childhood; even then he turns the ear from unseemly words; presently, too, he moulds the heart by kindly precepts, correcting roughness and envy and anger. He tells of noble deeds, equips the rising age with famous examples, and to the helpless and sick at heart brings comfort. Whence, in company with chaste boys, would the unwedded maid learn the suppliant hymn, had the Muse not given them a bard?

The state is here depicted not as a homogeneous mob, but as an aggregate of discrete particulars, each of which is separately acknowledged and addressed by the poet.[28] The art of poetry thus institutionalizes and embodies conventional satisfactions for the expectations and demands of the various elements in the social configuration:

> centuriae seniorum agitant expertia frugis,
> celsi praetereunt austera poemata Ramnes.
>
> (*Ars Poetica,* 341–342)

---

28. Brink, *Ars Poetica,* pp. 352–354.

The centuries of the elders chase from the stage what is profitless; the proud Ramnes disdain poems devoid of charms.

In the Horatian version, therefore, art quite literally reflects man's conventional life, and its very formal principles embody public convention. Because it is so constituted, art represents the public face of wisdom; a play should be marked with moral commonplaces,[29] just as the chorus, while fitting in a formal sense with the plot (ll. 193–202), has as its subject matter "instances of piety and conventional good sense."[30] Indeed, the subjects of poetry generally, its objects of imitation, are not so much instances of universals as the multiple particulars of common life. Insofar as Horace conceives of drama, and especially comic drama, as imitative,[31] what it imitates is *vitae morumque,* or familiar life in all its variety. Character is inconceivable to Horace apart from the Roman concern with *mores:*

> Tu quid ego et populus mecum desideret audi,
> si plosoris eges aulaea manentis et usque
> sessuri, donec cantor 'vos plaudite' dicat,
> aetatis cuiusque notandi sunt tibi mores,
> mobilibusque decor naturis dandus et annis.
>
> (ll. 153–158)

Now hear what I, and with me the public, expect. If you want an approving hearer, one who waits for the curtain, and will stay until the singer cries "Give your applause," you must note the manners of each age, and give a befitting tone to shifting natures and their years.

Quintilian, in observing the importance of a knowledge of *mores* for both orator and poet, remarks upon the difficulty of translating the Greek *ethos* into Latin: *"ethos* is a word for which in my opinion Latin has no equivalent: it is however rendered by *mores* and consequently the branch of philosophy known as *ethics* is styled *moral* by us. But close consideration of the nature of the subject leads me to think in this connection it is not so much *mores* in general that is meant as certain peculiar aspects, for the term *mores* includes every attitude of the

---

29. See Brink, *Ars Poetica,* p. 344, and Fairclough's note on this passage in the Loeb edition.

30. Brink, *Ars Poetica,* p. 256.

31. See Craig La Drière, "Horace and the Theory of Imitation," *American Journal of Philology,* 40 (1939), 288–300.

mind" (6.2.8–9). It is precisely the broad inclusiveness of the term that Horace emphasizes, not only at ll. 311–316, but more extensively at ll. 153–178. The changefulness of human life from hour to hour there echoes the earlier lengthy evocation of the mutability of linguistic usage. The public expects to find itself mirrored in the poet's art, not merely in its *genus* as man, but in the various social species, the "shifting natures" (l. 158) that in turn reflect shared values and conventions. The definition of comedy later attributed by Donatus to Cicero—the mirror of custom (*speculum consuetudine*)[32]—is precisely that which later commentators applied to the Horatian dictum that the poet depicts "life and manners" (l. 317): "What," says Acron, "is comedy but the image of daily life?" Landino simply observes that "the good imitator tries to imitate the life and manners of men."[33] The art of poetry embodies the conventional specifications of common life in conventional poetic forms.

This is evident even in Horace's distinction between tradition and innovation (l. 119). The poet either goes to the general and collective source of tradition, or takes the alternative of inventing *de novo* by depicting the particular circumstances of life and manners. As a consequence, the only "universal" in Horace's *Ars* is the body of shared values and conventions that history has made available in literary tradition or that usage has made available in contemporary experience. While Aristotle refers such traditional or conventional materials to the higher test of the universal,[34] they represent in themselves, for Horace, the ultimate authority in the poetic art.

In the light of the conventionality that Horace attributes to the subject matter of poetry, both in its particular sense as derived or "imitated" from life and manners and in its general derivation from tradition, one may assign to the whole spirit of the *Ars* the formula that Horace specifically applies to the problem of diction: "I will," says Horace, "seek a new style created from the familiar" (l. 240). The poetic

32. See Marvin T. Herrick, *The Fusion of Horatian and Aristotelian Literary Criticism, 1531–5*, Illinois Studies in Language and Literature, 32 (Urbana: University of Illinois Press, 1946), p. 28; cf. *Epistles*, 2.1.118–169, and La Drière, "Horace and the Theory of Imitation," p. 294 and n. 22.

33. Herrick, p. 29.

34. *Poetics*, 1455a34–b13. See Brink, *Ars Poetica*, p. 205. Brink's comparison of *Ars Poetica* 119–128 with ch. 9 of the *Poetics* is highly imaginative and suggestive, and I am very much indebted to it. But his insistence on finding Peripatetic parallels with the *Ars* involves him in some special pleading to make Horace carry the weight of Aristotle. See esp. *Prolegomena*, pp. 106–107. The much closer parallel to Horace occurs at *Poetics*, ch. 17; and this chapter emphasizes, if anything, the substantial difference between the Horatian concepts and the Aristotelian "universal" and "particular" of *Poetics* 9.

art involves a dynamic interplay between the integrity of formal control and the conventionality of the resources and materials of art. The achievement of decorous unity is the crowning product of individual and knowing control over resources provided by the panorama of human experience:

> tantum series iuncturque pollet
> tantum de medio sumptis accedit honoris

—such is the power of order and connection, such the beauty that may crown the commonplace (ll. 242–243).

The connection between poetic art and the familiar or conventional aspects of human experience means that any *ars* will recite traditional practices and opinions. The recital of various decorums of genre (ll. 73–89) that follows the invocation of linguistic usage is therefore most properly understood in connection with it.[35] The genres, that is, are not so much founded upon universal correspondences between structures and meanings as upon their conventional association in historical practice. With their unique features and demands, the genres reflect the eternal fact that *mutavit mentem populus levis* (*Epistles,* 2.1.108). Just as public usage resembles nature in changing the shape and color of the surrounding world, so do public taste and poetic practice together give birth and shape to conventional poetic forms. While the Aristotelian "history" of comedy and tragedy always has in view the perfected and final form, the point of reference for Horace is the origin of poetic form, the foundations and precedents followed by tradition.[36]

Accordingly, the Horatian view implies that if poetic forms and genres derive from the matrix of history and tradition, they should be composed and judged with reference to that matrix. It is therefore significant that Horace adds to his discussion of the sources of "good writing" a general comparison of Greek and Roman *ethos* (ll. 323–333). One of the sources of art resides by implication in history and national character; the relative achievement of Greek and Roman poets can only fully be understood in the light of the values and motivations predominant in each civilization. That Horace's attention to history amounts to more than a naive theory of progress[37] is clear enough from

35. La Drière, review of Wolf Steidle, pp. 242–243. Notice, however, the different assumptions guiding lines 89–99, which seem to posit more absolute criteria for genre and diction.

36. See Brink, *Ars Poetica,* p. 161.

37. As basically described in J. F. D'Alton, *Horace and His Age: A Study in Historical Background* (1917; rpt., New York: Russell and Russell, 1962), pp. 268–269; cf. the same writer's *Roman Literary Theory and Criticism* (1931; rpt., New

his remarks concerning the history of the chorus and the history of Old Comedy (ll. 202–220, 281–284). Both the chorus and the Old Comedy are related, not to some later and more "perfect" form, but to a specific audience, and by implication to specific moral and political changes. Just as in the *Epistle to Augustus* (ll. 93–103) Horace relates the literary decline of Greece to political and moral corruption, so in his history of the chorus and of Old Comedy he traces the artistic pattern of decline from simplicity to corruption by outlining its later enjoyment of license and appetite for extravagance.

Horace's frequent appeals to history amount to more than isolated insights. They are not "perspectives" or "points of view" tacked on as afterthoughts; rather, they are integral to his conception of the poetic art, and corollary to his understanding of convention. The art of poetry, as Horace is at pains to show throughout, is the natural product of man's impulse to formalize the variety of his experiences, pleasures, and beliefs. The various specifications of this impulse, however, are manifest particulars, shared conventions that reflect the changing life of man. Horace's magnificent comparison of linguistic usage with changing forms in nature is more than simply imaginative: throughout the *Ars* Horace calls upon history to justify the comparison. Just as Aristotle's philosophic outlook enables him to examine *techne* in the light of universal *physis,* so Horace's regard for history emphasizes the distance between unchanging principles and their conventional specifications in the arts. History shows that each particular functions in reciprocal relations with other particulars; contingencies upon one particular influence the balance of the entire matrix. If there be an architechtonic order, it is so difficult of access that history and tradition represent the most reliable among provisional guides to success.

Thus, in their differing assessments of convention, history and philosophy function as alternative modes of thought. Euripides had expressed the difference between them by contrasting the unity of cosmic nature with the savage turmoil of practical and civil life:

York: Russell and Russell, 1962), esp. pp. 191–203; E. E. Sikes, *Roman Poetry* (New York: Dutton, 1923); and J. W. H. Atkins, *A History of Literary Criticism in Antiquity* (Cambridge: Cambridge University Press, 1934). All of these writers point to an important aspect of ancient literary criticism, which they label the "historical point of view." But in their admiration for historical scholarship they do an injustice to antiquity: first, in understanding the "historical point of view" to mean the same as "the idea of progress"; and second, in conceiving this aspect of ancient thought to be a "point of view," as if it were a perspective tacked on to thoughts unrelated to it. As I am trying to show throughout this chapter, the "historical point of view" is a fundamental and integral part of a complex of ideas and assumptions.

> Happy are they who discover history,
> Not in the suffering of citizens,
> Nor in the unjust deeds of violence,
> But in beholding the splendid order
> Of unchanging and eternal nature.[38]

According to Euripides, the objects of civic history stand opposed to the unchanging nature contemplated by natural science, or by the philosophic mind more generally. History insidiously undermines the philosophic view that human *mores,* conventions, and institutions share the permanent and abiding value of nature.

At the same time, however, history can provide what philosophy cannot—a practical guide to success within the world of contingency that is its frame of reference. It is not surprising, therefore, that rhetoric contracted an early alliance with history. Rhetoric and history, both essentially skeptical in outlook, envisage man's actions and inventions as particular responses to contingent circumstances. Because human discourse enables man to adapt to circumstance, rhetorical analysis gives rise to historical understanding, and historical insight provides a basis for rhetorical success. For these reasons Cicero observes that history is "the branch of literature closer than any other to oratory" (*De Legibus,* 1.2.5), and Lucian posits as the prime requirements of the historian poetical and rhetorical sophistication (*De Conscribenda Historia,* secs. 34, 58).

Such rhetorical thinking is so pervasive in the *Ars Poetica* that Horace even subjects poetic structure to its social setting. Just as the objects of imitation originate either in tradition or in life and manners, and just as style reflects the varieties of usage, so, too, does the formal disposition of these elements depend upon a special relationship with the public:

> cui lecta potenter erit res,
> nec facundia deseret hunc nec lucidus ordo.
> ordinis haec virtus erit et venus, aut ego fallor
> ut iam nunc dicat iam nunc debentia dici

(ll. 40–43)

Whoever shall choose a theme within his range, neither speech will fail him, nor clearness of order. Of order, this, if I mistake not, will be the excellence and charm that the

---

38. My translation of frag. 910, in August Nauck, ed., *Tragicorum Graecorum Fragmenta* (Leipzig: Teubner, 1889), p. 654. The fragment is cited in Jaeger, I, 385.

> author of the long-promised poem shall say at the moment
> what at that moment should be said.

Order must possess charm as well as excellence, and so attaches to the audience through the general demand for rhetorical efficacy, and hence ultimately to the social context suggested by the Orphic myth. As opposed to Aristotelian *mythos*, Horatian *ordo* is a matter of timing, and shares the rhetorical assumption that "the most effective arrangement must take account of the prejudices and weaknesses of an audience and the contingencies of individual cases."[39] Like the Sophists and rhetoricians before him, Horace tacitly acknowledges that decorum is relative to changing conditions, that, as Gorgias had maintained, "the harmony which assigns identity is a product of the moment, the proper circumstance."[40]

It is for just such reasons that Horace thinks historically in the *Ars Poetica*. Received poetic forms and techniques represent a series of such adjustments through time, and so tradition, precedent, and collective experience provide the means and materials that constitute the poetic art. The history of poetry, its successes and failures, forms the more comprehensive counterpart and background to the dialogue between the poet and his critic-friend (ll. 419–453); in a collective sense, history is a dialogue between many poets and many critics: it images the long and arduous interchange of trial and experience between the constructive and critical capacities.

The consequence of locating rhetoric, poetics, or any *techne* in the context of social history is a replacement of uniform standards with relative ones. Always tied to particulars and contingencies, historical thinking, Sextus observes, is nontechnical and unmethodical by philosophic standards: "there is no technical knowledge of things which vary from hour to hour."[41] Similarly, in Tacitus' *Dialogue on Oratory*, the connection of eloquence with historical change displaces the philosophic ideal of *techne* in the direction of practice. "The true basis of eloquence," Tacitus insists, "is not in theoretical knowledge only, but in a far greater degree in natural capacity and practical experience" (33.4). This is because the norms of discourse are social, conventional rather than natural, so that "the forms and types of oratory change with the times" (30.3.5). Thus focused upon convention, upon the social basis of its norms and upon their changes in time, rhetorical thinking

39. Brink, *Ars Poetica*, p. 127.

40. Nancy S. Streuver, *The Language of History in the Renaissance* (Princeton: Princeton University Press, 1970), p. 12, on *Gorgias*, frag. 82B6.

41. Sextus Empiricus, *Pyrrhonean Hypotheses*, 1.254–260.

represents a skeptical alternative to the philosophic view of art as a rational science of production in conformity with nature. Looking back upon the history of rhetoric, Tacitus saw that such thinking was an integral part of the ancient technical tradition. Together with the philosophic view of nature, it helped to shape a highly complex intellectual framework capable of a variety of emphases and approaches.

4. THE MEDIEVAL REDEFINITION

The advent of Christianity brought with it a major revaluation and redefinition of the classical arts and sciences. Confronted with the Incarnation, as Alain de Lille observed, the arts were invalidated: "Nature falls silent, Logic is conquered, Rhetoric and Reason fail."[1] The singular and transcendent glory of the Divinity made more painfully evident what Boethius called the mutability of secular life, "the differences in languages, fashions, and conversation." Unlike the contemplative ideal, Boethius explained, "the customs and laws of diverse nations do so much differ from one another, that the same thing which some commend as laudable, others condemn as deserving punishment."[2] When the converted Augustine looked back upon his education in the classical arts, he lamented its massive perpetration of unquestioned social values: "How must one condemn the river of custom! Who can stand firm against it?" In contrast with the narrow scope of secular tradition, "that true and inward goodness . . . makes its judgments not from convention but from the most right and undeviating law of God Almighty."[3]

But although the insecurity of merely human covenants threatened to invalidate the arts altogether, such early Christian thinkers as Augustine and Jerome were determined to retain and purify them. In late antiquity, the chief means of preservation was the compilation of technical handbooks or compendia. Christianity adopted the framework of ancient technical thinking embodied in these handbooks, and the *artes* came to represent "the basic schema of the world of thought"[4] in the Middle Ages. But in preserving the technical schema,

1. Alain de Lille, *Anticlaudianus,* quoted in Ernst R. Curtius, *European Literature and the Latin Middle Ages,* trans. Willard R. Trask (Princeton: Princeton University Press, 1953), p. 42.

2. Boethius, *The Consolation of Philosophy,* trans. "I.T." (1609), rev. H. F. Steward (1918; rpt., Cambridge: Harvard University Press, 1968), 2.7.

3. St. Augustine, *The Confessions,* trans. Rex Warner (New York: New American Library, 1963), pp. 33, 61.

4. Curtius, p. 42.

the early Christian thinkers were compelled to reevaluate its conceptual basis.

Nearly all medieval definitions and classifications of the arts preserved the ancient distinction between nature and convention, and emphasized their opposition in principle, for only through a rational standard of natural fitness could the arts serve the soul. Thus Augustine justified secular learning by remarking that "it is not by faith alone, but by trustworthy reason, that the soul leads itself little by little to most virtuous habits and the perfect life."[5] In keeping with their necessary task, the arts themselves partake of reason; dialectic crowns the arts of the *trivium,* not only because of its greater rigor and complexity, but also because it pervades and shapes each of the other arts (*De Ordine,* 2.13.38). The significant exception to this identification of the arts with reason is rhetoric, an art necessitated by the fact that men are swayed by custom: "unwise men generally follow their own feelings and habits rather than the narrow road of truth." Because of its connection with convention, rhetoric is the most benighted of the arts, "a portion more replete with lack than with enlightenment" (*De Ordine,* 2.13.39). Because it is the least rational of the arts, its source lies "not in rational rules but in imitation."[6] In Augustine's view, only by becoming an "art of preaching," by substituting the truth of Scripture and the example of St. Paul for the instability of secular political life, can rhetoric become an art compatible with both faith and reason.

The encyclopedic tradition further emphasized the rational stability of art by pointing to the freedom from corporal limitation in the seven "liberal" arts. Using the etymological method characteristic of the encyclopedic tradition, Cassiodorus, for example, observes that

> the word book [*liber*] comes from the word "free" [*liber*]; a book, in other words, is the bark of a tree, removed and freed—the bark on which the ancients used to write oracular responses before the invention of papyrus. In view of this, therefore, we are permitted to make short books or extended ones, since we are allowed to limit the size of books in accordance with their nature . . . "Art" [*ars*] is so called because it limits [*artet*] and binds us with its rules; according

5. St. Augustine, *Divine Providence and the Problem of Evil: A Translation of St. Augustine's "De Ordine,"* trans. Robert P. Russell (New York: Cosmopolitan Science and Art Co., 1942), 2.19.50.

6. St. Augustine, *De Doctrina Christiana,* trans. D. W. Robertson, Jr. (New York: Bobbs-Merrill, 1958), 4.1.2, 3.4–5.

to others this word is taken over from the Greek expression *apo tes aretes,* which means "from excellence."[7]

As they elaborated the procedure of separating the *Organon* from Aristotle's other works, the later encyclopedists traditionally categorized the linguistic arts of the *trivium* as "rational," "logical," or "instrumental."[8] As such, these arts were specifically contrasted not only with the theoretical sciences but, more important, with the "practical" and the "mechanical" or "servile" arts.[9] As a result, the arts of the trivium were theoretically removed from the limitations of both matter and contingency.

Despite their varying degrees of rational purity, however, all of the arts were understood to reflect divine wisdom. Hugo of St. Victor, for example, maintains that the arts aid in man's rehabilitation; the arts, he says, "ought to regard either the restoring of our nature's integrity, or the relieving of those weaknesses to which our present life lies subject."[10] Burdened with the task of restoring fallen human nature, the arts reflect nature in its most perfect and ideal form: "the products of artificers, while not nature, imitate nature, and in the design by which they imitate, they express the form of their exemplar, which is nature" (*Didascalion,* 1.4). For the encyclopedic tradition as a whole, art "is no longer concerned with the exercise of skill, but with the formal principles of knowledge."[11] John of Salisbury, for example, remarks in his defense of the arts that "art is a system that reason has devised in order to expedite, by its own short cut, our ability to do things within our natural capacities."[12] Given the rationality of the arts, it is not surprising that for John "nature is the mother of all the arts, to which she has given reason as their nurse for their protection and improvement" (*Metalogicon,* p. 33).

The elevation of reason to a position of sovereignty over the en-

7. Cassiodorus, *Institutiones,* ed. R. A. B. Mynors (Oxford: Clarendon Press, 1937), Praefatio, bk. 2; trans. Leslie Webber Jones, *An Introduction to Divine and Human Readings* (New York: Columbia University Press, 1946), pp. 143–144.

8. See O. B. Hardison, *The Enduring Monument* (Chapel Hill: University of North Carolina Press, 1962), pp. 3–4.

9. See Katherine Gilbert and Helmut Kuhn, *A History of Esthetics* (Bloomington: Indiana University Press, 1954), pp. 156–160.

10. Hugo of St. Victor, *Didascalion,* trans. Jerome Taylor (New York: Columbia University Press, 1961), 1.5.

11. Ernst Schlosser, *Die Kunstliteratur* (1924), quoted in Edgar De Bruyne, *The Esthetics of the Middle Ages,* trans. Eileen B. Hennessy (New York: Ungar, 1969), p. 29.

12. John of Salisbury, *Metalogicon,* trans. Daniel D. McGarry (Berkeley: University of California Press, 1955), p. 34.

cyclopedic arts coincided with an equally thorough demotion of convention. In keeping with the etymological bias of his compendium, Cassiodorus includes no mention of *usus* in his discussion of language. The power of usage represents for Isidore the most negative of influences, the principal obstruction to compiling a reliable encyclopedia on the basis of etymology. The impossibility of universal knowledge dates from the building of the tower of Babel, whence "the diversity of languages arose."[13] Thereafter, the genealogy of the world's nations was obscured by tribes who cast aside their names and took on new ones, "either from kings, or countries, or customs, or other causes" (*Etymologiae,* 9.2.132). Furthermore, following the dispersal at Babel, *usus* replaced *natura* in human learning. "Not all names were given by the ancients in accordance with nature," Isidore laments, "but certain also according to whim, just as we sometimes give to slaves and estates names according to our fancy. Hence it is that the etymologies of some names are not found, since certain things have received names not according to the quality in which they originated, but according to man's arbitrary choice" (*Etymologiae,* 1.29.2–3).

Since the art of rhetoric had fallen into almost total disuse, the encyclopedic treatments of rhetoric show little awareness of the potential threat it poses to the test of natural fitness. The function of rhetoric, Cassiodorus observes, is "to persuade, by speaking on civil questions, to the extent permitted by the nature of things and persons" (*Institutiones,* 2.2.1). But instead of exploring what had classically been the source of a conflict between "speech addressed to matters" and "speech addressed to hearers," Cassiodorus drops the distinction between "things" and "persons," and goes on to enumerate the parts and kinds of rhetoric after the simplistic fashion of his sources, the *Ad Herrenium* and Cicero's *De Inventione.* Both Isidore and Martianus Capella are similarly derivative and unsophisticated. Even in the later and more sophisticated compendia of Hugo of St. Victor and John of Salisbury, where the importance of practice and experience in the social setting receives its greatest emphasis, the experiential dimension of rhetoric is clearly subordinated to the rational. Thus Hugo qualifies the importance of experience by observing that

> all sciences, indeed, were matters of use before they became
> matters of art. But when men considered that use can be
> transformed into art, and what was vague and subject to
> caprice can be brought into order by definite rules and pre-

13. Isidore, *Etymologiae,* 4.1.1, trans. Ernest Brehant, *An Encyclopedist of the Dark Ages* (New York: Columbia University Press, 1912).

cepts, they began to reduce to art the habits which had
arisen partly by chance, partly by nature—correcting what
was bad in use, supplying what was missing, eliminating
what was superfluous, and furthermore prescribing definite
rules and precepts for each usage.   (*Didascalion,* 1.11)

Citing Horace on usage, John of Salisbury similarly observes that practice and convention provide the material for the rational art of grammar; but the art itself is so defined by virtue of its rational regularity
(*Metalogicon,* pp. 39, 49–51). In none of the encyclopedic writers is
there anything like the depiction of the dynamic relations between
social practice and rational control in Cicero's *De Oratore* or Horace's
Ars Poetica.

In accordance with ancient grammatical practice, most medieval
writers discuss the art of poetry under the aegis of one or more of the
trivium arts, usually grammar. Only with the composition of several
separate treatises in the later twelfth century does poetry receive full
and explicit recognition as a distinct art meriting technical treatment.
Yet even this recognition is marked by surprisingly little theoretical
reflection on the status or aim of the art with reference to other arts
or to kinds of knowledge generally. John of Garland's reflections on
art in the *Parisiana Poetria* are limited to the observation that "anyone who presents an art ought to define his terms, make distinctions,
and include examples."[14] Geoffrey of Vinsauf expresses the nature of
artistic control metaphorically: "If a man has a house to build he does
not rush into action . . . he mentally outlines the successive steps in
a definite order. The mind's hand shapes the entire house before the
body's hand builds it. Its mode of being is archetypal before it is
actual."[15] Although Geoffrey distinguishes between the "order of nature" and the "order of art" in disposing of material, he argues that
"deft artistry inverts things in such a way that it does not pervert
them" (*Poetria Nova,* 1.87–100). The scanty theoretical indications are
that the poetic art shares the rational order of nature, even when
seeming to contradict it.

At the same time, the concept of convention is either completely
overlooked or relegated to a minor role in these treatises. Despite his

14. John of Garland, *Parisiana Poetria,* trans. Trawgott Lawler (New Haven:
Yale University Press, 1974), 1.26–27.

15. Geoffrey de Vinsauf, *Poetria Nova,* ed. Edmond Faral, *Les arts poétiques du
XIIe et du XIIIe siècles* (1924; rpt., Paris: Librairie Honoré Champion, 1962),
1.43–48. Trans. Margaret F. Nims (Toronto: Pontifical Institute of Medieval Studies,
1967).

frequent citation of Horace, John of Garland includes no mention of *usus;* his mention of *Ars Poetica,* ll. 46–48, on the problem of coinage would be the logical place for an invocation of linguistic usage but none is made. The rigid decorums of Virgilian precedent, furthermore, show none of the plenitude and variety that characterize Horace's discussions of "life and manners." Geoffrey does refer decorum of style to the triple test of ear, mind, and usage (*usus*), but he devotes several lines to each of the first two criteria, while limiting his discussion of *usus* to its appearance in the summary formulas (*Poetria Nova,* 4.1946–1968). Matthieu de Vendôme grants a somewhat more substantial role to convention, perhaps because of his more frequent citation of Horace. Not only does he quote *Ars Poetica,* l. 72, in observing that usage serves as a proper antidote to stylistic excess, but he cites "proverbial wisdom (that is, commonplaces)" as one of the ways of beginning a poem.[16] Yet even these acknowledgments are incidental or residual, and in no way affect the general outlook of the text. Despite their almost total reliance upon precedent and tradition, the twelfth-century poetic handbooks show little awareness or interest in the problem of convention, and in their infrequent theoretical statements about art adhere primarily to the earlier Christian and encyclopedic assumptions.

These assumptions were summarized and systematically reinforced by Aquinas, whose discussion of art was perhaps the most extended and elaborate in the Middle Ages. By adapting Aristotle's *Ethics* to his purpose, Aquinas guaranteed in systematic fashion the subordination of artistic production to rational intelligence. For while the speculative and practical powers differ with respect to their different ends in truth and goodness, every practical act requires the aid of reason. Thus artistic habits share with speculative habits the attribute of virtue: "art is nothing other than the right judgment about things to be made."[17] This means that art, like the speculative habits, derives its virtue from its rational consistency: "Art gives only the ability to act well." Because art shares with the speculative habits the contemplation of unchanging principles, its virtue "consists essentially and originally in a permanent disposition to act in accordance with reason.[18] Thomas therefore observes that "when anyone endowed with art produces bad work, this is not the work of his art; but contrary to it: as

16. Matthieu de Vendôme, *Ars Versificatoria,* ed. Faral, 4.26, 1.16.

17. St. Thomas Aquinas, *Summa Theologiae,* 1a2ae, q. 57., a. 3; Dominican Fathers translation (New York: McGraw-Hill, 1969), vol. 23.

18. Etienne Gilson, *The Philosophy of St. Thomas Aquinas,* trans. Edward Bullough (St. Louis: B. Herder, 1937), p. 311.

when, though knowing the truth, a man lies, his words are contrary to, and not in accordance with, his knowledge." The value of artistic productions "consists in their conforming to the measure demanded by art, which is their rule."[19] Any actual productions falling short of this criterion reflect contingencies of practice or material; art itself, though operative within the sphere of changing things, remains as impervious to change as any other virtue.

Thus, in reexamining the conceptual basis of the technical tradition, and by insisting upon the transcendent powers and aims of art, Aquinas, like most thinkers of the Middle Ages, implicitly maintained the contrast between nature and convention as alternative tests of fitness. By the later Middle Ages, this contrast begins to reemerge as an explicit and highly conspicuous opposition. Boccaccio, for example, draws a vivid distinction between the rational foundation of poetry and the merely conventional basis of law; poetry, he claims,

> constitutes a stable and fixed science founded upon things eternal, and confirmed by original principles; in all times and places this knowledge is the same, unshaken by any possible change. Not so with the law; the Slav, for example, knows not the same laws as the African . . . city ordinances and statutes of the realm may greatly increase or diminish the power of a law; and the proclaimed adjournment of the court may silence them. Laws even become antiquated and sometimes actually dead; for some were long ago held in very high regard which in our times are either wholly neglected or obsolete; and consequently not invariable like poetry. In a word . . . we should speak of the practice [*facultas*] of law, not the science [*scientia*] of law; and how much a science transcends mere practice the wise of all times know—both ancient and modern.[20]

Boccaccio's alternatives of *facultas* and *scientia* are echoed in Richard of Bury's distinction between convention and reason. Contrasting the arts with the study of law, Richard remarks that "many laws achieve force by mere custom [*consuetudine sola*], not by syllogistic necessity, like the arts . . . For whatever receives its stability from use alone [*sola consuetudine*] must necessarily be brought to nought

19. St. Thomas Aquinas, *Quaestiones Disputatae,* q. 1, a. 13., trans. John Patrick Reid, *The Virtues (In General)* (Providence: Providence College Press, 1951).

20. *Boccaccio on Poetry,* trans. Charles G. Osgood (Princeton: Princeton University Press, 1930), pp. 25–26; cf. p. 150n12.

by disuse." Richard's preference for letters over law reflects the manifest difference in aim and principle between law and science:

> every science is delighted and desires to open its inward parts and display the very heart of its principles, and to show forth the roots from which it buds and flourishes . . . for thus from the cognate and harmonious light of truth of conclusion to principles, the whole body of science will be full of light, having no part dark. But laws, on the contrary, since they are human enactments for the regulation of social life, or the yokes of princes thrown over the necks of their subjects, refuse to be brought to the standard of *synteresis*, the origin of equity, because they possess more of arbitrary will than of rational judgment.[21]

Significantly, Richard contrasts the open radiance of reason and the *artes* with the close obscurity of law and convention based upon the practical impetus of will. This reevaluation practically reverses the classical figure that compares the closed fist of dialectic with the open hand of rhetoric. In Cicero's version, as in the rhetorical tradition generally, Zeno's Stoic analogy is taken as a compliment to rhetoric: "relaxing and extending his hand, he said eloquence was like the open palm." To Aristotle's observation that rhetoric is broader and more open to contingency than dialectic, Cicero adds the observation that "dialectic is narrower." Despite the rhetorician's need for dialectic, its close obscurity requires the addition of a "certain grace of style; the orator must open up the dialectical habit of discussing briefly and compactly to the greater clarity and fullness of the ordinary judgment and the popular intelligence" (*Orator*, 3.113–117). In Richard's version, by contrast, the open brilliance, clarity, and fullness of ancient rhetoric are appropriated for the lucid integrity of *scientia* and the changing world of "human enactment" is banished into darkness.

Such reversals demonstrate the extent to which the Middle Ages witnessed a genuine and thorough reevaluation of the ancient technical tradition. At the same time, however, this reevaluation did not actually change the conceptual basis of that tradition. On the contrary, by consistently opposing the values of permanence and order to the values of accommodation and contingency, the theorists of the Middle Ages maintained and further polarized nature and convention as alternative principles of fitness and rectitude. The alternative as-

21. Richard of Bury, *Philobiblon*, trans. E. C. Thomas (1960; rpt., Oxford: Basil Blackwell, 1970), p. 119.

sumptions and procedures to which these principles gave rise became an explicit focus of debate with the Renaissance revival of rhetorical ideals. This revival, with its emphasis upon the practical rehabilitation of the arts through their application to the panorama of human experience, brought renewed vigor to the rival claims of reason and experience and so to the alternatives of nature and convention as artistic norms. Among humanists aware of these rival claims, the concept of art once again became highly problematic and fraught with difficulties. The orator, Petrarch observed, was essentially a man of affairs who found his place "in large cities and in the press of the crowd." This meant in turn, said Leonardo Bruni, that the orator "appears to support those things which take part in ordinary life and practice, not to invent things which are strange and abhorrent and of no use to it." The need for practical utility brought renewed importance to the social character of rhetoric; Lorenzo Valla asserted that "as *mores* and laws differ among nations and peoples, and the differing nature of language among them each is holy and inviolate . . . usage [*consuetidine*] ought to be fixed as a kind of civil law." At the same time, however, adherence to convention was balanced by the need for more abiding fitness. Along the entire valley of the Arno, Dante observed, men had "changed their nature" by succumbing to the public contagion of "bad custom [*mal uso*]" (*Purgatorio,* 14.39–41). No practical humanist could ignore the power of convention, but convention could not itself serve as sufficient guide to man's right life. The crowd, Petrarch complained, "is not able to see anything with the mind; it judges all things according to the testimony of its eyes. It is the task of a higher spirit to recall [man's] mind from his senses, and to remove his thoughts from the common practice."[22]

The alternatives of nature and convention, reason and experience, were a problem not simply in the art of rhetoric, but in all the arts, for which rhetoric, with its renewed claims on behalf of experience, served as a model of normative ambivalence. Thus when Roger Ascham turned to the precedent of Cicero's *De Oratore* in exploring the specific art of archery in his *Toxophilus* (1545), he was attempting a definitive formulation of the normative difficulties besetting all the practical arts and aims of humanism. Against the claims of Toxophilus, the practitioner of archery, that the certainty of excellence resides in constant "use," in the inarticulate adjustments that archers

22. The passages from Petrarch, Bruni, and Valla are cited in Jerrold E. Seigel, *Rhetoric and Philosophy in Renaissance Humanism* (Princeton: Princeton University Press, 1968), pp. 43, 111, and 163, respectively.

make in practice, the philosopher Philologe advances the alternative claim that rational control surpasses practice in importance. "For all Use, in all things," Philologe maintains, "yf it be not stayed with Cunnyng, wyll verie easely bryng a man to do that thynge, what so ever he goeth aboute, with muche illfavoredness and deformitie."[23] By way of contrast, rational control takes the form of art, and works "to oversee, and correcte use: which use if it be not led, & governed wyth cunnyng, shall sooner go amisse, than strayght" (p. 62). The possibility of such artistic knowledge hinges upon the underlying "nature" presumed to exist in archery: "And where ye doubte whether there can be gadered any knowledge or arte in shootyng or no, surely I thinke that a man being wel exercised in it and sumwhat honestly learned withal, might soone with diligent observing and marking of the whole nature of shootynge, find out as it were an arte of it . . . there lieth hid in the nature of shootynge, an Arte" (p. 60).

It is not surprising that in response to this demand Toxophilus revives the arguments of Antonius in Cicero's *De Oratore,* for in his use of rhetorical assumptions, Toxophilus also addresses himself to the burden of the medieval inheritance. "I lacke learnynge," he claims, "whych shulde set out the Arte or waye in any thynge. And you must knowe that I was never so well sene, in the Posteriorums of Aristotle as to invent and search out general Demonstrations for the setting forth of any newe Science" (p. 63). In support of his skeptical approach to art, Toxophilus cites Cicero's qualification of perfection by the complexity of experience in the *Orator:* "although as Cicero saith a man maye ymagine and dreame in his minde of a perfite ende in any thynge, yet there is no experience or use of it" (p. 64). In other words, inarticulate and irregular adjustments to the contingencies of practice militate against the formulation of abiding principles. Toxophilus is ultimately persuaded of the rational basis of art, that "there lieth hid in the nature of shootynge, an Arte." But after rendering the outlines of this art, he returns to the opposing claims of practice, and questions whether any art can overcome the diversity of practices in use. "All the discommodities whiche ill custome hath grafted in archers, can neyther be quycklye poulled out, nor yet sone rekened of me, they be so many" (p. 101). Customary practice constitutes the primary obstacle to the rational control of human endeavor: "Use and custome, separated from knowledge and learnyng, doth not onely hurt shootynge, but the most weyghtye thynges in the worlde beside: And therefore I mar-

23. Roger Ascham, *Toxophilus,* in *English Works,* ed. William Aldis Wright (1904; rpt., Cambridge: Cambridge University Press, 1970), p. 60.

vaile moche at those people whyche be the maynteners of uses withoute knowledge, having no other word in theyr mouthe but thys use,
use, custome, custome" (p. 101).

Ascham's dialogue is most directly concerned with the conflict between the powers of reason and experience in the agency or efficient
cause of art—the artist himself. But its implications bear upon the
formal cause of art as well. Just as experience shapes the individual,
so it shapes collective habits or conventions, which in turn become an
alternative to reason as a source of artistic norms. Accordingly, "thys
use, use, custome, custome" threatens to affect "the most weyghtye
thynges in the worlde" by enforcing "uses withoute knowledge." The
threat expresses itself most clearly when social norms part company
with nature and become mere arbitrary fashion.

This was a special concern for the arts of speech in the Renaissance.
John Hoskins, for example, balanced against his tribute to the unity of
Logos, cited at the beginning of this chapter, a lament at the multi-
plicity of verbal conventions:

> there are now such schisms of eloquence that it is enough for
> any ten years that all the bravest wits do imitate some one
> figure which a critic hath taught some great personage. So
> it may be within this two hundred years we shall go through
> the whole body of rhetoric. It is true that we study according
> to the predominancy of courtly inclinations: whilst mathe-
> matics are in request, all our similitudes come from lines,
> circles, and angles; whilst moral philosophy is now a while
> spoken of, it is rudeness not to be sententious. And for my
> part, I'll make one. I have used and outworn six several
> styles since I was first Fellow of New College, and am yet
> able to bear the fashion of [the] writing company.[24]

The essentially negative metaphor of fashion serves as Hoskins' evaluation of convention as a norm. But almost contemporaneously, Samuel Daniel seized upon the same metaphor, only to turn it against the
logocentric concept of art as understood by Hoskins. In Daniel's view,
the perfection of speech "hath as many shapes as there be tongues or
nations in the world, nor can with all the tyrannical Rules of idle
Rhetorique be governed otherwise then present custome and present
observation will allow. And being now the trim and fashion of the
times, to sute a man otherwise cannot but give a touch of singularity;

---

24. Hoskins, *Directions for Speech and Style,* pp. 38–39.

for when he hath all done, hee hath but found other clothes to the same body, and peradventure not so fitting as the former" (p. 363).[25]

Here fitness is a function of convention rather than the *Logos*. These two opinions reflect a central problem in Renaissance thought. Both Hoskins and Daniel are mindful of the powers of convention, but their differing evaluations suggest alternative visions of the powers and functions of the humane arts. With Daniel's view the classical concept of art finds itself on the threshold of a major redefinition. Envisioning art, as it does, as reflecting and changing with the diversity of experience over time and space, this redefinition eventually required a change in approach to the arts themselves. Originating with an acknowledgment of the varieties of practice and opinion, and thus from one implicit point of emphasis in the technical tradition, this approach eventually displaced the entire normative outlook of that tradition with a critical and historical assessment of the arts in the context of a changing human condition. Thus the demise of normative thinking originated from within classicism itself, in a critique that mature classicism had always conducted against itself. The modern and decisive emergence of this critique, brought about through changes in the concept of convention in moral, political, and historical thought, and its consequences for the verbal arts, are the subjects of the following chapters.

25. Daniel, *A Defense of Rhyme*, in G. Gregory Smith, II, 363.

II. Convention in the Sixteenth Century

1. THE "DUBLE NAME" OF CUSTOM: THE REFORMATION ATTACK ON CONVENTION

When Renaissance thinkers turned to the ancient technical tradition for guidance in rehabilitating the arts, they saw themselves confronted with a distinct problem. For the mature classicism of antiquity, adherence to convention was by no means always reckoned incompatible with the ultimate demand for natural rectitude and fitness. But for a great many Renaissance humanists, nature and convention were decidedly alternative ideals, and the conflict between them was an explicit source of debate. This debate was in part a product of the Christian hunger for absolutes, which had led to distrust of convention as a norm throughout the Middle Ages, but it was greatly aggravated by influences specific to Renaissance thought.

Some of these influences are represented in a sixteenth-century spelling manual in which a humanist's effort to establish normative principles revolves around the problematic character of convention. In his *Elementarie* (1582), Richard Mulcaster proposes to establish an "artificiall method" for regularizing the chaotic state of English orthography. In keeping with this aim, Mulcaster posits as a technical ideal the articulation of natural principles; his method uses, he claims, "such pollicies in the waie and passage to artificiall perfection, as nature hir selfe doth use in hir ascending to hir naturall height."[1] The means to "artificiall perfection" are "artificiall principles, which man's wisdom having considered the entendment of natur doth devise for himself, so manie in number, and so fit in qualitie, as theie maie take

1. Richard Mulcaster, *The First Part of the Elementarie* (Menston, Eng.: Scolar Press, 1970), p. 28.

67

sure hold of all natural inclinations and abilities, & bring them to perfection" (p. 30).

By concentrating on the relation of artistic precept to the structure
and function of nature, Mulcaster suggests that "art" operates with
reference to and in harmony with inherently natural principles. In
elaborating the theoretical basis for his proposals, however, Mulcaster
observes that verbal "art" is actually composed of voluntary as well as
cognitive elements, for it presides over a personified triumvirate of
sound, custom, and reason. Orthographical symbols, he observes, derive their efficacy

> not by them selves or anie vertew in their forme (for what
> likenesse or what affinitie hath the forme of anie letter in his
> own natur, to answer the force or sound in man's voice?)
> but onelie by consent of those men which first invented
> them and the pretie use thereof perceaved by those, which
> first did receive them. Whereby the people . . . agreed . . .
> that such a sound in the voice should be resembled by such a
> signe to the eie . . . whereunto theie subscribed their
> names, and set to their seals the daie and year, when their
> consent past. (p. 65)

Thus convention enters the realm of "art" as the voluntary practice
on which all formal regularization is to be based. It is then the business
of "reason" to gather "all those roming rules, that custom had beaten
out, into one bodie" and to dispose them "so in writing, as everie one
knew his own limits, reason his, custom his, sound his" (p. 74). For this
reason, Mulcaster proposes that spelling reform take cognizance of convention as well as reason, so that "the first doth the thing for the second to assure, and the second assureth, by observing of the first" (p. 74).

In order to advance his proposal, however, Mulcaster must defend
the role of convention against those who "have rated at custom, as a
most pernicious enemie to truth and right, even in that, where custom
hath most right, if it have right in anie" (p. 79). Convinced of the importance of linguistic usage, Mulcaster laments that the crux of his
argument hinges upon a concept almost universally despised. His opponent is not an individual competitor, but a whole climate of opinion created by anonymous and numberless men who "in their quarrel
to custom . . . seke first to bring it into generall hatred" (p. 84). Given
the controversial atmosphere that "aggravate[s] the discredit where-
with theie charge Custom," Mulcaster asks, "will there anie that fa-
voreth vertew, protect custom, being such a venim to all vertewes. and
such a poison to all vertewous effects?" (p. 85).

Against this obstacle, Mulcaster can only assert that some "good writers seme to favor custom," suggesting that, since all reasonable men agree, the source of controversy lies in some grave misapprehension. "Is there then," he asks, "not some error in the name, & maie not *custom* be misconstrewed?" (p. 86). After some consideration of the grounds on which the two sides meet, Mulcaster concludes that "it cannot otherwise be, but that the duble name is that which deceives" (p. 86).

This "duble name" suggests, perhaps as forcefully as any phrase could, that in the Renaissance the concept of convention was highly controversial. Ascham had indeed complained that his contemporaries had "no other word in theyr mouthe but thys use, use, custome, custome."[2] Moreover, the apparent moral implications of Mulcaster's problem emphasize the *kind* of controversy in which convention was likely to be involved. His intellectual adversaries are not simply fellow orthographers, but moral and political philosophers, lawyers and divines. The scope and strength of moral opposition to the concept of convention thus suggest its fundamental importance to Renaissance thinkers.

It is now quite common to suggest that any civilization may be understood to rest upon an underlying "system of norms" that determine its structure and direct its functions.[3] At the risk of oversimplification, one might argue that Renaissance civilization was quite consciously so constructed. That is, not only was Renaissance civilization "norm-conscious" in that it understood human life to be governed by fundamental laws or ends, commands or principles, but it tended to think of these same norms as isomorphic, applicable and operative in all spheres of human activity. For this reason Mulcaster was right in complaining that the "duble name" of "custom" was made to bear the weight of educational and moral, legal and religious implications and connotations. He wished for but could not foresee the time when a modern term like "convention" would circumvent some of these difficulties.

The concept of convention was therefore pervasively controversial in Renaissance thought because it was "normative" in character; it was, for the Renaissance, the *kind* of concept upon which men based their arguments and to which they appealed as a "principle." Because by far the greater part of what is loosely termed "Renaissance literary

2. Roger Ascham, *Toxophilus*, in *English Works*, ed. William Aldis Wright (1904; rpt., Cambridge: Cambridge University Press, 1970), p. 60.

3. See Paul Schrecker, *Work and History: An Essay on the Structure of Civilization* (Princeton: Princeton University Press, 1948).

criticism" followed the specifically prescriptive tradition of poetic and rhetorical *artes* or handbooks, as well as the general Renaissance habit of thinking in normative terms, the various assessments and applications of "convention" in literary thought necessarily reflected the characteristics and attitudes of other types of normative discourse. Indeed, the concept was profoundly shaped by the intersecting contexts of Renaissance moral, political, and religious thought, and especially by the reassessment of Christian ideals that was part of the Protestant Reformation.

When he invoked the "duble name" of custom, Mulcaster may have had in mind a contemporary morality play in which the "duble name" of custom appears personified as a double agent who incorporates two meanings of convention, each of which was generated by the Reformation of the European churches. Charged with reforming zeal, the anonymous *New Custom* (1559) depicts the conversion of Perverse Doctrine from the wiles of Hypocrisy, Cruelty, and Avarice to the purity of the Light of the Gospel and New Custom. This conversion hinges, however, upon the "duble name," or identity, of New Custom, the Reformed Church; Perverse Doctrine is prepared for his conversion by a shock of recognition when New Custom reveals his true identity as Primitive Constitution. As the Prologue observes, New Custom has a "duble name":

> For the primitive constitution, which was first appointed
> Even by God himself and by Christ his annointed;
> Confirm'd by th' Apostles, and of great antiquity:
> See, how it is perverted by men's wicked iniquity,
> To be called New Custom or New Constitution,
> Surely a name of too much ungodly abusion.[4]

This contrast between the "primitive constitution" and "new custom" suggests that the "duble name" of custom rests upon a contrast of ancient, ancestral, and received rites and practices as against recent innovations. The constant recourse of the reformers to the Pauline Epistles, the Acts of the Apostles, and to patristic material in general would seem to imply that in part the difficulties over the role of custom in the Reformation were simply historical in character,[5] or, in other words, that the *nature* of customary or conventional authority was un-

---

4. *New Custom,* in *Old English Plays,* ed. W. Carew Hazlitt (1874; rpt., New York: Benjamin Blom, 1964), III, 5.

5. See Horton Davies, *Worship and Theology in England, from Cranmer to Hooker* (Princeton: Princeton University Press, 1970), pp. 67–69.

questioned and that all controversy merely stemmed from differing historical assessments of the traditional priority of particular customs or conventions. Thus, John Foxe, for example, summoned history to justify Protestant practice; the function of history was not to question the nature of example and precedent, but to find the "purest," the oldest and most sacrosanct of traditions. "We have the old acts and histories of ancient time," he explained, "to give testimony with us, wherein we have sufficient matter for us to shew that the same form, usage, and institution of this our present reformed Church, are not the beginning of any new church of our own, but the renewing of the old ancient Church of Christ."[6]

Foxe's monumental historical venture, however, rested ultimately on doctrinal, not historical, grounds. In publishing an anonymous "Dialogue between Custom and Verity," for example, Foxe observes that the dialogue teaches men "not to measure religion by custom, but to try custom by truth of the Word of God: for custom may soon deceive, but the word of God abideth for ever." The dialogue itself, like many Reformation tracts, views customary usage or tradition not as the source of religious truth, but as its opponent. Thus at the heart of the quest for historical purity rests the conception of a revealed truth transcending all tradition. The "fundamental" nature of this truth, its utter priority, therefore calls into question the validity of all traditional practice and authority. Even the oldest usages and traditions are inferior to revealed truth, for their mode of transmission, and perhaps even their origins, are purely social in character. The historical dimension of time alone is insufficient to validate authority, for history demonstrates that all tradition is subject to the accretion of impurities and errors. Historical priority is merely relative. Thus Thomas Cranmer's *Confutation against Unwritten Verities* marshals testimony from the Old Testament to the Fathers that "custom is of no strength in this case of proving a religion."[7] John Jewel applies this principle with magisterial aloofness in observing several decades later that "the truth of God neither is furthered by the face of antiquity, nor hindered by the opinion of novelty, for oftentimes the thing that indeed

6. John Foxe, *Acts and Monuments,* ed. George Townsend (rpt., New York: AMS Press, 1965), 1.9. For the possible influence of Foxe in *New Custom,* see Leslie Martin Oliver, "John Foxe and the Drama *New Custom,*" *HLQ,* 10 (1949), 407–410.

7. Thomas Cranmer, *Miscellaneous Writings and Letters,* ed. John Edmund Cox (Cambridge: Parker Society, 1846), pp. 51–52. Cf. John Bradford, *Writings,* ed. Aubrey Townsend (Cambridge: Parker Society, 1848), I, 376; Thomas Becon, *Works,* ed. John Ayre (Cambridge: Parker Society, 1843), II, 379; and William Whitaker, *A Disputation of Holy Scripture Against the Papists,* ed. and trans. William Fitzgerald (Cambridge: Parker Society, 1849), pp. 612–613.

is new is commended as old, and the thing that indeed is old is condemned as new . . . Heresy is reproved not so well by novelty as by verity. Whatsoever thing serveth against the truth, the same is an heresy, yes, although it be a custom never so old."[8]

The reasons for such rigid opposition to traditional and customary authority, and the numerous arguments advanced in its behalf are of central importance to the shaping of Renaissance concepts of convention. In their quest for purity, the English reformers were led to reflect upon the nature and value of conventional norms as they related to two major concepts: the purity of Scripture and the integrity of the Christian community. The first of these concepts called attention to the presence of convention in religious thought by drawing a distinction between the sometimes difficult verbal surface of Scripture and the fundamentally human and comprehensible nature of its meaning. The second attempted to invalidate the role of tradition and convention in religious life by distinguishing the universal nature of the Christian faith from the historical and particular nature of secular communities.

Much of the impetus toward purity and simplicity in the Christian churches stemmed from a redefinition of the nature of Scripture at the beginning of the Reformation. When John Colet delivered his lectures at Oxford on St. Paul's Epistle to the Romans, he expounded on the epistle as a whole, and "not as an armoury of detached texts."[9] Until Colet's time, most scholastic commentators had held "a traditional belief in the *plenary* and verbal inspiration of the Bible, and remorselessly pursuing this belief to its logical results, had fallen into a method almost exclusively textarian."[10] Colet's method, clearly indebted to the revival of rhetorical thought, is to distinguish between the particular historical circumstances that contribute to the wording of the text and its universal human meaning. Calling attention to St. Paul's sense of decorum, Colet observes that "having regard to persons, places, circumstances, and time . . . he adapted his words so as to be most useful."[11] Accordingly, Colet attempts to develop an inter-

8. John Jewel, *Defense of the Apology for the Church of England,* in *Works,* ed. John Ayre (Cambridge: Parker Society, 1848), IV, 778. Cf. I, 49, 154–155.

9. Frederic Seebohm, *The Oxford Reformers* (1867; rpt., New York: Everyman's Library, 1914), p. 19.

10. Seebohm, p. 17.

11. John Colet, *Exposition of St. Paul's Epistle to the Romans,* in *Letters to Radulphus . . . Together with Other Treatises,* trans. J. H. Lupton (London: George Bell, 1876), p. 60. Cf. *An Exposition of St. Paul's Epistle to the Corinthians,* trans. J. H. Lupton (London: George Bell, 1874), pp. 22–23, 34.

pretive procedure responsive to St. Paul's habits of decorum as a writer. In his expositions of both Romans and 1 Corinthians, Colet draws upon historical evidence in order to establish the circumstances that called forth particular forms of eloquence.[12] In his later letters on the Mosaic account of the Creation, Colet draws an even more radical distinction between the human message of Scripture and its conventional verbal surface; Moses, he says, recounts the Creation "after the manner of some popular poet, that he may the better study the spirit of simple-minded rustics; imagining a succession of events, and works, and times, such as could by no means find place with so great an Artificer."[13] While taking pleasure in such expression, Colet concerns himself primarily with the meaning of the texts; it is his aim, as he wrote to Erasmus, to "leave all roundabout roads and go by a short cut to the truth."[14]

Following the lead of Colet, Erasmus advises the reader of Scripture that the human meaning of the text is to be discovered, not from arcane knowledge of "instances, relations, quiddities, and formalities,"[15] but from awareness of the human circumstances to which it is addressed:

> If we know from study of history not only the positions of these nations to whom these things happened, or to whom the Apostles wrote, but also their origins, manners, institutions, religion, and character, it is wonderful how much light and, if I may so speak, *life* is thrown into the reading of what before seemed dry and lifeless . . . To get at the real meaning, it is not enough to take four or five isolated words; you must look where they came from, what was said, by whom it was said, to whom it was said, at what time, on what occasion, in what words, what preceded, what followed.[16]

12. See, e.g., Colet's *Exposition of St. Paul's Epistle to the Corinthians,* pp. 9–10.

13. Colet, *Letters to Radulphus on Genesis I,* pp. 9–10; cf. pp. 14, 20, 27. Cf. Leland Miles, *John Colet and the Platonic Tradition* (La Salle, Ill.: Open Court, 1961), p. 32n1.

14. Quoted in Johan Huizinga, *Erasmus and the Age of Reformation* (1924; rpt., New York: Harper Torchbooks, 1957), p. 109.

15. Erasmus, *Paraclesis,* in *Christian Humanism and the Reformation: Selected Writings of Desiderius Erasmus,* trans. John C. Olin (New York: Harper Torchbooks, 1965), p. 101.

16. Quoted in Seebohm, p. 205. Cf. James Kelsey McConica, *English Humanists and Reformation Politics* (Oxford: Clarendon Press, 1965), p. 24.

In his appeal to historic circumstance over scholastic quiddity, Erasmus shares with Colet the rhetorical and archaeological bias that was characteristic of the humanist revival. At the same time, however, the purpose of such contextual knowledge is merely instrumental. Like Colet, Erasmus calls attention to the historical context of Scripture only to emphasize the underlying humanity of its message. Thus the reader is admonished to approach the New Testament not "in the frame of mind with which he approaches the *Attic Nights* of Gellius, or the *Miscellanea* of Angelo Poliziano, namely in order to gauge the depth of thought or rhetorical power or hidden erudition. We are concerned here with something that is sacred, something that is commended to the world by its simplicity and purity."[17]

This conceptual contrast between the universal simplicity of the "philosophy of Christ" and the particular complexity of political, social, and verbal circumstance led Erasmus to reflect upon a similar contrast in the Church of his own day. This contrast threw into bold relief the circumstantial and conventional nature of Christian ceremony. Compared with the simple worship of Christ, the veneration of saints, Erasmus observes, seems to "vary with different nations. Paul, for example, is a favorite with the French for the same purposes that Jerome is among our countrymen; and the things James or John perform in this place or in that, neither can perform everywhere."[18] Such observances distract men from fundamental simplicity; the authorities in each nation revere national saints and "detest the man who disregards national custom, yet excuse themselves from disregarding the most ancient custom of the universal Church!"[19] The true Christian, therefore, must "beware lest thou this wise think: . . . this is the custom and manner of living of kings, this wise live great men, this do both bishops and popes."[20] Taking Christ as his example, Erasmus scorns precedent and custom, in order to apply "not the manner of men to Christ, but Christ to the living of men."[21]

With the application of this contrast to the Church of his own day,

17. Erasmus, epistolary greeting to the reader, *Novum Instrumentum* (1515), in *Erasmus and His Age: Selected Letters of Desiderius Erasmus,* ed. Hans J. Hillerbrand (New York: Harper Torchbooks, 1970), p. 95.

18. Erasmus, *Enchiridion,* trans. Raymond Himelick (Bloomington: Indiana University Press, 1963), p. 99.

19. Erasmus, "A Fish Diet," in *Colloquia,* trans. Craig R. Thompson (Chicago: University of Chicago Press, 1965), p. 346.

20. Erasmus, *Enchiridion,* trans. (1533?) as *A Book Called in Latin "Enchiridion Militis Christiani" and in English "The Manual of a Christian Knight"* (London: Methuen, 1905), p. 188.

21. Erasmus, *Enchiridion,* trans. (1533?), p. 189.

Erasmus anticipates the redefinition of the Christian community undertaken as the central task of the Reformation. This redefinition, at the hands of Luther, Calvin, and their successors, focused in large part upon ideas of law, authority, corporate identity, and social practice in such a way as to necessitate repeated and careful scrutiny of the nature and value of convention. Thus in his attack on ceremonialism in *The Babylonian Captivity of the Church,* Luther follows Erasmus in calling attention to the "centuries of ancient custom" that have obstructed devotion "purely and simply to that alone which Christ Himself instituted."[22] He fixes upon the concept of convention, however, not merely through an Erasmian contrast with simplicity, but through a more theoretical consideration of the nature of the Christian community. This community is united by "the one faith, the one gospel, one and the same sacrament";[23] it abides by the dictum of St. Paul: "We are all one body."[24]

Since membership in this community is spiritual, based on baptism and faith in Christ, it is potentially universal and transcendent of conventional limitation; it "does not care about pope or custom."[25] This independence stems from a contrast elaborated frequently in Luther's works: "the Kingdom of Christ is not a temporal, transitory, earthly kingdom, ruled with laws and regulations, but a spiritual, heavenly, and eternal kingdom that must be ruled without and above all laws, regulations and outward means."[26]

Like St. Augustine's contrast between the City of God and the City of Man, Luther's ideal of a spiritual community shares the hostility to conventional norms that was a cornerstone of the original Stoic vision of a world community. Both Stoicism and Augustinian Christianity hinged upon a contrast between the law of nature and the conventional laws of nations.[27] According to Stoic philosophy, all men are united by a universal law expressing a "fundamental moral fitness be-

22. *The Babylonian Captivity,* in *Martin Luther: Selections from His Writings,* ed. John Dillenberger (New York: Anchor Books, 1961), p. 271.

23. *Letter to the German Nobility,* in Luther, *Selections,* p. 414.

24. 1 Corinthians 12:12, quoted in *Letter to the German Nobility,* in Luther, *Selections,* p. 407.

25. *Receiving Both Kinds in the Sacrament* (1522), trans. Abdel Ross Wentz, in *Luther's Works,* ed. Jaroslav Pelikan and Walter Hansen (St. Louis: Concordia Publishing House, 1958–1967), XXXVI, 70.

26. *Commentary on Psalm 117,* trans. Edward Sitter, *Luther's Works,* XIV, 14.

27. See George H. Sabine, *A History of Political Theory* (New York: Holt, Rinehart, and Winston, 1961), pp. 142–166; and R. W. Carlyle and A. J. Carlyle, *A History of Medieval Political Thought in the West* (London: William Blackwood, 1928), I, 7–11.

tween human nature and nature at large."[28] This law derives its universality from the harmony between the natural order of creation and the rational nature of all men; "there is both one Universe, made up of all things, and one God immanent in all things, and one Substance, and one Law, one Reason common to all intelligent creatures, and one Truth."[29] The proper end or principle (*telos*) of human activity is therefore "life in accordance with nature . . . in accordance with our own human nature as well as that of the universe, a life in which we refrain from every action forbidden by the law common to all things, that is to say, the right reason which pervades all things."[30]

The Stoic doctrine of natural law thus opposes what the Sophists had upheld as the positive or conventional character of human law: "True law is right reason in agreement with nature; it is of universal application, undying and everlasting . . . And there will not be different laws at Rome or Athens, or different laws now and in the future, but one eternal and unchangeable law will be valid for all nations and all times."[31] While Stoicism shared the ethical bias of Plato and Aristotle, it was in origin cosmopolitan, and in principle opposed to the limitations of the city-state. When Diogenes, the Cynic forebear of the Stoics, arrived from Sinope to thumb his nose at Athenian provincialism, he "allowed convention no such authority as he allowed to natural right . . . the only true commonwealth was, he said, that which is as wide as the universe."[32] In contrast to the realization and expression of natural rights and duties within the structure of the Aristotelian *polis*, Stoic doctrine posited the essential equality of men and the self-sufficiency of the individual, whose *polis* is the world community.

Roman jurisprudence—with its concepts of equity, equality and *jus gentium*—was in part an effort to transform this ethical standard of nature into a conception of "legal competence and rights"[33] on a worldwide basis. Despite the pragmatic success of the Roman legal apparatus, however, the idea in its most philosophical sense remained hostile to what were bound to seem, by contrast, the restrictions of collective habit. The ideal that ought to prevail everywhere, Cicero laments, is corrupted "by bad customs . . . so great that the sparks

28. Sabine, p. 149; see also Sir Frederick Pollock, "The History of the Law of Nature," in *Jurisprudence and Legal Essays* (New York: St. Martin's Press, 1961), p. 124.

29. Marcus Aurelius, 7.9.

30. Diogenes Laertius, 7.88.

31. Cicero, *De Republica*, 3.22; cf. *De Legibus*, 1.15–16; and *De Finibus*, 2.14, 18.

32. Diogenes Laertius, 6.71–72.

33. Sabine, p. 161.

of fire, so to speak, which Nature has kindled in us are extinguished."[34] This discrepancy, which receives even greater emphasis in later Roman Stoicism, returns the contrast between a universal society and conventional politics almost to its original Cynic form. In the asceticism of Seneca, the earlier Roman ideal of the state gives way to the ideal of a higher society of rational beings. Thus Seneca remarks that "we live according to a pattern, and, instead of arranging our lives according to reason, are led astray by convention." The only solution for the rational man is to recognize that he lives in two worlds:

> Let us grasp the idea that there are two commonwealths—the one, a vast and truly common state, which embraces both men and gods, in which we look neither to this corner of earth nor to that, but measure the bounds of our citizenship by the path of the sun; the other, the one to which we have been assigned by the accident of birth. This will be the commonwealth of the Athenians or of the Carthaginians, or of any other city that belongs, not to all, but to some particular race of men.[35]

A similar resistance to convention underlies St. Augustine's *City of God*. "True justice," he declares, "has no existence save in that republic whose founder and ruler is Christ."[36] This does not mean that there can be no earthly city; indeed, a people can be "any assemblage of reasonable beings bound together by a common agreement as to the objects of their love" (19.24). But by this logic, even a band of robbers may rightly be called a commonwealth, for there must be among them a conventional, relative, and internal justice (19.24).[37]

Balanced against the conventional nature of the earthly city stands the City of God, which "calls citizens out of all nations, and gathers together a society of pilgrims of all languages, not scrupling about diversities in the manners, laws, and institutions whereby earthly peace is maintained and secured" (19.17). The universality of this city—or more properly, society—resembles the Stoic cosmopolis in its adherence

34. *De Legibus*, 1.12; I have rendered *consuetudinis*, for which the Loeb translator has "habits," as "customs."

35. *De Tranquillitate Animi*, 4.1.

36. *The City of God*, trans. Marcus Dods (New York: Modern Library, 1950), 2.21; cf. 19.21.

37. See J. N. Figgis, *The Political Aspects of St. Augustine's "City of God"* (1921; rpt., Gloucester, Mass.: Peter Smith, 1960), p. 60.

to an equality transcending conventional limitation; it is an acknowledgment of the Pauline principle that "there are varieties of gifts, but
the same Spirit; and there are varieties of service, but the same Lord;
and there are varieties of working, but it is the same God who inspires
them all in every one."[38] The basis of this unity differs in substance
from the Stoic conception; but in form and principle it remains similarly spiritual and transcendent, substituting for the equality of men in
reason and nature their equality in weakness and radical distance from
God.[39]

The "Kingdom of Christ" invoked by Luther out of St. Augustine
therefore envisions a Christian community essentially spiritual in nature. In keeping with its spirituality, the Christian community takes
as its constitution Scripture, which "should apply to all men of all
times. For although in the course of time customs, people, places, and
usages may vary, godliness and ungodliness remain the same through
the ages."[40] In the *Institutes* Calvin wields this primitive constitution
as a weapon against subjection of the Christian community to conventional limitations; invoking St. Paul, he warns all Christians against
being misled "by vain philosophy, according to the constitutions of
men" and condemns "all *ethelothreskeias,* that is, fictitious modes of
worship which men themselves devise or receive from others."[41] The
true Christian must think of himself as living in two worlds, for "in
man government is twofold: the one spiritual, by which the conscience
is trained to piety and divine worship; the other civil, by which the
individual is instructed in those duties, as men and citizens, we are
bound to perform" (3.19.5).

The role of conventional institutions in the secular or political world
was seldom a serious theoretical problem for the earlier reformers, for
the validity of such institutions was largely assumed. Following the
lead of St. Paul and St. Augustine, who had argued that insofar as the
City of God sojourns in the earthly city, it "makes no scruple to obey
the laws of the earthly city,"[42] most of the early reformers maintained
not only that the community of Christians in its earthly element was
bound to secular authority, but also, as Luther's *Letter to the German
Nobility* attests, that secular authority might be used as an instrument

38. 1 Corinthians 12:4–7. Cf. *City of God,* 22.18.

39. Ernst Troeltsch, *The Social Teaching of the Christian Churches,* trans.
Olive Wyon (New York: Macmillan, 1931), I, 76; cf. pp. 100–101.

40. Luther, *Lecture on Psalm 1,* in *Works,* XIV, 290.

41. John Calvin, *Institutes of the Christian Religion,* trans. Henry Beveridge
(Grand Rapids: W. B. Eerdmans, 1953), 4.10.8.

42. St. Augustine, *City of God,* 19.17; cf. 19.12, 15, 26.

to serve spiritual interests.[43] The ecclesiastical question most explicitly concerned with the nature and function of convention, therefore, involved the Christian community not in its secular aspect, but in its spiritual aspect. Was the Christian community in its spiritual aspect in any way conventional or subject to conventional limitation? Here St. Augustine was less emphatically clear. The early reformers, however, believed that they had found an answer in St. Augustine's view that even in the Church the reprobate were mingled with the elect. According to Protestant interpretations of Augustine, the true Christian community is constituted by an order of grace, and its members are the spritually elect; stemming from the righteousness of Abel, this community is not a single Church contrasted with a diversity of states, but a spiritual order "predestined to reign eternally with God."[44] Thus, Calvin maintains that individual souls must "be subject to no bondage, be bound by no chains" (*Institutes,* 4.10.1–3). While it is helpful, given the fallen nature of man, for an external Church to administer *la parolle de Dieu,* it cannot make, but can only interpret, the fundamental law of Scripture (*Institutes,* 4.10.27); the members of this external Church cannot be said to constitute the spiritual elect. The spiritual community, in other words, cannot be bound by convention; "whoever observes any rule, tradition, or ceremony with the opinion that thereby he will obtain the forgiveness of sins, righteousness, and eternal life—will hear the judgment of the Spirit pronounced against him."[45]

The "duble name" of custom in the English reformation derived, therefore, not from a conflict between two historical interpretations of tradition, but from a doctrinal debate about the nature and value of traditional or merely social norms themselves. Furthermore, this debate was carried out on normative grounds, and sought to define and compare on the basis of principle the different types of normative

43. Cf. Calvin, *Institutes,* 3.19.5; 4.10.5; Philip Melancthon, *On Christian Doctrine,* trans. Clyde L. Manschreck (New York: Oxford University Press, 1965), pp. 180–183; William Tyndale, *The Obedience of a Christian Man* (1528), in *Doctrinal Treatises,* ed. Henry Walter (Cambridge: Parker Society, 1849), vol. I; and *An Homily against Disobedience and Wilful Rebellion,* in *Sermons or Homilies Appointed to Be Read in Churches* (London: Society for Promoting Christian Knowledge, 1914). For concise accounts of the origin of the doctrine and its impact in England, see J. W. Allen, *A History of Political Thought in the Sixteenth Century* (1928; rpt., New York: Barnes and Noble, 1960), pp. 15–35, 52–60, 125–133; and Christopher Morris, *Political Thought in England: Tyndale to Hooker* (London: Oxford University Press, 1953), pp. 27–67.

44. St. Augustine, *City of God,* 18.49.

45. Luther, *Lectures on Galatians,* in *Works,* XXVII, 9; cf. pp. 25, 44, 110, 276.

guidance available to men. Such theoretical considerations lay at the heart of English ecclesiastical and political thought from the time of Henry VIII to the restoration of Charles II. It was in part this large body of thought, controversial in nature, that helped to shape the concept of convention during the sixteenth and seventeenth centuries.

Because the Augustinian bias of the early reformers centered on a contrast between the transcendence of spiritual norms and the inadequacy of customary ones, Reformation thought in England was in large part devoted to the doctrinal questions of authority and tradition, and implicitly to the concept of convention. The defense of customary practices was therefore faced with the theoretical challenge of reconciling the continuity of transcendent norms with the changing configurations of collective habit. Accordingly, two basic sets of attributes accumulated around the concept of convention, corresponding to the positive content of Protestant teaching and its essentially negative response to human practice. On the one hand, attempts were made to show that custom was merely a corollary of the "ancient and primitive constitution," so that custom might be understood as the essentially unchanging vehicle of revealed precedent. On the other hand, attempts were made to show that the qualities of discontinuity and mutability attributed to custom were in fact expressions of a beneficial power of accommodation, enabling men to live in harmony with changing circumstance.

Quite naturally, these two arguments were at first asserted independently, because each assumed a view of social norms that seemed to contradict the other. Where the one attempted to validate social norms as the impermeable repository of fundamental truth, the other sought sanction for their mutability in the principle of prudent adjustment to circumstance. In the course of ecclesiastical debate, and especially through the influence of English legal and political thought as the Anglican Church became increasingly a politic society, these two sets of attributes came to be understood as aspects or dimensions of a single type of normative guidance, a type subject to change yet nonetheless coterminous with unchanging norms. This synthesis marks a major transition in Renaissance thought, for it was the point at which convention began to be acceptable as an adequate test of rectitude and fitness.

Given the concept of Christian community advanced in Luther's *Babylonian Captivity*, it is not surprising that Henry VIII, as a prince of Christendom at that time still on good terms with Rome, should have replied in defense of authority. Significantly, Henry defended authority on the basis of tradition and custom, "opposing to the authority of a single buffoon the authority of so many holy fathers, the custom of so many centuries."[46] With the help of his unacknowledged collaborators, Henry arrived at an equation of authority with custom by first establishing the existence of an unwritten apostolic tradition on a scriptural basis,[47] and by then positing length of usage and breadth of consensus as the confirmation of its legitimacy. The authority of the Church thus derived from "the use of so many ages, and the consent of so many people."[48] Given the unanimous consent of so many nations, " 'tis forbidden to change, or move the things which have been for long time immoveable."[49]

Henry's recourse to the concept of custom was intended to establish the coherence and legitimate pedigree of traditional practices along a temporal dimension and to defend the power of consensus to lend legitimacy to tradition. But it failed to establish the coinherence of this tradition with the community whose constitution, Luther had maintained, resided only in Scripture. In other words, Henry's argument on the basis of usage, length of time, and numbers was vulnerable to Luther's distinction between traditional order and the order of grace. Because Henry argued for an unwritten tradition in addition to Scripture, he could not lay to rest the idea that scriptural truth might invalidate tradition. Thus Luther remarks, in his reply, that Henry's view rests only on relative grounds; given only the justification of time and usage, "by what reasoning will we prove that the faith of the Turks is erroneous, which has lasted now for about a thousand years? . . . Foolish, ridiculous, and most truly Henrican and Thomistic are these words, as if a spiritual matter were to be measured by prescriptions of time and usage or the law of men, like an estate or some plot of land."[50] As Luther had elsewhere maintained: "If custom were sufficient, the heathen would have the very best excuse, for their custom of worshipping idols is more than four thousand years old . . . no custom can change anything that is fixed in Scriptures and articles of

---

46. *Assertio Septem Sacramentorum,* in *Responsio ad Lutherum,* trans. Sister Scholastica Mandeville, *The Complete Works of St. Thomas More* (New Haven: Yale University Press, 1969), V, 53. I quote portions of the *Assertio* not printed in the More edition from *Assertio Septem Sacramentorum,* trans. T.W. (London, 1687), hereafter cited as *Assertio (1687).*

47. *Assertio,* in More, *Works,* V, 99; see also Heiko A. Obermann, *The Harvest of Medieval Theology* (Cambridge: Harvard University Press, 1963), and Carlyle and Carlyle, II, 101–114, 154–162.

48. *Assertio (1687),* p. 31.

49. *Assertio (1687),* p. 6.

50. Luther, *Contra Henrican Regem Angliae,* in *Responsio ad Lutherum,* p. 223.

faith. Custom is limited to the external and variable works and pos-
tures which characterize neither the Christian nor the priestly estate."[51]

In addition to Henry's assertion of a primarily temporal and traditional dimension, emphasizing the essentially static and continuous
aspect of custom, Luther's position provoked a second type of response,
which emphasized precisely the elements of variation and discontinuity
that Luther had attacked. According to this second view, custom, while
essentially unstable, nevertheless acts as a flexible form of guidance,
providing a relative measure of uniformity and harmony in the varied
flux of practical experience. As Erasmus became increasingly disturbed
by Luther's disruptive and divisive influence on the Church, he was
attracted by the power of custom as a source of unity and uniformity.
While he could not deny Luther's distinction between the integrity
of Christian faith based on Scripture and the relativity of convention,
Erasmus came to feel that the distinction "harms Christian *concord*
more than it helps piety."[52] While acknowledging that "certain individuals cannot bring themselves to be persuaded that what in these
times is termed sacramental . . . was instituted by Christ," he proposes that "they ought at least to agree to retain it as something that
is salutary and useful to many."[53] Erasmus bases this proposal on his
earlier distinction between truth and circumstance; St. Paul, he observes, "has differentiated between the permissible and the expedient
(1 Cor. 2:1–6). The truth may be spoken but it does not serve everyone
at all times and under all circumstances." In the interests of Christian
peace and *concordia,* Erasmus turns to the principle of decorum that
Colet had invoked out of St. Paul, and maintains that the distinction
between Scripture and convention is not absolute: "Holy scripture
knows how to adjust its language to our human condition . . . This
does not mean that changes really take place in the nature of God.
These are rather *modes of expression.* The same *prudence,* I believe,
should adorn all who have taken up preaching the divine word."[54]

While Erasmus' proposal for a moderate and flexible respect for existing convention was intended to establish a harmonious relationship
between Scripture and tradition as coordinate guides to man's right

51. Luther, "Answer to the Superchristian, Superspiritual, and Superlearned
Book of Goat Emser" (1521), in *Works of Martin Luther,* ed. Charles M. Jacobs
(Philadelphia: A. J. Holman, 1930), III, 325.

52. Erasmus, *A Diatribe or Sermon Concerning Free Will,* in *Discourse on Free
Will,* trans. Ernest F. Winter (New York: Ungar, 1961), p. 8. Cf. Richard Popkin,
A History of Scepticism (1960; rpt., New York: Harper Torchbooks, 1964), pp. 5–7.

53. Erasmus, *On Mending the Peace in the Church,* in *The Essential Erasmus,*
ed. John P. Dolan (New York: New American Library, 1964), p. 391.

54. Erasmus, *Discourse on Free Will,* pp. 11, 12; my italics.

life, it did not deny the fundamental distinction between them. Consequently, Luther attacked what Erasmus had himself admitted as the skeptical basis for his recommendations of conformity, prudence, and decorum. As long as the distinction between the absolute nature of Scripture and the relative character of convention, between the Kingdom of Christ and the realm of human experience, remained stronger than the bonds between them, Luther could continue to maintain that "the Holy Spirit is no skeptic, and what He has written into our hearts are no doubts or opinions, but assertions, more certain and more firm than all human experience and life itself."[55]

Thus the early arguments of neither Henry nor Erasmus could produce a view of custom capable of rivaling the integrity of Scripture as the proper guide for human acts. This failure was compounded by the fact that each emphasized separately a dimension or quality of customary practice to the detriment of the other. If, on the one hand, as Henry argued, customary practice was but the reflection of ancient precedent, then any practice that could be shown to have changed with time could not properly claim the sanctity of "custom." His argument was historically vulnerable. If, on the other hand, as Erasmus had maintained, customary practice was merely a relative and superficial response to circumstance, there could be no positive assurance that it was continuous with the ends contained in Scripture except by explicit reference to God's unalterable word. His argument was philosophically vulnerable.

In the course of the sixteenth century, however, these weaknesses gradually became a source of strength as the various upholders of ecclesiastical ceremony, regulation, and polity sought to reconcile the two dimensions of human experience—stasis and flux, continuity and change—in the single normative principle of customary practice. The reconciliation of such apparently contradictory principles seemed at first to require the aid of miracles, and not surprisingly the earliest efforts at synthesis, such as Thomas More's *Responsio ad Lutherum* (1523), sought to sanctify the miracle of custom on spiritual grounds. With the later establishment and defense of the Anglican Church, however, the miracle of More's Catholic argument became increasingly secularized and the concept of convention took shape as the civic and social miracle that reconciles change and continuity within the order of human things.

For his miraculous synthesis of the two views of custom, More found warrant in Bishop John Fisher's *Sermon Made Agayn the Pernicyous*

---

55. Luther, *The Bondage of the Will,* in Winter, *Discourse on Free Will,* p. 103; cf. p. 6.

Doctryn of Martin Luther (1521). Fisher begins his defense of the
Church with points similar to those already outlined by Henry and
Erasmus, arguing for the validity of unwritten tradition, the legitimiz-
ing power of custom, and the value of conformity in producing Christian *concordia*.[56] To this last virtue, which had been for Henry the
expression of political consensus, and for Erasmus the last refuge of a
troubled and skeptical mind, Fisher adds a spiritual dimension. Conformity, or *concordia*, expresses spiritual harmony; the continuity of
tradition is evidence that "the holy spirit of trowth was sent . . . to
abyde with us for ever" (p. 324). In the narrowest sense, Fisher argues
that this spirit speaks through "the fathers & doctours of the chyrche,"
but in a broader and more generous sense he concludes that the spirit
that Luther finds working only through the Scriptures, or in individuals through God's will, coinheres in the present among those who
"conform themselves, *concordi sensu*, with the early fathers through
whom the Spirit has spoken."[57]

More filled the highly spiritual outlines of Fisher's argument, however, with a solid and pragmatic content, and related it in concrete
terms to history, Scripture, and law, in such a way as to expand and
legitimize the province of convention. The presence of tradition in the
Church, says More, is evidence that "the holy Spirit of God interiorly
inspires His church with truth, that that interior Spirit renders all
taught of God, that he alone makes those who dwell in a house to be of
one mind."[58] More's concept of tradition, unlike Henry's, is by no
means static; it combines with the Henrican sanctity of unbroken usage
the Erasmian concept of usage as the flexible principle of accommodation and adjustment. More's combination of these concepts puts teeth
in Fisher's view of the social coinherence of spirit. The working of
God's Holy Spirit through human tradition is dynamic, incremental,
apocalyptic:

> from time to time as it liketh his majesty to have things
> knowen or done in his church, so is not doubt but he tem-
> pereth his revelations, and in such wise doth insumate and
> inspire them into the breasts of his Christian people, that
> by the secret instinct of the holy ghost they consent and

56. See Fisher's *Sermon Made Agayn the Pernicyous Doctryn of Martin Luther*,
in *English Works*, ed. John E. B. Mayor (London: Early English Texts Society,
1874), pp. 332–333; and Edward· L. Surtz, S.J., *The Works and Days of John Fisher*
(Cambridge: Harvard University Press, 1967), pp. 106–112.

57. Edward J. Surtz, S.J., Introduction to *Responsio ad Lutherum*, pt. 2, More,
Works, V, 744.

58. More, *Responsio ad Lutherum*, *Works*, V, 623–625.

agree together in one . . . But as it may be that many things be those not all at once revealed and understanden in the Scripture, but by sundry times and ages more things and more by God unto his church disclosed, and that it shall be like his high goodness and wisdom to dispense and dispose; so in things to be done may fall in his church variety, mutation, and change.[59]

In More's view the Christian community does not exist in opposition to changing norms, but resides within them. There can be no human definition of this community apart from the historic definitions realized in a context of changing experience. Consensus and adaptation producing *concordia* among men at moments in time, and the legitimization and confirmation of this concord through time, combine to make custom and tradition, not the final causes, but at least the means, of man's spiritual definition. Given the ongoing presence of the Holy Spirit, Christians need not agree "upon the best and upon the truth, but only to avoid all discord and division, and by common consent . . . to agree all in one, meaning thereby, as methinketh, that if the Church of Christ, intending well, do all agree upon any one thing concerning God's honour or man's soul, it cannot be but that thing must needs be true."[60]

More argues not only as a late medieval Catholic defending the need of law to ameliorate man's fallen nature, but as an English common lawyer, seeking through the historical evolution of law the articulate emergence of justice as a principle. "The law of the gospel," he maintains, "does not apportion possessions, nor does reason alone prescribe the forms of determining property, unless reason is attended by an agreement, and this a public agreement in the common form of mutual commerce, which agreement, either taking root in usage or expressed in writing, is public law."[61] Following a principle of the common law tradition that defined custom and tradition as the gradual and incremental means of accommodation and adjustment from which normative principles emerge, More relates transcendent principles to customary practice in such a way as to resolve their opposition in the theories of the Protestant reformers.

In one sense More's concept of convention is quite radical; though it buttresses convention with the sanctity of time and the commodity of

59. More, *A Dialogue concerning Heresies*, in *English Works*, ed. W. E. Campbell (New York: Dial Press, 1931), II, 97–98.

60. More, *English Works*, II, 158.

61. More, *Responsio ad Lutherum*, *Works*, V, 276–277.

consensus, it legitimizes and expands the province of convention as a
social, legal, and indeed spiritual norm. In other words, the products of
human experience are not simply to be measured by a higher principle,
but are themselves the source and confirmation of higher principles.
In this sense More comes close to arguing that men are what they agree
to be or decide to become. In another and more final sense, however,
this radical aspect of his thought is offset by an essentially medieval
one: the definition of man's place and function in the world through
adjustment and accommodation over time is not a process of self-definition, but the gradual disclosure of God's purpose for man. Custom
and tradition are not finally the sources, but the means, of man's definition, and it is not within the power of convention to alter this definition at the source. The importance of More's view is that by inte-
grating convention with a higher principle, instead of opposing the
two, he was able to suggest that convention was not an arbitrary obstruction, but an essential means of discovering man's spiritual definition. Its shortcoming, however, was that in relating convention to
providence More had chosen the very principle of continuity that all
the reformers had agreed was explicitly revealed in Scripture and was
therefore impervious to further definition or specification through the
acts of men. Once the place of this principle of continuity in More's
argument was denied, his view of convention could only appear hideous
to the sixteenth-century Protestant mind; in the absence of a guiding
principle, the view that tradition is altered by a continuous process of
voluntary change and accommodation could only lead to the conclusion
that the rules by which men live are wholly mutable and arbitrary.

The process of civil and ecclesiastical enactment, controversy, and
apologetics that led to the establishment of an English Church in the
later sixteenth century may therefore be understood as a search for an
alternative basis or principle of continuity by which the flexible role
of convention in the Church might be justified in the absence of scriptural warrant. From the very beginning, this search was frankly pragmatic. The Six Articles Act (1539), for example, sought religious uniformity solely on the basis of the "innumerable commodities, which
have ever ensued . . . of concord, agreement, and unity in opinions."[62]
Such frankness alone, however, was wholly inadequate. Hugh Latimer,
for instance, objected that "we ought never regard unity so much that
we would, or should, forsake God's word for her sake."[63] In his petition

---

62. *Documents Illustrative of English Church History*, ed. Henry Gee and William
H. Hardy (London: Macmillan, 1896), p. 302.

63. Hugh Latimer, *Sermons*, ed. George E. Corrie (Cambridge: Parker Society,
1844), I, 487.

to the king, Philip Melancthon similarly inveighed against Henry's efforts in the absence of scriptural warrant, pointing out that "it is no light offense to set up new kinds of worshiping and serving of God without his Word, or to defend the same: such prescription God doth horribly detest, who will be known by his Word only."[64] Recalling the earlier promise of Henry's break with Rome, Melancthon pleads for reform "by the evident and substantial testimony of the primitive church." The defense of conventional order was thus in need of two supports: a defined area of jurisdiction whose boundaries would not conflict with Scripture and, once this area was defined, a theory that would justify convention itself as an adequate normative principle.

On the first of these points there was relatively widespread agreement. Concerning the primacy of Scripture there was "no discernible difference between the conformist and the non-conformist position. Both placed Scripture in a position of highest authority."[65] Beginning with the composition of the Edwardian prayer books (1549–1552), the primitive constitution of Scripture became the established criterion for reform on all sides. The First Prayer Book posited as its goal "an ordre for prayer muche agreeable to the mind and purpose of the olde fathers," based upon "the holy Scriptures, or that which is evidently grounded upon the same." At the same time, however, the Prayer Book acknowledged the need of a residue of conventional ceremony because "wythoute some Ceremonies it is not possible to kepe any ordre of quyete dyscyplyne in the churche."

Because it drew a sharp distinction between the stability of the primitive constitution and the conventional nature of ceremony, the First Prayer Book approached the latter with great diffidence, asserting only that the ceremonies "that remaine are retained for a discipline and ordre, which (upon just causes) may be altered and changed . . . [but] are not to be esteemed equal with goddes lawe."[66] Despite such early hesitation, there nevertheless grew up around this need for order the concept of an extrascriptural jurisdiction, or *adiaphora*, in which conventional norms might prevail. Nicholas Ridley, following the lead of the Edwardian prayer books, used the silence of Scripture to outline such an area,[67] and from Ridley's first conflict over the use of vestments

64. Philip Melancthon, *Epistle . . . against the cruel Act of the Six Articles,* in John Foxe, *Acts and Monuments,* V, 354.

65. John Henry Primus, *The Vestments Controversy* (Kampen, Neth.: J. H. Kok, 1960), p. 118.

66. *The First Prayer Book of Edward VI* (1910; rpt., New York: Everyman's Library, 1952), Preface, pp. 3–4; pp. 287–288.

67. See John Hooper, *Early Writings,* ed. Samuel Carr (Cambridge: Parker Society, 1848), I, 479; the "Reply of Bp. Ridley to Bp. Hooper on the Vestment con-

with Bishop Hooper, under Edward VI, through the second vestments controversy under Elizabeth and the Admonition Controversy, the concept of *adiaphora* came to be asserted in increasingly secular and pragmatic terms. Among the party closest to the Crown, and especially in the thought of Matthew Parker, conventional limitations, "one uniformity of rites and manners," were necessary only so that "the people might thereby quietly honour and serve Almighty God in truth, concord, unity, peace, and quietness." The discretionary use of convention arises, in other words, out of the purely practical and administrative need for accommodation. Thus, onto Ridley's distinction between the authority of scriptural precedent and the indifference of scriptural silence Parker superimposes a dichotomy between internal conviction and external action; this latter sphere is governed by laws not "equivalent with the eternal word of God," but "concerning decency, distinction, and order for the time."[68]

To many of the returned Marian exiles, this argument was seen for the "politic" invention that it was, savoring, as Jewel put it, of "too much prudence."[69] Nevertheless, a number of them conceded to "prudence" and turned to the example of St. Paul, who was the Christian incarnation of the humanist ideal of rhetorical decorum: "we ought to beware, lest . . . we should bring the Church at large into some grievous peril. And I do not think this opinion of mine is at variance with the mind of Paul, who was wont to become all things to all men, that he might gain some; and who thought good to circumcise Timothy, lest he should alienate the Jews of that place from the Christian religion, and that he might exercise his ministry with greater advantage."[70]

Such pleas for prudence, accommodation, and adaptability further alienated the Puritan party because they had the effect of emphasizing the dimension of accommodation, or the temporary and provisional aspect of custom. They called attention to what Erasmus had earlier seen as the discontinuity of tradition, the fact that human endeavor constantly needs to adapt itself to circumstance. The early reformers

---

troversy," in John Bradford, *Writings*, II, 382; John Whitgift, *Works*, ed. John Ayre (Cambridge: Parker Society, 1850), I, 64; Whitgift's *Defense of an Answer* in Donald J. McGinn, *The Admonition Controversy* (New Brunswick: Rutgers University Press, 1949), p. 299; and W. H. Frere and G. E. Douglas, ed., *Puritan Manifestos* (London: The Church Historical Society, 1954), pp. xi–xxxv.

68. Matthew Parker, *Advertisements* (1566), in Gee and Hardy, pp. 467–468.

69. *The Zurich Letters*, ed. Hastings Robinson (Cambridge: Parker Society, 1842), vol. I, Letter 24.

70. Richard Cox to Rudolf Gualter, *Zurich Letters*, II, 344.

had argued against Erasmus, as the Puritans would continue to argue against the Church party, that this need was rendered superfluous by the continuity of Scripture. The mere delineation of a discretionary area that might be guided by convention, and the argument that such an area is conducive to good order, left unresolved the question of the rightness of this order. The excuse of necessity alone was insufficient; in the view of many reformers "there be many thinges doone either unadvisedlie, or of necessity; and yet we should not have them be drawn into a custom."[71] The weakness of conventional order was not simply due to the greater strength of Scripture; rather, having been demystified by the Anglicans themselves, the concept of convention was in need of a secular miracle to replace the providential miracle that for More had reconciled change and continuity in the social sphere. In other words, the pragmatic justification of conventional usages was in need of a principle that would insure that inherent in the process of adjustment was a nontemporal dimension of stability—that the rightness sought was not an arbitrary accommodation leading man away from his true ends, but an adjustment made in the interest of realizing them.

The principle was found in the miracle of history, in a theory of history that reconciled change and continuity in the concept of corporate identity. In the work of John Whitgift, one of the most gifted and systematic of Anglican apologists, the continuity of corporate identity through time begins to emerge as the guarantor of customary norms. Whitgift defends the role of conventional practices in the Church through the familiar concept of liberty in things indifferent. But he argues for this liberty on the historical grounds of a continuous order as well as on the pragmatic grounds of stable order. Unlike the earlier apologists, he refers not only to "the circumstances of time, place, and person" but also to "the whole state of things *now in this church and realm of England.*"[72] The order to which he refers exists not as a temporary circumstance but as a continuous entity in history. Accordingly, he argues that in order to reestablish a primitive constitution, the Puritans would have to contradict the continuity of history: "All the laws of this land that be contrary to these judicial laws of Moses must be abrogated; the prince must be abridged of that prerogative which she hath . . . To be short, all things must be transformed: lawyers must cast away their huge volumes and multitudes of cases, and content themselves with the Books of Moses."[73]

71. "Of Custome," in *The Common Places of the most famous and renowned Divine Doctor Peter Martyr*, trans. Anthonie Marten (London, 1574), p. 98.

72. John Whitgift, *Works*, I, 4; my italics.

73. Whitgift, *Answer to an Admonition*, in McGinn, p. 399.

The rightness of accommodation through changeable conventional forms, in other words, is justified through Whitgift's conception of the church as a "politic society" retaining its identity within history. The preservation of this identity through history amounts to a secularized version of the continuity More had seen in providence; the "huge volumes and multitudes of cases" are weighty testimony in its favor.

From this testimony, Whitgift infers that the key to the miraculous normative power of convention resides in historical process. Having arrived at this hypothesis, he leaves the actual miracle unexplained. He does not show, in other words, *how, in principle,* the historical continuity preserved by conventional adjustment is of equal value with the continuity of Scripture or in keeping with man's highest ends. It was at this intersection of historical reflection that the increasingly secular arguments of ecclesiastical debate converged with developments in legal and moral thought and grounded the power of convention in the continuity of nature itself. As in so many other respects, it was Whitgift's student, Richard Hooker, who stood at the converging point.

2. "Use Becomes Another Nature": Custom in Sixteenth-Century Politics and Law

While Whitgift had carried the Anglican defense of *adiaphora* to an important threshold by suggesting that in the nature of historical process lay the explanation that would reconcile the evident mutability and variety of conventional norms with the ideals of permanence and continuity, it was one of Richard Hooker's great achievements to offer a theory of history that would articulate this reconciliation on the basis of principle. Hooker's account of law is comprehensive, but among the many types of divine, natural, and human law that constitute his frame of reference are those ceremonial rites and orders, customary forms and apparently arbitrary practices that constitute a class of norms whose rationale was neither immediately conspicuous nor articulate. For nearly a century this class of norms had been a focus of debate, and Hooker's *Laws of Ecclesiastical Polity* is continuous with this debate, taking as one of its principal aims the defense of "such customes or rites as publiquelie are establisht," and "thinges the fittnes whereof is not of it selfe apparent."[1]

It is well known that the strength of Hooker's argument lies in his

---

1. Richard Hooker, *Of the Laws of Ecclesiastical Polity,* in *The Folger Library Edition of The Works of Richard Hooker,* ed. W. Speed Hill (Cambridge: Harvard University Press, 1977), 5.6.1, 5.7.4. For bks. 6–8 the edition cited is *Works* (Oxford: Clarendon Press, 1865), vol. II.

lucid reconciliation of the orders of faith and reason, which makes
Scripture "the evidence of Gods owne testimonie added unto the naturall assent of reason" (1.12.1), and in his subsequent justification of
human activity on the principles of nature and reason adopted from
the Thomistic hierarchy of laws.[2] In Hooker's view, the difference between scriptural and merely human norms does not amount to a conflict in man's nature or destiny; rather, it expresses the need for guidance in different aspects of his being. Hooker's appeal to the norm of
nature is thus a final and decisive step in the increasingly secularized
discussion of convention. Indeed, it is partly because Hooker places the
whole framework of human law on this broadly philosophic footing that
he is able to arrive at a definition of historical change compatible with
unchanging standards of rectitude. At the same time, however, Hooker's
theory of natural law is by itself no sanction for customary norms. On
the contrary, the Augustinian critique of convention, as noted earlier,
drew upon the same Stoic teachings out of which the medieval natural
law tradition was born. In other words, the natural law tradition was
no less hostile to the apparently arbitrary influence of convention than
the Augustinian protestantism to which Hooker's argument was addressed. Hooker himself follows this tradition when he paraphrases
Cicero in observing that "lewde and wicked custome, beginning perhaps at the first amongst few, afterwards spreading into greater multitudes, and so continuing from time to time, may be of force even in
plaine things to smother the light of naturall understanding" (1.8.11).

Having thus invoked the principles of reason and nature as the normative basis for human activity, Hooker is faced with the further task of
showing how those elements of human activity that are purely or apparently conventional can be reconciled with the unchanging dictates
of right reason.[3] He resolves this difficulty in two ways. First, he builds
into his account of natural law an analysis of human acts, and then
draws an extended analogy between the structure of such acts and the
structure of collective acts, and especially between the rational habit of
prudence in the individual and the conventional guidance of law in
societies. The inarticulate temporal development of habit, which enables individuals to fulfill the natural law, is thus projected upon
societies as the historical development of customary norms. Second,

2. See Alexander Passerin D'Entreves, *The Medieval Contribution to Political
Thought* (1939; rpt., New York: Humanities Press, n.d.), pp. 117–124; and Peter
Munz, *The Place of Hooker in the History of Thought* (London: Routledge and
Kegan Paul, 1952), ch. 2, and Appendix A.

3. For the view that Hooker fails in this task, see Munz, p. 110, and H. F.
Kearney, "Richard Hooker: A Reconstruction," *Cambridge Journal*, 5 (1952), 300–
311.

Hooker substantiates this analogical framework with a practical content derived specifically from sixteenth-century English legal and political theory. By drawing upon the two closely related concepts of "custom" as the basis of legal power and "consensus" as the source of political power, Hooker reconciles within his framework the power of tradition with the power of accommodation, the dimension of continuity with the dimension of change.

Hooker thus prepares for his defense of conventional norms at the very outset of his natural law theory, when he prefaces his account of law with a portrait of man himself. Like the rest of created nature, man is incomplete and has yet to fulfill the ends for which he was created (1.5.1). It is thus "by proceeding in the knowledge of truth and by growing in the exercise of vertue" that "man amongst the creatures of this inferiour world, aspireth to the greatest conformity with God" (1.5.3). The means to this fulfillment of the divine and natural law is the rational will: "the object of wil, is that good which reason doth leade us to seeke" (1.7.3). The "two principall fountaines" of human action are therefore *"Knowledge* and *Will,* which will in things tending towards any end is termed *Choice"* (1.7.2).

In any specific act of choice, however, these faculties may cooperate in either of two ways, because "the sentences which reason giveth are some more, some lesse general" (1.8.4). In the first instance, the rational will may have direct recourse to final principles, for "the maine principles of reason are in themselves apparent" (1.8.5). In such cases, reason enables man to comprehend not only "whatsoever may be easily knowne to belong to the dutie of all men, but even whatsoever may possibly be knowne to be of that qualitie so that the same be by *necessarie* consequence deduced out of cleere and manifest principles" (1.8.11).

In fact, however, this ideal model is complicated by the context of particularity in which man is compelled to act as a consequence of his fallen nature. Given this practical site of action, it becomes difficult to discover first principles from which a course of action might be necessarily deduced. "Goodnes doth not moove by being, but by being apparent; and therefore many things are neglected which are most pretious, only because the value of them lyeth hid" (1.7.6). In the absence of self-evident principles, there arises the potential for conflict and the need for prudent deliberation between reason and will. Such deliberation, however, "is a thing painful and the painfulnes of knowledge is that which maketh the will so hardly inclinable thereunto. The root hereof divine malediction" (1.7.7). Habits formed in the will, and especially in the lower appetite, act to impede the influence of reason; "custome inuring the mind by long practise, and so leaving there a sensible impression, prevaileth more then reasonable perswasion what way so ever" (1.7.6).

In the face of these difficulties, Hooker turns to the habitual character of the virtue of prudence, to the power of habit to rectify deliberation. The habit of prudence, he observes, is developed in two ways. "Education and instruction are the meanes, the one by use, the other by precept to make our naturall faculty of reason, both the better and the sooner able to judge rightly betweene truth and error, good and evill" (1.6.5). One of these means, "instruction by precept," is most clearly in accord with natural law philosophy, for it produces a habit that seeks goodness through a "knowledge of the causes whereby it is made such" (1.8.2). However, the second means, "education . . . by use," is less immediately articulate, for it proceeds by "observation of those signes and tokens, which being annexed alwaies unto goodnes, argue that where they are found, there also goodnes is, *although we know not the cause by force whereof it is there*" (1.8.2; my italics). Unlike the clarity of "precepts," the evidence of "signs and tokens" requires the gradual accumulation of experience in contingent matters, and in this respect the habit of prudence is formed not through intuition or ratiocination, but through a process of practice, experiment, and adjustment. For this reason Aquinas had maintained that memory is the first of the parts of prudence:

> Prudence . . . is engaged with contingent human doings. Here a person cannot be guided only by norms which are simply and of necessity true. He must also appreciate what happens in the majority of cases. Aristotle remarks that like should be concluded from like; accordingly, principles should be proportionate to the conclusions which we draw. Now to know what is true in the majority of cases we must be empirical; Aristotle says that intellectual virtue is produced and developed by time and experience. Experience is stocked with memories . . . consequently recalling many facts is required for prudence.[4]

This emphasis upon the power of "time and experience," upon "experience . . . stocked with memories," pervades Hooker's account of human acts, and it is the basis for his view of prudence in the individual. It is also the basis for his analogy between individual and collective acts, for like the habits of individuals, the laws of societies embody "experience . . . stocked with memories." The confusing con-

4. St. Thomas Aquinas, *Summa Theologiae*, 2a2ae; q. 49, a. 1.

text of particular and contingent goods, which vitiates the individual act, becomes an even greater problem in the social context. Men have always known, Hooker declares, that "no man might in reason take upon him to determine his owne right, and according to his owne determination proceede in maintenance therof, in as much as every man is towards himselfe and them whom he greatly affecteth partiall; and therfore that strifes and troubles would be endlesse, except they gave their common consent all to be ordered by some whom they should agree upon" (1.10.4).

It is crucial to observe that in Hooker's view not only do the institution of "public societies" and the promulgation of laws arise from the complex nature of the human act and the potential conflict it engenders, but the very structure of collective acts forms an analogue or counterpart to the structure of the individual act. For enlightened men, prudence offers sufficient guidance to the means conducive to the common good. But because "the greatest parte of men are such as prefer their owne privat good before all things" (1.10.6), it is necessary to restrain their wills with an external form of guidance or prudence. This collective counterpart to prudence is law, "a directive rule unto goodness of operation." In part, its function is "instructive" or preceptual; because not all men are self-sufficient in virtue, it is right and proper for them to obtain from others the education that brings them to virtue: "because there is difficultie and possibilitie many ways to erre, unless such things were set downe by lawes, many would be ignorant of their duties . . . and many that know what they should do, would neverthelesse dissemble it" (1.10.5). In part, however, law is also constraining: "lawes do not only teach what is good but they injoyne it, they have in them a certain constreining force" (1.10.7). In this sense law acts as a counterpart to habitual rectitude. Just as the individual will habitually embraces the means conducive to the good it desires, so the collective will necessarily embraces the means leading to the common good.

This parallel becomes the basis for Hooker's justification of the function and value of conventional norms. Just as in the individual act, so in the legal acts of societies reason and will cooperate in either of two ways. All human laws "be either such as establish some dutie whereunto all men by the law of reason did before stand bound; or els such as make that a dutie now which before was none" (1.10.10). In the first case, as in the individual act, the collective will desires as its object an end that universal reason posits as an unconditional good. "That which plaine or necessarie reason bindeth men unto may be in sundry considerations expedient to be ratified by humane law" (1.10.10). Such human law is termed "mixed" because, though it is enacted by human societies, it nevertheless derives necessarily from unconditional natural principles.

In the second case, where laws "make that a duty which before was none," different circumstances prevail. The choices of societies, like those of individuals, are almost always choices of particular or intermediate goods. These choices are guided by "merely" human laws, whose province is not necessarily first principles, but "any thing which reason doth but probablie teach to be fit and convenient" (1.10.10). This second type of "fitness or convenience" most crucially and decisively raises the spectre of convention, "for if once we descend unto probable collections what is convenient for men, we are then in the territorie where free and arbitrarie determinations . . . take place" (1.8.11). The question quite naturally arises, "howe it commeth to passe that . . . there shoulde be found even in good lawes so great varietie as there is" (1.10.9). The answer is that because laws represent the public habit of prudence, they arise as adjustments to contingent matters and their rationale lies buried in time or circumstance. As in the human act, there are in collective acts "sundry particular endes, whereunto the different disposition of that subject or matter, for which lawes are provided, causeth them to have especiall respect in making lawes" (1.10.9). Thus laws, established as forms of guidance in contingent matters, "must have an eye to the place where, and to the men amongst whome . . . one kinde of lawes cannot serve for all kindes of regiment" (1.10.9).

By calling attention to the radical variety of conventional norms, this view of law seems to emphasize the Anglican principles of accommodation and adjustment to the detriment of continuity. Hooker has prepared for this difficulty, however, through his analogy to human acts. Just as prudence guides the will in choosing contingent goods as means to final natural goods, so law specifies the contingent means to attainment of the common good. This assures that conventional adjustments are ultimately but not always conspicuously conducted with a view to first principles; "our ende ought alwaies to bee the same, our waies and meanes thereunto not so" (4.2.3). Like the highest goods desired by individual will, the public will desires the common good that "the law of nature doth require" (1.10.5). Nevertheless, like all intermediate goods, the means to this good may vary with circumstances: "nature tieth not to any one, but leaveth the choice as a thing arbitrarie" (1.10.5). This does not mean that the "indifference" of conventional laws and practices stems from their irrelevance to man's highest good; on the contrary, they are instrumental to it. "All publike regiment of what kind soever seemeth evidently to have risen from deliberate advice, consultation, and composition betwene men, judging it convenient and behoofull" (1.10.4). As the means is to the end, so is the species to the genus: convention specifies the particular means to a natural and generic end or good. This ratio is confirmed by the analogy of language, for "he which affirmeth speech to be necessarie amongest all men throughout the worlde, doth not thereby import that all men must necessarily speake one kinde of language" (3.2.1). Thus Hooker justifies the place of convention in collective life by assserting it as the means of adjustment and accommodation through which the fundamental continuity of human nature is preserved. The rightness of conventional order in "things indifferent" is therefore not an obstacle to man's fulfillment of his destiny, but coterminous with it.

Although Hooker's theoretical framework suggests the potential compatibility of conventional norms with natural ends, the actual task of achieving a practical reconciliation presents considerably greater difficulties. These difficulties arise in connection with the practical question of sovereignty, for although in theory the common will is shaped by collective habits of rectitude in the same way that the individual is guided by prudence, the actual means or apparatus by which the common will embraces habits conducive to common good requires further explanation. In other words, it remains for Hooker to determine where the actual power to promulgate and rule by law resides, to locate the power that gives to law its binding force. It is at this point that Hooker turns from the tradition of natural law to English common law and constitutional theory by positing as the basis of sovereignty the two related concepts of custom and consensus. Laws, he observes, are on the one hand made by an act of consent, expressed individually, through representatives, or by a monarch who rules through silent and indirect consent; or, on the other hand, they are inherited through custom, the counsel of the past for guidance in the present. Custom and consensus are related, for custom is the temporal vehicle of consensus; it is the mode of longevity through which the immortality of consensus is expressed:

> to be commanded we do consent, when that societie whereof we are parte hath at any time before consented, without revoking the same after by the like universall agreement. Wherefore as any mans deed past is good as long as him selfe continueth: so the act of a publique societie of men done five hundreth yeares sithence standeth as theirs, who presently are of the same societies, because corporations are immortall: we were then alive in our predecessors, and they in their successors do live still.   (1.10.8)

Hooker herein draws upon the common law tradition that the rule of law is supreme,[5] but in attributing such normative power to custom and consensus he submits his theory of natural law to the very principles of limitation and divisiveness upon which the earlier reformers had seized. Such principles, they had observed, were subject to the infirmities of will and the vagaries of time, both of which make norms diverse and variable. By Hooker's own admission, "disimilitude in great things is such a thing which draweth great inconvenience after it, a thing which Christian religion must always carefully prevent. And the way to prevent it is . . . the framing of . . . the rule of one only Law, to stand in no less force than the law of nations doeth, to be received in all kingdoms" (8.3.5). Having asserted natural law as a principle compatible and on parity with the continuity of Scripture, Hooker faces the further task of demonstrating, in a practical way, how the unity of this law is expressed in the variety of custom.

This was a task that Hooker shared with the English common lawyers of the sixteenth century as they attempted to defend the customary basis of English law against the natural law rationale of the Roman code. The dimensions of the problem are quite thoroughly explored in Thomas Starkey's comparison of English and Roman law in his *Dialogue Between Cardinal Pole and Thomas Lupset* (c. 1535). Not surprisingly, Pole's advocacy of Roman law begins with the familiar Senecan invocations of the Golden Age and skeptical citations of the variety of social practice to support the view that man is "custummably blyndyd."[6] Near the conclusion of the dialogue, however, Pole turns from a theoretical to a practical attack on custom by contrasting the rational uniformity of the Roman code with the unreliable variety of customary law predominant in England. The surest solution to current injustices in England is to "schake of al . . . tyrranical custumys and unresonabyl bandys" of the common law, and "to have the cyvyle law of the Romanys to be the commyn law here of England" (pp. 115, 195). The problem with English law is its customary character, its lack

5. See Edmund Dudley, *The Tree of Commonwealth*, ed. D. M. Brodie (Cambridge: Cambridge University Press, 1948), p. 102; and John Aylmer, *An Harborowe for Faithfull and Trewe Subiectes* (Strasbourg, 1559), sig. H3v. The problem of sovereignty in Hooker is discussed in D. W. Hanson, *From Kingdom to Commonwealth: The Growth of Civic Consciousness in English Political Thought* (Cambridge: Harvard University Press, 1970), pp. 275–276; and E. T. Davies, *The Political Ideas of Richard Hooker* (London: Society for Promoting Christian Knowledge, 1946), p. 75 ff.

6. Thomas Starkey, *A Dialogue Between Cardinal Pole and Thomas Lupset*, ed. J. M. Cowper (London: Early English Texts Society, 1878), pp. 9–11, 30.

of rational principle: "our law and order thereof is over-confuse. Hyt is infynyte and wythout ordur or end. There ys no stabyl grounde therin, nor sure stay; but every one that can colour reson makyth a stope to the best law that ys before tyme devysyd" (p. 192).

By contrast, the Roman law provides "rulys more convenyent to the order of nature" (p. 193). This "convenience to the order of nature" is not simply a philosophical advantage; it is pragmatic as well. The tripartite apparatus of local law (*jus civile*), the law of nations (*jus gentium*), and natural law (*jus naturale*) embodied in the Roman code is not primarily philosophical; rather, it reflects the practical expansion of Roman jurisdiction from the city to the world.[7] Pole's attack on customary laws thus stems from a pragmatic view of universality; the Roman law most resembles natural law because it is "now the commyn law almost of al Chrystyen natyonys" (p. 193). Having survived as an unaltered written code, the Roman law represents, in contrast to national custom, a near approximation of universality in pragmatic terms; "yf Nature schold hyrselfe prescrybe the partycular meanys whereby mankynd schold observe hyr lawys, I think sche wold admyt the same" (p. 194).

Pole's pragmatic attack on the insularity and irrationality of customary norms suggests the type of difficulty Hooker faced in providing his abstract theory of convention with a practical justification in accord with natural law. The nature of his solution would seem in one sense to support Izaak Walton's remark that "the foundation" of Hooker's *Laws* "was laid in the Temple,"[8] for Hooker turns to the pragmatic defense of customary norms as argued by the English common lawyers. Hooker invokes this defense by observing that although "lawes humane must be made according to the generall lawes of nature" (3.9.2), any alteration of customary law "though it bee from worse to better hath in it inconveniences, and those weightie" (4.14.1). This is especially so "if it be a lawe which the custome and continuall practise of many ages or yeares hath confirmed in the mindes of men . . . It amazeth them, it causeth them to stand in doubt whether any thing be in it self by nature either good or evil, and not al things rather such as men at this or that time agree to accompt of them, when they behold even those thinges disproved, disanulled, rejected, which use had made in a maner naturall" (4.14.1). In drawing so close a parallel between "use" and

7. See *The Institutes of Justinian*, trans. G. B. Moyle (Oxford: Clarendon Press, 1889), 1.1.4; and A. P. d'Entreves, *Natural Law: An Introduction to Legal Philosophy* (London: Hutchinson's University Library, 1951), pp. 28–30. Cf. Sabine, pp. 166–172.

8. Izaak Walton, *The Lives of John Donne, Sir Henry Wotton, Richard Hooker, George Herbert, and Robert Sanderson* (London: Oxford World Classics, 1927), p. 208.

"nature," Hooker has recourse to a central tenet of the common law tradition. This tradition had grown out of the medieval and primarily Germanic conception of law as immemorial custom. According to this conception, "the fact that any state of affairs has existed for a considerable time creates the presumption that it is lawful and right."[9] Presumptive reasoning posits an equation of the continuity of providence and nature with the continuity of tribal or national practice; good law is therefore ancient law; it is neither made nor written; legal innovation is presumed to be merely a discovery or restoration of older customary practice.[10] These principles were made an explicit part of the philosophic apparatus of English law with Bracton's observation at the outset of his legal compendium (c. 1256) that "though in almost all lands use is made of *leges* and the *jus scriptum,* England alone uses unwritten law and custom. There law derives from nothing written but from what usage [*usus*] has approved."[11] Accordingly, Bracton remarks that his work is to be considered "under ethics, moral science as it were, since it treats of customary principles of behavior" (2.20).

Thus where the conception of universal law implicit in the Roman code had dictated that the authority of ancient custom and usage was invalid in the face of reason or *lex scripta,* medieval customary law had asserted that the code did not extend so far as to overrule *usum et mores.*[12] As Pole's position in Starkey's *Dialogue* indicates, however, the normative character of usage continued to be challenged by the conceptual basis of the Roman law during the Renaissance. Ironically, this challenge was met in England by an alliance between the common lawyers and the early religious reformers, whose ordinary scorn for unwritten traditions has already been noted. The principal vehicle in England for the natural law apparatus of the Roman code was canon law, which equally aroused the antipapist zeal of religious reformers and the jealousy of common lawyers, who associated it with "attempts to encroach upon the king's authority for the benefit of foreigners" and the "meddling and vexatious jurisdiction of the spiritual courts."[13]

9. Sabine, p. 202.

10. See Sabine, pp. 198–221; Fritz Kern, *Kingship and Law in the Middle Ages,* trans. S. B. Chrimes (1956; rpt., New York: Harper Torchbooks, 1970), pp. 149–176; and C. H. McIlwain, *The Growth of Political Thought in the West* (New York: Macmillan, 1932), pp. 170–194.

11. Henry de Bracton, *On the Laws and Customs of England,* trans. Samuel E. Thorne (Cambridge: Harvard University Press, 1968), 2.19.

12. McIlwain quotes this phrase from the twelfth century *Libri Feudorum,* in *Growth,* p. 171; cf. Justinian, *Institutes,* 1.2.11.

13. Sir Frederick Pollock, quoted in "The Law of Nature and the Common Law," in W. S. Holdsworth, *A History of English Law* (London: Methuen, 1909), II, 512.

The response of the common lawyers was therefore to appropriate the concepts of nature and reason and to incorporate them in the theoretical framework of the common law in such a way as to justify a body of customary law already long in existence.[14]

This strategy of incorporation is central to Christopher St. Germain's *Doctour and Student* (1528), an influential treatise that set the tone for sixteenth-century common lawyers and thus helped to pave the way for Hooker's argument. St. Germain remarks that in England law is "groundyd" on six principles; these are the law of reason, the law of God, and custom, maxims, local customs, and statutes.[15] Although he admits that in theory custom "may not prevayle" against divine law or reason, he asserts that in practice it is nearly impossible to bring such abstract standards to bear upon the laws of England. Though "some men have affyrmed that all of the law of the realm is provable by the lawe of reason . . . that can not be provyed as me semeth" (p. 37).

The various forms of the law of reason may be found implicit in the English law, but "there is no special written law concerning such law of reason" (p. 37). It is "not moche usyd in the lawes of Engelonde to reason what law is groundyd upon the lawe of fyrste reason primarye or the lawe of reason secondarye, for they be most openly knowen of them selfe" (p. 37). More important, however, the rationale of "mixed" law is impossible to determine because "that law is derived from some one maxim, or even from many maxims of English law as aforesaid, and often there is no easy approach to deduction from them" (p. 37). In other words, English customs and maxims (which are merely the judicial reduction of customs to easily stated principles) are themselves irreducible principles, and therefore insusceptible to deduction from other rational principles. Customary practice culminates in "dyvers pryncyples that be called by those learned in the law maxyms the whiche have ben alwayes taken for law in this realme so that it is not

---

Cf. Stanley Chodorow, *Christian Political Theory and Church Politics in the Mid-Twelfth Century* (Berkeley: University of California Press, 1972), pp. 96–111; Carlyle and Carlyle, II, 101–113; F. W. Maitland, "English Law and the Renaissance," in *Selected Historical Essays,* ed. Helen M. Cam (Cambridge: Selden Society, 1957), pp. 135–151; Philip Hughes, *The Reformation in England* (New York: MacMillan, 1951), I, 24–30; and John D. Eusden, *Puritans, Lawyers, and Politics in Early Seventeenth-Century England* (New Haven: Yale University Press, 1958), pp. 126–141.

14. See C. H. McIlwain, *The High Court of Parliament* (New Haven: Yale University Press, 1910), p. 97, and Franklin LeVan Baumer, *The Early Tudor Theory of Kingship* (New Haven: Yale University Press, 1940), pp. 6–7.

15. Christopher St. Germain, *Doctour and Student,* ed. T. F. T. Plucknett and J. L. Barton (London: Selden Society, 1974), pp. 31 ff.

lawfull for none that is lernyd to deny them for every one of those maxymes is suffycyent auctorytie to hym selfe to such an extent that it is fruitless to argue with those who deny them" (p. 57). The consequence of this "suffycyent auctorytie" is that, if the laws of England are in any sense "groundyd" on the law of reason, then reason must be indemonstrably incorporated in customary practice.

This is the explicit argument of Sir John Fortescue's *De Laudibus Legum Angliae* (1546). Insofar as English law conforms with natural law it is unexceptional, he observes; yet it is superior to other forms of law, including the Roman code. Instead of offering a theoretical explanation, however, Fortescue defends this superiority by undertaking a historical sketch of the "characteristics" of "the customs, and also the statutes of England":

> The kingdom of England was first inhabited by the Britons, then ruled by Romans, again by Britons, then possessed by Saxons, but finally by Normans whose posterity hold the realm at the present time. And throughout the period of these nations and their Kings, the realm has been continuously ruled by the same customs as it is now; customs, which, if they had not been the best, some of those Kings would have changed for the sake of justice or by the impulse of caprice, and totally abolished them, especially the Romans, who judged almost the whole world by their laws. Similarly, others of the aforesaid Kings, who possessed the Kingdom of England only by the sword, could, by that power, have destroyed its laws. Indeed, neither the civil laws of the Romans, so deeply rooted by the usage of so many ages, nor the laws of the Venetians, which are renowned above all others for their antiquity—though their island was inhabited, and Rome unbuilt at the time of the origin of the Britons—nor the laws of any Christian Kingdom, are so rooted in antiquity. Here there is no gainsaying nor legitimate doubt but that the customs of the English are not only good but the best.[16]

The test of perfect justice is therefore not only deduction from the principles of natural law, but also the suitability of law to national character and historical circumstance. The measure of this suitability is determined by history, by experience and long usage; such measure-

16. Sir John Fortescue, *De Laudibus Legem Angliae,* trans. S. B. Chrimes (Cambridge: Cambridge University Press, 1949), pp. 39–41.

ment is a "presumptive" form of reasoning. The continuity of customary laws has "testified silently in their behalf, there is a greater weight of experience, a greater weight of presumption, impelling us to believe them satisfactory to the historic society where they obtain."[17] As it is put in Starkey's *Dialogue,* "there be . . . certayn custumys and manerys by long use and tyme confyrmyd and approvyd" (p. 15).

The most certain guidance in assimilating human law with nature resides, therefore, not in a superempirical body of rational law, but in the silent testimony of experience. Accordingly, Fortescue's Prince is counseled in the manner later recommended by St. Germain: he is to study precedent, the "certain universals which those learned in the laws of England and mathematicians alike call maxims" (p. 21). These principles are not above the law, but by virtue of the power of experience, are embodied in it; they "are not known by force of argument, nor by logical demonstrations, but they are acquired . . . by induction through the senses and the memory" (p. 23). The very process by which the Prince will learn and assimilate these principles becomes an analogue to the historical process by which such principles are defined: "Hence you will realize that if by instruction you will understand the laws of which you are now ignorant, you will love them since they are the best; and the more you reflect on them, the more agreeably will you enjoy them. For all that is loved transfers the lover into its own nature by usage, wherefore, said Aristotle, Use becomes another nature" (p. 17).

Through this pragmatic assimilation of nature to the inarticulate level of trial and error, the common law provides Hooker with a practical content in keeping with his theoretical framework. In fact, Fortescue's formula, by which "Use becomes another nature," is but the inverse of Hooker's framework, in which the formation of habits in the will serves as prelude to his account of law. In the human act, the habit of prudence counsels the will in its choice of means to natural ends; in the acts of societies, human law serves as the counterpart to prudence by providing a rule of guidance to the common good desired by the common will. In practical terms, this will expresses itself through the sovereign power of custom, that form of legal habit which history and experience have established and confirmed as the valid form of guidance for the common good. Such legal customs are the social counterpart of habit in the will. Although the shape of custom may appear unwarranted by superempirical standards, "we must not think but that there is some ground of reason even in nature . . . The thinges which

17. J. G. A. Pocock, *The Machiavellian Moment* (Princeton: Princeton University Press, 1975), p. 16. Cf. F. W. Maitland, "English Law and the Renaissance," in Cam.

so long experience of all ages hath confirmed and made profitable, let not us presume to condemne as follies and toyes, because *wee some-times knowe not the cause and reason of them"* (4.1.3; my italics). Given the confinement of man's quest for perfection to a realm of spa-tial and temporal limitation, the "ways of wisdom" must be many. In addition to the aid wisdom sends to men through Scripture and nature, "in some thinges she leadeth and trayneth them onely by worldly ex-perience and practise" (2.1.4). In order that this form of wisdom be not folly, custom comes to man's aid to secure and render coherent the variety of experience through time:

> It is therefore the voice both of God and nature not of learn-inge onlie, that especiallie in matters of action and policie "The sentences and judgments of men experienced, aged and wise, yea though they speake without any proofe or demonstration are no lesse to be harkned unto, then as beinge demonstrations in them selves; because such mens longe observation is as an eye wherewith they presently and plainlie behold those principles which sway over all actions" . . . That which showeth them to be wise is the gatheringe of principles out of theire owne particular experimentes. (5.7.2, on *Ethics*, 6.2)

The very principle of experience through which Hooker justifies the authority of custom as "second nature," however, raises the possibility that the changing configurations of circumstance may render custom obsolete. Indeed, "the wisedome which is learned by tract of time, findeth the lawes that have bene in former ages establisht, needefull in later to be abrogated" (4.14.1). Because the sovereignty of custom lies ultimately in the confirmation of experience, and not in the in-herent rightness of conventional forms, "that which hath bene once most sufficient, may wax otherwise by alteration of time and place" (3.10.3). Thus in addition to the sovereignty derived from "silent al-lowance famously notified by custom reaching beyond the memory of man," there arises the need for accommodation to changing circum-stance "by express consent, whereof positive laws are witnesses" (8.2.11). This second practical form of expression not only suggests that change and accommodation, rather than continuity, are the decisive factors in the framing of human laws, but challenges the stability of custom by suggesting that sovereignty is political rather than legal, that law is made rather than inherited. In order to preserve the rightful place he has established for custom, Hooker must therefore provide a practical explanation of political sovereignty in keeping with it. He must, in other words, show that the political power of framing laws in response to circumstance derives from the same underlying principle of collective experience that insures the continuity of convention with man's highest ends.

Hooker derives the needed explanation from a corollary of the common law defense of custom, the concept of consensus. Just as Fortescue had justified the superiority of English customs through the testimony of history and experience, so he goes on to maintain the superiority of English statutes by the means through which they are made: "they are not made by the prince's will, but also by the assent of the whole realm . . . they are necessarily replete with prudence and wisdom, since they are promulgated not by the prudence of one counsellor nor of a hundred only, but of more than three hundred chosen men" (p. 41).

What is most significant in Fortescue's logic is not the particular theory of mixed monarchy, parliamentary power, or constitution that it might imply—for indeed Fortescue is quite hazy as to any such specific formulation—but the pragmatic assumption that underlying all particular forms of political sovereignty is the ultimate sovereignty of consensus. On the basis of such consensual logic the common law mind habitually spoke "of custom both as established by royal or ministerial action and as existing from uncreated antiquity; . . . the distinction between statutes as making new law and declaring old were both apparent and habitually slurred over."[18] The common and crucial element in Fortescue's defenses of both custom and consensus is their embodiment of collective prudence. Prudence is a habit born of experience—of the experience of ages past in the long run, of as many men as possible in the short. The power to rule by law, in other words, is secondary to the power of consensus that creates it; it is a corollary of the wisdom that accepts what history and experience have established as custom. Just as the establishment of custom assumes the consensus of the body for which it has proved beneficial, so the power of ruling and legislating derives ultimately from "a body of men united by consent of law and by community of interest."[19]

In the course of the sixteenth century, this emphasis upon consensual origins and common interest tended to displace arguments from natural analogy or necessity[20] as the basis of political thought. The great representative of this tendency, whose thought in some re-

18. Pocock, *Machiavellian Moment*, p. 27.

19. Fortescue, p. 31, quoting the *City of God*, 19.23.

20. Examples of which appear, respectively, in Sir Thomas Elyot, *The Book named "The Governor,"* ed. S. E. Lehmberg (New York: Everyman's Library, 1962), p. 7; and John Hayward, *An Answer to the First Part of a Certain Conference* (London, 1603), sig. C2v.

spects resembles Hooker's, was Sir Thomas Smith, who argued in *De Republica Anglorum* for the ultimate sovereignty of "a society or common doing of a multitude of free men collected together and united by common accord and covenauntes among themselves, for the conservation of themselves as well in peace as in warre."[21] This implies that the conferring of political sovereignty is a formal but nevertheless circumstantial response, intended to preserve the more fundamental continuity of the commonwealth, "for all chaungeth continually to more or less, and still to diverse and diverse orders, as the diversity of times do present occasion, and the mutability of mens wittes doth invent and assay newe wayes, to reforme and amende that wherein they do finde fault" (p. 33). From the perpetual continuation of this process Smith deduces an analogy between the commonwealth and the human personality which differs essentially from medieval versions. Instead of emphasizing in medieval fashion the anatomical relation of various parts to the whole, Smith's analogy focuses on the continuing identity of both human and political bodies as they move through time, adapting themselves to circumstance and changing in configuration while remaining essentially the same: "the nature of man is never to stand still in one manner of estate, but to grow from the lesse to the more . . . neither of a man's bodie it selfe, nor of the politique bodie which is compact of the same" (pp. 12–13). It is very much in keeping with this Heraclitean analogy between the body and the commonweal that Hooker defends the power of societies to adapt to circumstance: "All things natural have in them naturally more or less the power of providing for their own safety; and as each particular man hath this power, so every politic society of men must needs have the same, that thereby the whole may provide for the good of all the parts therein" (8.14.3). This power emphasizes the conventionality of political forms at the same time that it guarantees their legitimacy as expressions of the natural tendency in man to seek a common good. It is, in other words, needful "often to vary, alter, and change customs incident unto the manner of exercising that power which doth itself continue always one and the same" (7.2.2).

By thus linking the power of accommodation with the continuous identity of commonwealths, Hooker reconciles the prerogative of political sovereignty with the sovereignty of customary law. In another and more theoretical sense, he reconciles the power of accommodation with the power of tradition, the power of making and changing norms with the power that confirms and legitimizes them. The source of both

21. Sir Thomas Smith, *De Republica Anglorum*, ed. L. Alston (Cambridge: Cambridge University Press, 1906), p. 20.

these powers is consensus. Put yet another way, the commonwealth is both a process and a product of consensus. It is a product in the sense that common wisdom arising from experience has consulted with the common will to establish habitual forms of guidance. Through the formation of legal habits, tradition serves to establish the formal identity of a commonwealth. Though willed as an end, however, this formal identity is not a final product (like works of art), but an instrumental one. It is the means through which the continuing action of adjusting means to ends is guaranteed. Accordingly, the formal identity of a commonwealth not only embodies the guidelines for action, but contains the further power to act. The state, in other words, is a temporal process of perpetuation.

By thus combining the two concepts of custom and consensus from the pragmatic tradition of English legal and political thought, Hooker suggests the compatibility of legal with political rule on the basis of consensus. In a more theoretical sense, however, this enables him to show that the single principle of convention functions in two dimensions, preserving continuity through change, maintaining identity while adapting to circumstance.

Finally, and most important, by placing this entire discussion within the language and logical framework of the human act, Hooker suggests that the human capacities for change and for normative stability are not only mutually compatible, but together coterminous with nature itself. Insofar as Hooker's effort is prompted by the "duble name" of custom, it does not deny, but continues to maintain, the distinction between "custom and verity." Every custom must continue to be "judged of by the ende for which it was made, and by the aptnes of thinges therein prescribed unto the same end" (3.10.1). But by positing a harmonious hierarchy of ends, and by establishing an aspect of man's being that enacts its quest for fulfillment through conventional means, Hooker suggests that guidance is to be sought not only in transcendent norms, but also in the products of human experience itself, "the cust005 and orders of this present world" (Preface, 8.6).

3. A World on Wheels:
Convention in Sixteenth-Century Moral Philosophy

As the culmination of a century of debate, Hooker's effort to rehabilitate the "duble name" of custom represents a shift of focus from a realm of absolute and unchanging ends to an arena of contingent and provisional norms responsive to the changing configurations of experience. Although based upon the proposition that political and legal acts are ultimately justified by natural principles, Hooker's

effort quite frankly suggested that the fitness of particular acts is determined by reference not to nature, but to convention. Hooker therefore not only defended the arts of politics and law against the Protestant reformers, but in defending them, altered their normative basis.

Hooker's orchestration of the arts of morals, politics, and law demonstrates that this alteration was not an isolated phenomenon, but
part of a larger and more general revision of the normative basis of
the arts in the sixteenth century. The normative outlook inherited
from the technical tradition of antiquity and the Middle Ages provided the Renaissance with a highly isomorphic intellectual framework, so that a shift in the normative basis of one discipline was quite
naturally reflected in others. When Ben Jonson remarked that the
poet should master *"civil prudence . . .* furnish'd out of the body of
the State,"[1] he was expressing his awareness of a normative change that
affected eloquence as well; the art of poetry, formerly considered a
theoretical or logical art, was tending to be reclassified as a species of
the practical sciences, which included politics and moral philosophy.[2]
Thus changes in the status of the verbal arts, like those in other arts,
were governed in large part by changes in the normative framework
that embraced them all.

It is therefore not surprising to find that the increasing prominence
of the concept of convention in the verbal arts reflects its growing importance not only in the arts of politics and law, but also in Renaissance moral philosophy. Like ecclesiastical, political, and legal debate
in the sixteenth century, moral controversy often centered on the "duble name" of custom, and the normative outcome was much the same.
Although moral philosophy in sixteenth-century England began with
the rigid humanist assertion of the inherent natural fitness of moral
acts, it witnessed a gradual displacement of nature by convention as
the test of moral fitness as early moral humanism gave way first to the
curious ambivalence of the courtesy books and then to the moral relativity of the skeptics and libertines at century's end. Moreover, this
normative shift generated a reassessment of the value of normative
thinking in principle. Confronted with the variety and diversity of experience, the normative approach of moral philosophy increasingly
gave way to more critical and comparative approaches to rectitude. Instead of following a regimen dictated by a contemplative understand-

1. Ben Jonson, *Timber, or Discoveries,* in *Works,* ed. C. H. Hereford and Percy
and Evelyn Simpson (Oxford: Clarendon Press, 1947), VIII, 640.
2. See O. B. Hardison, *The Enduring Monument* (Chapel Hill: University of
North Carolina Press, 1962), ch. 1; and Bernard Weinberg, *A History of Literary
Criticism in the Italian Renaissance* (Chicago: University of Chicago Press, 1961), I, i.

ing of nature's highest ends, the moral thinker of the later Renaissance found his moral nature by constantly interpreting and revising his responses to a complex and shifting panorama of experience. The substantial revision of moral thought in England between the time of Thomas More and the end of the sixteenth century therefore involved a complex interplay between a nascent pragmatism and a normative framework in the process of change. The concept of convention as a moral norm was at once a cause and a beneficiary of this revision.

Ironically, the way for this revision was in part prepared by the early humanist attempts to make reason and nature prevail over the intransigent and unthinking inertia of habituation. Nature and convention were thus the normative alternatives posed, for example, by Thomas More's Utopian civilization. Choosing their duties and occupations by natural inclination,[3] the Utopians observe a fashion "uniform and unchanging" (More's *Works*, IV, 133–136), and practice a "universal behavior" (IV, 147). Like their dependency on an agrarian economy and their refusal to use cosmetics (IV, 137, 193), these measures are in keeping with their aim to provide only "the few needs and conveniences demanded by nature" (IV, 131).

Significantly, this quest for the "conveniences demanded by nature" is reflected at the higher level of ethical and political conduct, where in the absence of revelation the Utopians adhere to an ethic that mingles Stoic and Epicurean tenets.[4] They define virtue "as living according to nature, since to this end we were created by God. That individual, they say, is following the guidance of nature who, in desiring one thing and avoiding another, obeys the dictates of reason" (IV, 163).

In positing and reflecting on this standard, More's satiric contrast between Utopian and European institutions and practices becomes an inquiry into the principles underlying them. Just as his portrayal of Utopian economy and policy begs comparison with European practice, so the Utopian philosophy questions the rightness of European ways of thinking at the level of principle: "For just as the senses as well as right reason aim at whatever is pleasant by right reason . . . so they hold that whatever things mortals imagine by a foolish consensus to be sweet to them in spite of its being against nature (as though they had the power to change the nature of things as they change their names) are all so far from making for happiness that they are even a great hindrance to it" (IV, 167).

---

3. Sir Thomas More, *Utopia*, ed. Edward Surtz and J. H. Hexter, in *Complete Works* (New Haven: Yale University Press, 1964), IV, 127.

4. See J. H. Hexter, *More's "Utopia": The Biography of an Idea* (Princeton: Princeton University Press, 1952), p. 51.

Claiming as it does the power to change things as it changes their names, "foolish consensus" opposes at the level of principle the life dictated by nature and right reason. Indeed, the Utopians themselves maintain that the extravagant pleasures sought by the "mob of mortals" do not "arise from the nature of the thing itself [*ipsius rei natura*], but from their own perverse habit [*perversa consuetudo*]" (IV, 171–173).

The extent of this perversity is magnified by the Utopian achievement in the absence of those conventional institutions on which Christian civilization prides itself. Explicit social codes and positive laws are useless if they originate only in a "foolish consensus": "If a person does not regard nature, do you suppose he will care anything about words?" (IV, 197). More's focus on the merely conventional basis of European practices emphasizes not only the insecurity of conventional norms, but also their power to divide the human family and blind men to the truth. Indeed, the very strangeness to European eyes of the natural life of Utopia is testimony to "what opposite ideas and feelings are created by customs" (IV, 153). More's rejection of unsupported or unmotivated conventions[5] is typical of the early humanist position, and it rests upon the same Stoic contrast between immanent and transcendent norms that had been long subsumed by Christian thought and most recently wielded against "custom" by the Protestant reformers. Unlike its theological counterpart, however, the contrast in the secularized version of humanist moral and educational theory retained not only the broad conceptual distinction between immanent and transcendent, changing and unchanging principles, but also the specific philosophic nomenclature that designated these principles "convention" and "nature."

More important, however, the practical program of humanist ethics also differed from its theological counterpart in balancing its Stoic opposition to conventional norms with practical consideration of the need for habitual norms in the formation of moral virtue. At once more pragmatic and less radical than the extreme Protestant advocates of grace and total conversion, the humanists proposed as a means to moral rectitude an active program of human self-improvement through education and practice. An offspring of the humanistic marriage of idealism with rhetorical pragmatism, this program hinged upon the recognition that "morall vertues are not gotten by knowing onely what they be, but through the long practise of many vertuous

5. The inferiority of unsupported convention as compared with the Utopian ethic of natural law, however, should be balanced against the further inferiority of that ethic to divine revelation.

operations, whereby they fasten themselves to the minde, as being . . . converted into an habite."[6] According to the humanist program, the habitual mode of existence and operation of virtue in human agents requires not only natural disposition and rational knowledge of virtue, but "use and exercise" to "bring foorth the fruits thereof."[7] As a result, the opposition of natural principles to merely customary ones was slightly modified by an educational ideal that insisted upon their mutual dependency; although "nature is the best mistris we can have . . . the custome of vertuous behaviour and wholesome doctrine being taken in tender yeares, is converted not onely into an habite, but even into nature."[8] This conception of the cumulative movement of repeated experience toward the fixity of nature introduced to the moral sphere a normative principle already embraced by the English legal tradition, that "it is as difficult to break custome long used, as to change or alter nature";[9] and it legitimized by filling with a philosophic content the popular sixteenth-century proverb: "custome is as it were another nature."[10]

Such humanist syntheses were intended only to provide some common ground between natural norms and practical habits, and never to suggest that habits could themselves become an alternative source of norms. Nevertheless, few humanists could embrace the power of habit without seeing in its very inarticulateness a challenge to the norm of nature. In defending virtue as the habitual "observance of the mean relative to us," Aristotle had maintained that virtue is empirically determined by prudence with reference to the agent and his circumstances. By contrast, the typical Renaissance definition of virtue as adherence to nature tended to imply that the standard of moral virtue is external to and predetermines moral acts themselves.[11] Virtue,

6. Lodowick Bryskett, *A Discourse of Civill Life,* ed. Thomas E. Wright (Northridge, Cal.: San Fernando Valley State College, 1970), p. 154.

7. Pierre de la Primaudaye, *The French Académie,* trans. T.B. (London, 1602), p. 59.

8. Bryskett, p. 46.

9. William Baldwin, *A Treatise of Morall Philosophie,* ed. Robert Hood Bowers (Gainesville, Fla.: Scholar's Facsimiles, 1967), p. 364.

10. Baldwin, p. 364. Perhaps the most frequent and immediate source is Erasmus, *Adagia,* 3825, "Usus est altera natura"; see *Utopia,* pp. 458–459. See also Morris Palmer Tilley, *A Dictionary of Proverbs in England in the Sixteenth and Seventeenth Centuries* (Ann Arbor: University of Michigan Press, 1950), pp. 136, 693; and Charles G. Smith, *Shakespeare's Proverb Lore* (Cambridge: Harvard University Press, 1963), pp. 33–34, 91.

11. The difference may be attributed not only to the influence of Stoic teachings, but to Aquinas; compare, for example, *Ethics,* 1106b36–1107a4 with *Summa Theologiae,* 2a2ae, q. 91, a. 3.

one humanist maintained, is "the participation of the eternall Law in the reasonable creature."[12] Although the virtues are "grounded in those parts which are without reason," they are yet "apt to be ruled by reason."[13] This means that habitual responses to experience developed in the absence of overriding natural ends are morally inadequate: "custome without truth is but an old errour."[14] Though it brings to fruition standards posited by natural inclination and wisdom, "use without the two former is unperfect."[15] As for "that prudence, which is gotten onely by use, and by a man's own experience, it is too long, dangerous and difficult, because it is not able to make us wise but after our own perill."[16]

Through its combination of high moral idealism with pragmatic educational aims, the humanist program was therefore confronted and critically occupied with what Mulcaster had called the "duble name" of custom. Without some critical attempt at definition, customary practices might equally be invested with sanctity or cloaked with shame:

> Custome is to be observed in good and commendable things, and not in wicked and unlawfull . . . And if it happen that any abuse do grow and shrowd it selfe under the name of custome, the same ought to be taken away and abolished . . . For good customes are agreeable to Nature, in which respect it is said, that custome is another nature. But that which is contrary to nature . . . ought not to be named a custome, but a vile abuse, be it never so much cloked with the name of custome.[17]

Such attempts to distinguish between the good and evil faces of custom were further qualified and compromised by the complex framework in which human acts occur. Here not only the habitual mode but also the social setting of moral acts was at issue. On the one hand, there was frequently a temptation to maintain that the inherent fitness of moral acts was impervious to circumstance; Juan Luis Vives, for example, claimed in *De Tradendis Disciplinis* that "To be sure, no one can deny that everything has changed, and continues to change, every day, because these changes spring from our volition and indus-

12. Baldwin, p. 148; cf. pp. 146–150, passim.
13. Bryskett, p. 154.
14. Baldwin, p. 260.
15. Primaudaye, p. 164.
16. Primaudaye, p. 167.
17. Bryskett, p. 64.

try. But similar changes do not ever take place in the essential nature of human beings, i.e., in the foundations of the affections in the human mind, and the results they produce on actions and volitions."[18] On the other hand, the importance of experience in forming moral virtue and the variety of experience itself combined to exert a pull away from a center of inherent moral fitness toward a periphery of changing issues and circumstances. In this sense, virtue becomes radically practical; it is what Vives called the "skill of accommodating all things of which we make use in life, to their proper places, persons, and functions" (p. 228). Unlike that part of man which contemplates "the universall things which nature hath produced," the prudent faculty that seeks such fitness is concerned "about such things as are subject to change; and may be & may not be; may be done and may not be done; and (when al is said) are fortunable: of which there is no certaine and infallible truth, as there is of things eternall . . . For she onely forseeth and knoweth what is convenient or seemely."[19]

These two opposed criteria, the "seemliness" or "convenience" of moral acts and their inherent natural fitness, engendered an ambivalence in humanist attempts to isolate the source of rectitude. According to Erasmus, fitness may arise "sometimes from the very nature of things, sometimes from human custom and opinion . . . as it is true that there is nothing too ridiculous for custom to sanction, so it is undeniable that . . . there is a certain decorum among the sensible and judicious."[20] Just as attempts were made to reconcile a universal code of conduct with the power of habit in the individual, so attempts were made to complement inherent virtue with the comeliness demanded by circumstance. Such formulas, however, were themselves ambiguous, suggesting as they did that in specific application to time and place natural precepts might so be altered as to lose their original shape. Thus the need for "seemliness" in human acts contributed crucially to the sixteenth-century shift of focus from the natural to the conventional aspects of human affairs. By suggesting that the fitness of human acts is relative to the contexts in which they are performed, the ideal of "seemliness" not only set an alternative criterion for rectitude, but also emphasized its arbitrary, dynamic, and intersubjective character.

One of the principal vehicles of this shift in focus was the modification of the Ciceronian ideal of propriety by the Italian courtesy books

18. Juan Luis Vives, *De Tradendis Disciplinis*, trans. Foster Watson (1913; rpt., Totowa, N.J.: Rowman and Littlefield, 1971), p. 232.

19. Bryskett, p. 187.

20. Erasmus, *The Colloquies*, trans. Craig R. Thompson (Chicago: University of Chicago Press, 1965), pp. 213–214.

popular in the later sixteenth century. The purpose of Cicero's ideal of moral *decorum* was to emphasize the inseparability of propriety and moral rectitude (*De Officiis*, 1.94). This ideal was reflected in the standard of natural fitness posited not only in such humanistic works as More's *Utopia*, but also in the countless sixteenth-century "mirrors" and "estates" satires, whose approach to individual conduct assumed a perfect harmony between the propriety of social orders and the hierarchy of nature itself.[21] In addition to the duties demanded by both universal and particular nature, however, Cicero observes that man has other *officia* that vary with the change of external circumstance or deliberate choice (*De Officiis*, 1.115). This variety largely stems from the necessity of reverence toward others; "for indifference to public opinion implies not merely self-sufficiency, but even total lack of principle" (*De Officiis*, 1.99). This element of public opinion completes an essentially rhetorical conception of moral acts, for in addition to the fitness derived from the ideal forms of universal nature and the varied but hierarchically stable *ethos* of individual character, human acts contain as well an element of *pathos*. As in the more purely rhetorical distinction between a speech composed with a view to its subject and a speech composed with a view to its audience, the element of *pathos* suggests the need to complement propriety in the unchanging philosophic sense with propriety in its practical and contingent sense, to complement natural fitness with adaptation to time and circumstance. Not the intransigence of an Ajax, but the wiles of a Ulysses represent the proper balance of *ethos* with *pathos;* while we ought to keep to "that role to which we are best adapted . . . if at some time stress of circumstances shall thrust us aside into some uncongenial part, we must devote to it all possible thought, practice, and pains, that we may perform it, if not with propriety, at least with as little impropriety as possible" (*De Officiis*, 1.113–114).

Where humanist ideals gave way to more purely courtly ones, where the conditions of civic freedom or learned exile gave way to courtly service and diplomacy, this element of *pathos* became the basis for a highly rhetorical conception of human personality. Not only did this conception shift the framework for discussion of human morality from universal nature and the hierarchical stability of *ethos* to the flux of *pathos,* but it did so in explicitly rhetorical terms. As Daniel Javitch has observed, the prescriptions set forth to fashion Castiglione's cour-

21. See, e.g., John E. Mason, *Gentlefolk in the Making* (Philadelphia: University of Pennsylvania Press, 1935), chs. 1–2; and Ruth Kelso, *The Doctrine of the English Gentleman in the Sixteenth Century*, University of Illinois Studies in Language and Literature, 14 (Urbana: University of Illinois Press, 1929), chs. 2–3.

tier "are often transferred, themselves, from the realm of verbal and pictorial art . . . Many of the . . . artifices necessary for appearing to good advantage are derived from traditional rhetorical techniques."[22] The element of "seemliness" in conduct, like that of oratory, depends for its effect upon adjustment to circumstance; like good courtiers, "orators also have alwaies had such a diversitie among them, as (in a manner) every age hath brought forth and set by one sorte of Orators peculiar for that time, which have been unlike and disagreeing not onely to their predecessors and followers but also among them selves."[23] This type of rhetorical analogy emphasizes the circumstantial and experiential origin of norms for "seemliness," which "are learned, not so much by readyng, as by using company, for when an other speaketh, wee marke what liketh and what disliketh, and by that wee knowe what we ought to avoyde, and what to followe."[24]

Given its rhetorical outlook, the courtesy literature seizes and extends the practical dimension of the humanist moral program only to wield it skeptically as a weapon against the ancient moral tradition. "There is more certainty in the principles of practice," writes Robert Johnson, "then in the most necessary demonstrations, or clearest discourses of reason: and these men that are intendants, and practised in the occurents of Court, are fitter for any active employment."[25] Not only do Castiglione and Guazzo write in dialogue form because "there can be no certaine and determinate science from particular to particular," but they explicitly contrast their efforts with the antecedent tradition of moral philosophy.[26] This skeptical and pragmatic approach is justified by "the diversity of manners which occurre in conversation" and the "difference of the life and manners of men."[27] It is difficult

22. Daniel Javitch, "Poetry and Court Conduct: Puttenham's *Arte of English Poesie* in the Light of Castiglione's *Cortegiano*," *MLN*, 77 (1972), 868; see also John Simon White, *Renaissance Cavalier* (New York: Philosophical Library, 1959), pp. 33–36. For discussion of differences between humanist and courtly ideals, see Lauro Martines, "The Gentleman in Renaissance Italy: Strains of Isolation in the Body Politic," in *The Darker Vision of the Renaissance,* ed. Robert Kinsman (Berkeley: UCLA Center for Medieval and Renaissance Studies, 1974), pp. 77–93; and George K. Hunter, *John Lyly* (Cambridge: Harvard University Press, 1962), pp. 1–35.

23. Baldassare Castiglione, *The Book of the Courtier,* trans. Sir Thomas Hoby (1561), ed. W. H. D. Rouse (1928; rpt., New York: Everyman's Library, 1956), p. 62.

24. Stephano Guazzo, *The Civile Conversation,* ed. Sir Edward Sullivan (London: Constable, 1925), I, 130.

25. Robert Johnson, *Essaies, or Rather Imperfect Offers,* ed. Robert Hood Bowers (Gainesville: Scholar's Facsimiles, 1955), sig. C7v.

26. See Guazzo, I, 53, 110; Castiglione, pp. 3, 16, 31.

27. Guazzo, I, 54.

for Castiglione, "to picke out the perfect trade and way, and (as it were) the floure of the Courtiership" because "use maketh us many time to delite in, and to set little by the selfe same things: whereby sometime it proceedeth that maners, garments, customes, and fashions, which at sometime have been ever in price, become not regarded, and contrariwise, the not regarded, become of price . . . Therefore it is manifestly to be discerned, that *use hath greater force than reason,* to bring up new inventions among us, and to abolish the olde" (p. 16; my italics).

Not only did this new ideal precipitate a shift of focus from the natural to the conventional basis of human conduct, but it emphasized the arbitrary and dynamic origins of convention. By creeping in "unawares from time to time," the "violence of custome . . . hath at this day in manner vanquished reason."[28] Unlike the permanence of right reason, "custome and use, is as it were, bred and borne of time," so that "with the times the manners of men are altered."[29] While right reason serves to unite men under the universal rule of nature, the principle of convention is essentially divisive: "Opinion and Custome (as daily experience teacheth) do leade every one, be hee never so foolish or barbarous, to believe his own country condicions, and self conceytes to bee best."[30] Guazzo remarks upon the subtlety of this influence when he observes that

> if it seem no marvaile unto you to see these divers fashions and customes, according to the diversitie and great distance of the Countries, doe but consider howe much we differ within the circuite of Italy, in the Rome, Tuscane, Lombardie, and other partes of it . . . and you shall finde, howe onely the river Po and Tanar make Countries to differ in language, apparell, life, and manners, which are no further distant one from an other, then from one side or banke of the river to the other. (I, 65)

In keeping with the end of rhetorical "seemliness," this shift in moral focus reevaluated the influence of convention in human acts. Unlike the ambivalent early humanist approach, the later courtesy literature more readily embraced conformity with convention as the means to

---

28. Castiglione (Hoby's preface), p. 2; Guazzo, I, 62.

29. Giovanni della Casa, *Galateo of Manners and Behaviours,* trans. Robert Peterson, ed. Lewis Einstein (Boston: Merrymount Press, 1914), p. 97; Haly Heron, *The Kayes of Counsaile: A New Discourse of Morall Philosophie,* ed. Virgil B. Heltzel (Liverpool: University Press of Liverpool, 1954), p. 21.

30. Anon., *The English Courtier and the Country-gentleman* (London, 1586; another issue of *Cyvile and yncyvile life,* London, 1579), sig. Aiii.

decorous life. Castiglione, for example, discusses an error "generallye seene in olde men" who plangently "commend the times past, and blame the times present: dispraysing our doings and maners, and whatsoever they did not in their youth" (p. 86). The source of this error is their failure to understand that

> these fashions are brought up much by custome, and gen-
> erally men delite in them, as at that time they were con-
> tented to goe in their jacket, their breechless hose, and in
> their lowe shoes with latchets, and (to appeare fine) carry
> all daye long a Hauke upon their fist, without purpose . . .
> and used many other foolish fashions, the which they are
> nowe stale, so were they at that time much set by . . .
> Therefore may it be lawfull for us also to follow the cus-
> tome of our times, without controlement of these olde men.
> (p. 91)

Although Castiglione's defiance is here directed only at those things "which of them selves are neither good nor badde," this type of re-evaluation approached moral relativity when carried to the extreme. The pull of "convenience" away from the moral center of universal nature implied "that many things which are evil seem at first sight good, and many seem evil, and yet are good" (p. 99). Because "eche man desireth to bee well thought of, albeit there bee no valoure or goddnes in him," we must adopt as norms "not those, that we judge in our own conceits to be good: but suche, as be current by custome, & used in our own time."[31] Unlike earlier humanists, the courtly writers unabashedly advised that "we must not take uppon us to alter customes at our will. For time doth beget them, and time doth weare them out."[32] In order to achieve success, the ideal courtier must "frame himself according to the inclination of them he accompanieth him selfe withall."[33] Taking his cue from Castiglione, Robert Johnson

---

31. Della Casa, pp. 31, 51.

32. Della Casa, pp. 104–105.

33. Castiglione, p. 121. It should be noted, however, that in bk. 4 Castiglione's Courtier becomes the Counsellor, whose task, like that of Elyot's Governor, is "to win for himself . . . the favor and mind of the prince whome he serves." Thus White maintains that in bk. 4, Castiglione's "proclaimed aesthetic individualism takes a definitely ethical turn," p. 58. See also Joseph Mazzeo, *Renaissance and Revolution: The Remaking of European Thought* (New York: Random House, 1965), p. 147; Lawrence V. Ryan, "Book Four of Castiglione's *Courtier:* Climax or Afterthought?" *SRen,* 19 (1972), 156–179; and Wayne A. Rebhorn, *Courtly Performances: Masking and Festivity in Castiglione's "Book of the Courtier"* (Detroit: Wayne State University Press, 1978), pp. 26–29 and ch. 6.

observes that "one of the chiefest rules" of wisdom is "to dissemble according to the appearance and fashion of the time" (sig. C7v). "It is not inconvenient, but necessary," says Guazzo, "to folow the diversitie of manners and customes, according to the diversitie of Countries, and to imitate Alcibiades, to whom it was counted a praise, that he had so readie a wit to frame himself to the diversitie of the life and manners of other countries, and according to the saying, When one is at Rome, to live as they doe at Rome" (p. 65).

The extent to which such endorsement of convention altered sixteenth-century moral thought is perhaps best demonstrated by Philibert de Vienne's *Philosopher of the Court,* an anticourtly satire, whose gross irony escaped the notice of its translator.[34] "The vertue of man," says Philibert, "consisteth not in that whiche is only good of it selfe, folowing the opinion of Philosophie: but in that which seemeth to them good, & in no other than a certaine maner of living."[35] With hideous complacency, the author announces that "our new and moral Philosophie" is

> a manner of lyving according to the manner of the Courte, and differeth from the Philosophie of the Auncients, in that their vertue . . . is to live according to the instinct of Nature: and ours is too lyve according to the manner of the Courte. And even as it was aunciently affirmed, that if we followe Nature and doe no more than oure naturall reason sheweth us, wee should never doe evill: so, if wee followe the manner and customes, in due and true order of the Courte, we shall ever doe that is seemelye, good, and well.
> (pp. 17–18)

In light of this courtly ethic, it is useless "too embrace and followe vertue for the love of hir self"; instead, "wee shoulde or oughte to live vertuously, to the ends to obtayne honor and reputation" (p. 20). In explicit contrast to the antecedent moral tradition, virtue "is whollie set and placed in the court: even as the same of the auncients is placed in nature" (p. 22). The means to virtuous conduct is not to know oneself, but "to see and knowe the world . . . to understande the customes, lyving, and maners of sundrie nations" (pp. 24–25). Because there can be "no judgements of the inwarde dispositions of anye, more certayne than by the outward countenance and open shewe of

34. See Daniel Javitch, "The Philosopher of the Court: A French Satire Misunderstood," *CL,* 23 (1971), 97–124.

35. Philibert de Vienne, *The Philosopher of the Court,* trans. George North (London, 1575), p. 12.

oure lyving," it is best "to do as Romans do . . . to dissemble and accommodate oure selves to everie one" (pp. 84, 98). "To be open and simple," by contrast, "is meete for beastes and ydiotes" (p. 100).

Quite predictably, the challenge of this moral alternative, brought to England by "Nufangleness,"[36] did not pass unnoticed. Indeed, it provided ample grist for the spate of anticourtly satire and pastoral debate of the later sixteenth century. The frequent portrayal of the court as "a perpetuall dreame, a botomless whorlepole, an inchanted phantasy, and a maze," where "opinions are followed and reason let passe" and where men "for the obteining a little favour, do against nature,"[37] reflects an energetic resistance in England to the displacement of an ethic based on nature. The idealization of the pastoral mode draws much of its life from an implicit conflict between a stable and natural moral center and the shifting panorama of conventional "seemliness" at its periphery. As noted in Chapter I, the ideal of nature was not so frequently a primitivistic protest against all artifice as it was a civilized criticism of that part of artifice which is merely arbitrary and conventional. It is "both nature *and* reason" which leads men from the court to the country, where the mode of fitness is natural, and where it is more proper "to be a Milstone, not to stirre at every motion, then a feather in a Weathercocke, to turne with every gayle of winde."[38] The objection to the substitution of convention for nature is not a repudiation of artifice, but a protest against unreason. The aspect of artifice seized upon is the mutability of "divers fashions, chainging with the Moone."[39]

> Seest thou not, I say, what a deformed thing this fashion is, how giddily 'a turns about all the hotbloods between fourteen and five-and-thirty, sometimes fashioning them like Pharoah's soldiers in the reechy painting, sometime like god Bel's priests in the old church window, sometime like the shaven Hercules in the smirch'd worm-eaten tapestry, where his codpiece seems as massy as his club?[40]

36. Robert Greene, *A Quip for an Upstart Courtier*, in *Works*, ed. Alexander B. Grosart (rpt., New York: Russell and Russell, 1964), XI, 294.

37. Antony de Guevara, *A Looking Glasse for the Court*, trans. Frances Bryan (London, 1575), pp. 44, 32, 16.

38. Nicholas Breton, *The Court and the Country*, in *A Mad World My Masters, and Other Prose Works*, ed. Ursula Kentish-Wright (London: Cresset Press, 1929), pp. 187, 221; my italics.

39. Philip Stubbes, *The Anatomie of Abuses*, ed. Frederick J. Furnivall (Vaduz: Kraus Reprints, 1965), p. 74.

40. *Much Ado About Nothing*, 3.2.130–138. See also Francẹs Elizabeth Baldwin, *Sumptuary Legislation and Personal Regulation in England*, Johns Hopkins Studies

It is important to note that such protests themselves contributed to the growing reputation of convention. As the practical ethic of the humanist program receded into a literary ideal, the dreary and familiar evidence of "reechy paintings" and "smirch'd worm-eaten tapestries" attested that

> Custome chalengeth a large prerogative, which (in process of time) maketh hirselfe almost equal with Nature in force & conditions. For, if we consider the whole regiment of the world . . . we shal find almost nothing in so large an Empire that is not subject to the rule of custome: firste the generall fruite and propagation of kinde, is by custome naturallye increased and maintained, by Custome Emperours and Kings are crowned, by custome Knights and Lordes created, and by custome Justice administered, truth exalted, dueties regarded, Desertes rewarded, mighte encouraged, and to be shorte, all kynde of good vertues easilye attained and worthyly embraced . . . these are by custome specially maintained.[41]

Such concessions were augmented and considerably intensified by the skeptical and fideistic revivals of ancient Pyrrhonism in the later sixteenth century. These developments, together with a growing sense of mutability, and the vogue of melancholy associated with it, combined to magnify the power of convention by remaking nature in its image. Where the humanists proposed the rectification of habit through a practical subordination of activity to universal and unchanging natural ends, the skeptics of the later sixteenth century frequently reversed this arrangement, suggesting not only that such ends were mutable, but also, in the extreme cases, that this mutability was itself a reflection of the variety of habitual response.

Thus Cornelius Agrippa's *Vanitie and uncertaintie of Artes and Sciences* expanded the opposition of the earlier religious reformers to the transience of customary practices by attacking the very continuity of nature itself. The insecurity of unaided nature, Agrippa argues, is a function of the fall of man; the law of nature "is altered at every chaunge of time, of the state, and of the Prince, whiche tooke the firste beginninge of the sinne of our first parent, whiche was cause of all our miseries, from whence the first Lawe of corrupt nature proceeded which

in Historical and Political Science, 44 (Baltimore: The Johns Hopkins University Press, 1926), p. 194.

41. Heron, p. 88.

they tearme the Lawe of nature."[42] The most conspicuous complement to Agrippa's Calvinist theology, however, is his almost exclusive use of one of Sextus' ten Modes (*tropous*) of refutation—the Mode of Convention.[43] In order to demonstrate the uncertainty of moral philosophy, he surveys the variety of ancient philosophical schools, concluding that "if there be any Philosophie or Doctrine of manners, as some will, I suppose that this doth not so mutche consist of weake reasons of Philosophies, as of divers use, custome, observation, & practice in common life, and that it is mutable according to the opinion of times, places, and menne" (sig. T3v). Not only are established rules of conduct "right or wrong, according to the use of time, and agreements of menne," but all human achievements are similarly the products of convention. Unlike the majesty of Scripture, the "sciences are nothinge els, but the ordinaunces and opinions of men, so noysome as profitable" (sig. C1). The sweep of Agrippa's fideistic gaze extends from the practical to the productive sciences, fixing in each instance on the conventional bias that undermines human effort: "All the frate of litterature, or grammar, consisteth but in the onely use and authoritie of the Elders, to whom it is liked that everie thing shoulde be so called and written . . . none of them, whether he were a Greeke or a Latine, hath rendered a reason, how the partes of speech should be distinguished" (sig. C3v).

A similarly Calvinist theology motivates Fulke Greville's attack upon the "seas of errors" and "vaine Idols of humanity" in his *Treatie of Humane Learning*.[44] Subject "unto Time," and "like fleshy visions, never permanent. / Rising to fall, falling to rise again" (*Works,* II, 24),

> These Arts, moulds, workes can but expresse the sinne
> Whence by man's follie, his fall did beginne.
>
> (p. 24)

The vehicle of this expression is convention. Ideally, human "art should not like a curtizan / Change habits, dressing graces every day" (II, 35). In their fallen condition, however, the arts can only achieve the illusion of following nature by erecting "formes of opinion, Wit, and Vanity," mere "shadowes" grounded not on truth but

42. Cornelius Agrippa, *Of the Vanitie and uncertaintie of Artes and Sciences,* trans. James Sanford (London, 1569), sig. S5v.

43. On Agrippa's use of Sextus, see Charles G. Nauert, Jr., *Agrippa and the Crisis of Renaissance Thought,* Illinois Studies in the Social Sciences, 55 (Urbana: University of Illinois Press, 1965), pp. 142–143, 293–300; and Popkin, p. 25.

44. Fulke Greville, *Treatie of Humane Learning,* in *Works,* ed. A. B. Grosart (London, 1870), II, 19, 20.

> On precepts of the heathen, humours of Kings,
> Customes of men, and Time's unconstant wings.

(II, 43)

Supported philosophically by the cyclical cosmology of the preacher of Ecclesiastes, and concretely reinforced by the seeming evidence of mutability in recent social and religious upheavals,[45] and in natural portents and disasters, this fideistic focus on the transience of human effort was widened by a general sense of mutability and decay in the later sixteenth century.[46] From the perspective of a pervasive and fashionable melancholy, the variety and diversity of human practices became so striking as to demand redefinition of nature itself. Recast in the image of variety, nature was divided into a shifting congeries of irregular segments and particulars: "ech age . . . hath his tyme, each nation his nature, and each nature his property."[47] The continual shifting of these configurations, like the movement of the heavens and the elements, reflected with redoubled energy back upon the sphere of human efforts to order and stabilize experience. Thus, as John Norden pessimistically expressed it,

> men their maners and their properties
> Doe alter so, that all things alter too,
> Subject to them, and to their faculties:
> As *time* doth men, so *men invention* woo,
> > And many things do follow as the *founders* doo.
> > Man onely erreth from right *reasons* way,
> > Fed by fond fancie, guide unto estray.[48]

---

45. Thus John Norden observes in *Vicissitudo Rerum,* ed. D. C. Collins (Oxford: Shakespeare Association, 1931), st. 40, that

> Such changes never have beene seene of yore,
> In *Countries* and in *Kingdomes,* as of late,
> *Manners,* and *Lawes,* and *Religious* lore,
> Never were prized at so meene a rate;
> > Such are the changes of this *earthes* estate,
> > It may be sayd, *Times* wings beginne to frie
> > Now couching low, that erst did soare so hie.

46. See Victor Harris, *All Cohaerence Gone* (Chicago: University of Chicago Press, 1949), pp. 87–128.

47. John Banister, *The Historie of Man* (London, 1578), sig. Biiv., quoted in D. C. Allen, "The Degeneration of Man and Renaissance Pessimism," *SP,* 35 (1938), 220.

48. Norden, st. 151.

The concept of convention realized in Agrippa's bookish fideism and in the highly mannered, often Calvinistic mutability literature is more vividly and concretely explored in the *Essays* of Montaigne, whom Samuel Daniel commended for his "bolde sallies out upon / *Custome, the mightie tyrant of the earth.*"[49] "Whatsoever I ayme at," Montaigne observes, "I must needs force some of customes contradictions, so carefully hath she barred all our entrances" (1.35.239). "Custome is a violent and deceiving schoole-mistris," and "there is nothing . . . that either she doth not, or cannot" (1.22.105, 113). The quest for truth is everywhere limited by the boundaries of convention: "humane reason is a tincture in like weight and measure, infused into all our opinions and customes, what forme soever they be of: infinite in matter: infinite in diversitie" (1.22.109).

This diversity is a function of the human condition. "The world runnes all on wheeles," and "constancy it selfe is nothing but a languishing and wavering dance" (2.2.23). Consequently, "nothinge can be certainely established . . . both the judgeing and the judged being in continuall alteration and motion" (2.12.323). Nonetheless, because man "must have his steps numbred and ordered" (2.12.271), he attempts to set bounds to his experience. Given his sensual nature and the practical sphere of his existence, these limits are established practically, as custom "by little and little, and as it were by stealth, establisheth the foot of her authoritie in us" (1.22.105). Man is thus the product of two forces, the *condition universelle* embodied in the flux of nature, and the pressures of his times, the "particular configuration of forces and issue within the limits of contemporary experience."[50] The first of these forces inevitably implies the second. Because "we sucke . . . the milke of our birth," we find that "whatsoever is beyond the compasse of custome, wee deeme likewise to be beyond the compasse of reason" (1.22.114). Accordingly, man's encounter with man seems "strange . . . and wondrous" (3.13.341), for "men call that barbarisme which is not common to them. As indeed we have no ayme of truth and reason, than the example and *Idea* of the opinions and customes of the countrie we live in" (1.30.219). So readily does the conventional configuration of the times govern human nature that the very "lawes of conscience, which we say to proceed from nature, rise and proceed of custome: every man holding in special regard, and inward veneration the opinions approved, and customes received about

49. Commendatory verses to *The Essays of Michael Lord of Montaigne*, trans. John Florio (New York: Everyman's Library, 1965), I, 13.

50. Ricardo Quinones, *The Renaissance Discovery of Time* (Cambridge: Harvard University Press, 1972), p. 219; cf. Montaigne's *Essays*, 3.2.23–29.

him, cannot without remorse leave them, nor without applause ap-
plie himselfe unto them" (1.22.114). Appealing to "divers customes,
fashions, and usages" (3.13.341), Montaigne's cultural relativism suggested to John Donne that "that is the common opinion in one Age
which is not in another; yea, in one Kingdome at the same time, which
is not in another." If human laws, says Donne, "were necessary consequences from that law of nature, they could not be contrary in divers
places and times, as we see lawes to be." Thus, he confesses, "this
terme the law of Nature, is so variously and unconstantly deliver'd"
that "I read it a hundred times before I understand it once, or can
conclude it to signifie that which the author should at that time
meane." Since "scandall makes an indifferent thing heinous at that
time; which, if some person go out of the roome, or winke, is not
so,"[51]

> Ther's nothing simply good, or ill alone,
> Of every quality comparison,
> The onely measure is, and judge, opinion.[52]

Unlike Agrippa, Norden, or Greville, however, Montaigne and
Donne are cheerful skeptics. Just as the early redefinitions of the nature and function of convention were accompanied by a reevaluation
of its "duble name" that began with humanist pragmatism and ended
with the less reluctant concessions of the courtesy books, so too, the
displacement of unity and stability by variety and change in the concept of nature elicited not only an ascetic or fideistic flight to absolutes, but also a positive response of acceptance and affirmation. This
second response, through its endorsement of natural process and variety, led also to a greater willingness to rest satisfied with mutability,
diversity, and limitations inherent in the "second nature" of convention. Through his vigorous and supple approach to the varieties of experience Montaigne served as the example and stimulus for this trend.
Unlike Agrippa and the Protestant reformers, Montaigne reaffirmed
the value of conventional human institutions and achievements while
at the same time acknowledging their limitations. Given the inade-
quacies of the human mind and the dynamic character of existence,
"there is great reason why the spirit of man should be . . . strictly
embarred"; indeed, "there are few soules, so orderly, so constant, and

51. John Donne, *Biathanatos,* ed. J. William Hebel (New York: Facsimile Text Society, 1930), pp. 85, 77, 36, 173–174.
52. Donne, *Metempsychosis,* ll. 518–520, in *The Complete Poetry of John Donne,*
ed. John T. Shawcross (New York: Anchor Books, 1967), p. 329; cf. "Elegy xvii:
Variety," ll. 46–54.

so well borne, as may be trusted with their owne conduct, and . . . saile in the liberty of their judgments beyond common opinions" (2.12.272). "The greatnesse of the minde," Montaigne says, "is not so much, to draw up and hale forward, as to knowe how to range, direct and circumscribe it selfe" (3.13.379). The measure of order imposed by even conventional norms is preferable to anarchy: "since I am not capable to chuse, I take the choice from others; and keepe my selfe in the state, that God hath placed me in. Else could I hardly keepe my selfe from continuall rowling" (2.12.285).

More important, however, this impulse to enter the "closed comedy" of *obligations civiles* coexists for Montaigne with a desire for the "open comedy" of *occupation particulières*.[53] Though "we must live by the Worlde, and such as we finde it, so make use of it," a man should preserve his individual nature, and "know how to enjoy himselfe apart" (3.10.263). In other words, "a wise man ought inwardly to retire his minde from the common presse, and hold the same liberty and power to judge freely of all things, but for outward matters, he ought absolutely to follow the fashions and formes customarily received" (1.22.118). The integrity of individual nature, as Montaigne presents it, therefore provokes a significant departure from earlier attitudes toward convention. Although "there is nothing wherein the world differeth so much, as in customes and lawes," the proper response to this situation is neither total capitulation nor total disengagement. The Stoic or ascetic attempt to flee from change, "to passe it over and escape it . . . is mere folly," for "insteade of transforming themselves into Angels," such idealists "transchange themselves into beastes" (3.12.380, 385). By the same token, however, "there is no course of life so weake and sottish, as that which is managed by Order, Methode, and Discipline" (3.13.344). Like the complete rejection of conventional limitations, the "nice-delicatenesse" of being "tide to one certain particular fashion" results in a state of unthinking and inhuman petrifaction.

In effect, therefore, the earlier speculative and prescriptive approach to human norms gives way to a critical and comparative attitude in Montaigne's thought. While living in a world of manifold conventions, we ought "not servily be subjected to common lawes, but rather with judgement and voluntary liberty apply ourselves unto them" (2.8.68). Man's individual reason "is not a speculative but an empirical faculty that enables man to apprehend this world through direct and vicarious experience."[54] Accordingly, the wisest of philosophers are neither those

---

53. Quinones, p. 212; cf. pp. 220–221.

54. Robert Ornstein, "Donne, Montaigne, and Natural Law," *JEGP*, 55 (1956), 227.

who think they have found the truth in dogmatic abstractions, nor even those who, confessing that the truth cannot be found, conform to custom, but those who, acknowledging both their ignorance and the difficulty of the quest, have gone on searching for the truth in a critical confrontation with experience.[55]

Thus, Montaigne's skeptical displacement of the unity of nature with the manifold of convention subserves his image of man as an inquiring individual who seeks the signs of truth in the variety of conventional forms. Similarly, Donne's early libertine attack on natural law is continuous with his vigorously critical quest for truth.[56] "The inquity and burden of . . . custome," as well as the consequently various interpretations of natural law, demonstrate the ultimate importance of individual integrity: "Naturall law is so generall, that it extends to beasts more than to us, because they cannot compare degrees of obligation and distinctions of duties and offices, as we can. For we know that some things are naturall to the *species,* and other things to the particular *person* and that the latter may correct the first. And therefore when Cicero consulted the oracle at *Delphos,* he had his answer, *Follow your own nature.*"[57] The demand that man should be "Emperor of himselfe" and "doe according to reason"[58] in a manifestly unreasonable world, where "the golden laws of nature are repealed" and "we are made servants to opinion,"[59] elicits an understandably terrified response. In Donne's *Satyre III,* the insupportable flight of men toward the security of diverse religious sects, can lead a "careless Phrygius" to "abhorre / All," or an equally supine Gracchus to "love all as one," in thinking that

> As women do in divers countries goe
> In diverse habits, yet are stille one kinde;
> So doth, so is Religion.
>
> (ll. 66–68)

In this context, the fear of damnation "great courage, and high valour is" (l. 16), for "To adore, or scorne an image, or protest, / May all be

---

55. Montaigne, *Essays,* 2.12.207–221. See Donald M. Frame, *Montaigne's Discovery of Man: The Humanizing of a Humanist* (New York: Columbia University Press, 1955), p. 66.

56. See Louis I. Bredvold, "The Naturalism of Donne in Relation to Some Renaissance Traditions," *JEGP,* 22 (1923), 471–502; and George Williamson, "The Libertine Donne," *PQ,* 13 (1934), 276–291.

57. Donne, *Biathanatos,* p. 45.

58. Donne, *Biathanatos,* pp. 47, 45.

59. Donne, "Elegy xvii: Variety," ll. 47, 50, in Shawcross, p. 74.

bad" (ll. 76–77). Neither refusal to seek the "image" of truth in conventional forms, nor premature conformity with them can satisfy man's obligation to quest courageously for truth; he must

> doubt wisely; in strange way
> To stand inquiring right, is not to stray;
> To sleepe, or runne wrong, is: on a huge hill,
> Cragged, and steep, Truth stands, and hee that will
> Reach her, about must, and about must goe.

(ll. 77–81)

Fraught with "hard deedes, the bodies paines; hard knowledge too," man's search for truth is an arduous and necessarily indirect approach, attempting critically to assess the veracity of a multitude of opinions. Although the image of the "Sunne, dazling" suggests that truth is achieved through more than human power, the final lines support the human element emphasized throughout; like flowers at the water's edge, men must rely on human institutions, however flawed and precarious they may be. The paradox that man draws life from the very fluid force whose "tyrannous rage" (l. 106) can blindly sweep life away demands a wholehearted, yet cautious and discriminating, effort to form attachments with the shifting variety of conventional institutions.[60] Man must not withdraw, but "husband and improve" his contacts with the world, learning to "love the outward acts of Religion, though an *Hypocrite,* and though a natural man may doe them," for it is only by his judgment of "the quantitie in the light of the Moone" that he learns to gauge "the position and distance of the Sunne."[61]

Both Montaigne and Donne exemplify the pragmatic tendencies of later sixteenth-century moral thought. To the extent that convention tended to replace nature as the normative test of fitness, the entire tradition of moral prescription increasingly gave way to the individual's critical and comparative engagement with the varieties of experience. This engagement becomes Samuel Daniel's principal defense of the arts in *Musophilus* (1599). Provoked at once by the Calvinism of Greville and the skepticism of Montaigne,[62] *Musophilus* is pervaded

60. I am here indebted to the reading of Thomas V. Moore, "Donne's Use of Uncertainty as a Vital Force in *Satyre III," MP,* 67 (1969), 41–49.

61. Donne, "Sermon Preached at St. Paul's on Christmas Day, 1621," in *The Sermons of John Donne,* ed. George R. Potter and Evelyn M. Simpson (Berkeley: University of California Press, 1957), III, 368, 366.

62. See the edition of *Musophilus* by Raymond E. Himelick (West Lafayette, Ind.: Purdue University Press, 1965), p. 39; J. I. M. Stewart, "Samuel Daniel and

by a painful awareness that "this rowling world" (l. 677) would gladly "runne wilde, that it might make / One foremeless forme of confusion" (ll. 681–682). So inconstant are the norms observed by men that

> Either Truth, Goodness, Virtue are not still
> > The selfsame which they were, and alwayes one,
> > But alter to the project of our will,
> > Or we, our actions make them wait upon,
> > Putting them in the livery of our skill,
> > And cast them off againe when we have done.
> > > (ll. 307–312)

Like the refined adjustments of Montaigne and Donne, however, Daniel's response to the shifting panorama of opinion is neither sudden flight to absolutes nor uncritical capitulation to convention, but a qualified assertion of the viability of arts and letters in a less than perfect world. Musophilus maintains the capacity of human learning to retain integrity, "a recompense sufficient / Unto her selfe" (ll. 609–610); she need not "like to a wanton Curtezen, / Open her breasts for show, to winne her praise" (ll. 591–592), but may

> > undeceived with the Paralax
> > Of a mistaking eye of passion, know
> > By these mask'd outsides what the inward lackes;
> > Measuring man by himselfe, not by his show.
> > > (ll. 617–620)

There is, in Daniel's view, too much severity in those who "stand from off the earth beyond our sight" (l. 212), for the attempt "to pull backe th' on-running state of things" (l. 713) may make "the cure prove worse than the disease" (l. 740). The premature attempt to reach too far upward or backward from the present is a dangerous act of panic; it is fruitless to

> > > amend
> > By pulling down; and thinke you can proceed
> > By going backe unto the farther end.
> > > (ll. 750–752)

Montaigne," *RES,* 9 (1933), 311–312; Himelick, "Samuel Daniel, Montaigne, and Seneca," *N&Q,* n.s. 3 (1956), 61–64; and "Montaigne and Daniel's 'To Sir Thomas Egerton,'" *PQ,* 36 (1957), 500–504.

Instead, we should

> descend from that high stand
> Of over-looking Contemplation,
> And cast our thoughts, but to, and not beyond
> This spacious circuit which we tread upon.
>
> (ll. 537–540)

Instead of flying to a perspective so long that it invalidates all human effort, Daniel rests upon a critical but active confrontation with experience. Men's "hie knowledges," as Daniel elsewhere observes, "doe but give them more eyes to looke out into the uncertaintie and confusion," and so he walks with Montaigne "the plaine tract I finde beaten by Custome and the Time, contenting me with what I see in use."[63] Accordingly, Daniel redefines the meaning of cultural tradition, for it conveys, not the *fait accompli* of unchanging norms, but the accumulated record and reflection of innumerable encounters with experience. For Daniel, no less than for Arnold, literature is a "criticism of life"[64] and goes "arm'd into the list" with men themselves, in order that

> their experience may not come behind
> The times conceipt, but leading in their place
> May make men see the weapons of the mind . . .
> For should not grave and learn'd *experience*
> That lookes with th' eyes of all the world beside,
> And with all ages holdes intelligence,
> Go safer than deceipt without a guide?
>
> (ll. 839–841, 914–918)

The critical but active stance of Montaigne, Donne, and Daniel represents the fulfillment of a movement in the sixteenth century toward acceptance of the diversity of "second nature." Relating the variety of conventional forms to the flux and plenitude of nature itself, this movement is epitomized in Spenser's image of man as the interpreter of a shifting world of manifold particulars. Like Agrippa, Greville, and Norden, Spenser frequently laments the transience of "civill uses lore":

63. Samuel Daniel, *A Defense of Rhyme,* in G. Gregory Smith, *Elizabethan Critical Essays* (1904; rpt., Oxford: Oxford University Press, 1967), II, 374.

64. Douglas Bush remarks that *Musophilus* is "a sixteenth-century *Culture and Anarchy* in verse," *Mythology and the Renaissance Tradition in English Poetry* (1932; rpt., New York: Pageant Book Co., 1957), p. 29.

> For that which all men then did vertue call,
> Is now cald vice; and that which vice was hight,
> Is now hight vertue, and so us'd of all;
> Right now is wrong, and wrong that was is right;
> As all things else in time are chaunged quite:
> No wonder; for the heavens revolution
> Is wandred farre from where it first was pight,
> And so doe make contrarie constitution
> Of all this lower world, toward his dissolution.[65]

Throughout Spenser's work, the instability of social or conventional norms reflects the mutability of fallen nature. In *The Faerie Queene,* Spenser's heroes repeatedly confront a polysemous social world, whose fallen nature manifests itself in "wicked customes," "evill fashion," and "ungentle usage."[66]

Like Montaigne's revision of Agrippa, and Daniel's revision of Greville, however, Spenser's response to this condition in the *Cantos of Mutabilitie* transcends Norden's negative vision of mutability by ending in affirmation. Indeed, as Harry Berger has shown,[67] the subject of the cantos is not so much the condition of mutability itself as the history of man's interpretive response to it; using a technique of "conspicuous allusion," Spenser recites the historical variety of interpretive responses to the given fact of mutability. Beginning in the antique heroic mode,' he traces the figure of Mutabilitie from the theogony of the fall of the Titans, through the investment of divinities in cosmological speculation, to her uninvited entry to the anthropomorphized court of the newer Pantheon.

These differing historical versions of mutability give way to a comic version of the fall of man, which represents a further cultural (that is, Christian) interpretation; and the final judicial process of canto 7, with its use of formal debate, of pageantry, and of emblematic imagery, echoes the more recent medieval response to mutability. Like the previous episodes, this one supersedes those before it, not only in historical order, but also in encompassing and "demythologizing" earlier attempts to cope with the world's variety, for here we learn that Jove was created in just such an attempt:

65. Edmund Spenser, *The Faerie Queene,* ed. J. W. Hales (New York: Everyman's Library, 1969), bk. 5, proem, 3–4.

66. *Faerie Queene,* 6.1.6; 5.2.28; 6.3.42.

67. Harry Berger, *"The Mutabilitie Cantos:* Archaism and Evolution in Retrospect," in his *Spenser: A Collection of Critical Essays* (Englewood Cliffs: Prentice-Hall, 1968).

> But you, Dan Jove, that only constant are,
> And King of all the rest, as ye doe clame,
> Are you not subject eke to this misfare?
> Then, let me aske you this withouten blame;
> Where were ye borne? *Some say* in Crete by name,
> Others in Thebes, and others other-where;
> But, wheresoever they comment the same,
> *They all consent* that ye begotten were
> And borne here in this world; ne other can appeare.
>
> (7.7.53; my italics)

Having shown through his "recapitulation of the phases of experience from pagan through medieval models of imagination"[68] that the mutable "second nature" of imagination reflects the variety of conventional responses to the conditions of human existence, Spenser summons Nature herself to offer a further interpretation:

> I well consider all that ye have said,
> And find that all things stedfastnesse do hate
> And changed be; yet, being rightly wayd,
> They are not changed from their first estate;
> But by their change their being do dilate,
> And turning to themselves at length againe,
> Do worke their owne perfection so by fate.
>
> (7.7.58)

This transformation of Nature's mutability to an image of dilation and proliferation is typical of the delight with which Spenser so frequently regards the multiplicity and variety of natural forms. The magnificent pageant of canto 7, like the delightful variety of the Garden in *Muiopotmos* or the "infinite shapes of creatures" born in the Garden of Adonis in obedience to God's command "to increase and multiply" (3.6.34–35), emphasizes the positive aspects of change and diversity. Nature's own interpretation in the *Mutabilitie Cantos* thus reflects the cyclical pattern developed by Louis LeRoy in his treatment of mutability in *The Interchangeable Course, or Variety of Things* (1594). All things "that are moveable," he says "doe begin, and end; are borne, and die; do increase, & diminish uncessantly; endeavoring notwithstanding (as much as they may) to come near and participate of eternity: not by remaining alwaies one and the same but by continuing their kindes by the meanes of generation; which is an immortall worke

---

68. Berger, p. 148.

in this mortalitie."[69] This natural proliferation is reflected in the activities of men, who "desire to change their habitations, and dwellings; having a mutable mind, impacient of rest, and desirous of novelties: By reason whereof, they cease not from going one to an other, changing of maners, tongues, letters, lordships, and religions" (sig. D4). In contrast to Agrippa, Norden, or Greville, however, LeRoy views this variety as having "wholie and altogether the agreement, and sympathy of heaven, and earth; from whence as from a perpetuall spring floweth this universal abundance, by which this world is incessantly restored, and renewed" (sig. F6v). Though "the vicissitude in all human affairs, armes, learning, language, arts, estates, lands, and maners" is embodied in a cyclical pattern of rise and fall, this pattern comes to replace the vision of the four Kingdoms expounded out of the Book of Daniel with an image of much greater plenitude and proliferation (sig. Y1). Accordingly, the pattern of the world's progress is not simply cyclical; each cycle initiates another explosion outward toward diversity and complexity. This pattern of dispersal is mirrored in the arts, which move from a center of simplicity toward a circumference of variety. The contagious and changing element of convention serves human civilization in much the same way that physical generation serves nature:

> Bookes are different also according to the disposition of the times, and inclinations of the countries wherein they are made: even as wines are divers according to the territorie, quality of the aire, and disposition of the yere; the nature of the vine, & industry of the keeper. Every age hath his peculiar kind of speech; every nation and age his phrase: the Greekes and Latins writing after one sort; the Hebrewes, Chaldees, and Arabians after an other.   (sig. F4v.)

The consequence of this vision is a willingness to acknowledge the conventional element of civilization and affirm its beneficial power. In order to silence "the old complaint" of men "affectionate to antiquitie," LeRoy exposes the illusory foundations of the premature conservatism of men "that embarke themselves on the sea, and beginning to saile, according to the measure as they are distant from the land; it

---

69. Louis LeRoy, *Of the Interchangeable Course, or Variety of Things*, trans. R.A. (London, 1594), sig. Z3v. See John L. Lievsay, "An Immediate Source for *Faerie Queen*, bk. V, Proem," *MLN*, 59 (1944), 469–472; Kathrine Koller, "Two Elizabethan Expressions of the Idea of Mutability," *SP*, 35 (1938), 228–237; and Herbert Weisinger, "Ideas of History during the Renaissance," *JHI*, 6 (1945), 417–435.

seemeth unto them, that the bank, or shore, the hills, trees, and houses do leave them" (sig. Y4v). Instead of panic and flight to the illusion of a Golden Age, LeRoy proposes a critical engagement with the present, in an effort "to bring forth new inventions, agreeable to the manners, and affairs of this time" (sig. Z2).

This connection between the plenitude of nature and the variety of conventional forms underlies Spenser's presentation of conventional responses to change in the *Mutabilitie Cantos*. Beginning with the simple vision of the Golden Age, and following the cyclical pattern articulated by Nature herself, the movement of these responses forward and outward into history, in which each response invalidates its predecessor by subsuming it in a more complex vision, establishes the relativity of human vision to a proliferating cultural matrix. This cultural pattern, which mirrors the movement of nature itself toward increasing complexity and diversity, is portrayed not only in the *Mutabilitie Cantos*, but also in *The Faerie Queene* in such characters as Artegall, whose administration of justice must be revised from the savage rigor imaged by the iron Talus, to the more complex response of Mercilla, whose equity tempers justice with regard for circumstance. Similarly, book 6 depicts several stages in the growth of civilization, from the primitive rituals of cannibals to Colin Clout's apocalyptic vision of "Great Gloriana" in the center of the graces on Mount Acidale.[70]

Indeed, the entire movement of *The Faerie Queene*, from virtues proper to the individual (Holiness, Temperance), through those relating him to others (Chastity, Friendship), to those relating him to civilization (Justice, Courtesy), capitulates the movement toward cultural diversity and complexity traced in the *Mutabilitie Cantos*. Spenser never detaches such movement from its foothold in nature and grace, nor would it ever have occurred to him to relinquish the ideal of abiding rectitude and fitness. Yet the facility and delight with which Spenser explores and manipulates the literary conventions of a variety of cultures suggest not only a recognition, in the manner of Montaigne, of the critical importance of the human powers of accommodation and adjustment, but also a realization, in the manner of Hooker, that the diversity of adjustments made by cultures and civilizations are coterminous with nature itself. Man, in other words, is by his very nature a creator of conventions; if God has made the world, man is at least the

70. See Berger, "A Secret Discipline: *The Faerie Queene*, Book VI," in *Form and Convention in the Poetry of Edmund Spenser*, ed. William Nelson (New York: Columbia University Press, 1961), pp. 57–65. I am also in debt to Berger's Introduction to *Spenser*; to his "Archaism, Immortality, and the Muse," *Yale Review*, 58 (1969), 214–231; and "The Spenserian Dynamics," *SEL*, 8 (1968), 1–18.

maker of world views.[71] As Gabriel Harvey once remarked, "Nature herself is changeable and most of all delighted with vanitye; and art, after a sort her ape, conformeth herself to the like mutabilitye."[72] It is in recognition of this relationship that the ways of Spenser's

> delightful land of Faery,
> Are so exceeding spacious and wyde,
> And sprinckled with such sweet variety
> Of all that pleasant is to eare or eye.
> *(Faerie Queene,* book 6, Proem)

Thus Spenser's vision of mutability epitomizes both the shift in the sixteenth-century moral outlook from a quest for unchanging natural norms to a recognition of the prevalence of conventional ones, and the subsequent shift in attitude from a prescriptive hostility toward convention to a critical and comparative engagement with it in the changing configurations of moral experience. Like Hooker, who advised men to turn their gaze from the rigidity of absolutes to "the customs and the orders of this present world," Spenser summarizes a major movement of the sixteenth century when he undertakes his adaptation of the moral tradition to "the use of these dayes."[73]

4. NEO-STOIC AND BACONIAN NATURE: SEVENTEENTH CENTURY PROSPECTS

The history of the concept of convention in the sixteenth century is partly the history of its changing relationships with the concept of nature. The concept of convention developed by appropriating and accumulating powers and functions from nature, only to be readopted as the "second nature" of fashion and custom, whose changefulness reflected a redefined nature's mutability and variety. The vast differences between the stable unity of Utopian nature and the prolific energy and diversity of nature in LeRoy and Spenser serve as only one measure of this transformation.

Needless to say, this movement toward acceptance of conventional norms did not go unopposed. In addition to the fideistic flights proposed by the likes of Agrippa and Greville, the later sixteenth and

71. The phrase is Berger's, in *Spenser: A Collection of Critical Essays,* p. 176.
72. Gabriel Harvey, *The Letter-Book,* p. 170, quoted in William Blisset, "Spenser's Mutabilitie," in *Essays in English Literature to the Victorian Age,* ed. Miller MacLure (Toronto: University of Toronto Press, 1974), p. 40.
73. Spenser, Letter to Raleigh, *Faerie Queene,* p. 2.

early seventeenth centuries witnessed repeated efforts to reconstruct an edifice of unchanging and rational order in opposition to the apparent flux of life governed by opinion and customary norms. The somewhat enervated revival of the concepts of universal nature and right reason in the rise of Neo-Stoicism,[1] as well as the novel but related vision of order in Baconian nature, constituted the pair of opposing views against which the concept of convention was to be measured in the seventeenth century.

However different in other respects, these two visions of nature were alike in their unalterable opposition to conventional norms. "There is nothinge in the world," says the Neo-Stoic Guillaume du Vair,

> which tendeth not to one end or other . . . May we not safely conclude, that man hath also his ends, as well as all other creatures; which is set before him as the furthermost marke and butte, whereto all his actions should be directed: and sithence that the happiness of all things is their perfection, and their perfection the fruition of their end, shall not the happiness and felicitie of man consist in the full obtaining and attaining unto that which is proposed unto him, and whereunto all his actions are to be preferred?[2]

Beyond man's power to alter, these ends are dictated by a universal and natural order; and because man's nature is rational, he follows this order by following his reason. The flux of opinion and convention is abhorrent, because it exists in opposition to natural order. The passions that sway men's souls from reason are the vain and empty products of habit; as one example, the excessive love of country reflected in the false clamor for *pietas* is but "floting and fleeting wordes, savoring of nothing, but an unpleasant juice of POPULAR OPINION . . . You would have it to be from nature: But the truth is, it groweth of custome, or of some decree of ordinance."[3] Similarly opposed to the transience of opinion, William Cornwallis in his *Essayes* confesses that he keeps the "Pamphlets and lying Stories and News and twoo penny

1. For brief accounts of this development, and the revival of ancient Stoic texts surrounding it, see Herschel Baker, *The Dignity of Man* (Cambridge: Harvard University Press, 1947), pp. 301–312, and *The Wars of Truth* (Cambridge: Harvard University Press, 1952), pp. 110–116; and Robert Hoopes, *Right Reason in the English Renaissance* (Cambridge: Harvard University Press, 1962), pp. 132–145.

2. Guillaume du Vair, *The Morall Philosophie of the Stoicks*, trans. Thomas James, ed. Rudolf Kirk (New Brunswick: Rutgers University Press, 1951), pp. 53–54.

3. Justus Lipsius, *Two Bookes of Constancie*, trans. Sir John Stradling, ed. Rudolf Kirk (New Brunswick: Rutgers University Press, 1939), p. 95.

Poets . . . in my privy," because he finds in them no truth, but only the variety of fashion, "the difference of wits and dispositions, the alterations of Arguments pleasing the world, and the change of stiles."[4] Although *ratio est naturae imitatio,* we willingly "put on all habits saving Vertues. Our haire shall go off or on as occasion serves; we will pull our browes and indure any paine to imitate the fashion" (p. 63). The Neo-Stoic response to this irrational situation is the cultivation of rational self-sufficiency, "to lift up our hearts from the earth," as du Vair explained, and "place them in a quiet and peaceable estate" (p. 108). "Because a mans wordes and gestures are framed by long custome and imitation of others," warns du Vair, "we should not sort ourselves too much with the common sort of people, or haunt the theaters and common places of assemblie . . . for it is not possible but a man should draw some vile humour or other from the common people" (p. 124).

This hatred of the unsavory contagion of the theater and the marketplace, the source of what Greville had called "these vaine Idols of humanity," marks a point of alliance between the backward-looking concept of nature posited by Neo-Stoic "right reason" and the forward-looking vision of Baconian nature. The affinities between these otherwise different views are apparent in the antipathy to "the reign or tyranny of custom,"[5] which Bacon shares with Milton, who equally objected to "the inveterate blots and obscurities wrought upon our mindes by the suttle insinuating of Error and Custome."[6] "The predominance of custom is everywhere visible," says Bacon; so much so that "men profess, protest, engage, give great words, and then do just as they have done before, as if they were dead images and engines moved only by the wheels of custom . . . But if the force of custom simple and separate be great, the force of custom copulate and conjoined and collegiate is far greater. For there example teacheth, company comforteth, emulation quickeneth, glory raiseth, so as in such places the force of custom is in his exaltation."[7] Indeed, the Neo-Stoic contempt for convention expressed in his early *Essays* helped to motivate Bacon's later quest for greater certainty and stability through a "chain" of "second causes," of natural "ordinances and decrees which

4. William Cornwallis, *Essayes,* ed. Don Cameron Allen (Baltimore: The Johns Hopkins University Press, 1946), pp. 50–51.

5. Sir Francis Bacon, "Of Custome and Education," in *Essays,* ed. Clark Sutherland Northrup (Boston: Houghton Mifflin, 1908), p. 124.

6. *Complete Prose Works of John Milton* (New Haven: Yale University Press, 1959), II, 222–223.

7. Bacon, *Essays,* pp. 124–125.

throughout all . . . changes are infallibly observed."[8] In order that "knowledge may not be as a courtesan, for pleasure and vanity only . . . but as a spouse, for generation, fruit, and comfort," Bacon proposes a program in which man is once again "the servant and interpreter of Nature," and "can do and understand so much and so much only as he has observed in fact or in thought of the course of nature."[9] Accordingly, this new definition of nature, like that in Neo-Stoicism, takes up a stance in opposition not only to those flaws in the universal and individual nature of man, but also to those idols of the marketplace and theater which originate in "the commerce and consort of men."[10]

Because the concept of convention continued to be shaped by its changing relationships with concepts of nature, these attempts to rehabilitate human effort on the footing of a stable and universal nature comprised the standards against which convention would be measured in the seventeenth century. In their mutual agreement that "a truth resting supinely on authority or one incompatible to reason was no better than error,"[11] these two redefinitions opposed the concept of nature to norms of tradition and authority in such a way as to reinforce awareness of their conventional character. And although each of these two redefinitions led to a unique vision, the one positing the absolute standards of right reason and nature in a golden world of antiquity, the other positing them in an unlimited future to be reached through the progressive momentum of the present, their mutual opposition to convention generated a third type of vision, whose comparative and historical assessment of human achievement would be asserted as a reply to ancient and modern prejudices alike. This vision will be a major subject of Chapters IV and V.

8. Bacon, *Works*, IV, 32; III, 268, 265. See Ronald S. Crane, "The Relation of Bacon's *Essays* to His Program for the Advancement of Learning," in *Schelling Anniversary Papers* (New York: Century, 1923), pp. 87–105.

9. Bacon, *Works*, III, 295; IV, 47.

10. Bacon, *Works*, IV, 55; cf. III, 439 ff.

11. Baker, *Wars of Truth*, p. 161.

III. Convention and the Sixteenth-Century Arts of Speech

Like the moral and political arts, the verbal arts in Renaissance England were confronted with a philosophic conflict at their normative center. Perhaps to an even greater extent than the moral and political arts, the arts of speech were called upon to mediate between the nature and structure of reality, on the one hand, and the changing expectations, habits, and shared assumptions of men on the other. Historically, this was to some degree a uniquely linguistic problem, for as Aristotle had pointed out, the complete act of speech involves not only *res* and *verba,* but a speaker and his hearers as well. As instruments for the "establishing of a right relation between reader and subject," the verbal arts were forced to "be both efficacious and proportionate to the nature of what they help to express."[1]

The potential conflict between these demands had long preoccupied the technical tradition, but it became increasingly pronounced in the setting of debate that comprised the normative crisis of Renaissance thought. This crisis cohered around ideals of rectitude and fitness fundamental to normative thought itself, and thus encompassed all the arts. When Nicolas Grimald, for example, boasted that "propriety was observed" in his *Christus Redivivus* (1540), he turned immediately from literature to a larger context: "As in everyday life and conduct (*vita & moribus*), it is considered especially difficult to perceive and note in each instance what is proper (*decoru*)—a subject that is learnedly treated by philosophers in their ethical teachings—so in poetical compositions, to fashion diction in harmony with the matter and the

---

1. Rosemond Tuve, *Elizabethan and Metaphysical Imagery* (1947; rpt., Chicago: University of Chicago Press, 1972), pp. 189–190.

characters demands a man of keen insight, of refined judgement, un-
usual diligence and blessed with great leisure." As an abstract ideal,
propriety extends over a wide range of activity, encompassing the
whole of life and manners. Underlying its extensiveness, however, is
the basic notion of fitness or "harmony," according to which all things
are disposed to their "proper place."[2]

This notion, more than any other, acted as the guide to Renaissance
activity in all its forms. Accordingly, the formal instruments, or arts—
both practical and productive—through which this guidance was expressed, assumed and articulated an ideal of rectitude or fitness against
which the value of particular acts and productions should be measured.
Moreover, while using different materials to different ends, all of the
arts shared a basic agreement that their common ideal of rectitude and
their common use of a normative framework allowed for comparison
that might more clearly establish in a philosophic sense the character
of fitness itself. In comparing statecraft with poetry, for example,
Thomas More observes that each

> performs its role neatly and appropriately. This is the phi-
> losophy [of statecraft] which you must employ. Otherwise
> we have the situation in which a comedy of Plautus is being
> performed and the household slaves are making trivial jokes
> at one another and then you come on stage in a philoso-
> pher's attire and recite the passage from the *Octavia* where
> Seneca is disputing with Nero. Would it not have been
> preferable to take a part without words than by reciting
> something inappropriate to make a hodge-podge of comedy
> and tragedy?[3]

On the one hand, More can compare these two arts on a philosophic
level because they share the principle of fitness as a common ideal. On
the other hand, this elevation to the level of theory produces a conflict over the specific terms in which fitness might actually be defined.
Because it follows closely on the heels of More's debate with Hythloday in *Utopia*, the comparison occurs in a setting of ambivalence and
controversy. Out of this setting arise alternative definitions of fitness:
Hythloday's assertion that political wisdom involves unerring obedi-

2. *The Life and Poems of Nicolas Grimald*, ed. L. R. Merrill (New Haven: Yale
University Press, 1935), pp. 95, 109.

3. Sir Thomas More, *Utopia*, ed. Edward Surtz and J. H. Hexter, in *Complete
Works* (New Haven: Yale University Press, 1964), IV, 99.

ence to unchanging dictates of nature, and More's suggestion that the test of political rectitude is adjustment to the changing shape of political situations. When More goes on to compare politics with poetry, this unresolved contrast between alternative moral and political principles is brought to bear upon poetry as well. Politics and theater therefore confront a similar normative issue, for in the political context of More's argument it is an open question whether the artistically indecorous Senecan intruder illustrates a contradiction of unchanging natural principles or a violation of the historic and social expectations and habits of the audience.

Like politics, sixteenth-century literary theory was animated by the tensions between these alternative modes of fitness. It has been suggested that "though one sometimes finds that the wish to persuade controls the truth of things represented . . . the [Renaissance] critics of poetry do not advise the poets to persuade in this way."[4] In fact, however, like the moral and political arts, the arts of speech in sixteenth-century England witnessed the gradual displacement of the criterion of natural fitness by the idea that rectitude arises from the often arbitrary and unpredictable character of experience engendered by the power of human habit. Though "nature" continued to be asserted as the object of artistic expression and the test of artistic fitness, it was increasingly modified by concessions to the power of convention. As a result, there was a growing need, as in the practical arts, to complement the earlier normative framework with more critical, comparative, and historical procedures. As the verbal arts ceased to be treated as logical sciences and were increasingly classified with the practical arts of politics and ethics, they were correspondingly subjected to the influences of time and circumstance, which were all the time bearing more heavily upon these arts. If the integrity of nature was to continue to be asserted as the norm and justification of the arts of speech, it would be necessary to relate this norm, by a "separation of opinions," to the apparent complexity of artistic practice. In attempting to do so, the theorists of the later Renaissance turned in part from contemplation of the structure and function of nature itself to an assessment of the verbal arts in relation to their human setting.

As in the moral and political arts, this transition involved a dy-

---

4. Dorothy Schuchman McCoy, *Tradition and Convention: A Study of Periphrasis in English Pastoral Poetry from 1557–1715* (The Hague: Mouton, 1965), p. 33. See also T. McAlindon, *Shakespeare and Decorum* (London: Macmillan, 1973), pp. 9–10; and Thomas Kranidas, *The Fierce Equation: A Study of Milton's Decorum* (The Hague: Mouton, 1965), ch. 1, and esp. pp. 23, 47–48.

namic interplay between logical and rhetorical criteria. Indeed, these criteria were intrinsic to the development of the verbal arts, not only through the rival claims of philosophic and rhetorical schools in antiquity, but through the virtual identification of poetics and rhetoric with logic that the early Renaissance inherited from the Middle Ages. Because logic was the most advanced of the medieval trivium arts of grammar, rhetoric, and logic, it was frequently understood as the generic art to which the other verbal arts were subordinate as species.[5] Both Hugo of St. Victor and John of Salisbury classified language study under the heading of logic, as did the Arab interpreters of Aristotle.[6] This logical heritage accounts in part for the bias toward nature and reason as the tests of fitness in the early Renaissance. Thus Stephen Hawes, for example, posits reason as the test of poetic fitness in his *Pastime of Pleasure* (1512). The poets, he claims

> fayned / no fable without reason
> For reasonable is / all theyr moralyte
> And upon reason / was theyr conclusyon
> That the comyn wyt / by possybylyte
> Maye well adiuge / the perfyte veryte
> Of theyr sentence / for reason openly
> To the comyn wyt / it doth so notyfy.[7]

This standard applies not only to the "fayning" of fables, but to their "dysposycyon" and to "elocucyon" as well. The application of a logical criterion to poetics under the procedural auspices of rhetoric (invention, disposition, elocution) underlines what the sixteenth-century logician Ralph Lever was later to observe: that the "artes are knit together in such a bande of knowledge, that no man can be cunning in anye but he must have some knowledge in many."[8] The verbal arts were thus clustered isomorphically around a normative center; the

5. See, e.g., Alain de Lille's *Anticlaudianus*, in *Readings in Medieval Rhetoric*, ed. J. M. Miller, M. H. Prosser, and T. W. Benson (Bloomington: Indiana University Press, 1973), pp. 222–227; and C. S. Baldwin, *Medieval Rhetoric and Poetic* (New York: Macmillan, 1928), p. 150.

6. See O. B. Hardison, *The Enduring Monument* (Chapel Hill: University of North Carolina Press, 1962), p. 12; Bernard Weinberg, *A History of Literary Criticism in the Italian Renaissance* (Chicago: University of Chicago Press, 1961), I, 2–13; and J. E. Spingarn, *A History of Literary Criticism in the Renaissance* (1899; rpt., New York: Harcourt Brace & World, 1963), pp. 16–18.

7. Stephen Hawes, *The Pastime of Pleasure*, ed. William Edward Mead (London: Early English Texts Society, 1928), ll. 953–959.

8. Ralph Lever, *The Art of Reason, rightly termed, Witcraft* (1573) (Menston, Eng.: Scolar Press, 1972), p. 90.

poet, as Ben Jonson remarked, was to be brought "downe through the disciplines of Grammar, Logicke, Rhetoricke, and the Ethicks."[9]

This clustering originally concealed the opposition of rational and rhetorical criteria, for both rhetoric and poetics were treated as species of logic. To begin with, rhetoric and poetics were rarely distinguished.[10] Quintilian had recommended the study of poetry as propaedeutic to eloquence, and rhetorical analysis had been applied to both prose and verse by the grammarians of late antiquity and the early Middle Ages. As a result, from the time of its incorporation into the trivium, poetry was conceived as a species of rhetorical excellence. Even when accorded separate treatment, as in the twelfth-century arts of poetry, the conceptual framework and terminology for the analysis of poetry was derived from rhetoric. This procedure was continued in the *arts de séconde rhétorique* of late fifteenth- and early sixteenth-century France.[11] Thus Thomas Sébillet observed that "l'Orateur et le Poete" were "tant proches et conjoinz, que semblables et égauz en plusieurs choses, différent principalement en ce, que l'un est plus constraint de nombres que l'autre."[12] When George Gascoigne remarked that "the first and most necessarie poynt that ever I founde meete to be considered in making of a delectable poeme is this, to ground it upon some fine invention,"[13] or when Jonson claimed that "the Poet is the nearest Borderer upon the Orator, and expresseth all his vertues, though he

9. Ben Jonson, *Timber, Or Discoveries*, in *Works*, ed. C. H. Hereford and Percy and Evelyn Simpson (Oxford: Clarendon Press, 1947), VIII, 637.

10. See Donald Lemen Clark, *Rhetoric and Poetry in the Renaissance* (1922; rpt., New York: Russell and Russell, 1963); C. S. Baldwin, *Renaissance Literary Theory and Practice* (New York: Columbia University Press, 1939); William G. Crane, *Wit and Rhetoric in the Renaissance* (1937; rpt., Gloucester, Mass.: Peter Smith, 1964); Sister Miriam Joseph, *Rhetoric in Shakespeare's Time* (New York: Harcourt Brace & World, 1962); Hardin Craig, *The Enchanted Glass* (New York: Oxford University Press, 1936), chs. 6–7; A. W. Allison, "Poetry and Rhetoric: In Defense of Elizabethan Criticism," *Virginia University Studies*, 4 (1951), 203; Ian Sowton, "Hidden Persuaders as a Means of Literary Grace: Sixteenth-Century Poetics and Rhetoric in England," *Toronto University Quarterly*, 32 (1962), 55–69; and Martin T. Herrick, "The Place of Rhetoric in Poetic Theory," *Quarterly Journal of Speech*, 34 (1948), 1–22.

11. See Grahame Castor, *Pléiade Poetics* (Cambridge: Cambridge University Press, 1964), ch. 2; Warren Patterson, *Three Centuries of French Poetic Theory* (Ann Arbor: University of Michigan Press, 1935), I, i, esp. pp. 216–230; and Spingarn, *Literary Criticism in the Renaissance*, pp. 109–110.

12. Thomas Sébillet, *Art poétique françoys*, in S. John Holyoake, *An Introduction to French Sixteenth-Century Poetic Theory* (New York: Barnes and Noble, 1972), p. 16.

13. George Gascoigne, *Certayne Notes of Instruction*, in G. Gregory Smith, ed., *Elizabethan Critical Essays* (1904; rpt., Oxford University Press, 1967), I, 46.

be tyed more to numbers,"[14] they were following a tradition in which rhetoric and poetics were closely aligned.

This alignment, as will be seen later, ultimately promoted and sustained the essentially rhetorical view that poetic fitness is in large part conventional. In the earlier sixteenth century, however, the affiliation of poetics with rhetoric implied an ideal of natural fitness instead, for rhetoric was understood not as an alternative to logic but as a rational science subordinate to it. The logical heritage of the Middle Ages had suppressed the ancient antagonism between logic and rhetoric, so that Thomas Wilson could advise that "every man should desire, & seek to have his *Logique* perfit, before he looke to profite in *Rhetorique,* considering the ground and confirmation of causes, is for the most part gathered out of *Logique.*"[15] For the early Renaissance, "Logique" almost always meant place-logic, or the use of the "commonplaces." Thus in order to determine "whether the thinges that he hath founde in his mynde be convenient to the purpose," Leonard Cox refers the aspiring orator specifically to "certayn placys as the Rhetoriciens call them out of whom he that knoweth the facultye may fetche easyly suche thynges as be mete for the matter that he shal speke of."[16] The rhetorician, as Montaigne declares, "borroweth the places of arguments from the Logitian."[17] The "places of Logique," says Wilson, aid rhetorical invention because they "give good occasion to finde out plentifull matter . . . And therefore they that will prove any cause, seeke onely to teach thereby the trueth, must search out the places of *Logique,* and no doubt they finde much plentie."[18]

The development of place-logic, beginning with Cicero's *Topics* and carried on by Boethius and Rudolf Agricola, has a long and interesting history,[19] but its most significant outcome was the virtual identification of logical and rhetorical composition, both of which used as a common basis for "invention" the "store house of places wherein Argumentes

14. Jonson, *Discoveries,* in *Works,* VIII, 567.

15. Thomas Wilson, *The Arte of Rhetorique,* ed. G. H. Mair (Oxford: Clarendon Press, 1909), p. 113.

16. Leonard Cox, *The Arte or Crafte of Rhetoryke,* ed. Frederick Ives Carpenter (1899; rpt., New York: AMS Press, n.d.), pp. 43–44.

17. Montaigne, *Essays,* trans. John Florio (New York: Everyman's Library, 1965), II, 307.

18. Wilson, *The Arte of Rhetorique,* p. 6.

19. See William Kneale and Martha Kneale, *The Development of Logic* (Oxford: Clarendon Press, 1962), p. 179; William G. Crane, pp. 50–53; Sister Miriam Joseph, pp. 18–23; W. S. Howell, pp. 15–22; Walter J. Ong, "Tudor Writings on Rhetoric," *SRen,* 15 (1968), 39–69; and Ong, *Ramus, Method, and the Decay of Dialogue* (Cambridge: Harvard University Press, 1958), esp. pp. 98–126.

rest," for "how to finde out matter, and set it in order, may be comen to all men."[20] Because logical and rhetorical invention were virtually the same procedure, rhetorical invention was "comprehended in certayn placys" of logic:

> Logicke is a playne and a sure way to instructe a man of the trouthe of every thinge. And that in it the natures, causes, parties and effectes of thinges ar by certaine rules discuss'd and serchyd out / So that nothinge can be perfectly and properyely knowen but by rules of Logicke which is nothynge but an observacyon or a diligent *markynge of nature* / whereby in every thynge mannes reason doth consyder what is fyrste / what laste / what propre / what impropre.[21]

This "markynge of nature" through the logical procedure of invention underlay the early sixteenth-century theory that reason and nature are the test of "what is fyrste / what laste / what propre / what impropre" in poetry. A basic logical bias led to rigid interpretations of poetic fitness, which referred decorum to the nature of the poetic subject, its genus, species, properties, whole and parts. Thus when George Whetstone declared that "to worke a Commedie *kindly,* grave old men should instruct, yonge men should showe the imperfections of youth, Strumpets should be lascivious, boys unhappy, and Clownes should speake disorderlye,"[22] he wrote in recognition of an established logical bias, that poems

> should then like definitions be
> Round, neat, convertible, such as agree
> To persons so, that, were their names conceal'd,
> Must make them known as well as if reveal'd:
> Such as contain the kind and difference,
> And all the properties arising thence.[23]

---

20. Thomas Wilson, *The Rule of Reason, conteining the Arte of Logique* (London, 1552), sig. Liv; Richard Sherry, *A Treatise of Schemes and Tropes* (1550), ed. Herbert W. Hildebrandt (Gainesville, Fla.: Scholar's Facsimiles and Reprints, 1961), sig. B2.

21. Cox, *The Arte or Crafte of Rhetoryke,* p. 45; my italics.

22. George Whetstone, Preface to *Promos and Cassandra,* in O. B. Hardison, ed., *English Literary Criticism: The Renaissance* (New York: Appleton-Century-Crofts, 1963), p. 220; my italics.

23. Edward, Lord Herbert of Cherbury, "Elegy for Doctor *Dunn,*" in *Poems,* ed. G. C. Moore Smith (Oxford: Clarendon Press, 1923), p. 58, ll. 39–44.

This overlap of logical, rhetorical, and poetic invention posits as the basis of all discourse the logical structure of nature. In all discourse, invention is the procedure "wherein plentifully is searched and considered, what kinde of matter, how much variety of sentences, what sorts of figures, how many similitudes, what approbations, diminutions, insinuations, and circumstances are presently needfull, or furthering to the matter in handling.[24] The extension of this common procedure to all the verbal arts resulted in the basic tendency of rhetorical or poetic invention to contain or absorb specifically logical *loci.* Thus Richard Rainolde, for example, takes the student of rhetoric successively through the logical places that "prove" the greatness of a man by establishing genus through specific "properties" or differences, by enumerating the "parts" of education that contribute to the "whole," by noting his *actus,* or "manner of doing," and relating it to such "adjuncts" as his personal qualities and to such "adjacents" as supply their variants, by listing such circumstances of his "placing" as wealth, power, and friends, and by concluding by comparing with arguments drawn from sources similar to the subject:

> You shall bryng to his praise, *Genus eius,* that is to saie: of what *kinde* he came of, which doth consiste in fower poinctes:
>
> $$\left.\begin{array}{l} \text{of what nacion} \\ \text{of what countrie} \\ \text{of what auncestors} \\ \text{of what parents} \end{array}\right\}$$
>
> After that you shall declare, his educacion; the educacion is contained in these poinctes:
>
> $$\text{In} \left\{\begin{array}{l} \text{Institucion} \\ \text{Arte} \\ \text{Lawe} \end{array}\right\}$$
>
> That put to that, which is the chiefe grounde of all praise: his actes doen; which doe proceede out of the giftes, and excellencies of the minde, as the fortitude of the minde, the might and strength of the same, and magnanimitie.
>
> Of the bodie, as a beautiful face, amiable countenance, swiftenesse, the might and strength of the same. The excellencies of his fortune, as his dignitie, power, authoritie, riches, substaunce, and friendes.

24. Angel Day, *The English Secretorie,* ed. Robert O. Evans (Gainesville, Fla.: Scholar's Facsimiles and Reprints, 1967), p. 14.

In the fift place use a *comparison*, wherein that whiche
you praise, maie be advaunced to the uttermost.[25]

This logical bias obtains even at the level of diction, where the
"fryste care" is "to speake evedentlye after the dignitye and nature of
thinges."[26] Consequently, the conscious Renaissance parallel between
stylistic devices and logical places in artistic practice has important
theoretical implications as well. By insisting on the logical basis and
structure of stylistic devices, the figurists established a close relationship between the style of discourse and the *nature* of its subject.
"Every mans stile," George Pattenham explains, "is for the most part
according to the matter and subject" because there needs to be a
"lovely conformitie, or proportion, or conveniencie betweene the
sence and the sensible." It therefore "behooveth the maker or Poet to
follow *the nature* of his subject."[27] The test of verbal fitness or "conveniencie" resides in the structure of nature itself: "everything that
is added to the particular subject is drawn *from the nature* of the subject, either by metaphor, or epithet, or other means that are inherent
in nature itself."[28]

This approach to style produced a sharp contrast between the artistic and merely conventional uses of speech. Although "the proper
use of speech is to utter the meaning of our mynde with as playne
wordes as may be," says Richard Sherry, yet "to set out the matter more
plainly we be compelled to speake, otherwyse than after common
facion."[29] In order to achieve the "lovely conformitie . . . betweene
the sence and the sensible" that is the aim of artistic speech, the poet
must depart "from the common course of ordinary speech and capacitie
of the vulgar judgement."[30] The artistic control of speech is "by trans-
lacion taken for the forme, fashion, and shape of anye thynge expressed
in wrytynge."[31] Accordingly, while poetic diction depends on the conventional lexicon for its material, its aim is to strip the lexicon of its
conventionality, and to rearrange its elements with reference to logical

---

25. Richard Rainolde, *The Foundacion of Rhetorike*, ed. Francis R. Johnson
(New York: Scholar's Facsimiles and Reprints, 1945), sig. K4.
26. Sherry, *A Treatise of Schemes and Tropes*, sig. B2.
27. George Puttenham, *The Arte of English Poesie*, ed. Gladys Doidge Willcock
and Alice Walker (Cambridge: Cambridge University Press, 1936), pp. 232, 262, 231.
28. Fracastoro, *Naugerius*, trans. Ruth Kelso, University of Illinois Studies in
Language and Literature, 14 (Urbana: University of Illinois Press, 1924), p. 70;
my italics.
29. Sherry, *A Treatise of Schemes and Tropes*, sig. A6.
30. Puttenham, p. 137.
31. Sherry, *A Treatise of Schemes and Tropes*, sig. B5.

structure, producing "a fashion of wordes, Oration, or sentence, *made new by Arte,* tourning from the common maner and custome of wrytyng or speaking."[32]

While this explicitly logical basis influenced the concept of poetry implicit in the *artes* or handbook tradition by drawing the procedures of composition inward toward a structured center of rational and natural fitness, it also influenced other forms of discourse, or theories, about poetry by logically limiting and categorizing the terms in which propositions about poetry could be made. Ironically, this second influence of place-logic served to counteract the first, for embedded in the logical places themselves was a structural distinction that framed alternative sets of data *about* discourse. The distinction emphasized the difference between unchanging natural principles and social or temporal contingencies, and thus implicitly embodied an ancient quarrel. Applied to propositions *about* the arts of speech, it could give rise alternatively to theories that emphasized either the natural fitness of verbal norms or their relationship to a variety of contingent issues, such as changing ends, effects, circumstances, and expectations. The source of these alternatives lies in the tabular structure of the places themselves, as exemplified in the table from Wilson's *Rule of Reason* shown on page 147.[33] Of foremost importance in Wilson's arrangement of the topics is the dichotomy between those sources of arguments "which are in the substaunce or nature of the thyng," and those which are "not in the substance, or nature of the thynge, but without it."[34] This division of topics reflects the division by Wilson, and by the scholastic logicians generally, of the five "predicables," or types of predicates, that propositions may have. The types of predicates arise either from the subject itself (the "predicables" of genus, species, difference, and property) or from sources connected with the subject (the "predicable" of accident), so that the sources of argument are said to be either internal or external to the subject under discussion.[35]

The distinction is essential to sixteenth-century poetic theory because the basic difference between internal and external arguments gives rise to two general types of theoretical discourse. Though the

32. Henry Peacham, *The Garden of Eloquence,* ed. William G. Crane (Gainesville, Fla.: Scholar's Facsimiles and Reprints, 1954), sig. B1.

33. No two logicians, of course, used exactly the same procedure, as witnessed by the complaint of Sherry, sig. F4v. See also Sister Miriam Joseph, p. 30; Ong, *Ramus,* pp. 121–123; and Sister Joan Marie Lechner, *Renaissance Concepts of the Commonplaces* (New York: Pageant Press, 1962), pp. 77–96.

34. The first of these quotations is from sig. L4v of *The Rule of Reason,* the second from the table itself, sig. L4.

35. See Howell, pp. 17–19; Crane, pp. 51–52.

Division of the Places, from Wilson's *Rule of Reason*

The division of the places, whiche are XXIIII in number

Some are inward places, called *Loci interni*, and thei are	Particularlie in the verie substaunce, as	The definicion The generall worde The kinde The propertie The whole The partes The yoked woorde
	and partlie incidente to the substuance, as	Woordes adjoined The maner of doyng The thing conteined
Some are outward places, called *Externi*, that is not in the substaunce, or nature of the thynge, but without it and these are	Either knitte with a nigh affinitie, called *Cognata*, of the whiche some are causes, as	The efficiente cause The ende
	some are those which spryng of the causes caled *Eventa*, as	The effecte The thing appointed for some ende
	Either applied to the thing, not beeyng the cause thereof, but only gevyng a name thereunto, called *Applicita*, as,	The Place The Tyme Thynges annexed
	Or els thei be accidentes, whereof there be	Things chauncyng Sentences of the sage The name of a thing Thynges compared Thynges like
	Or els thei are repugnances, as	Discordances Thynges differyng

Note: This table is based on the second (1552) edition of Wilson's *Rule of Reason*, sig. L4. The reproduction in William G. Crane's *Wit and Rhetoric in the Renaissance* (1937; rpt., Gloucester, Mass.: Peter Smith, 1964), p. 54, duplicates the erroneous printing of the table in the 1551 edition. The correctness of the second edition is confirmed by reference to Agricola's table, from which Wilson's is taken (see Walter J. Ong, *Ramus, Method, and the Decay of Dialogue* [Cambridge: Harvard University Press, 1958], p. 127) and by the subsequent editions of 1553, 1567, and 1580.

two are by no means mutually exclusive, discourse which draws upon terms arising from the subject itself will generate propositions about its nature, its genus, species, properties, parts, and mode of operation, while discourse which draws upon related terms will place the subject in a matrix of cause, effect, place, time, circumstance, contingency, precedent, and comparison. The very logical framework for the possibilities of discourse therefore marks the points of departure for the two major Renaissance views of poetic fitness, one of which maintained for all time the natural integrity and abiding fitness of poetic norms, while the other related such fitness to a complex and changing configuration of intersubjective and historical issues.

Argument from terms internal to the subject quite clearly produced an inclination to interpret the subject as an unchanging nature. Beginning with the first such term, Wilson observes that "a definition is a perfect sentence whereby *the very nature of the thyng it selfe*, is set furth and expounded."[36] It is, says John Hoskins, "the shortest and truest exposicion of *the nature of any thinge*."[37] After definition come the various types of division that comprehend the remaining internal terms: "As a definition therefore doth declare what a thing is, so a division sheweth how many things are contained in the same." The first of these divisions is classification, which involves genus and species, as well as "the propertie" that determines species, for "the difference, & the propertie declare natures workyng in all thynges livying." The next division is a partion "of the whole and his partes," which "is nothynge els but the right maner of a perfecte division."[38] The final division discriminates among those terms "partlie incidente to the substance," the subject and its adjuncts and "maner of doyng" (which includes both *actio* and *passio*). In other words, an essence or substance may be discussed through its quality ("thing contained"), or through qualities inferred by the application of other terms ("wordes adjoigned") or through the manner in which it acts or is acted upon ("the maner of doyng").[39]

This set of "internal" places, comprehending "the substance or nature of the thing," quite naturally lent theoretical support to the logical bias of poetic practice in the early sixteenth century. Ascham's classification of the arts of speech in *The Scolemaster*, for example, relies quite heavily on such places:

> The true difference of authors is best known *per diversa genera dicendi* that every one used; and therefore I will

36. Wilson, *The Rule of Reason*, sig. L4v; my italics.

37. John Hoskins, *Directions for Speech and Style*, ed. Hoyt T. Hudson, Princeton Studies in English, 12 (Princeton: Princeton University Press, 1935), p. 158; my italics.

38. Wilson, *The Rule of Reason*, sigs. C2, L7.

39. See Abraham Fraunce, *The Lawyer's Logicke*, fol. 39v, 38r; and Sister Miriam Joseph, p. 319.

here divide *genus dicendi,* not into these three, *tenue, medi-
ocre, et grande,* but as the matter of every author requireth;
as,

In genus $\begin{cases} \text{Poeticum} \\ \text{Historicum} \\ \text{Philosophicum} \\ \text{Oratorium} \end{cases}$

These differ one from another in choice of words, in framing of sentences, in handling of arguments, and use of right
form, figure, and number, proper and fit for every matter:
and every one of these is diverse also in itself; and the first,

Poeticum, in $\begin{cases} \text{Comicum} \\ \text{Tragicum} \\ \text{Epicum} \\ \text{Melicum.} \end{cases}$

And here, whosoever hath been diligent to read advisedly
over Terence, Seneca, Virgil, Horace, or els Aristophanes,
Sophocles, Homer, and Pindar; and shall diligently mark
the difference they use in propriety of words, in form of
sentence, in handling of their matter; he shall easily perceive what is fit, and *decorum* in every one, to the true use
of perfect *Imitation.*[40]

Ascham's brisk citation of the literary kinds and his insistence on
decorum throughout their various parts play the subservient role of
clarifying and organizing his main discussion of a nonlogical mode of
transmission, namely, imitation. Nevertheless, his use of logical organization shows that "literary invention—both 'finding' and 'making'—
in the Renaissance was largely generic, and . . . transfer of ancient
values was largely in generic terms, accomplished by generic instruments and helps."[41] Moreover, the basis of Ascham's classification is
not the authors or agents themselves, but "matter," usually regarded
in logic as part of "the verie substaunce" and therefore comprehended
by logical definition.[42] Accordingly, Ascham establishes nature as the
norm and test of fitness through two kinds of logical argument, analogy
and deduction. "The whole doctrine of comedies and tragedies," says
Ascham, "is a perfect Imitation, or fair lovely painted picture of the

40. Roger Ascham, *The Scolemaster,* ed. Edward Arber (London: Constable,
1923), pp. 137–138.
41. Rosalie Colie, *The Resources of Kind: Genre-Theory in the Renaissance*
(Berkeley: University of California Press, 1973), p. 17.
42. See, e.g., Lever, *The Art of Reason,* pp. 176–177.

life of every degree of man" (p. 117). By analogy between nature and the "matter" of poetry, Ascham establishes its species, which, as Wilson had declared, is "a maner of argumentation, where any thyng is proved by an other, for the likenes, that is found in them both."[43] On the basis of this analogy, Ascham then argues by deduction for the "use of right form, figure, and number, proper and fit for every matter." The implied procedure is, in Wilson's words, "an absolute gatheryng or reasonyng, whereby the last sentence [e.g., a proposition about diction], whiche we would prove, is confirmed by other proposicions and sentences, more universal, & better knowen, than the thing which is proved."[44] Ascham's use of the concepts of genus and species in connection with poetic fitness therefore leads him to establish nature as the test of artistic goodness, "for all the workes of nature, in a maner be examples for arte to folow" (p. 116).

This aim for natural *perfiteness* motivates Ascham's hostility to historical change and the variety of conventions that it generates. The chief obstacle to *perfiteness* is "our rude and beggarly ryming, brought first into Italie by *Gothes* and *Hunnes*, whar all good verses and all good learning to, were destroyed by them: and after caryed into France and Germanie: and at last receyved into England" (p. 145). The instrument of this contagion is convention; Chaucer, Norton, Surrey, Wyatt, and Phaer would have been "more like unto the Grecians than unto the Gothians, in handling of their verse," if they "had bene directed to follow the best examples, and not have bene caryed by tyme and custome" (p. 145). Similarly, the contagion of Chaucerian and Petrarchan conventions is followed "as one here in England did folow Syr *Tho. More:* who, being most unlike unto him in writ and learnyng, nevertheless in wearing his gowne awrye upon the one shoulder, as Syr *Tho. More* was wont to do, would nedes be counted lyke unto him" (pp. 146–147). Those who follow the vernacular conventions "do so for lacke of knowledge what is best" (p. 147). Instead of following "the fair and rightest way" embodied in the transcendent norms of nature and the ancients, they "wander still in [their] foul wrong" (p. 149). The loaded moral imagery of Ascham's contrast suggests the "duble name" that the Reformation had brought to convention, and Wilson makes the analogy explicit when he laments the waywardness of rhetorical fashion:

> That is right by custome, which long tyme hath confirmed, being partly grounded upon nature, & partly upon reason

---

43. Wilson, *The Rule of Reason*, sig. J7v.
44. Wilson, *The Rule of Reason*, sig. G6.

> . . . we turning natures light, into blind custome, without
> God's will, have used at length to believe, that he was really
> here with us in earth, and worshipped him not in spirite,
> but in Copes, in Candlesticks, in Belles, in Tapers, and in
> Censers, in Crosses, in Banners, in shaven Crownes, and
> long Gownes, and many good morowes else . . . The which
> childish toyes, time hath so long confirmed, that the trueth
> is scant able to trie them out, our hearts be so hard, and
> our wits so far to seeke.[45]

Like the transcendent norms of religions, the nature and abiding
norms of poetic fitness are obscured by the blind intransigence of
habits and customary practices sanctioned only by time or social
fashion: "for ignorance men can not like, and for idleness, men will
not labor, to come to any *perfiteness* at all."[46]

By way of contrast with the type of discourse generated by arguments drawn from "the substaunce or nature of the thing," those arguments drawn from the "outward places . . . not in the substance, or
nature of the thynge" are capable of generating a considerably different type of discourse. Instead of justifying its propositions with terms
derived from the inherent nature, genus, species, properties, parts, and
so on, of its subject, this type of discourse supports its propositions
with arguments that in various ways impinge upon the subject. Of the
nearest affinity to the subject are its efficient and final causes, which
are related to it productively. In its final cause the subject reaches out
beyond itself to a variety of ends. Of equal importance is the agency,
for as Lever remarks, "workmen are . . . many sundrye wayes devided." Closely related to agency and end are effect and means, for as
is the efficient cause, so will the effect and means be long, short, good,
bad.[47]

Furthermore, the arguments drawn from "place" and "time" establish a whole sequential and temporal context for the proposition. Thus
Lever explains that time is not merely divided into past, present, and
future; "it may also be many other wayes devided, by reason of the
manifold varietie of matters that chaunce in it. As the time of warre, ye
time of peace, the time of dearth, the tyme of plenty, the tyme of syck-
nesse, the time of health." The "thynges annexed" constitute those circumstances that, unlike adjacents ("woordes ajoigned") are not necessarily, but accidentally, related to a subject and are therefore capable of

45. Wilson, *The Arte of Rhetorique*, pp. 33–34.
46. Ascham, *The Scolemaster*, p. 147.
47. Lever, *The Art of Reason, rightly termed, Witcraft*, pp. 178, 180–182.

change. "Things chauncyng" further complicate the matrix, for they bring into consideration antecedents, concurrences, and consequents: "divers things using to chance at once, are witnesses and assurances one of another."[48] Finally, in addition to the different sources of comparison and contrast, and not the least important to Renaissance poetic theory, are the arguments drawn from human testimony. While Lever's list makes mention of "Law" and "custome,"[49] Wilson's more expansive list includes such arguments as "have been used in this common life. As . . . the judgements of learned men, the common opinion of the multitude, olde custome, auncient fashions, or any such like."[50]

Not only the testimony of "common opinion," "olde custome," and "auncient fashion," but such arguments as means, ends, time, place, circumstance, comparison, and contingency, all drawn from places furnishing arguments "not in the substaunce, or nature of the thynge," are capable of generating and supporting propositions about poetic norms vastly different from those derived through the "internal places." In the broadest terms, such external places are likely to suggest that fitness is not absolute and inherent in the rational nature of poetry itself, but flexible and conventional, conditioned by the diversity and complexity of circumstance.

The difference between these types of conclusion was recognized by the Renaissance logicians themselves, who distinguished between the "necessity" of propositions derived from the internal places and the "contingency" of propositions derived from the external places. Propositions derived from the internal places, or "nature of the thing," tended to be "absolute" in character. Any statement derived from the internal places, Lever observes, "is necessarily required in the essential being of an other, and it is devided into seven partes. The Saywhat (definition), the general terme (genus), the speciall term (species), the proper terme (property), the whole, the parte, and the offspryng (subject and adjuncts)." By contrast, statements derived from the external places or terms in some way related to the subject tended to be "relative" in character. Lever remarks on the presumed "weakness" or relativism of such arguments when he observes of comparison, for example, that "learned men in arguing, make small accompt of any similitude. For by a similitude you maye as soone prove a wrong matter as a right."[51]

48. Lever, *The Art of Reason, rightly termed, Witcraft*, pp. 42, 190.

49. Lever, *The Art of Reason, rightly termed, Witcraft*, p. 197.

50. Wilson, *The Rule of Reason*, sig. O4.

51. Lever, *The Art of Reason, rightly termed, Witcraft*, pp. 145, 196; cf. Wilson, *The Rule of Reason*, sig. L2; and see Sister Miriam Joseph, p. 337.

Thus although the literary theorists of the early sixteenth century lacked a distinctly Aristotelian concept of *mimesis,* they possessed an intellectual bias and logical instruments that led them to conclude that the human habit of *ars* or *techne* was based upon the rational structure and function of nature. They were first of all able rationally to justify the classifications and partitions inherited from the grammatical and rhetorical traditions by defining and distinguishing in pseudo-Aristotelian fashion the constituent species, elements, and qualities of poetry on the basis of internal principles analogous to natural structures. Moreover, they were able to distinguish between the logical consequences of such procedures and those that referred the art merely to conventional and conditional principles. When Vicenzo Maggi, for example, lectured on the *Poetics* and the *Ars Poetica* at Ferrara in 1550, he distinguished sharply between the Aristotelian and Horatian approaches to the art. Aristotle, he observes, treats the nature of poetry itself (*de re in se*), Horace very little so (*quasi nihil de re*).[52] Horace is said to deal with such extrinsic matters as the poet and his audience, and merely passes on "the laws [*legibus*] which the poet must observe." Such "laws" might well be placed among what Wilson calls the extrinsic sources of testimony, including such things as "common opinion," "olde custome," and "auncient fashion." Aristotle, on the other hand, says Maggi, clearly "speaks of poetics so that we may know its parts both quantitative and qualitative." Indeed, the first sentence of the *Poetics,* as Maggi outlines it, demonstrates Aristotle's approach to the *res in se;* it comprehends, he says,

A.   Genera et partes
1. Genera
2. Partes
   a. De poesi in se
   b. De generibus
   c. De fabula
   d. De partibus qualibus et quantis
   e. De omnis quae pertinent ad janc materiam
B.   Modum quae uult servare in tractandis propositis

Thus by underlining alternative approaches to the arts of speech, the framework of Renaissance logic helped to revive an ancient issue, and gave rise to comparative and historical modes of discourse at odds with the logical bias toward natural fitness. As humanist writers looked back upon their classical heritage, they found a pressing need for both

52. Weinberg, I, 378.

alternatives. On the one hand, efforts to restore ancient eloquence to the present perforce assumed timeless and abiding standards of fitness; on the other hand, the altered character of contemporary social and linguistic habits imposed a need for flexible adaptability. Thus where the "internal" places provided generic helps for the recovery of ancient norms, the "external" places provided argumentative means for adapting these norms to new social and historical contingencies. Arguments for adaptation tended to cohere around three different clusters in the "external" places: the categories of time, place, circumstance, and comparison, all of which underlined differences in social settings; the category of agency, which subjected the habit of art to the inarticulate influence of social settings; and the categories of end, effect, and means, which asserted a vital and dynamic connection between the arts of speech and the changing expectations, values, and assumptions of men in time.

To begin with, the logical categories of time, place, circumstance, and comparison provided argumentative support for innovation based on differing social and linguistic conventions. Ascham, for example, used these categories in order to "excuse *Terence,* because in his tyme, and a good while after, Poetrie was never perfited in Latin" (p. 105). The faulty diction and meter of Plautus and Terence is not to "their reproach, but the fault of the tyme, wherein they wrote" (p. 144). Against the natural integrity and rational transcendence of art Ascham therefore balances the transience and variety of related circumstances that impinge upon it; history and the heritage of linguistic convention constitute a matrix into which the art of poetry is set, "for no perfection is durable" (p. 142). Ascham never relinquishes the norm of natural perfection, and he attributes variations in milieu to a natural pattern of rise and fall, after the manner of the preacher of Ecclesiastes. Other theorists, however, often interpreted the varied patterns marked by time and place as formal expressions of changing conventions, and thus conceded the relativity of poetic norms in a manner that sanctioned departures from classical precedents. Thus Du Bellay appealed to differences in time, place, and circumstances in order to argue that the French recovery of eloquence must differ from its Roman model because of differences in "l'origine des deux nations, leurs faictz, leurs loix, meurs & manières de vivre."[53]

As with Renaissance moral philosophy, however, it was perhaps through consideration of the "efficient cause" or agent himself that the power of convention was most obviously brought to bear upon the

---

53. Du Bellay, *La déffense et illustration de la langue françoyse,* ed. Henri Chamard (Paris: Marcel Didier, 1948), p. 184.

poetic art. While for the early Renaissance the source and test of poetic fitness was the principle of nature, the mode of existence and operation of this principle, as in moral philosophy, was understood to be habitual. Because the standard of natural fitness was presumed to have been achieved preeminently by the ancients, arguments were frequently made for a wholesale transfer of this achievement through the purely rational power of precepts.[54] In contrast to this approach, however, and more in line with the practical program of humanist ethics, most of the early theorists followed the rhetorical tradition by insisting upon the importance of practice in the formation of habit. Because of the habitual character of human agency "all our actions that proceed from nature are sooner & better learned by use & exercise, then by Art, or Precepte . . . we begin not by Art, but by Nature; and proceed by use, custome, authoritye, and exercise."[55] As in humanist moral philosophy, this shift of focus from the art mediated to the process of mediation called attention to the limits placed upon habit by the temporal and intersubjective setting in which it is formed, "for as ye use to heare, so ye learne to spake: if ye heare no other, ye speake not your selfe: and whom ye onelie heare, of them ye onelie learne."[56] The habitual status of art in human agents thus suggested that its transmission was not wholly rational, but social as well, and engendered what Joseph Webbe called "the controversy between art and use." Balancing a rational standard of fitness against its habitual mode of existence in the individual, the ideas of habit and agency implied a similar tension on a more collective and cultural level, "making that which was usurped by the tenure of Art, rule, and precept, to be more surely holden under use, custome, and authoritie."[57]

As a result, the attempt to effect a wholesale transfer from antiquity of presumably natural and perfect standards met with opposition from the process of mediation itself.[58] Most notably, this opposition arose at the level of diction, where the European vernacular seemed at times to require redefinition of such standards themselves. Thus, following the precedent of Dante's *De Vulgari Eloquentia*, Du Bellay observes that the proper virtue of style resides in "motz propres, utisez & non

54. See, e.g., Robert Whittinton, *Vulgaria*, ed. Beatrice White (London: Early English Texts Society, 1932), pp. 35–38.

55. Joseph Webbe, *An appeale to truth, in the controversy between art and use* (London, 1622), p. 12.

56. Ascham, *The Scolemaster*, p. 116.

57. Webbe, *An appeale to truth*, p. 5.

58. See Richard Foster Jones, *The Triumph of the English Language* (Stanford: Stanford University Press, 1953), p. 181; and Elizabeth J. Sweeting, *Early Tudor Criticism, Linguistic and Literary* (Oxford: Basil Blackwell, 1940), p. 48.

aliènes du commun usaige de parler . . . il est impossible de la rendre avecques la mesme grace dont l'autheur en a usé: d'autant que chacune Langue a je ne sçay quoy propre seulement à elle."[59] It is with special regard for the transactional basis of the problem that Thomas Hoby similarly declares that as "the practising emonge sundrye Nations, hath always bene of force to transport from one to an other (in a maner) as merchaundise, so also new woordes, whiche afterwards remaine or decaye, according as they are admitted by custom or refused."[60]

The cultural diversities embedded in the logical arguments of "place," "time," and "agency" introduced the problem of convention to theoretical discourse about art, but this introduction was reinforced by the dictinctive function of the verbal arts themselves, namely, mediation. Accordingly, the places of "ende" and "effecte" exerted an additional pull away from absolute or natural norms toward more purely conditional or conventional ones. While the perceived affinities of the arts of discourse could lead them toward the integrity of natural structure at the pole of logic, the arts could equally be drawn toward the variety of possible structures generated by rhetorical function. The rhetorical ends of teaching, persuading, and delighting posited the power of speech in its intended effect upon an audience. Accordingly, Wilson explains that "not onely is it necessarie to know what manner of cause we have taken in hande when we first enter upon any matter, but also it is wisedome to consider the tyme, the place, the man for whom we speake."[61] This reference back to the "places" of time, place, and circumstance extends the range of their reference. Because speech involves "a certaine bestowing of things, and an apt declaring what is meete for every part, as time and place doe best require,"[62] circumstance dictates artistic choices. The key to eloquence resides, as Du Bellay puts it, "plus en la discretion & bon jugement de l'orateur qu'en certaines reigles & préceptes: veu que les événementz du tens, le circonstance des lieux, la condition des personnes & la divérsité des occasions sont innumérables."[63]

Consequently, the rhetorical, transactional character of poetic art served as counterbalance to the self-contained and rationally structured qualities demanded by poetic art's connection with logic. Thus Wilson, for example, prescribes that the writer must "use such wordes as seeme

59. Du Bellay, *Déffense et illustration*, pp. 35–36.
60. Baldassare Castiglione, *The Boke of the Courtier*, trans. Sir Thomas Hoby (1561), ed. W. H. D. Rouse (1928; rpt., New York: Everyman's Library, 1956), p. 12.
61. Wilson, *The Arte of Rhetorique*, p. 8.
62. Wilson, *The Arte of Rhetorique*, p. 157.
63. Du Bellay, *Déffense et illustration*, p. 33.

for that kinde of writing most convenient," but such "convenience" is dictated in part by what is "usuall and accustomable." "The folie is espied," he says, "when either we will use such wordes as fewe men doe use, or use them out of place, when an other might serve much better."[64] On the one hand, the logical bias of early Renaissance poetics requires a "lovely conformitie . . . betweene the sence and the sensible." On the other hand, while the parallels between the figures and the places of logic facilitate such fitness, "our maker must take heed," Puttenham warns, "that he be not to bold . . . for unless usual speach and custome allow it, it is a fault and no figure."[65]

As was the case in humanist moral philosophy, and as the structure of the logical places demonstrates, the very framework of the Renaissance arts of discourse entertained at once the dual criteria of nature and convention as the tests of fitness. These two criteria most frequently met where the special bias of logic met the special bias of rhetoric and grammar: virtually constituted in its early stages both by the "diligent markynge of nature" inherited from logic and by the rhetorical demands "more surely holden under use, custome, and authoritie," Renaissance poetics became the ground where these criteria most often cooperated or clashed. Throughout the Middle Ages *usus* had held its place in germinal form as a grammatical principle. As such, it emphasized the changeful and intersubjective character of the verbal medium: "in forme of speche is chaunge . . . In sondry landes sondry ben usages."[66] With the recovery of rhetorical tradition, and through renewed emphasis on the transactional function of the verbal arts, the norm of usage gained increasing currency in poetic theory. Based on the need for "handsomenes and fashion more answerable to these times, wherein fashions are so often altered,"[67] this norm was frequently contrasted with the idea of inherent rational fitness. It was increasingly argued that "Art . . . is not capable of use, because use is various or changeable." Against the fixity of rational standards was opposed the thought that "whatever confused Custome hath received, must and will passe without contradiction," so that "Art and Use are almost opposite."[68] In the early rhetorical and logical treatises, these two principles existed side by side, no more in conflict than the "places" of logical

64. Wilson, *The Arte of Rhetorique*, pp. 169, 166, 165.
65. Puttenham, p. 162.
66. Chaucer, *Troilus and Chryseyde*, bk. 2, ll. 22–28.
67. William Webbe, in praise of Robert Wilmot's *Tancred and Gismund . . . Newly revived and published according to the decorum of these daies*, quoted in Jones, p. 174.
68. Webbe, *An appeale to truth*, pp. 22, 43–44.

arguments themselves. But in framing the possibilities and varieties of discourse, these treatises granted to convention a foothold that it would not easily relinquish.

2. "Conveniency to Nature" and the "Secretes of Privitie": Nature and Convention in Defense of Poetry

As part of a complex technical aggregate, poetic theory in the earlier sixteenth century was subject to the various normative demands of the other arts of speech. By the latter half of the century, however, poetics was recognized as a distinctive verbal art, and treated as such in the polemical defense of poetry in England. Yet even this essentially belletristic defense remained firmly within the framework of the *artes* tradition, not only through continued assertion of nature as the norm of fitness, but also through the technical application of this norm to characteristically poetic aims and procedures. Sir Philip Sidney's *Apologie for Poetrie* (1595) is thus not only a judicial oration in defense of poetry,[1] but also an *ars poetica* that systematically expounds its nature, function, kinds, and parts in accordance with the tradition of *ars* or *techne*. Despite his objections that "we much cumber ourselves" with "artificial rules" and "imitative patterns," Sidney follows the main line of normative tradition when he goes on to maintain that "as the fertilest ground must be manured, so must the highest-flying wit have a Daedalus to guide him."[2] His aristocratically aloof disclaimers do not conceal the fact that part of his intention is to prescribe "the right use both of matter and manner" (p. 140).

In keeping with this interest, Sidney not only defends poetry in the name of *ars,* but embodies an *ars* in his defense. He is at pains throughout to distinguish between "poetry" on the one hand and "poesy"— what Jonson was to call the poet's "skill or crafte of making"[3]—on the other. "Poetry" gives rise to "sweet delights" (p. 98). It is, like the completed history of Herodotus, the product of skilled artifice (p. 97); and as an artifact it is subject to the contempt of those "professing learning" (p. 96). By way of contrast, however, "Poesy . . . is an *art* of imitation, for so Aristotle termeth it in his word *mimesis*, that is to say, a representing, counterfeiting, or figuring forth—to speak metaphori-

1. See Kenneth Orne Myrick, *Sir Philip Sidney as a Literary Craftsman* (Cambridge: Harvard University Press, 1935), ch. 2. Though Virginia R. Hyman does not specifically regard the *Apologie* as an *ars,* she does point to the rational mode of exposition that underlies it; see "Sidney's Defense," *SEL,* 10 (1970), 50.

2. Sir Philip Sidney, *An Apologie for Poetrie,* ed. Geoffrey Shepherd (1965; rpt., New York: Barnes and Noble, 1973), p. 132. Hereafter cited as *Apologie.*

3. Ben Jonson, *Discoveries,* in *Works,* VIII, 636; see Shepherd's note, p. 152.

cally, a speaking picture—with this end, to teach and delight" (p. 101).[4]

Sidney's comparison of this art with the powers and functions of other arts not only demonstrates the technical orientation of the *Apologie,* but also indicates his bias toward the specifically Platonic-Aristotelian definition of art:

> There is no art delivered to mankind that hath not the works of Nature for his principal object, without which they could not consist, and on which they depend, as they become actors and players, as it were, of what nature will have set forth. So doth the astronomer look upon the stars, and, by that he seeth, setteth down what order Nature hath taken therein. So do the geometrician and the arithmetician in their diverse sorts of quantities. So doth the musician in times tell you which by nature agree, which not. The natural philosopher thereon hath his name, and the moral philosopher standeth upon the natural virtues, vices, and passions of man; and "follow Nature" (saith he) "therein thou shalt not err." The lawyer saith what men have determined; the historian what men have done. The grammarian speaketh only of the rules of speech; and the rhetorician and logician, considering what nature will soonest prove and persuade, thereon give artificial rules, which still are compassed within the circle of a question according to the proposed matter. (p. 100)

Since the arts subject themselves like actors or players to the script of Nature, the measure of goodness in the arts is their articulation of principles and precepts that conform to natural structure and process. The arts are to be measured not only by their fruits, but against each other, insofar as they all seek in various ways to fulfill the norms of nature.

In comparison with the other arts, the art of poetry, as Sidney describes it, seems at first sight to violate this criterion, for the poet,

> disdaining to be tied to any such subjection, lifted up with the vigor of his own invention, doth grow in effect into another nature, in making things either better than Nature

---

4. "Art" in my italics. While the metaphor of "speaking picture" seems to denote a property of "poetry" rather than "poesy," Sidney's "represent-ing, counterfeit-ing, or figur-ing forth," merits comparison with Else's interpretation of Aristotle on *techne,* cited in Chapter I, section 2.

bringeth forth, or quite anew, formes such as never were in Nature, as the Heroes, Demigods, Cyclops, Chimeras, Furies, and such like: so as he goeth hand in hand with Nature, not enclosed within the narrow warrant of her gifts, but freely ranging only within the zodiac of his own wit.   (p. 100)

The free-ranging "vigor" of poetic "invention," the "golden world" that poetry delivers, and the affinity of the poetic maker to the Divine Maker, all demonstrate that the distinctive quality of the poetic art "standeth in the *Idea* or fore-conceit of the work, and not in the work itself" (p. 101).

In establishing the *"Idea* or fore-conceit" as the center of poetic art, Sidney immediately removes it from the flux of phenomenal nature; "Poesy," as he later says, "should be *eikastike*" rather than *phantastike* (p. 125).[5] In using this Neo-platonic framework, however, Sidney does not portray poetic art as purely visionary in character or remove it from technical subordination to principle and rule. Rather, he establishes a "scientific substructure"[6] as the basis of the art, thus arguing not so much for poetry's depiction of the ideal as for the transcendent status of the technical norms through which this depiction is achieved. Poesy (and not simply poetry) is *eikastic* in virtue of its status as an *ars*, whose norms derive from "knowledge of universal patterns."[7] The ideal is not so much related mimetically to the art as an object of imitation as it is related productively to the art as its normative basis; as

5. Cf. *Sophist*, 235B–236C, and *Republic*, 506B–518D. Sidney's Platonism is most strongly emphasized by Irene Samuel, who argues for Sidney's direct and extensive knowledge of Plato ("The Influence of Plato on Sir Philip Sidney's *Defense of Poetry*," *MLQ*, 1 [1940], 383–391), and by A. C. Hamilton, who argues that Sidney's Platonism is independent and eclectic ("Sidney's Idea of the 'Right Poet,'" *CL*, 9 [1957], 51–59). The most convincing case is put by John P. McIntyre, who emphasizes the Neo-Platonism of the Florentine Academy as Sidney's immediate source, demonstrating the coalescence of Platonic distinctions between the ideal and real with Christianity's conceptions of pre- and postlapsarian states in Sidney's terms "erected wit" and "infected will." However, McIntyre underestimates the equal importance of Aristotelian influence, and maintains that Sidney's "fore-conceit" denotes the Platonic ideal as the *object* of imitation to the exclusion of Aristotle's "probable action"; "Sidney's 'Golden World,'" *CL*, 14 (1962), 356–365. For a view of the *objects* of imitation similar to McIntyre's, see Cornell M. Dowlin, "Sidney's Two Definitions of Poetry," *MLQ*, 3 (1942), 573–581.

6. The phrase is Forrest G. Robinson's, *The Shape of Things Known: Sidney's Apology in Its Philosophical Tradition* (Cambridge: Harvard University Press, 1972), p. 136.

7. Samuel, p. 386.

Pico had put it, "each cause which operates by art or intelligence must first of all contain the form of that which it wishes to produce."[8] Sidney's analogy between the poetic maker and the Divine Maker is meant to convey the priority and transcendent status of the artistic knowledge governing production; as he phrased it in his translation of Du Plessis Mornay's Platonic theology, "the Craftsman maketh his worke by the pattern which he had erst conceyved in his mynde, which patterne is his inwarde work: so God made the world and all that is therein."[9] Sidney's insistence on the transcendence of such "patterne" is a function of his defense of poetry as the product of *ars,* his "firm conviction that poetry is a science and that it should be accepted as such."[10]

In turning from his Platonic defense of the normative status of the art "to a more ordinary opening of him" (p. 101), Sidney undertakes a technical exposition of the art "by his works, and then by his parts" (p. 103). This transition from epistemological status to mode of operation marks a shift in emphasis from Platonic to Aristotelian concepts of art as well.[11] While the epistemological status of the art, "the skill of the artificer [cf. Du Plessis' "inward skill or arte" and Jonson's "skill or crafte of making"] standeth in that *Idea* or fore-conceit of the work," its mode of operation is to "imitate [or] borrow nothing of what is, hath been, or shall be; but range, only reined with learned discretion, into the divine consideration of what may be and should be" (p. 102). In virtue of this "consideration," the poetic art lays greatest claim to fulfilling "the highest end of the mistress-knowledge, by the Greeks called

8. Quoted in Shepherd's notes, p. 158.

9. *A Worke concerning the trewenesse of the Christian Religion,* in *The Prose Works of Sir Philip Sidney,* ed. Albert Feuillerat (1912; rpt., Cambridge University Press, 1962), III, 268. Shepherd cites the passage in his notes, p. 158. See also Jay L. Halio, "The Metaphor of Conception and Elizabethan Theories of the Imagination," *Neophilologus,* 50 (1966), 454–461.

10. Robinson, p. 136.

11. A sharper distinction between what Sidney says about the normative status of the art and what he says about its mode of operation might help to sort out the confusions over Platonic and Aristotelian elements in the essay (see note 5, above). This is best achieved by recognizing the *Apologie*'s frankly normative bias, and by comparing it with other works in the handbook tradition, to which in many respects it belongs. It is also noteworthy that Sidney quite consistently predicates those Platonic qualities pertaining to the epistemological status of the art intransitively ("*standeth* in that *Idea* or fore-conceit") and predicates those Aristotelian qualities pertaining to its mode of operation transitively ("*informs* a conjectured likelihood"). This is clearly an Aristotelian rather than a Platonic notion, for as the object of imitation (rather than the status of technical norms), the ideal purely and simply *is.*

architechtonike, which stands (as I think) in the knowledge of a man's self, in the ethic and politic consideration, with the end of well-doing, and not of well-knowing only" (p. 104).

In keeping with this claim, therefore, poetic art aims to depict not the Platonic ideal, but "all virtues, vices, and passions so in their own natural seats laid to the view, that we seem not to hear of them, but clearly to see through them" (p. 108). The "ethic and politic consideration" dictates that while the poetic art is impervious to nature's flux, it is nevertheless "reined with a learned discretion" and in its mode of operation "goeth hand in hand with Nature." It is, in very nearly the full Aristotelian sense, a *mimesis praxeos.* The poet by "an example only informes a conjectured likelihood," and "frame[s] his example to that which is most reasonable, be it in warlike, politic, or private matters" (p. 110).

For the basis of this "likelihood," the poet looks not "to the particular truth of things," but "to the general reasons of things" (p. 107). Thus it is, says Sidney in comparing poetry and history, that

> Aristotle himself, in his discourse of poesy, plainly deter-mineth this question, saying that Poetry is *philosophoteron* and *spoudaioteron,* that is to say more philosophical and more studiously serious than history. His reason is, because poesy dealeth with *Katholou,* that is to say, with the universal consideration, and the history with *Kathekaston,* the particular: "now," saith he, "the universal weighs what is fit to be said or done, either in likelihood or necessity (which the poesy considereth in his imposed names), and the particular only marks whether Alcibiades did, or suffered, this or that."   (p.109)

Through its ability to articulate such universal principles, poetic art shares the transcendent status of *episteme;* but in its mode of operation it is analogous to natural process, bodying forth its production in conformity with principle, creating "in effect another nature." Moreover, the principles that govern this production are the same rational principles of probability and necessity that govern nature. Although the art of poetry does not copy individual works of nature, it operates in conformity with natural principle. In its appeal to "second and abstract notions," the poet's art most nearly resembles that of the metaphysician, who, though "he be counted supernatural, yet doth he indeed build upon the depth of Nature" (p. 100). It is due to this conformity with natural principle that the philosophers were the first to take from poetic art "the right discerning true points of knowledge" (p. 128).

Having established the transcendent status of the art as well as its analogies with natural structure and process, Sidney turns immediately at the *partitio* to an examination of the art "by his workes." Having there substantiated the status of the art by logical definition and examined its mode of operation, he next undertakes "more narrowly" to examine the art "in his parts, kinds, or species (as you list to term them)" (p. 116). Although some of these are "turned according to the matter they deal with, some by the sorts of verse they liked best to write in" (p. 103), the principal basis of Sidney's classification is *res*, the objects of imitation.

Accordingly, while Sidney's concept of genre takes some note of traditional verse forms, his bias toward nature as the norm of poetic art leads him, after the fashion of Aristotle's Italian commentators, to treat the literary kinds with reference to an implicitly hierarchical scheme supposedly derived from the scale of nature itself. Pastoral ranks among the "lowest" of the kinds, its "poor pipe" singing the "misery" of "them that lie lowest" (p. 116). Comedy, taking as its object "the common errors of our life," depicts "the most ridiculous and scornful sort that may be" (p. 117). Tragedy, by contrast, is "high and excellent"; and Heroic "is not only a kind, but the best and most accomplished kind of Poetry," for its "lofty image of such worthies most inflameth the mind with desire to be worthy."

Moreover, the same artistic principle that engenders these distinctions in kind assures that each possesses an internal integrity. The dramatist, for example, should observe the unities of time and place, refusing to violate the "common reason" with a structure "inartificially imagined" (p. 134). Furthermore, the natural integrity of the kinds dictates against such "gross absurdities" as "mongrel tragi-comed[ies]," which are "neither right tragedies, nor right comedies, mingling kings and clowns . . . with neither decency nor discretion" (p. 135). Even where Sidney seems to allow for the possibility of "conjunction" among the kinds, his use of natural metaphor suggests the cross-breeding of natural species: "some poesies have *coupled together* two or three *kinds,* as tragical and comical, whereupon is *risen* the tragi-comical" (p. 116). This offspring, as he later says, is "mongrel."

Such natural integrity obtains even at the level of diction, for the poet must arrange "each syllable of each word by just proportion according to the dignity of the subject" (p. 103). There are, Sidney claims, "two principal parts" of poetry—"matter to be expressed by words and words to express the matter" (p. 133). The relationship between the two is conceived in terms of natural fitness, for *"oratio* next to *ratio,* speech next to reason," is "the greatest gift bestowed upon mortality" (p. 122). The proper relationship obtains, Sidney implies,

when style is logically governed by the nature of *res*, the things themselves. This is, as Gabriel Harvey remarked, "a pithie rule in Sir
Philips *Apologie for Poetrie*. The invention must guide & rule the
Elocution: *non* contra."[12] The poet's alternative to the habitual copy
and commonplace approach of the rhetorical handbooks is, as Sidney
elsewhere says,

> pronouncing grace, wherewith his mind
> Prints his owne lively forme in rudest braine.[13]

This normative bias is the source of Sidney's hostility to what he sees
as merely conventional styles and devices. "Caught up" with "certain
swelling phrases," the followers of Petrarchan conventions "coldly . . .
apply fiery speeches, as men that had rather read lovers' writings . . .
then that in truth they feel those passions" (pp. 137–138). The "courte-
san-like painted affection" of inkhornism, the excesses of alliteration,
and the "absurd surfeit" of Euphuism are all part of the contagion
fostered by unreasoning but "diligent imitators of Tully and Demos-
thenes," who "keep Nizolian paper-books of their figures and phrases"
(pp. 138–139). In bowing to the "opinion of a seeming fineness," they
violate "the end of speech," which is "the uttering sweetly and properly
the conceits of the mind" (pp. 139–140). Insisting that such propriety
derives naturally from "a good invention" (p. 124). Sidney shares with
Gascoigne a bias against unmotivated conventions; only by attempting
"some depth of devise in the Invention," as Gascoigne says, can the
poet produce something more than "a tale of a tubbe," and "avoyde the
uncomely *customes* of common writers."[14]

As one means of avoiding such contagion, Sidney proposes that the
inarticulate copy and commonplace technique of imitation should be
subordinated to a methodical instruction in artistic principles. "Exercise we do, but that very fore-backwardly"; the problem, he maintains,
is that "where we should exercise to know, we exercise as having
known" (p. 133). Thus Sidney would apply to imitation the Ramist
"double analysis" that articulates both rhetorical and dialectical structure, and follows "that fundamental principle . . . of tracing causes

12. Gabriel Harvey, *Marginalia*, in G. Gregory Smith, I, 360; see Shepherd's note,
p. 219, and Robinson, pp. 110–111.

13. Sidney, *Astrophel and Stella*, in *Silver Poets of the Sixteenth Century*, ed.
Gerald Bullett (New York: Everyman's Library, 1947), sonnet 58.

14. George Gascoigne, *Certayne Notes of Instruction*, in G. Gregory Smith, I, 47–
48; my italics.

and not merely effects."[15] This would illuminate even routine and habit with the light of reason, securing it to the "imaginative ground-plot of a profitable invention" (p. 124), and thus rectifying the mere "opinion of a seeming fineness." This bias toward rational integrity, as throughout the *Apologie,* insures that the art of poetry "hath the most conveniency to Nature of all other" (p. 114).

"Conveniency to Nature" thus serves as the explicit philosophical basis of Sidney's *Apologie.* In addition, however, this "conveniency" is quite consciously colored by a social bias, more heavily emphasized in other sixteenth-century defenses of poetry, which implies that while the norms and procedures of the art are dictated by universal nature, their preservation and transmission are entrusted to a custody that is social, customary, and traditional. Sidney's aristocratic tone not only colors the scale of nature from which he draws the hierarchy of genres; it impinges as well upon his ideal of rational community by raising the suggestion that such order is social as well as intellectual. This suggestion in itself presents no threat to the norm of nature, for the ideal of a rational society stems from opposition to unmotivated conventions. But when Sidney distinguishes between the ideal nature of the art and its present practice, he complains that "base men with servile wits undertake it . . . as if all the Muses were got with child to bring forth bastard poets" (p. 132). Implicit in this complaint is a distinction between mere poetasters catering to public desire and the true "knights of the . . . order" (p. 132), who constitute the community of right poets. Like most sixteenth-century defenders of poetry, Sidney thus imposes upon the standard of nature a social distinction between elite and public,[16] and wields it almost without exception against the opposition at large.

This social bias was seldom, if ever, divorced from its intellectual foundation, but it called attention to the necessarily conventional aspects of art, most notably in the social posture of coterie that was a corollary of the defense of poetry and a source of the coy and esoteric reserve of the group surrounding Sidney and including Spenser and

15. Gabriel Harvey, *Ciceronianus,* ed. Harold S. Wilson, trans. Clarence A. Forbes, University of Nebraska Studies in the Humanities (Lincoln: University of Nebraska Press, 1945), p. 73.

16. See also John Rainolds, *Oratio in Laudem Artis Poeticae,* ed. William Ringler, trans. Walter Allen, Jr., Princeton Studies in English (Princeton: Princeton University Press, 1940), p. 39. For the social factors giving rise to this coincidence, see Vernon Hall, *Renaissance Literary Criticism: A Study of Its Social Content* (New York: Columbia University Press, 1945), pp. 53–56, 119–127, 197–202; and Guy A. Thompson, *Elizabethan Criticism of Poetry* (1914; rpt., Folcroft, Pa.: Folcroft Press, 1969), pp. 48–60.

Harvey. In his gloss on Spenser's *Shepheards Calender* (1579), for example, "E.K." declares that "I was made privie to his counsell and secret meaning in them, as also in sundry other works of his . . . whose commendations to set out were verye vaine, the thinges though worthy of many yet being knowen to few."[17] Harvey similarly declares that in Sidney's *Arcadia* "there want not some suttle Stratagems of importance and some politique Secretes of privitie."[18] The coincidence of an intellectual contrast between knowledge and ignorance with a social contrast between privilege and exclusion suggests in these and other cases that while artistic norms are natural, access to them stems from membership in an elite.

The power of this suggestion to modify the concept of nature is most apparent when reason gives way to retrospection in the mythographical recitations that inevitably shore up the defenses of poetry. Thomas Lodge, for example, in *A Defense of Poetry, Music, and Stage Plays,* offers the commonplace that "poetes were the first raysors of cities, prescribers of good lawes, mayntayners of religion . . . inventors of laws, and lastly the very fot-paths to knowledge and understanding."[19] As the group that constitutes the origin and center of society, the poets preside as priests over the rites and practices that constitute tradition. Accordingly, because the powers of poetry are coeval with its origins, the proper understanding of poetry is a retrospective knowledge of tradition: "men that have knowledge what tragedies and comedies be wil commend them, but it is sufferable in the folish to reprove that they know not, becaus ther mouthes will hardly be stopped . . . the reder shal perceive the antiquity of play-making, the inventors of comedies, and therewithall the use and commodity of them" (pp. 79–80). The knowledge lacking in the opponents of drama does not so much pertain to the "nature" of drama as to its origin and "use," its place within a tradition of *praxis*. Reason alone, without a knowledge of tradition, is inadequate, for while reason might make all men wish that "all abuse of playing were abolished . . . the antiquity causeth

---

17. E.K., "Epistle Dedicatory to the Shepheards Calender," in *The Shepheards Calender and Other Poems,* ed. Philip Henderson (New York: Everyman's Library, 1932), p. 16.

18. Gabriel Harvey, *Foure Letters and certaine Sonnets: Especially touching Robert Greene, and other parties, by him abused . . . ,* in G. Gregory Smith, II, 238. For the views of two writers not part of this coterie but very much aware of its social dimensions, see the remarks of William Webbe and Thomas Nashe, in G. Gregory Smith, I, 245; II, 224.

19. Thomas Lodge, *A Defense of Poetry, Music, and Stage Plays,* in G. Gregory Smith, I, 75. Subsequent references to this work in the text are given by page number only.

me to allow it" (p. 84). Holy in the eyes of those who are privileged to stand within the tradition, "those instruments which you mislike in playes grow of auncient custome" (p. 84). Excluded from the priesthood, barbarians must "begg at knowledge gate awhile" (p. 71).

The traditionalist bias of this poet-priest ideal was strongest in two of the more esoteric concerns of the defenders: the allegorical vindication of poetry and the problem of poetic diction, related to allegory through a recondite association of quantitative verse with musical and Orphic powers. Both of these concerns subjected the ideal of nature to the power of convention by emphasizing the social rather than rational character of allegorical and prosodic norms. Part of Lodge's strategy in excluding the attackers from the priesthood of artistic tradition, for example, is his insistence that they lack a lexicon for the properly allegorical reading of poetry:

> Did you never reade that under the persons of beastes many abuses were dissiphered? have you not reason to waye that whatsoever Virgile did write of his gnatt or Ovid of his fly was all covertly to declare abuse? . . . You say that Poets are subtil; if so, you have learned that poynt of them; you can well glose on a trifling text. But you have dronke perhaps of Lethe; your gramer learning is out of your head; you forget your Accidence; you remember not that under the person of AEneas in Virgil the practise of a diligent captaine is discribed, under the shadow of byrdes, beastes, and trees the follies of the world were dissiphered; you know not that the creation is signified in the Image of Prometheus, the fall of pride in the person of Narcissus; these are toyes, because they savor of wisedome which you want.   (p. 65)

On the one hand, Lodge suggests that the "wisedome" wanting is the common grammatical knowledge available to all, but on the other hand, this knowledge, as in Sidney's *Apologie* and indeed in nearly every sixteenth-century defense, is linked decisively with the sense of coterie or priesthood. The early poets, says Sidney, wrote "under the veil of fables . . . there are many mysteries contained in Poetry, which of purpose were written darkly, lest by prophane wits it should be abused" (p. 142).[20]

---

20. The relative importance of allegory in Sidney's *Apologie* and, by implication, the larger problem of his position on poetic obscurity and clarity are by no means clear, for he sometimes insists that allegory is lucid: "the poet is the food for the tenderest stomachs, the poet is indeed the right popular philosopher, whereof

This socially biased interpretation of allegory was not without precedent, but it tended to suppress the naturalist disposition that was one historical basis for allegorical theory and that would have been more in accord with the overall stance of the defenders. Augustine, for example, had found warrant for allegory in the rational relationship between created nature and ideas.[21] As developed in the aesthetics of the Victorine school, this relationship assures that allegory is neither imaginary nor literary, but real and theological; it arises, not from the figurative meanings of words, but from the structure of nature itself.[22] The natural fitness of *verba* to *res* subserves the higher fitness between nature and ideas; nature is itself an allegory. "It is clear," says Bonaventure, "that the whole world is like a mirror, bright with reflected light of the divine wisdom; it is like a great coal radiant with light."[23] This interpretation was available in the Renaissance view of nature as "that universall and publick Manuscript, that lies expans'd unto the eyes of all."[24] Allegory in the naturalist tradition was thus possible because "the order of God's creatures in themselves is not only admirable and glorious, but eloquent."[25]

In contrast with the open radiance and clarity implicit in this view, there was a second view of allegory, equally traditional, that emphasized the arbitrary and purely conventional relationships of symbols to ideas, and it was to this view that most defenders of poetry turned. In expounding the Dream of Scipio in Cicero's *Republic*, Macrobius had maintained that Nature's "sacred rites" "are veiled in mysterious

---

Aesop's tales give good proof; whose pretty allegories, stealing under the formal tales of beasts, make many, more beastly than beasts, begin to hear the sound of virtue from these dumb speakers"; *Apologie*, p. 109. Myrick labors at great length in opposition to the then prevalent view that "Sidney's Theory of Poetic Truth" was allegorical rather than Aristotelian, ch. 6. More recently, Michael Murrin has attempted to place Sidney in a middle and ambivalent position, between the allegorical bias of Lodge and Harington on the one hand and the "neo-classicism" of Puttenham and Jonson on the other, *The Veil of Allegory* (Chicago: University of Chicago Press, 1969), ch. 7.

21. See Augustine, *On Free Choice of the Will*, trans. Anna S. Benjamin and L. H. Hackstaff (Indianapolis: Bobbs-Merrill, 1964), 2.16; and Etienne Gilson, *The Christian Philosophy of St. Augustine*, trans. L. E. M. Lynch (New York: Random House, 1960), pp. 21–22.

22. See DeBruyne, chs. 1 and 4; and Angus Fletcher, *Allegory: The Theory of a Symbolic Mode* (Ithaca: Cornell University Press, 1964), pp. 130–135.

23. Quoted in W. K. Wimsatt and Cleanth Brooks, *Literary Criticism: A Short History* (1957; rpt., New York: Vintage Books, n.d.), p. 147.

24. Sir Thomas Browne, *Religio Medici*, in *Selected Writings*, ed. Sir Geoffrey Keynes (Chicago: University of Chicago Press, 1968), pp. 20, 22.

25. John Hoskins, *Directions for Speech and Style*, p. 2.

representations so that she may not have to show herself even to initiates. Only eminent men of superior intelligence gain a revelation of her truths; the others must satisfy their desire for worship with a ritual drama which prevents her secrets from becoming common."[26]

Instead of pointing to the allegory of nature itself, *verba* are used in this instance to "cloak" or "veil" it; words figuratively obscure natural relationships. On the basis of this distinction Bede observed that "allegory is sometimes factual, sometimes verbal only,"[27] and Aquinas distinguished between allegory that operates "by words only" and allegory that works "by things themselves."[28] Boccaccio emphasized the purely verbal model because he valued allegorical obscurity over clarity as a means of preserving the purity of truth; poets use the veil of allegory, he argued, "to make truths which they would otherwise cheapen by exposure the object of strong intellectual effort and various interpretation, that in ultimate discovery they shall be more precious . . . You must read, you must persevere, you must sit up nights, you must inquire, and exert the utmost power of your mind . . . For we are forbidden by divine command to give that which is holy to dogs, or to cast pearls before swine."[29] Influenced by the *trobar clus* of the troubadours and the *difficulté vaincu* adopted by the *rhétoriqueurs*, the Pléiade in its early years cultivated an even more aristocratic and deliberate obscurity as part of a posture of *odi profanum vulgus*. "Les poètes," said Louis Le Caron, "pensant estre indignes de prostituer leurs sacrées inventions au profane vulgaire, les ont voulu couvrir de fables: afin qu'elles ne fussent entendues que des plus sages et doctes."[30]

The nominalist implications inherent in the rhetorical treatment of allegory as a "figure" or "garment" of style lent further support to the esoteric ideal of allegorical duplicity. Puttenham, for example, in his *Arte of English Poesie*, includes allegory among several figures that "be occupied of purpose to deceive the eare and also the minde, drawing it from plainnesse and simplicitie to a certaine doublenesse,

26. Macrobius, *Commentary on the Dream of Scipio*, trans. William H. Stahl (New York: Columbia University Press, 1952), 1.2.17–18.

27. Bede, *De Schematibus et Tropis Sacrae Scripturae*, in *Complete Works*, ed. J. A. Giles (London: Whittaker and Co., 1843), VII, 95; quoted in John MacQueen, *Allegory* (London: Methuen, 1970), p. 50.

28. Aquinas, *Summa Theologiae*, 1a; q. 1., a. 10. See MacQueen, p. 53, and Wimsatt and Brooks, p. 147.

29. Boccaccio, *Genealogia Deorum Gentilium*, in *Boccaccio on Poetry*, trans. Charles G. Osgood (Princeton: Princeton University Press, 1930), 14.12.

30. Louis Le Caron, *Dialogues philosophiques*, quoted in Robert J. Clements, *Critical Theory and Practice of the Pléiade* (Cambridge: Harvard University Press, 1942), p. 4.

whereby our talke is the more guilefull and abusing, for what else is your *Metaphore* but an inversion of sense by transport; your *allegorie* but a duplicitie of meaning or dissimulation under covert and darke intendments" (p. 154). According to such rhetorical theories, the poet deliberately "causes a division in his audience, separating the few from the many."[31] Duplicity acts to separate the uninitiated reader from what Stanyhurst calls "the diving searcher"[32] and Harington, "the Understander."[33] For Spenser, as for others, intellectual access to allegorical meaning is in part a social privilege, for while his audience is the Muses' "learned throng," he sings "of Knights and Ladies gentle deeds," and intends his book "to fashion a gentleman or noble person in vertuous and gentle discipline."[34] The truths with which he deals reside not in the clarity of nature's light but in "antique rolles," and "there lye hidden still."[35] With a smug assurance of his own privileged status, Harvey remarks that Spenser's *Dreams* are "a degree or two at the leaste above the reach and compasse of a common Schollars capacitie."[36] Yet more convinced of the priesthood's exclusivity, Chapman restricts his audience to a coterie capable of preserving the sanctity of traditional rites and practices; it consists of "those searching spirits, who learning hath made noble and nobility sacred," for "that Poetry should be as pervial as oratory, and plainnes her special ornament, were the plain way to barbarism."[37]

The sanction for such exclusivity was especially strong in the esoteric aura that surrounded the allegorical tradition of sixteenth-century satire. In an age when, as Raleigh observed, "whosoever . . . shall follow truth too neare the heeles, it may happily strike out his teeth,"[38] it was essential that the truth be cloaked in relatively exclusive conventions. Thus, while Bacon objected to the affected mystifications in the allegorical defense of poetry, he nevertheless conceded the

31. Murrin, p. 13.

32. Richard Stanyhurst, Dedication and Preface to *Aeneid,* in G. Gregory Smith, II, 136.

33. John Harington, *A Briefe Apologie of Poetrie,* in G. Gregory Smith, II, 203.

34. Spenser, *Faerie Queene,* bk. 1, prol., st. 1, and the Letter to Raleigh.

35. *Faerie Queene,* bk. 1, prol., st. 2.

36. Quoted in Murrin, p. 15.

37. George Chapman, Epistle to Matthew Roydon, *The Shadow of Night,* quoted in Margaret Bottral, "George Chapman's Defence of Difficulty in Poetry," *Criterion,* 16 (1937), 650. See also Arnold Stein, "Donne's Obscurity and the Elizabethan Tradition," *ELH,* 13 (1946), 98–118; Robert L. Sharp, "Some Light on Metaphysical Obscurity and Roughness," *SP,* 31 (1934), 497–518; and A. Alvarez, *The School of Donne* (New York: Pantheon Books, 1961), pp. 29–52.

38. Sir Walter Raleigh, Preface to the *Historie of the World,* in *Selections,* ed. G. E. Hadow (1917; rpt., Oxford: Clarendon Press, 1926), p. 61.

value of "poesy parabolical . . . when the secrets and mysteries of religion, policy, or philosophy are involved in fables or parables."[39] Motivated by what Joseph Hall called "feare of jeopardie,"[40] Renaissance satirists drew upon the posture of coterie in ancient satire and upon a nominalist interpretation of allegory in order to support the privilege of deliberately esoteric obscurity. This privilege entailed the replacement of universal norms with the shared conventions of the literary group. Part of "E.K." 's privileged social stance is thus his understanding that the type-names of the *Shepheards Calender* have the purpose of "counterfeicting the names of secret personages."[41] Implicitly, this social stance subjects the rationality of art to a measure of historicity, because the justification for conventions dies with the social groups that created them. Thus, while John Marston, for example, objects to the mere affectation of obscurity, he acknowledges that deliberate obscurity often reflects good artistic practice based on conventional norms from which the reader is historically excluded: *"Persius is crabby, because antient, & his jerks, (being particularly given to private customes of his time) dusky. Juvenall (upon the like occasion) seemes to our judgement, gloomy. Yet both of them goe a good seemely pace, not stumbling, shufling. Chaucer is hard even to our understandings: who knows not the reason? how much more those old Satyres which expresse themselves in termes, that breathed not even in theyr dayes."*[42]

The specter of convention raised by the allegorical defense appeared as well in a second application of the coterie posture—the defense of poetry's musical powers. As in the allegorical defense, this application arose, not out of a direct appeal to universal nature, but out of a restrospective account of poetic tradition. The early poets, says Sidney in the *Apologie,* had the power "to draw with their charming sweetness the wild untamed wits to an admiration of knowledge . . . Amphion was said to move stones with his poetry to build Thebes, and Orpheus to be listened to by beasts" (p. 96). Control over this power is described in priestly and prophetic terms; the ancients, Sidney

39. Bacon, *Works*, IV, 317.

40. Joseph Hall, *Virgidemarium*, ed. Samuel W. Singer (Chiswick: C. Whittingham, 1824), 5.1.8.

41. E.K., "Epistle Dedicatory to the Shepheard's Calender," in *The Shepheard's Calendar and Other Poems*, pp. 17, 16.

42. John Marston, *The Scourge of Villainy*, in *Works*, ed. A. H. Bullen (London: John C. Nimmo, 1887), III, 304–305. See Alvin Kernan, *The Cankered Muse: Satire of the English Renaissance* (New Haven: Yale University Press, 1959), pp. 56–61; Ellen Douglass Leyburn, *Satiric Allegory: Mirror of Man* (New Haven: Yale University Press, 1956), pp. 7–9; and Fletcher, *Allegory*, pp. 324–331.

claims, thought that in "such verses great tokens of their following fortunes were placed . . . which, although it was a very vain and godless superstition, as also it was to think that spirits were commanded by such verses—whereupon this word charms, derived of *carmina,* cometh—so yet serveth it to show the great reverence those wits were held in" (p. 98). For Sidney, as for most writers of the sixteenth century, "a powerful aura of allegory . . . surrounds their use of musical terminology. The effects· of the measured poetry and music could be understood, not only literally as the power believed to be generated by the kind of music used by the ancients . . . but also more widely as the results of an education, 'musical' in the Platonic sense, and based on long discipline in the moral and intellectual virtues."[43]

This view of a secret musical tradition helps to explain why the posture of esoteric coterie was adopted among such groups as the Academia della Nuova Poesia, Antoine de Baif's Académie du Musique et de Poésie, and the Pléiade in their efforts to reunite poetry and music. The esoteric posture is especially strong in de Baif's belief that

> Jadis Musiciens et Poétes et Sages
> Furent mesmes auteurs: mais la suite des ages,
> Par le tems qui tout change a separé les troys.
> Puissons-nous, d'entreprendre heureusement hardie,
> Du bon siècle améner la *coustume abolie,*
> Et les troys réunir sous la faveur des Roys.[44]

While ultimately directed outward toward the whole of humanity, and while based upon the universal harmony of nature, Baif's aims simultaneously suggest the necessity of an inner priesthood to restore, preserve, and administer *la coustume abolie.*

For the group surrounding Sidney, the preservation of musical tradition through the restoration of quantitative verse seems to have been one point of contact with the French academies and one motive for their posture as a priestly coterie.[45] While the norms of such verse pre-

---

43. Frances A. Yates, *The French Academies of the Sixteenth Century* (London: Warburg Institute, 1947), pp. 59–60; see also John Hollander, *The Untuning of the Sky: Ideas of Music in English Poetry, 1500–1700* (1961; rpt., New York: Norton, 1970), p. 175.

44. Quoted in Yates, p. 43; my italics. See also Bruce Pattison, *Music and Poetry of the English Renaissance* (London: Methuen, 1948), pp. 62–65.

45. See J. E. Phillips, "Poetry and Music in the Seventeenth Century," in *Music and Literature in England* (Los Angeles; Clark Memorial Library, 1953), and his "Daniel Rogers: A Neo-Latin Link between the *Pléiade* and Sidney's 'Areopagus,' " in *Neo-Latin Poetry of the Sixteenth and Seventeenth Centuries* (Los Angeles: Clark

sumably derive from natural laws of harmony, they are, as Spenser reports, expounded, practiced, preserved, and protected by a coterie. Sidney and Dyer, he writes to Harvey, "have proclaimed in their *areio pago* a generall surceasing and silence of bolde Rymers, and also of the verie beste to: in steade whereof, they have by their whole Senate, prescribed certain Lawes and rules of Quantities of sillables for English verse, having had thereof already great practice, and drawen mee to their faction." The desired reform requires the "great practise" of a coterie to subdue the language: "it is to be wonne with Custome, and rough words must be subdued with Use."[46] The quasi-legal terminology suggests the importance of social identity, for the reform is an attempt, as William Webbe puts it, "to put in practice and to establish for an accustomed right among the English Poets"[47] quantitative verse. The voluntary rather than rational basis of this "accustomed right" is urgently affirmed in Spenser's request "that we might both accorde and agree in one, lest we overthrowe one an other and be overthrowen of the rest."[48]

Like the use of coterie in the allegorical defense, the fear of being "overthrowen of the rest" suggests a conflict between the rites and practices of artistic priesthood and the larger realm of public convention. The reformers must contend against "the cankered enmitie of curious custome," Webbe complains. In attempting to restore quantitative verse, the reformers are doomed, "because it is straunge, and the other barbarous custome, being within the compasse of every base witt, hath worne it out of credite or estimation." Spenser, he claims, might have surpassed Virgil and Theocritus, "if the coarseness of our speech (I mean the course of custome which he would not infringe) had been no more let unto him than theyr pure native tongues were unto them."[49]

Webbe's contrast between "the course of custome" and the idea of a "pure native tongue" points up a problem that was to plague Renaissance efforts to define the relation of nature to the conventions of po-

Memorial Library, 1965). See also John Buxton, *Sir Philip Sidney and the English Renaissance* (London: Macmillan, 1954), pp. 95–116; and Vere L. Rubel, *Poetic Diction in the English Renaissance* (New York: Modern Language Association, 1941), p. 101n2.

46. Spenser-Harvey Correspondence, in G. Gregory Smith, I, 89, 99.

47. Webbe, *A Discourse of English Poesie,* in G. Gregory Smith, I, 278.

48. Spenser-Harvey Correspondence, in G. Gregory Smith, I, 99; for the context of Spenser's remarks, see William Ringler, "Master Drant's Rules," *PQ,* 29 (1950), 70–74.

49. Webbe, *A Discourse of English Poesie,* in G. Gregory Smith, I, 228, 279, 263.

etic diction. On the one hand, the aim of the quantitative experiment was, as Sidney says, to preserve the "number, measure, order, proportion" befitting a poetics that took its norms from nature. On the other hand, the conflict between such norms and current linguistic usage necessitated a special sanction to allow for the distinctiveness of poetic diction, making it "tollerable in a verse to sette wordes so extraordinaryly as other speech will not admitt."[50] Thus ensconced in privilege, these norms were bound to take on a coloring of convention. Moreover, the resistance of "curious custome" or public usage to such experiments seemed to suggest a natural order in the language itself. "The naturall course of most English verses," Webbe observes, "seemeth to run uppon the olde Iambicke stroake" because there is "such a naturall force or quantity in eche worde, that it will not abide anie place but one, without some foul disgrace."[51] Similarly, says Stanyhurst, "that nature wyl not permit us too fashion oure wordes in all poinctes correspondent too thee Latinistes, may easily appeere in such termes as we borrow of theym."[52]

The power of usage to transform pronunciation, by analogy with customary law, severely compromised the distinction between an *ars* based on nature and an *ars* based on convention. In the name of nature Stanyhurst pleads for convention: "That nothing may bee doone or spoaken agaynst nature, and that *Art* is also bound too shape yt self by an imitation too *Nature,* we must request theese *grammatical Precisians,* that as every countrye hath hath his peculiar law, so they permit everye language to use his particular loare."[53] Paradoxically, the seemingly natural quality of current usage and the apparent artificiality of the experimenters combined to shift the burden of conventionality to the "license" of the poet-priests, who "attribute greater prerogative too thee Latin tongue than reason wyl affurd, and less libertye too oure language than nature may permit."[54] Thus Harvey complains to Spenser,

> Is there no other Pollicie to pulle downe Ryming and set uppe Versifying but you must needes correcte *Magnificat:* and against all order of Lawe, and in despite of Custome, forcibly usurp and tyrannize upon a quiet companye of wordes that so farre beyonde the memorie of man have so

50. Webbe, *A Discourse of English Poesie,* in G. Gregory Smith, I, 274.
51. Webbe, *A Discourse of English Poesie,* in G. Gregory Smith, I, 273.
52. Stanyhurst, Dedication and Preface to *Aeneid,* in G. Gregory Smith, I, 142.
53. Stanyhurst, Dedication and Preface to *Aeneid,* in G. Gregory Smith, I, 144.
54. Stanyhurst, Dedication and Preface to *Aeneid,* in G. Gregory Smith, I, 141.

peacefully enjoyed their severall Priviledges and Liberties, without any disturbance or the least controlement? What? Is HORACES *Ars Poetica* so quite out of our Englishe Poets head that he must have his Remembrancer to pull hym by the sleeve, and put him in mind of *Penes Usum,* and *ius,* and *norma loquendi?* . . . never heard I any that durst presume so much over the Englishe . . . as to alter the Quantitie of any one sillable, otherwise than our common speeche and generall recyved Custome would beare them oute.[55]

Reverting to the principal argument of the common law, Harvey curtails the license of poetic diction, shifting the basis of artistic speech to convention, so that "we are licensed and authorized by the ordinarie use, and custome, and proprietie, and Idiome, and as it were, Majestie of our speeche: which I accounte the only infallible and soveraigne Rule of all Rules."

It would remain for others to articulate further and more clearly the relationship between nature and artistic convention, and to expand it beyond diction into other components of poetic art. Nevertheless, the sense of coterie connected with the allegorical and Orphic defenses of Sidney and others led them outward from an otherwise naturalistic poetics toward consideration of the intersubjective character of poetic norms resulting from their intended effects upon an audience. Indeed, the Orphic myth had always suggested that the true quality of poetic art was coeval with its social function, and Horace had used it to suggest that the formal dimension of poetic art was closely linked to its dynamic or rhetorical dimension. Not surprisingly, in order to justify and explain their concepts of allegory and diction as conventional, the defenders were forced to shift their focus from the "inwarde" seats of arguments to the "outwarde" seats of end, effect, place, time, circumstance, comparison, and testimony, including custom.

3. THE ARTLESSNESS OF ART: CONVENTION IN RENAISSANCE POETICS

As the informing principle of Sidney's *Apologie,* "conveniency to Nature" brings to bear upon the status, structure, and mode of operation of poetic art a universal and transcendent test of fitness. Sidney extends this test to poetic effects as well when he attacks contemporary poetasters, who obtain a "seeming fineness, but persuade few—which

---

55. Spenser-Harvey Correspondence, in G. Gregory Smith, I, 117.

should be the end of their fineness." In explaining this rhetorical failure, Sidney observes that he has "found in divers smally learned courtiers a more sound style than in some professors of learning; of which I can guess no other cause, but that the courtier, following that which by practice he findeth fittest to nature, therein (though he know it not) doth according to art, to show art, and not to hide art (as in these cases he should do), flieth from nature, and indeed abuseth art" (p. 139). Paradoxically, inarticulate effort may satisfy the ends of art more fully than the rational deliberation that characterizes art itself. When extended to the effects of art, the test of natural fitness demands the artlessness of art, the illusion that things could not have been otherwise. While the proper kind of human production requires the articulation of artistic norms in keeping with natural structure and process, nature further demands the subordination of these norms to natural effects in the finished product.

The ideal of "artless" art thus arises as an explicitly rhetorical concern for the effects of works upon their audience. As one of the least rhetorically biased of sixteenth-century treatises, Sidney's *Apologie* tenaciously defends the scientific integrity of poetic art, and thus in general assumes that such integrity itself secures the proper effectiveness of works. Like the role of social norms in allegory and diction, the rhetorical aspects of artless art are therefore subordinated in the *Apologie* to the overriding norm of nature, and invoked only tangentially in connection with artistic abuse. In the more frankly rhetorical outlook that was a major source of sixteenth-century theory, however, these aspects were the focus of a more direct concern with the communication of effects. Just as rhetorical considerations had challenged the norm of nature in antiquity, the rhetorical side of Renaissance theory continued to offset the rational ideal of artful control with the alternative demand for "artless" effects.

In Puttenham's *Arte of English Poesie* (1589), the most comprehensive and penetrating rhetorical treatment of poetry in sixteenth-century England, this demand becomes the basis for a theory of literature opposed in principle to Sidney's and thus coessential to the sixteenth-century normative debate. Puttenham's poet is, like Sidney's, a "Maker" (p. 3). He is also, however, a "counterfaictor" (p. 3), because "the good Poet or maker ought to dissemble his art" (p. 298). Accordingly, Puttenham says, "we do allow our Courtly Poet to be a dissembler only in the subtleties of his art: that is, when he is most artificiall, so to disguise and cloake it as it may not appeare, nor seeme to proceede from him by any studie or trade of rules, but to be his naturall" (p. 303). When not obtrusively working "by example or mediation or exercise as all other artificers do," the poet "is then most admired . . . most naturall and least artificiall" (p. 308).

In shifting the critical focus from the abstract status and structure of poetic art to its illusory effects, the paradox of artless art gives rise to the further paradox that art best achieves this illusion when guided, not by nature, but by convention. The reasons for this paradox are most explicit in one of Puttenham's principal sources, the courtesy books, where moral rectitude is often treated as a species of artistic illusion. As noted earlier, the approach to rectitude in these books encourages a virtual identification between moral and artistic fitness. Moreover, the essentially rhetorical character there attributed to both types of fitness demands that, like the rectitude of acts, the excellence of art should be measured by its effect. Castiglione, for example, maintains that "that may be saide to be a verie arte, that appeareth not to be arte, neither ought a man to put more diligence to any thing than in covering it: for in case it be open, it loseth credite clene, and maketh a man litel set by."[1] There is, he claims, a "not regarded purenesse which best pleaseth the eyes and mindes of men" (pp. 66–67). This simplicity is best achieved, not by direct recourse to natural norms, but by conformity with the illusory "second nature" of convention. The attempt to act according to an unchanging and natural standard of integrity produces a "maner of Preciseness and curiousness . . . too much in extremitie, which is alwaies a vice, and contrarie to that pure and amiable simplicitie, which is so acceptable to mens mindes" (p. 47). The courtier's quest for fitness "acceptable to mens mindes" requires that "he avoide curiositie." Like the psychagogic sweetness (*dulcia*) of the Horatian *Ars*, the "good grace [*sprezzatura*]" of the courtier's artless art is rhetorical in character. Instead of following the unchanging dictates of nature, the courtier turns to the shifting panorama of convention: "even as the Bee in greene medowes fleeth alwaies about the grasse, choosing out flowers: So shall our Courtier steale his grace from them that to his seeming have it" (p. 45). In order to achieve the artlessness of art, and "to keepe company pleasantly with every man," says Castiglione of the courtier, "let him do whatsoever other men do" (p. 42).

Explicitly sharing the bias of the "Courtiers, for whose instruction this travaile is taken" (p. 158), Puttenham theoretically justifies the affinity between convention and artless art by explaining the relationship of habitual acts to nature. "Custome and exercise" are "requisite to every action," and by virtue of their inarticulate, experiential char-

1. Castiglione, *The Boke of the Courtier*, p. 46.

acter, they are more closely linked to natural power than the more deliberate procedures entailed by rational precepts.

> What else is language and utterance, and discourse & per-
> swasion, then the vertues of a well constitute body and
> minde, little lesse naturall then [a man's] very sensuall ac-
> tions, saving that the one is perfited by nature at once, the
> other not without *exercise and iteration.* Peradventure also
> it wilbe granted, that a man discernes more brimly his col-
> lours, and heares and feeles more exactly *by use and often
> hearing* and feeling and seeing, & though it be better to see
> with spectacles then not to see at all, yet is their praise not
> egall nor in any mans judgement comparable: no more is
> that which a Poet makes by arte and precepts.   (p. 305; my
> italics)

Unlike the "spectacles" of artistic precepts, the power of "use" is intrinsic to natural acts themselves. The relationship of "use" and "iteration" to man's innate powers forms the basis for the artlessness of
art. The successful "counterfaictor" works not by "artes and methodes"
primarily, but "by long and studious observation [or] rather *a repetition or reminiscens naturall,* reduced unto perfection, and *made
prompt by use and exercise.* And so whatsoever a man speakes or per-
suades he doth it not by imitation artificially, but by observation naturally" (p. 300). To operate "by observation naturally," the poet turns
not to abstract principles, but to the familiar world of experience;
"there was no art in the world," says Puttenham, "till by experience
found out" (p. 5). The poet's habit of art is formed by experience, and
part of that experience is his retrospective appeal to the inarticulate
habits and expectations that form the public counterpart and setting
of the individual's development.

Aristotle helped to pave the way for these connections when he
posited familiarity and experience as one basis for artistic illusion.
One of the natural origins of poetry is

> the enjoyment people always get from representations . . .
> The reason is this. Learning things gives great pleasure not
> only to philosophers but also in the same way to all other
> men, though they share this pleasure to a small degree. The
> reason why we enjoy seeing likenesses is that, as we look, we
> learn and infer what each is, for instance "that is so and so."
> If we have never happened to see the original, our pleasure
> is not due to the representation as such but to the technique

or the colour or some other such cause. (*Poetics*, 1448b6–20)

The decisive element for representation as such is the familiarity of the audience with an original. The technique and medium attract attention only when the object of imitation is strange; when it is familiar, the medium tends to disappear. Although Aristotle's approach to poetic art ultimately dictates that this "original" is at bottom a universal principle (*ta katholou*), and thus that credibility is a function of philosophic probability, he nevertheless established for all time the dependence of artistic illusion on its credibility with an audience. Horace, as noted earlier, interpreted this relationship in social and empirical terms when he substituted the familiar world of tradition and contemporary *mores* for the universal as the basis of imitation. In the Renaissance, this empirical interpretation became the frequent source for a virtual identification of probability with credibility, and hence with the expectations of the audience. Acknowledging that "nothing must be brought upon the stage which would go counter to the wish and desire of the spectators," Vettori, for example, went on to observe that "poets must adapt themselves to [the audience's] judgment and express those things which are apt to persuade."[2] The principle guiding such accommodation is not natural fitness, but social familiarity. Maggi similarly argued that "just as the image of a thing gives greater pleasure to one who knows the things previously than one who does not . . . so one who knows previously that action which the poet imitates will learn and reason that this is the imitation of that action." Accordingly, because the poet cannot achieve his ends of teaching and delighting "unless he obtains the belief of his audience, he follows common opinion in this respect." The "falsehoods of the kind that are told by poets," Maggi claimed, are held to be verisimilar or true "insofar as they are received in the opinion of the crowd."[3]

The influence of opinion upon credibility therefore dictates that the criterion of belief is familiarity rather than reason, and that the test of poetic fitness is not nature, but convention. This led many theorists away from the Aristotelian approach and toward the Horatian view that art is fashioned from conventional resources and materials that are themselves created by intersubjective expectations and demands. Indeed, these demands were explicitly imposed by Helenius

2. Pietro Vettori, *Commentarii in Primum Librum Aristotelis de Arte Poetarum* (1560), quoted in Weinberg, I, 464.

3. Vincenzo Maggi, *In Aristotelis Librum de Poetica Communes Explanationes* (1550), quoted in Weinberg, I, 409, 412–413.

Acron, whose commentary was part of nearly every sixteenth-century text of Horace. The *Ars Poetica,* Acron maintained, "shows only to what extent is important the consideration of customs [*consuetudinis*], saying that sometimes a story through the suitableness of the persons introduced and the expressions of the mores, even though it may be without art [*sine arte*], without beauty, without gravity or sententiae, pleases more than high-sounding verses which are lacking in the observation of the mores."[4] Although Robortello's more extensive commentary on Aristotle included a wider range of possible mimetic criteria, he granted convention a substantial role in *mimesis;* the poet draws upon the universally true, the possible, and the traditional or conventional, for "poetics speaks only of those actions which exist, or which can exist, or which do exist according to what men used to think." The importance of this final criterion was further emphasized when it was made to play a decisive role among the kinds of poetic criteria. These kinds Robortello classified as follows:

Duplicit modo fingere, & mentiri poetas
1. in rebus secundum naturam [the possible]
   a. to anangkaion [the necessary]
   b. to eikos [the probable]
2. in rebus praeter naturam [the impossible]
   a. quae receptae iam sunt in opinionem vulgi [the traditional]
   b. non ante unquam auditis, aut narratis ab alio [the newly invented][5]

In its distinction between the integrity of such natural principles as necessity and probability, on the one hand, and those that are received or unfamiliar according to convention, on the other, Robortello's dichotomy defines the alternatives available to Renaissance poetic theory: an art that derives its integrity from natural and immutable principles, or an "artless art" whose hidden norms are shared assumptions; an art that looks for the test of fitness to the logical structure of nature, or an art that looks to the rhetorical convenience of convention; an art defined with reference, through analogy and syllogism, to the "internal places" of definition, division, genus, species, parts and whole, or an art defined inductively from the "external places" or contingencies of end, effect, time, place, circumstance, and tradition.

4. *Acronis et Porphyrionis Commentarii in Q. Horatium Flaccus,* quoted in Weinberg, I, 77.

5. Francesco Robortello, *In Librum Aristotelis de Arte Poetica Explicationes* (1548), quoted in Weinberg, I, 391, 393.

In his quest for "artless art," Puttenham, to a greater extent than other early English theorists, appeals to the second of these alternatives. This appeal is framed, however, by the terms of a naturalist poetics. All relations of fitness arise from the natural possibility of proportion; because any such relation "resteth in the good conformitie of many things and their sundry circumstances, with respect to one another, so as there be found a just correspondencie betweene them by this or that relation, the Greekes call it *Analogie* or a convenient relation" (p. 262). "The spirituall objects of the mind," he says, "stand no lesse in the due proportion of reason and discourse than any other materiall thing doth in his sensible bewtie, proportion, and comelynesse." Thus in verbal art there needs to be a "lovely conformitie or proportion, or convenience betweene the sense and the sensible." In poetic terms this means that "in all decencie the stile ought to conforme with the nature of the subject" (p. 151) so that if the "matter be high and loftie . . . the stile should be so to" (p. 149). Like Sidney's approach to style, and like the "office" or "estates" approach to moral rectitude, the fitness of *verba* to *res* is conceived analogically and syllogistically in relation to the hierarchical structure of nature itself, "for it it comely that every estate and vocation should be knowen by the differences of their habit: a clarke from a layman: a gentleman from a yeoman: a souldier from a citizen, and the chiefe of every degree from their inferiour, because in confusion and disorder there is no manner of decencie" (p. 283).

Considerably more skeptical than other thinkers in his approach to this hierarchy, however, Puttenham points to the circumstantial aspects of its structure, for "in the use of a garment many occasions alter the decencie, sometimes the qualitie of the person, sometimes the case, otherwhiles the countrie custome, and often the constitution of the lawes, and *the very nature of use itself*" (p. 285; my italics). Operating at the submerged and inarticulate level of experience, the power of use imparts a coloring of natural fitness to conventions:

> The countrie custome maketh things decent in use, as in Asia for all men to weare long gownes both a foot and horsebacke; in Europa short gaberdins, or clokes, or jakkets, even for their upper garments. The Turke and Persian to weare great talibants of ten, fifteene, and twentie elles of linnen a peece upon their heads, which can not be remooved: in Europa to were caps or hats, which upon every occasion of salutation we use to put of, as a signe of reverence. In th' East parts the men to make water couring like women, with us standing at a wall. With them to congratulat and salute

by giving a becke with the head, or a bende of the bodie, with us here in England, and in Germany, and all other Northerne parts of the world to shake hands. In France, Italie, and Spaine to embrace over the shoulder, under the armes, at the very knees, according to the superiors degree. With us the wemen give their mouth to be kissed, in other places their cheke, in many places their hand. (pp. 285–286)

In such varieties of norms Puttenham discovers "the humours and appetites of men how divers and chaungeable they be in liking new fashions, though many times worse than the olde, and not onely in the manner of their life and use of their garments, but also in their learn-inges and arts and specially of their languages" (p. 15). Like other fashions, formed by "use and exercise . . . & accepted by consent of a whole countrey & nation," linguistic habit comes eventually to be "called a language, & receaveth none allowed alteration, but by ex-traordinary occasions by little and little, as it were insensible bringing in of many corruptions that creep along with the time" (pp. 133–134). The "insensibility" of such changes, arising from the illusory relation of habit to nature, establishes the possibility of an "artless art" that plays upon convention, for

> Many a word yfalne shall eft arise
> And such as now bene held in hiest prise
> Will fall as fast, when use and custome will
> Onely Umpires of speach, for force and skill.
> (p. 148; *Ars poetica,* 70–72)

The principle of convention imposes on the arts a transactional char-acter that influences not only the material but the kinds and struc-tures of discourse. "By reason of the sundry circumstances, that mans affaires are as it were wrapt in, this *decencie* comes to be a very much alterable and subject to varietie, in so much as our speach asketh one maner of *decencie,* in respect of the person who speakes: another of his to whom it is spoken: another of whom we speake, and in what place and time and to what purpose" (p. 263). Conceived as a relation of means to ends rather than parts to whole or species to genus, artistic fitness is referred not to the logical structure of nature, but to a variety of rhetorical circumstances: "for maners of speaches, some serve to work in excesse, some in mediocritie, some to grave purposes, some to light, some to be short and brief, some to be long, some to stirre up affections, some to pacifie and appease them" (p. 140).

The ramifications of Puttenham's rhetorical bias for poetic theory are most apparent in the tone and method of his discourse. Indeed, John Harington had compared Puttenham's treatment of poetic art with Sidney's, and concluded that "though the poore gentleman laboreth greatly to prove, or rather to make Poetrie an art," Puttenham fails because he merely "reciteth as you may see, in the plurall number, some pluralities of patterns and parcels of . . . Poetrie."[6] It might be said, however, that this "pluralism" was a natural and deliberate corollary of Puttenham's poetic theory. "Since the actions of man with their circumstances be infinite," he says, "and the world likewise replenished with many judgements, it may be a question who shal have the determination of such controversie as may arise whether this or that action or speach be decent or indecent" (p. 263). With the skepticism that accompanied recognition of the transactional element, not only in the productive arts, but in the practical arts of morality and politics as well, Puttenham abandons direct intuition of universals for the empirical variety of particulars. "I see no way," he says, "so fit to enable a man truly to estimate of *decencie* as example, by whose veritie we may deeme the differences of things and their proportions, and by particular discussions come at length to sentence of it generally" (p. 263). By his own admission, the source of artistic knowledge therefore resides, not in universal nature, but in the complexity of history; prudent retrospection rather than scientific intellection is the basis for artistic knowledge:

> first wee wil sort you out divers points, in which the wise and learned men of times past have noted much decency or undecencie, every man according to his discretion, as it hath bene said afore: but wherein for the most parte all discreete men doe generally agree, and varie not in opinion, whereof the examples I will give you be worthie of remembraunce: & though they brought with them no doctrine or institution at all, yet for the solace they may geve the readers, after such a rable of scholasticall precepts which be tedious, these reports being of the nature of matters historicall, they are to be embraced: but olde memories are very profitable to the mind, and serve as a glasse to looke upon and beholde the events of time, and more exactly to skan the trueth of every case that shall happen in the affaires of man. (p. 264)

Because it derives retrospectively from "olde memories" rather than "scholasticall precepts," such normative guidance bears in a special

6. John Harington, *A Briefe Apologie for Poetry*, in G. Gregory Smith, II, 197.

way on poetic theory. This is nowhere more apparent than in Puttenham's treatment of literary kinds. While Sidney had treated these kinds, as well as their elements, with reference to their position in a logical framework analogous to the scale of nature, Puttenham refers them individually to their origins in social practice. The historical and pluralistic nature of his procedure is reflected in the typical content of his chapter headings:

XVIII.	Of the Shepheardes or pastorall Poesy called Eglogue, and to what purpose it was first invented and used
XIX.	Of Historicall Poesie, by which the famous acts of Princes and the vertuous and worthy lives of our forefathers were reported
XX.	In what forme of Poesie vertue in the inferiour sort was recommended (Encomia)
XXI.	The forme wherein honest and profitable Artes and sciences were treated (Philosophic poetry)
XXII.	Of what forme of Poesie the amours affections and allurements were uttered
XXIII.	The forme of Poeticall rejoysings (Triumphals)
XXIIII.	The forme of Poetical lamentations
XXV.	Of the solemne rejoysings at the nativitie of Princes children (Genethliaca)
XXVI.	The maner of rejoysings at marriages and weddings (Epithalamia)
XXVII.	The maner of Poesie by which they uttered their bitter taunts, and privy nips, or witty scoffes and other merry conceits (Satire, Epigram)
XXVIII.	Of the poeme called Epitaph used for memoriall of the dead.

The striking feature in Puttenham's approach to literary kinds is that while formally they are products, they are in origin *acts*. Only through "often use and iteration" do these acts acquire, through the fixity of habit, a distinctive shape. In giving shape and expression to various "affections" (p. 144) and "part[s] of mind" (p. 39), poetic forms and kinds become the conventional specifications of natural impulse. Thus because "pleasure is the chiefe parte of man's felicities in this world . . . Therefore nature and civilitie have ordained (besides the private solaces) publike rejoysings for the comfort and recreation of many. And they be *of diverse sorts and upon divers occasions growne*" (pp. 45–46; my italics). The form of the Genethliacon arises from just such a specific occasion: "The comfort of issue and procreation of children is so naturall and so great, not onely to all men but specially to Princes, as dutie and civility have made it a common custome to re-joyse at the birth of their noble children" (p. 49). Though different in their forms, lamentations bears a similarly customary relationship to their practical origins. Social as well as literary in origin, lament, like other poetic forms, is a *"mimesis* of the changing states of society":[7]

> the lamenting of deaths was chiefly at the very burialls of the dead, also at monethes mindes and longer times, by custome continued yearly, when as they used many offices of service and love towardes the dead, and thereupon are called *Obesequies* in our vulgare, which was done not onely by cladding the mourners their friendes and servaunts in blacke vestures, of shape dolefull and sad, but also by wofull countenances and voyces, and besides by Poeticall mournings in verse. Such funerall songs were called *Epicedia* if they were song by many, and *Monodia* if they were uttered by one alone, and this was used at the enterment of Princes and others of great accompt, and it was reckoneed a great civilitie to use such ceremonies, as at this day is also in some country used. In Rome they accustomed to make orations funerall and commendatorie of the dead parties in the publique place called *Prorostris.* (p. 49)

Not only do such social practices underlie the conventional literary kinds, but the constituent elements of each kind and its total structure may be referred to the substratum of experience out of which it arose. Thus,

> *Epithalamie* was devided by breaches into three partes to serve for three severall fits or times to be song. The firste breach was song at the first parte of the night when the spouse and her husband were brought to their bed & at the very chamber dore . . . & the tunes of the songs were very loude and shrill, to the intent there might no noise be hard out of the bed chamber by the skreeing & outcry of the young damosell feeling the first forces of her stiffe & rigorous young man, she being as all virgins tender & weake, & un-

---

7. Quoted from Willcock and Walker's Introduction, p. lvi. Puttenham's view of this relationship is discussed briefly but well by Constance I. Smith, "Some Ideas on Education before Locke," *JHI,* 23 (1962), 403–406.

expert in those manner of affaires . . . Aboute midnight or
one of the clocke, the Musicians came again to the chamber
dore . . . this part of the ballade was to refresh the faint
and weried bodies and spirits, and to animate new appetite
with cherefull wordes, encoring them to the recontinuance
of the same entertainments . . . In the morning when it
was faire broad daye . . . the same Musicians came againe
with this last part, and greeted them both with a Psalme of
new applausions . . . then by good admonitions enformed
them to the frugall & thriftie life all the rest of their dayes.
(pp. 51–53)

The history of the genre is thus embedded in its form. Such fanciful
and unscholarly accounts have led a recent historian of the "Rise of
English Literary History" to slight Elizabethan contributions to literary history, and to place its modern origins in the later eighteenth
century, "when biography and criticism coalesced, and when, under the
influence of political historiography, the narrative method began to be
used."[8] At issue in the Renaissance, however, were not only the techniques that established the presumed superiority of modern historical
method, but the attitudes that made such methods possible. Puttenham's imaginative account, more economically and more poignantly
perhaps than any modern history could, attempts to establish the vital
relationship between literary form and expression and the changing
configuration of human circumstance. In keeping with this principle,
Puttenham turns to the influence of history on literary expression.
Memory, he says,

> maketh most to a sound judgement and perfect worldly
> wisedome, examining and comparing the times past with the
> present, and by them both considering the time to come,
> concludeth with a stedfoote resolution, what is the best
> course to be taken in his actions and advises in this world:
> it came upon this reason, experience to be so highly com-
> mended in all consultations of importance, and preferred
> before any learning or science, and yet experience is no more
> than a masse of memories assembled, that is, such trials as
> man hath made in time before.   (p. 39)

In his respect for tradition, for "such trials as man hath made in
time before," Puttenham resembles Hooker more than he resembles

8. René Wellek, *The Rise of English Literary History* (Chapel Hill: University
of North Carolina Press, 1941), p. 1.

Sidney. His attempt to justify the poetic forms "which we in our vulgare makings do imitate and use . . . such as time and usurpation by custome have allowed us out of the Greeke & Latine" (p. 58) hinges on awareness of the power and relativity of habit. The artlessness of art, like the fitness of customary law, depends upon an inherently rational link between traditional practice and natural order that has been submerged by time. The proper understanding of art, like that of law, requires articulation of this missing link by relating established principles to the historical conditions and circumstances under which they arose, "since all artes grew firste by observation of natures proceedings and custome" (p. 128). Accordingly, the chief requirements of a poet are age and memory, from which are born the power of accommodation: "age brings experience, experience bringeth wisdom, long life yeldes long use and much exercise of speech, exercise and custome with wisedome, make an assured and volluble utterance" (p. 142).

On the one hand, this awareness of conventional influence on artistic norms engenders a conservative respect for established tradition. Like the English common law, which philosophically resisted the proposed "reception" of Roman law, the established English idiom, says Puttenham, resists the importation of Latin prosody: "For the most part wise and grave men doe naturally mislike with all sodaine innovations specially of lawes (and this the law of our auncient English Poesie) and therefore lately we imputed it to a nice & scholasticall curiositie in such makers as have sought to bring into our vulgar Poesie some of the auncient feete" (p. 113). Such schemes ought not "by authority of our own judgement be generally applauded at to the discredit of our forefathers maner of vulgar Poesie." Because of the hidden link between convention and the "natural" effect of artless art, it is "somewhat too late to admit a new invention of feete and times that our forefathers never used nor never observed till this day" (p. 119).

On the other hand, this skeptical attitude permits a tolerance for the diversity of traditions and the forms indigenous to them. Originating in a respect for the diversity of linguistic and social usage, Puttenham's attitude extends to his defense of such forms as metrical romance, for there "be sundry formes of poems and not all one" (p. 42). Moreover, as Puttenham says, "examining and comparing the times past with the present" involves consideration of "the time to come." This vital and dynamic relationship of poetic past to poetic future helps to change our picture of Renaissance poetics. In demonstrating that the criterion of logical significancy served almost exclusively as the Renaissance test of poetic fitness, Rosemond Tuve has claimed that there was little "relaxation of the criterion of significancy for images during this entire period, nor much change in the definition of it."[9] Puttenham's theory, however, suggests that there were vastly different ideas of *how* such significancy could be obtained. Contending as it does that the relation of artistic norms to nature is submerged by time and custom, Puttenham's theory suggests that poetic art achieves its ends, not by logically and systematically exploring the structure of nature, but by drawing upon and manipulating such intellectual structures as have been previously established and sanctioned by custom. This allows for novel applications of established norms, once the reasons for their existence have been obscured.

This possibility is explicitly developed in Castiglione's exposition of the "artless art" that so attracted Puttenham. In explaining the resources of figurative speech, Castiglione emphasizes, not the logical significance of such speech, but its established currency with an audience. "Do you not knowe," he says, "that figures of speech which give such grace and brightnesse to an Oration, are all the abuse of Grammer rules, but yet are received and confirmed by use, because men are *able to make no other reason* but that they delite, and to the verie sense of our eares it appeareth, they bring a life and a sweetnesse" (p. 60; my italics). The very power that gives currency to such techniques, however, also allows for further innovation, for, as Puttenham puts it, "commonly the firste attempt in any arte or engine artificiall is amendable, & in time by often experiences reformed" (pp. 58–59). The power of convention to conceal apparent artifice suggests that "straungenesse . . . proceedes but of novelitie and disacquaintaunce with our eares, which in processes of time, and by custome will frame very well" (pp. 156–157). Innovations may seem to violate the familiar "second nature" of convention, and "seeme nothing pleasant to an English eare, but time and usage will make them acceptable inough, as it doth in all other new guises, be it for wearing of apparell or otherwise" (p. 128). This dynamic and experiential sense of tradition inspires Puttenham's approach with both confidence and skeptical tolerance, as he attempts "but to fashion an art, & not to finish it: which time onely & custom have authoritie to do" (p. 128).

4. "THE SEPARATION OF OPINIONS": THE ROLE OF CONVENTION IN CRITICISM AND CONTROVERSY

The increasing prominence of convention as a normative principle in the literary theory of the later sixteenth century was accompanied

9. Tuve, *Elizabethan and Metaphysical Imagery*, p. 155.

by a corresponding shift in critical method. The displacement of the norm of nature by convention was implicitly the displacement of a universal and authoritative standard by a variety of particular and changing possibilities. Accordingly, in Renaissance literary theory, as in moral philosophy, the transition from nature to convention as the test of fitness engendered a corresponding methodological shift away from a purely normative or prescriptive approach and toward an attitude increasingly critical, historical, and comparative. Although it did not lead to complete abandonment of the older prescriptive approach, the conception of conventional fitness, with its emphasis on rhetorical efficacy, almost inevitably led theoretical discourse away from the "internal places" and toward the "external places" of time, place, circumstance, custom, and so on, where information about such effectiveness might best be found. As a result, the normative transition to convention required a method capable of extrapolating reliable norms from the various and complex demands imposed by rhetorical theory. In order to retain some measure of systematic coherence in the face of rhetorical chaos, the normative tradition was forced to become a critical tradition.

This shift in method is most fully reflected in the attitude of Ben Jonson, who observes in *Timber, or Discoveries* that "among diverse opinions of an Art, and most of them contrary in themselves, it is hard to make election; and therefore, though a man cannot invent new things after so many, he may do a welcome worke yet to help posterity to judge rightly of the old."[1] Confronted with the "diverse opinions of an Art," Jonson's response resembles Montaigne's view that we ought "not servily be subjected to common lawes, but rather with judgement and voluntary liberty apply ourselves unto them."[2] Taking as his motto *tanquam explorator*,[3] Jonson declares that the arduous critical task "is *Monte potiri*, to get to the hill: For no perfect Discovery can be made upon a flat or levell" (*Works*, VIII, 628). Like Donne's image of Truth on a hill in *Satyre III*, Jonson's description of this task suggests that man "about must, and about must goe," making his way critically among the variety of institutional forms. Choosing neither premature flight to absolutes nor uncritical capitulation to convention, the critic takes a stand in which intelligence confronts a periphery of circumstances and contingencies; such a critic merits Jonson's highest praise as a man who

1. Jonson, *Discoveries*, in *Works*, VIII, 617.
2. Montaigne, *Essays*, 2.8.68.
3. See Percy Simpson, " 'Tanquam Explorator': Jonson's Method in the 'Discoveries,' " *MLR*, 2 (1907), 201–210.

> like a Compasse keeping one foot still
> Upon your Center, doe your Circle fill
> Of general knowledge; watch'd men, manners too,
> Heard what times past have said, seene what ours doe.[4]

This critical encompassment of experience, like Donne's wise doubting, requires that

> wee must not goe about like men anguish'd and perplex'd for vitious affectation of praise, but calmely study the separation of opinions, find the errors have intervened, awake Antiquity, call former times into question; but make no parties with the present, nor follow any fierce undertakers, mingle no doubtful credit with the simplicity of truth, but gently stirre the mould about the root of the Question, and avoid all disgladiations, facility of credit, or superstitious simplicity; seeke the consonancy and concatenation of Truth; stoope only to point of necessity and what leads to convenience.   (VIII, 627)

Jonson posits as the aim of critical method the disengagement of "the simplicity of truth," but this aim is strikingly compromised by his final "stoope . . . to point of necessity and what leads to convenience." This compromise, or "convenience," is itself a function of the rhetorical basis on which Jonson defines the test of poetic fitness. Like Puttenham's poet or the rhetorically astute courtier, Jonson's artist "knowes it is his onely Art so to carry it, as none by Artificers perceive it" (VIII, 587). The poet is therefore not only a maker, but a "feigner" whose aim is to "make or fayne," who "fayneth and formeth a fable." Because he "writes things *like* the truth" (VIII, 635), the poet looks outward toward his audience, which is the custodian and arbiter of the values that he exploits. Since the "publicke fame . . . is the Judge,"[5] the artist's presentation of nature must appeal to social norms. To a greater extent than earlier theorists, Jonson thus concedes that the arts of discourse are "but convenient to the times and manners we live with" (VIII, 592).[6] This "convenience" accounts in large part for aesthetic corruption as well as success. "Wheresoever manners and fashions are corrupted," he observes, "Language is. It imitates the

---

4. Jonson, "Epistle to Mr. John Selden," in *Poems,* ed. George Burke Jonston (Cambridge: Harvard University Press, 1954), p. 136, ll. 31–34.

5. Jonson, "An Execration upon Vulcan," in *Poems,* p. 178, ll. 46–47.

6. See Ralph S. Walker, "Ben Jonson's *Discoveries:* A New Analysis," in *Essays and Studies,* 5 (1952), 32–51.

publicke riot. The excesse of Feasts and apparell are the notes of a sick State, and the wantonesse of language, of a sick mind" (VIII, 593). As the public face of wisdom, the arts of discourse reflect the impact of time and history upon shared values and assumptions. The extraordinary achievement of Bacon, says Jonson, was made possible because "within his view and about his times were all the wits borne that could honour a language or helpe study. Now things daily fall; wits growe downeward and *Eloquence* grows back-ward" (VIII, 591–592). This vital link between eloquence and public convention similarly underlies Jonson's plaints against "the garbage of the time"; it is "the Times have adultered [poetry's] forme."[7]

Jonson's critical stance will not allow him to concede all values to an overwhelming temporal flow. But as a result of its rhetorical link with public habit, poetic art must combine the integrity of formal control with reliance in practice upon means and materials that are conventional. "Speech," says Jonson, "is the instrument of Society," and sense, "the life and soule of Language . . . is wrought out of experience, the knowledge of human life and actions" (VIII, 621). Accordingly, "rules are ever of lesse force, and valew, then experiments" (VIII, 617). "Hee that was onely taught by himselfe, had a foole to his master" (VIII, 536); familiarity with convention, not only in the collective form of tradition, but in the current form of public mores and practices, is the key to poetic success. The model critic in this respect is not Aristotle, but *"Horace,* an author of much Civilitie; and (if any one among the heathen can be) the best master of both vertue, and wisedome; an excellent, and true judge upon cause, and reason; not because he thought so; but because he knew so, out of use and experience" (VIII, 642).

In translating the *Ars Poetica,* Jonson finds ample support for his claim; Jonson's Horace links poetic art with its audience through the mimesis of public convention:

> Hear, what it is the People, and I desire:
> If such a one's applause thou dost require,
> That tarries till the hangings be ta'en down,
> And sits, till th' *Epilogue* says *Clap* or *Crown:*
> The customs of each age thou must observe.[8]

7. Jonson, Dedicatory Epistle to *Volpone,* in J. E. Spingarn, *Critical Essays of the Seventeenth Century* (1908; rpt., Bloomington: Indiana University Press, 1968), I, 14–15. See also the attacks on current practice in *Discoveries,* in *Works,* VIII, 593–597, and in "Execration upon Vulcan," ll. 29–41, 65–82.

8. Jonson, *Horace His Art of Poetry,* in *Ben Jonson's Literary Criticism,* ed. James D. Redwine (Lincoln: University of Nebraska Press, 1970), ll. 219–223.

The critical relationship between applause, which measures poetic success, and the element of social familiarity, which insures verisimilitude, testifies to the importance of convention in poetic art. This is especially true for Jonson, for whom the plain style and comedy are inseparably linked as representative of artistic excellence. Jonson demands "pure and neat Language . . . yet plaine and customary" (VIII, 620), in keeping with the style of Horatian *sermo,* admired for its "ability to express emotion accurately."[9] He associates this element of familiarity with the grammatical commonplace that comedy is "to be *imitatio vitae, Speculum consuetudinis, Imago veritatis;* a thing through art pleasant, and ridiculous, and accommodated to the correction of manners."[10] The plainness of such comedy is not due to its lowliness on the scale of nature, but to its traffic with familiar social convention. "The Glass of custom (which is Comedy)," says Jonson's Mr. Probee, "is so held up to me, by the Poet, as I can therein view the daily examples of men's lives, and images of Truth, in their manners, so drawn from my delight, or profit, as I may (either way) use them."[11]

In effecting a transfer of the conventions and manners of common life into the conventions of poetic art, the poet becomes "a Master in manners," and his poetry "absolute Mistresse of manners."[12] In accord with this demand, Jonson's comedy of "humours" is concerned not simply with psychological obsession but with the moral contagion of public convention.[13] "Manners, now call'd humours, feed the stage,"[14] he remarks, and later claims that it was his aim to depict "some recent humours still, or manners of men, that went along with the times."[15] Connected with the changing configuration of public opinion as well as psychological make-up, the "humour" comes to take its place as both a social and a literary convention:

---

9. Wesley Trimpi, *Ben Jonson's Poems: A Study of the Plain Style* (Stanford: Stanford University Press, 1962), p. 78.

10. Jonson, *Every Man out of His Humour,* in *Works,* III, 3.6.204–209.

11. Jonson, *Every Man out of His Humour,* Chorus, act 2. See also John Heywood: "Cicero saith a comedy is the imitation of life, the glasse of custome, and the image of Truth," *An Apologie for Actors,* in O. B. Hardison, *English Literary Criticism: The Renaissance,* p. 225.

12. Jonson, Dedicatory Epistle to *Volpone,* in Spingarn, *Critical Essays,* I, 12; and *Discoveries,* in *Works,* VIII, 636.

13. See Redwine's Introduction to *Ben Jonson's Literary Criticism,* pp. xxiv–xxix, and his "Beyond Psychology: The Moral Basis of Jonson's Theory of Humour Characterization," *ELH,* 28 (1961), 316–334.

14. Jonson, Prologue to *The Alchemist,* in Redwine, p. 118.

15. Jonson, Induction to *The Magnetick Lady,* in Redwine, p. 124.

I bid the learned Maker look
On life, on manners, and make those his book,
Thence draw forth true expressions. For sometimes,
A poem, of no grace, weight, art, in rhymes
With specious places, and being humour'd right,
Most strongly takes the people with delight.[16]

As a substitute for Horatian *morataque recte,* the "humour" serves as the literary counterpart to the familiar elements of "life" and "manners" (*vitae morumque*), which should be reflected in poetic art. As such, it shows, as Acron had put it, "to what extent is important the consideration of customs."

As the reflection of social convention, the art of poetry is therefore bound to abide by convention's dictates: "Custome is the most certaine Mistresse of Language, as the publicke stampe makes the current money . . . the eldest of the present and the newest of the past language, is the best. For what was the ancient Language, which some men so doate upon, but the auncient Custome?" (VIII, 622). Bearing not only upon the linguistic material of poetic art, convention limits its formal possibilities as well. There are some figures "which will become our Language, that will by no means admit another . . . Therefore wee must consider in every tongue what is us'd, what receiv'd" (VIII, 624). Though all poetic innovations "are dangerous, and somewhat hard, before they are softened with use . . . things at first hard and rough are by use made tender and gentle" (VIII, 622). The power of usage to endow artistic speech with artless familiarity extends even to the level of formal composition, where there "is attain'd by Custome more than by care or diligence" (VIII, 623). By the same token, failure to abide by current practice results in ineffectual obtrusiveness: "Spenser, in affecting the Antients, writ no language" (VIII, 618). "Done himself, for not being understood, would perish."[17] Drummond's verses "smelled too much of the Schooles, and were not after the fancie of the tyme."[18]

Although Jonson firmly refuses to endorse any particular "fancie of the tyme,"[19] his concession to the hold of public expectations on poetic

16. Jonson, *Horace: His Art of Poetry,* ll. 453–458.

17. Jonson, *Conversations with William Drummond of Hawthornden,* ed. R. F. Patterson (London: Blackie and Son, 1923), p. 18.

18. Jonson, *Conversations,* pp. 10–11; see Ralph S. Walker, "Literary Criticism in Jonson's Conversations with Drummond," *English,* 8 (1951), 222–227, and esp. 224.

19. Implicit in Jonson's concessions to convention is thus the assumption that nothing is conceded uncritically: "when I name Custome, I understand not the

art leads him to question the value of any strictly prescriptive approach. In defending his failure to follow strictly ancient norms in his *Sejanus,* Jonson remarks that it is not "needful, or almost impossible, in these our Times, and to such Auditors as commonly Things are presented, to observe the ould state and splendour of *Drammatick Poems,* with preservation of any popular delight. But of this I shall take more seasonable cause to speake in my Observations upon *Horace* his *Art of Poetry,* which, with the Text translated, I intend shortly to publish."[20] By linking the poetic end of "popular delight" with the "Auditors" of "these our Times," and by referring this link to its most "seasonable" source, Jonson declares the independence of contemporary practice from ancient norms. Paradoxically, the element of rhetorical constraint introduces to poetic art an element of liberation. "I am not of that opinion," he declares, "to conclude a *Poets* liberty within the narrowe limits of lawes, which either the *Grammarians,* or *Philosophers* prescribe" (VIII, 641).

As in the case of the sixteenth-century moral and political arts, this movement away from a center of "philosophic" integrity and toward a periphery of practical contingencies entails a corresponding shift toward historical and comparative procedures. "Nothing can conduce more to letters," Jonson therefore maintains,

> then to examine the writings of the *Ancients,* and not to rest in their sole Authority, or to take all in trust upon them . . . For to all the observations of the Ancients, wee have oure owne experience: which, if wee will use, and apply, wee have better meanes to pronounce. It is true they open'd the gates, and made the way, that went before us; but as Guides, not Commenders . . . Truth lyes open to all; it is no man's severall . . . If I erre, pardon me: *Nulla ars simul & inventa est, & absoluta.* I doe not desire to be equall to those that went before; but to have my reason examin'd with theirs, and so much faith be given them, or me, as those shall evict. (VIII, 567)

Based upon appeal to "oure owne experience," Jonson's position assumes the superiority of neither ancient precedent nor contemporary

---

vulgar custome: For that were a precept no lesse dangerous to Language then life, if wee should speake or live after the manners of the vulgar," *Discoveries,* in *Works,* VIII, 622.

20. Jonson, Preface to *Sejanus,* in Spingarn, *Literary Criticism,* I, 10.

practice. Since "truth lyes open to all," it is subject to further evaluation in the light of subsequent experience. "Nothing is more ridiculous," he says,

> then to make an Author a *Dictator,* as the schools have done
> *Aristotle.* The dammage is infinite, knowledge receives by it.
> For to many things a man should owe but a temporary be-
> liefe, and a suspension of his owne Judgement, not an abso-
> lute resignation of himselfe, or a perpetuall captivity. Let
> *Aristotle,* and others have their dues; but if wee can make
> farther Discoveries of truth and fitnesse than they, why are
> we envied?   (VIII, 627)

In his hope for "farther Discoveries of truth and fitnesse," Jonson
does not oppose the achievement of antiquity with a hubristic belief in
the inevitability of progress; rather, he challenges the complacency of
stasis with the inevitability of change. The critical temper that pervades his work arises from his conception of the conventionality of
norms attendant on the changing shapes of civilizations. In keeping
with this conception, he removes poetic art from its traditional place
among the logical sciences, and deposits it together with eloquence
among the practical arts, which look outward and retrospectively toward the variety of social circumstance and contingency. The poet
"must have *Civil prudence,* and *Eloquence,* & that whole . . . furnish'd out of the body of the State, which commonly is the Schoole of
men" (VIII, 640). A prudent critic as well as artist, the poet must fashion his work in the fires of experience, and "bring all to the forge,
and file, againe; tourne it a newe" (VIII, 637–638).

Jonson's contemporaries were quick to recognize his critical pragmatism. As if in recognition of Jonson's awareness of the link between
artistic practice and the power of convention, John Selden praised
Jonson's "new pronouncements on old customs."[21] Thomas Cartwright
even more emphatically remarked that *"thou* taughtst *Custome,* and
not *Custome* thee."[22]

Jonson's critical stance is thus a comprehensive example of the
power of convention to supplement and even to supplant technical
prescription with a comparative and historical assessment of norms in
relation to their temporal and social setting. In the later sixteenth

21. John Selden, commendatory verses to the 1616 edition of the *Works,* quoted
in Trimpi, p. 77.
22. Thomas Cartwright, *The Plays and Poems,* ed. G. Blakemore Evans (Madison:
University of Wisconsin Press, 1951), p. 512, l. 24.

century, this stance was adopted with increasing frequency in response to the practical debates and controversies that were undermining the technical order. The participants in such debates, as Baxter Hathaway has remarked, were ultimately concerned with "the principles by means of which poems and other works of literature as fine art are composed and acquire value . . . if they had turned to a slavish imitation of the surfaces of the literary forms of antiquity without asking what could be modified to suit new times and customs, the impetus to general theory would have been less."[23] Though less riotous than in Italy, the critical controversies of the later Renaissance in England were no less concerned with normative principle at the highest level. In the matter of poetic diction, for example, the apparent conflict between nature and convention had already led theorists away from the "inwarde" seats of arguments, and toward the "outwarde" places of time and circumstance from which the issues seemed to arise. This was the case as well in conflicts over form and genre, and especially in those concerned with such "mixed" genres as romance and tragicomedy, for which there was little precedent in antiquity and little warrant in the abstract scale of nature upon which such precedents supposedly were based. Such controversies tended to enhance the theoretical significance of convention through the application of comparative and historical techniques to practical interests.

The romance-epic, for example, was a distinctively Renaissance invention, but its precursor, the medieval metrical romance, had been the object of critical scorn in England throughout the later sixteenth century as an instance of "the uncomely customes of common writers."[24] The native romance was treated as an outmoded and inartistic kind that was to be rectified and superseded by the purer forms encompassed by a rational poetics. When John Harington undertook to defend Ariosto's *Orlando Furioso* in England, he therefore set against the rigidity of abstract norms the accommodating power of convention. His principal source was Giraldi Cinthio, who had defended Ariosto in Italy by appealing to the courtly ideal of artless art, arguing in his *Discorsi* that "the writer ought to strive with the utmost effort, not so that the hard work on the composition will be visible, but so that the work will appear to be done naturally."[25] The key to such artistic

23. Baxter Hathaway, *Marvels and Commonplaces: Renaissance Literary Criticism* (New York: Random House, 1968), pp. 33–36.

24. Gascoigne, *Certayne Notes of Instruction,* in G. Gregory Smith, I, 47; see, e.g., the objections of Thomas Nashe, in G. Gregory Smith, I, 323; and Joseph Hall, "A Defiance to Envy," and 1.2 in *Virgidemarium.*

25. Giraldi Cinthio, *On Romances,* trans. Henry L. Snuggs (Lexington: University of Kentucky Press, 1968), p. 120.

illusion is verisimilitude, which depends upon "not only that which happens probably," but also that which has "been accepted by usage" (p. 49).

This second standard assumes a hidden link between the norms that govern poetic production and the setting in which they are produced. Accordingly, the grounds of artistic fitness on which Cinthio defends the romance are not its unmediated conformity with universal and unchanging natural principles, but its satisfaction of contemporary public demand. This second criterion introduces an element of relativity to poetic theory, and suggests that

> many things which in one time could appear censurable become laudable in another, through usage and authority given to them by whoever was able to do so. Many others which in early times appeared laudable came to be, through change of times, of customs, of human nature . . . either not well thought of or censurable . . . it is better to follow the usage of the time made reputable by worthy writers than to follow in the steps of those who wrote when such usage had not been introduced. Usage that the age and the time brings to us is of the greatest importance in all actions of the world. (pp. 43–44)

While Harington's defense of romance depends in part upon his neo-Aristotelian view that Ariosto observes such established and universal norms as unity of time, probability, and *peripeteia,* it relies substantially as well on Cinthio's theoretical linking of artistic norms with the changing shape of civilization:

> But now whereas some will say *Ariosto* wanteth art, reducing all heroicall Poems unto the methode of *Homer* and certain precepts of *Aristotle,* for Homer I say that that which was commendable in him to write in that age, the times being changed, would be thought otherwise now, as we see both in phrase & in fashions the world growes more curious each day then other. *Ovid* gave precepts of making love, and one was that one should spill wine on the boord & write his mistresse name therewith. This was a quaynt cast in that age; but he that should make love so now, his love would mocke him for his labour, and count him but a slovenly sutor. And if it be thus changed since *Ovids* time, much more since *Homers* time.[26]

26. John Harington, *A Briefe Apologie of Poetry,* in G. Gregory Smith, II, 215–216.

Because it could establish a relationship between shifting public values or beliefs and the changing shape of literary kinds, this mode of argument was brought to the defense of tragicomedy as well. Like opposition to the romance, the theoretical resistance to tragicomedy was based upon the premise that it violated natural fitness. "Mingling Kings and clownes . . . with neither decency nor discretion," tragicomedy was "neither right tragedy, nor right comedy." Both the lack of literary precedent and the very order of nature itself were evidence that in the hierarchy of literary kinds and their various *decora,* there was no place for this "mongrel" form.

John Lyly, however, defended the admitted impurity of such popular drama by appealing to the protean character of convention. "So nice is this world," he declares, "that for apparell there is no fashion, for musique no instrument, for diet no delicate, for playes no invention, but breedeth satiety before noone, and contempt before night."[27] The most extensive application of this argument to tragicomedy is Battista Guarini's *Il Verrato* (1588), in which Guarini argues that "all . . . variation in tragedy as in comedy arises from the public . . . And truly if public performances are made for the listeners, it is necessary that poems go on being changed according to the variations in manners and in times."[28] The audience acts as custodian of poetic fitness. Appealing to the theory of artless art, Guarini maintains that verisimilitude is not founded upon what is naturally probable, but "rather on what is *'persuabile,'* that which the audience will accept as likely to happen."[29] Though less systematically and more whimsically than Guarini, Lyly similarly justified the mixed elements of popular drama by appealing not to absolute standards, but to the origins of form in the distinctive setting of English society. This setting is the site of intersecting cultural contexts:

> Traffique and travel hath woven the nature of all nations
> into ours; and made this land like arras, full of devise;
> which was broad-cloth, full of workmanship. Time hath

27. John Lyly, Prologue to *Mydas,* in *Dramatic Works,* ed. F. W. Fairhold (London: John Russell Smith, 1858), II, 3. See the similar arguments of Lope de Vega in *The New Art of Writing Plays in This Age,* in Barret Clark, *European Theories of the Drama* (Cincinnati: Stewart and Kidd, 1918), pp. 89–90; and the comments of Tirso de Molina in his preface to *The Orchards of Toledo,* in Clark, pp. 94–95.

28. Battista Guarini, *Il Verrato* (1588), quoted in Weinberg, II, 660; see also Gilbert, *Literary Criticism,* p. 512; and Eugene M. Waith, *The Pattern of Tragicomedy in Beaumont and Fletcher* (New Haven: Yale University Press, 1952), pp. 46–50.

29. Weinberg, II, 683.

confounded our mindes, our minds the matter; but all commeth to this passe, that what heretofore hath beene served in severall dishes for a feast, is now minced in a charger for a gallimaufery. If we present a mingle-mangle, our fault is to be excused, because the whole world is become an hodge-podge.[30]

Thus, as the social instrument through which the power of time "hath confounded our mindes, our minds the matter," the concept of convention gained through controversy increasing prominence as both a theoretical principle and a methodological instrument. Appropriately, the implications of this prominence received their fullest exploration in the final phases of the controversy out of which they arose— the controversy over quantitative verse. The persistence of this controversy, despite its apparently limited importance in poetic practice, suggests that its concerns were at bottom theoretical rather than practical, involving in the abstract the relationship of changing conventions to the presumably stable and natural proportions to which art lays claim. While the resistance of customary speech to the "natural" harmonies of quantitative verse had led the contenders on all sides toward such "outwarde" places as time, place, circumstance, and precedent, there had been no comprehensive attempt to relate such factors in theory to the more universal and transcendent properties that seemed to inhere in harmony and proportion. In his *Defense of Rhyme* (1603), Samuel Daniel explores both the theoretical basis and the methodological implications of the concept of convention, using history as an instrument to trace the origins of convention to the power of nature itself.

Daniel's theoretical thrust was in part demanded by the position of his opponent, Thomas Campion, who in *Observations in the Art of English Poesie* insisted that "the world is made by Simmetry and proportion," and that the musical proportions of quantitative verse are "those numbers which Nature . . . destinates."[31] By contrast, "the vulgar and unartificiall custome of riming . . . is lame and unbeseeming" (pp. 327, 330). "For custome I alleage that ill uses are to be abolisht, and that things naturally unperfect can not be perfected by use." Any challenge to quantitative verse, Campion implies, would be a challenge to the "Simmetry and proportion" of nature itself.

---

30. Lyly, Prologue to *Mydas,* in *Dramatic Works,* II, 3–4.

31. Thomas Campion, *Observations in the Art of English Poesie,* in G. Gregory Smith, II, 329, 338. Subsequent references to this work in the text are given by page number only.

Although in other controversies the concept of convention had been used to emphasize the discontinuity of poetic norms, Daniel uses it in relation to the continuity of nature itself. "The Generall Custome and use of Rhyme in this Kingdome . . . having beene so long (as if from a Graunt of Nature) held unquestionable, made me to imagine that it lay altogether out of the way of contradiction, and was become . . . naturall."[32] In one respect, Daniel's does not differ significantly from earlier theories of convention, for it emphasizes the contribution of habit to the illusion of artlessness. "Custome . . . is before all Lawe, Nature . . . is above every Art" (p. 359). The affinity of custom to nature lies in the difference between inarticulate habituation and meddlesome impositions. "Such affliction doth laboursome curiositie still lay upon our best delights," Daniel complains, "as if Art were ordained to afflict Nature, and that we could not goe but in fetters. Every science, every profession, must be so wrapt up in unnecessary intrications, as if it were not to fashion but to confound the understanding: which makes me much to distrust man" (p. 365). By contrast with such "unnecessary intrications," custom silently and unobtrusively creates the norms that guide expression. "Every language hath her proper number or measure fitted to use and delight, which Custome, intertaininge by allowance of the Eare, doth indenize and make naturall" (p. 359).

In contrast with the discontinuity emphasized in controversies that exploited the concept of convention for its relationship to changing situations, Daniel grounds the phenomenon of change firmly in the sphere of nature. In effect, he attempts a synthesis of what had earlier been alternative views of poetic art, relating the variety of convention to the universal and unchanging dictates of nature. There is, he says, "but one learning, which *omnes gentes habent scriptum in cordibus suis,* one and the selfesame spirit that worketh in all. We have but one bodie of Justice, one bodie of Wisedome thorowout the whole world; which is but apparelled according to the fashion of every nation" (p. 372).

On the strength of this assertion René Wellek has claimed that in his view of norms Daniel is fundamentally unhistorical, that "his main argument is not historical at all, but rather an appeal to the eternal law of nature. 'Custom and Nature: both defend rhyme' . . . because men are everywhere and all the time the same."[33] In fact, however, the

---

32. Samuel Daniel, *A Defense of Rhyme,* in G. Gregory Smith, II, 357. Subsequent references to this work in the text are given by page number only.

33. Wellek, *The Rise of English Literary History,* pp. 10–11.

view of natural law that had been attached to custom in England had diverged distinctively, as noted previously, from the earlier view of a universal and rational law binding on all men in all respects. Through the testimony of accumulated wisdom and repeated acts, the individual and corporate powers of accommodation expressed in legal conventions approach the stability of nature itself. Considered as responses to the changing demands of experience, these customary norms define not uniform, but plural, means of fulfilling natural ends. The diversity of such norms does not mean that they are unnatural, but that they have achieved a degree of specification that enables them to satisfy generic norms of nature with due regard for the unique configurations of experience. Invoking the legal phrase of "time out of minde," in defense of the "plaine ancient verse" (p. 376), Daniel colors the powers of adjustment and change with this deep and solid sense of continuity:

> "Ill customes are to be left." I graunt it; but I see not howe that can be taken for an ill custome which nature hath thus ratified, all nations received, time so long confirmed . . . I doubt whether ever single numbers will doe in our Climate, if they shew no more worke of wonder than yet we see. And if ever they proove to become anything, it must be by the approbation of many ages that must give them their strength for any operation, as before the world will feele where the pulse, life, and energy lies.   (p. 362)

Endowing convention with the life of nature itself, Daniel not only sanctions normative diversity, but attaches to it a dignity in keeping with man's highest aspirations. It is, he claims, "a touch of arrogant ignorance to hold this or that nation Barbarous, these or those times grosse, considering how this manifold creature man, wheresoever hee stand in the world, hath alwayes some disposition of worth, intertaines the order of society, affects that which is most in use, and is eminent in some one thing or another that fits his humour and the times" (p. 367). This claim affirms the independence of nations and times: "all our understandings are not to be built by the square of *Greece* and *Italie*. We are the children of nature as well as they . . . Time and the turne of things bring about these faculties according to the present estimation: and *Res temporibus non tempora rebus servire oportet*. So that we must never rebell against use" (p. 367). At the same time, and perhaps more important, the element of human dignity implicit in all conventional forms establishes the need for an alternative to the normative approach in literary study. As Daniel's own appreciation of the

Middle Ages indicates, there lies beneath every convention, no matter how deeply buried by time, an expression of the dignity that binds all men. There is need to understand such expression as it is "disposed into diverse fashions, according to the humour of the Composer and the set of time" (p. 359), by looking tolerantly and retrospectively to its origin in "the set of time" itself.

IV. Contextualism and the Role of Convention in Historiography

1. HISTORICAL RHETORIC AND HISTORICAL EXPLANATION

In turning to the "set of time" in order to explain the diversity of norms and practices characteristic of different civilizations and epochs, Samuel Daniel was responding to the needs and character of a changing intellectual framework. In contrast with the uniformity of natural fitness over time, the concept of convention was in principle bound up with time and changing circumstance. That is why the ancient intellectual conflict between the principles of nature and convention was frequently expressed as a conflict between philosophy and history as alternative accounts of man. According to the philosophers, history neglected the relationship of human acts and institutions to abiding principles, and subjected them instead to chance and change, thus threatening to discredit ideals of permanent worth and rectitude. So long as history merely evidenced the inability of man to recognize and fulfill his natural ends, it could not serve the aims of philosophy.

The sophists and skeptics of antiquity, by contrast, had used the evidence of history to support their contention that convention ruled the life of man. In the Renaissance, however, the concept of convention gained its currency not as an antagonist to the philosophic tradition, but as a part of the moral and political branches of that tradition. Taking root in the iterative and habitual element of virtue emphasized by the humanists, the concept imparted an increasingly conventional coloring to the virtues themselves. Because of the practical importance of habit, Renaissance thought about the character of rectitude was confronted with the task of reconciling different particular habits—moral, political, and artistic—with the highest nature and destiny of man. Such efforts to establish continuity between unchanging

203

natural ends and the diversity of actual practices could only succeed by presupposing that the rational connections between ends and means had been submerged by time.

As a result, the philosophic, and primarily normative, quest for rectitude spawned a complementary retrospective study of the relationship of habitual practices to rectitude in time. The Renaissance contribution to historical thinking was thus a corollary of its thought about convention. This contribution has, until quite recently, been slighted.[1] In fact, however, by reflecting on convention the Renaissance historians changed the character of historical thinking and in many cases laid the foundations for modern historical thought.[2]

One of the developments generally thought to characterize modern historical consciousness is the belief that the events of history are the product and reflection of a particular configuration of issues and values in a particular historical setting. With this belief arises the need for the historian to consider the total context of this setting. A. O. Lovejoy has described this need in remarking that

> to study history is to seek in some degree to get beyond the limitations and preoccupations of the present: it demands for success an effort at self-transcendence. It is not impossible nor unprofitable for a rational animal—and it is imperative for the historian—to realize that his ancestors had ends of their own which were not solely instrumental to his ends, that the context and meaning of their existence are not exhaustively resolvable into those of the existence of their posterity.[3]

This belief in the past-ness of the past, and with it the effort to interpret the past in its own terms, has until recently been attributed to historical achievements in France in the later eighteenth century and in

1. See, e.g., James W. Thompson, *A History of Historical Writing* (New York: Macmillan, 1942), I, 626.

2. Two works especially concerned with this contribution are F. Smith Fussner, *The Historical Revolution: English Historical Thought, 1580–1640* (London: Routledge and Kegan Paul, 1962); and J. G. A. Pocock, *The Ancient Constitution and the Feudal Law: A Study of English Thought in the Seventeenth Century* (New York: Cambridge University Press, 1957), hereafter cited as *Ancient Constitution.*

3. A. O. Lovejoy, "Present Standpoints and Past History," in *The Philosophy of History in Our Time,* ed. Hans Meyerhoff (New York: Anchor Books, 1959), p. 180; see also William H. Dray, *The Philosophy of History* (Englewood Cliffs: Prentice-Hall, 1971), p. 30.

Germany in the early nineteenth.[4] In fact, however, these post-Enlightenment developments were anticipated by a general but widespread recognition in the later Renaissance of the importance of historical context. This recognition was part of the increasingly prominent view that norms of rectitude were conventional, and that man was both a creature and creator of customs, of social, political, and artistic institutions that in part determined and directed his actions. By relating particular norms and practices to their setting in a particular configuration of circumstances and contingencies, historical thinking provided a means of reconciling the diversity of conventions with the first cause of nature. While intended to serve the interests of an older philosophic view of man, however, this type of thinking resulted in a skepticism that might be characterized as a distinctively "historical" frame of mind—a frame of mind that capitulated to the integrity of historic process, and whose judgments were increasingly relative and contextual.

Although this kind of thought eventually challenged the validity of more philosophic and normative thinking, it began with the subordination of history to philosophy. The chief instrument of this subordination was the rhetorical tradition, which, as noted earlier, had always kept an eye on history for its illustrative value in discourse whose purposes were primarily nonhistorical.[5] Observing that history was the form of discourse "closer than any other to oratory" (*De Legibus,* 1.2.5), Cicero had urged the orator to "be acquainted with the events of past ages" because "the mention of antiquity and the citation of examples give the speech authority and credibility" (*Orator,* 34.120). Similarly, Quintilian had declared that history provides "a knowledge of historical facts and precedents, with which it is most desirable that our orator should be acquainted" (10.2.9). As a form of testimony, history was, in Cicero's often-repeated phrases: "vero testis temporum, lux veritatis, vita memoriae, magistram vitae, nuntia vestustatis" (*De Oratore,* 2.9.36).

Not only was this exemplary value of history reasserted by the Renaissance rhetoricians, but it was formally incorporated as a type of testimony among the logical places. In keeping with its ancillary role, history was frequently classified with poetics and rhetoric under the

4. See R. G. Collingwood, *The Idea of History* (1946; rpt., London: Oxford University Press, 1971); Henry Elmer Barnes, *A History of Historical Writing* (1937; rpt., New York: Dover Books, 1962); J. B. Bury, *The Idea of Progress: An Inquiry into Its Origin and Growth* (London: Macmillan, 1920); and Duncan Forbes, "Historismus in England," *Cambridge Journal,* 4 (1951).

5. See George H. Nadel, "Philosophy of History before Historicism," *History and Theory,* 3 (1964), 291–315.

general heading of logical science.[6] This classification was meant not only to reflect the use of *verba*, which history shared with other verbal arts, but also to demonstrate its subservience to logical and immutable propositions. Thus one Renaissance writer observes that "history teaches us the doctrine of philosophy."[7] Subordinate to the interests of principles themselves, history merely provides, as another puts it, "the concrete examples of the principles inculcated by philosophy."[8]

Distinguished from philosophic discourse in the manner rather than the content of its teaching, history therefore shared the normative framework and language of philosophy itself. "History," says Caxton, is the "moder of alle philosophye moevynge our maners to vertue."[9] Because man's unchanging duty was "much better shown by examples than by the precepts of a philosopher,"[10] it became the task of history "to note," as Sidney says, "the examples of vertue or vice."[11] This task was the basis for exemplary history from Petrarch's *De Viris Illustribus* and Boccaccio's *De Casibus Virorum Illustrium* to Lydgate's *Falls of Princes* and the *Mirror for Magistrates*. As a species of rhetorical *exemplum*, history, says Richard Braithwaite in *The Scholler's Medley*, was written as a form of portraiture in which "vertue never wants her character, nor vice her reproof."[12] Appealing not so much to the ran-

---

6. See Bernard Weinberg, *A History of Literary Criticism in the Italian Renaissance* (Chicago: University of Chicago Press, 1961), I, 8–11; and F. J. Levy, *Tudor Historical Thought* (San Marino, Calif.: Huntington Library, 1967), p. 242.

7. Coluccio Salutati, quoted in Myron P. Gilmore, "The Renaissance Conception of the Lessons of History," in *Facets of the Renaissance*, ed. William W. Werkmeister (1959; rpt., New York: Harper Torchbooks, 1963), p. 86.

8. Paolo Vergerio, quoted in Gilmore, p. 86.

9. William Caxton, Prologue to *Polychronicon*, in *Prologues and Epilogues*, ed. W. J. B. Crotch (London: Early English Texts Society, 1928), p. 65.

10. Daniel Heinsius, *The Value of History*, trans. George W. Robinson (Cambridge, Mass., 1943), p. 12.

11. Letter to Robert Sidney, 18 Oct. 1580, in *The Prose Works*, ed. Albert Feuillerat (1912; rpt., Cambridge: Cambridge University Press, 1963), III, 130; see also F. J. Levy, "Sir Philip Sidney and the Renaissance Idea of History," *Bibliothèque d'Humanisme et Renaissance*, 26 (1964), 608–617.

12. Richard Braithwaite, *The Scholler's Medley, or an Intermixt Discourse upon Historical and Poeticall Relations* (London, 1614), p. 7. See also Lily B. Campell, *Tudor Conceptions of History and Tragedy in "A Mirror for Magistrates"* (Berkeley: University of California Press, 1936); Willard Farnham, *The Medieval Heritage of Elizabethan Tragedy* (San Marino, Calif.: Huntington Library, 1936), chs. 1–4; Irving Ribner, *The English History Play in the Age of Shakespeare* (Princeton: Princeton University Press, 1957), ch. 1. For the relationships between history and the use of rhetorical *exempla* in the creation of literary-historical portraits, see Peter E. Bondanella, *Machiavelli and the Art of Renaissance History* (Detroit: Wayne State University Press, 1973), ch. 1; and David Riggs, *Shakespeare's Heroical*

dom particularity as to the recurrent patterns of experience, the historian acted "as a register to set downe the judgements and definitive sentences of God's court."[13]

Because it strongly emphasized the importance of moral pattern, and sought such patterns almost exclusively in biographical subject matter, exemplary history attached minimal significance to the historical setting in which men lived. Thus Braithwaite, for example, observes that the historian best performs his task by "approving of what is good, or may in it selfe be beneficiall to the State: and sleightly observing discourses of indifferency, as accomplements, ceremonies, circumstances and the like, resembling faire frontespieces which are made rather for ornament than use" (p. 8). With a similar emphasis upon moral utility, John Hales divides the historian's art according to the three types of "matter and things collected": the *epitome,* or "order of story"; *miscellenea,* or the recounting of such things as ceremony and "custom"; and *moralia,* or the exposition of a coherent moral pattern. Emphasizing the first and third of these aspects of the art by insisting on the relation between moral pattern and narrative coherence, Hales considers least important the accumulation of *miscellenea,* which are pleasant but "merely critical and scholastical."[14] In apparent violation of the function of exemplary history, the antiquarians were frequently attacked for their interest in and accumulation of seemingly irrelevant cultural information.[15]

While subordinate to philosophy, however, history became an increasingly prominent part of the humanists' pragmatic program of education. As an antidote to cloistered wisdom, Erasmus included in his educational ideal the reading of history, from which "the practical wisdom so essential to a man taking his part in public affairs will most surely be attained."[16] As a vicarious form of experience, Vives similarly observes, history enables man to use the experiences of others "as well as that of our own times."[17] "There is no doctrine, be it either divine

---

Histories: "Henry VI" and its Literary Tradition (Cambridge: Harvard University Press, 1971).

13. "Amiot to the Reader," in *Lives of the Noble Grecians and Romanes,* trans. Thomas North, ed. G. Wyndham (London: Tudor Translations, 1895), I, 15.

14. Quoted in John J. Murray, "John Hales on History," *HLQ,* 19 (1956), 237.

15. See Louis B. Wright, *Middle-Class Culture in Elizabethan England* (Chapel Hill: University of North Carolina Press, 1935), pp. 312–314.

16. *Desiderius Erasmus concerning the Aim and Method of Education,* trans. Craig R. Thompson (1904; rpt., New York: Columbia University Press, 1964), p. 129.

17. Juan Luis Vives, *On Education (De Tradendis Disciplinis),* trans. Foster Watson (1913; rpt., Totowa, N.J.: Rowman and Littlefield, 1971), p. 230.

or human," Thomas Elyot claims, "that is not either all expressed in history or at least mixed with history . . . so large is the compass of that which is named history, that it comprehendeth all thing that is necessary to put in memory."[18]

Just as the role of experience in the formation of habit had often led humanist moral philosophy away from a center of contemplative moral integrity and toward a variety of contingencies, so the exemplary value of vicarious experience transformed the character of history itself from an ancilla of philosophic norms to a repository of the norms themselves. In contrast to the uniformity of nature, the variety of experience encompassed by history suggested that "there is more certainty in the principles of practice, than in the most necessary demonstrations, or clearest discourses of reason."[19] As one of the moving forces behind this consensus, Guicciardini declares on the basis of historical evidence that "it is a great error to speak of the things of this world absolutely and indiscriminately, and to deal with them, as it were, by the book. In nearly all things one must make distinctions and exceptions because of differences in their circumstances. These circumstances are not covered by one and the same rule."[20] Similarly insisting on the importance of practical experience, Bacon remarks that "we are much beholden to Machiavel and others, that write what men do, and not what they ought to do." The contemplative ideal remains attractive, "but men must know," says Bacon, "that in this theater of man's life it is reserved only for God and the Angels to be lookers on."[21] Pierre Charron similarly argues that as a necessary substitute for *sapientia* in the life of action, *prudentia* best comprehends "the expressible Variety of Accidents, Circumstances, Appurtenances, Dependencies and Consequences; the Difference of Times, and Places and Persons."[22]

In transferring the source of wisdom from contemplative universals to the changing shapes of experience, the humanist ideal of *prudentia* thus greatly enhanced the standing of history as a distinctive art.

18. Thomas Elyot, *The Boke Named the Governour*, ed. S. E. Lehmberg (New York: Everyman's Library, 1907), pp. 228–229.

19. Robert Johnson, *Essaies, or Rather Imperfect Offers*, ed. Robert Hood Bowers (Gainesville, Fla.: Scholar's Facsimiles, 1955), sig. C7v; see also Eugene F. Rice, *The Renaissance Idea of Wisdom* (Cambridge: Harvard University Press, 1958), p. 177.

20. Francesco Guicciardini, *Maxims and Reflections (Ricordi)*, trans. Mario Domandi (1965; rpt., Philadelphia: University of Pennsylvania Press, 1972), C.6; cf. C.10, 12; B.70–71.

21. Bacon, *The Advancement of Learning*, bk. 2 in *Works*, III, 240–241.

22. Pierre Charron, *Of Wisdom*, trans. George Stanhope (London, 1729), 3.1.4.

"Historical Prudence," as Charron calls it, began to move away from subservience to more philosophic modes of normative discourse and toward a position from which it might, indeed, be said to rival them. Not philosophy, but "experience," says Charron, "is my Father, and Memory my Mother; or rather History, which is the Life and Soul of Memory."[23]

The product of this movement was the often subtle transformation of exemplary history into "politic" history, whose function was still the provision of examples, but examples that were no longer understood as practical demonstrations of philosophic norms and precepts; instead, they were themselves treated as the source of precepts. Specific rather than general in its conclusions, "politic" history increasingly removed normative discourse from the influence of the abiding natural principles inculcated by moral philosophy. In keeping with this transformation, the formerly "logical" art of history was frequently reclassified among the practical arts of statecraft. Taking as its "principle and proper work" the instructing of men "by the knowledge of actions past, to bear themselves prudently in the present and providently towards the future,"[24] history increasingly replaced the language of wisdom and virtue with the language of prudence and success, and the abiding integrity of natural norms with a variety of particular choices. In transferring normative discourse from a theoretical to a historical setting, the art of history suggested that the proper study of man was not the contemplation of his ends, but the scrutiny of his beginnings.

This shift in normative perspective was accompanied by major changes in the speculative and critical philosophies of history. Among the most important of the latter was a growing insistence that the historian's obligation extends beyond the mere recounting of events to the discovery of their causes. Even one of the authors of *A Mirror for Magistrates*, a prime instance of the older "exemplary" historiography, has John Typtoft complain that

> Unfruytfull Fabyan folowed the face
> Of time and dedes, but let the causes slip . . .
> Thus story writers leave the causes out,
> Or so rehears them, as they wer in doubt.

23. Charron, *Of Wisdom*, 3.1.5; see also Erwin Panofsky, "Titian's Allegory of Prudence," in *Meaning in the Visual Arts* (New York: Anchor Books, 1959), pp. 146–148.

24. Thomas Hobbes, Preface to *Thucydides*, ed. Richard Schlatter (New Brunswick: Rutgers University Press, 1974), p. 6. See Leo Strauss, *The Political Philosophy of Thomas Hobbes: Its Basis and Its Genesis*, trans. Elsa M. Sinclair (Chicago: University of Chicago Press, 1952), p. 82 ff.

> But . . . causes are the chiefest thinges
> That should be noted of the story wryters,
> That men may learne what endes and causes bringes.[25]

Similarly, Ascham remarks that the historian must "mark diligently the causes . . . and issues in all great attempts."[26] And Edmund Bolton later declares that since "the Causes of things . . . are wonderfully wrapt one within the other, he who relates Events without their Premisses and Circumstances deserves not the name of an historian."[27]

This need for explanation stemmed from a sense of disparity between human will and human achievement, an awareness that "what happens in history need not happen through anyone's deliberately wishing it to happen."[28] Christian thought had always insisted on this disparity by explaining historical events in terms of various providential schemes. Such modes of explanation were secularized, however, as the art of "politic" history, under the influence of a nascent pragmatism, ceased to function as the illustration of eternal principles and began to function as the source of practical guidance. The chief instrument of this secularization was a distinction between divine providence and temporal fortune.[29] Like providence, secular fortune caused disparity between intention and result in history. "So inconstant are the prosperities of fortune," Guicciardini declares, that "the doings of men are subject to alteration and chaunge."[30] Instead of forcing man into a position of acquiescence, however, the power of fortune presented him with a challenge. Unlike the power of providence, fortune or chance was itself limited by the laws of contingency. As such, it was a power with which the human mind could contend, for in scrutiny of the circumstances that thwart or aid human ambition there lies a "narrow opportunity for using prudence to advantage."[31] On the basis of this

---

25. *The Mirror for Magistrates,* ed. Lily B. Campbell (Cambridge: Harvard University Press, 1938), p. 197, ll. 22–35.

26. Roger Ascham, *A Report and Discourse of the Affairs and State of Germany,* in *Works,* ed. J. A. Giles (1864; rpt., New York: AMS Press, 1965), III, 6. See Walter F. Staton, "Roger Ascham's Theory of History Writing," *SP,* 56 (1959), 125–137.

27. Edmund Bolton, *Hypercritica: or A Rule of Judgement, for writing and reading our History's,* in J. E. Spingarn, *Critical Essays of the Seventeenth Century* (1908; rpt., Bloomington: Indiana University Press, 1957), I, 84.

28. Collingwood, p. 48.

29. See Felix Gilbert, *Machiavelli and Guicciardini: Politics and History in Sixteenth-Century Florence* (Princeton: Princeton University Press, 1965), p. 270.

30. Quoted in Rudolf B. Gottfried, *Geoffrey Fenton's Historie of Guicciardin* (Bloomington: Indiana University Press, 1939), p. 38.

31. Gottfried, p. 34. For helpful discussions of the ways in which the concept of fortune liberated rather than limited Renaissance historiography, see Myron P.

opportunity, Guicciardini summons men to the study of history: "we must not surrender, like animals, a prey to fortune; rather, we must follow reason, like men."[32] While similarly acknowledging the presiding influence of fortune in the form of historic contingencies, Machiavelli emphasizes the importance of examining such contingencies in an effort to prevail against them: "Fortune is the mistresse of one halfe of our actions; but . . . yet she lets us have rule of the other halfe, or little lesse. And I liken her to a precipitous torrent . . . fortune . . . shewes her power where vertue is not ordained to resist her, and thither turnes she all her forces, where she perceives that no provisions nor resistances are made to uphold her."[33]

In keeping with this opportunity, Machiavelli is at pains, according to the Elizabethan translator of his *Florentine History*, to set forth "the causes and effects of every action." Without mention of the causes, circumstances, and contingencies that constitute historic fortune, "our historie would be with more difficulty understood, and to the readers less pleasing."[34] Thus out of the need to stem the torrent of fortune arises the further need for explanation of its workings; as Braithwaite puts it, "he that discovers events and sequels without their present causes, is as one that would draw a River dry, without knowing whence the Spring is derived" (p. 7).

As part of the complex tissue of historical circumstance and contingency, the concept of convention came to play an important role in historical explanation. On the one hand, knowledge of human habits and institutions had long been cited as an office of the historian. Caxton, for example, had maintained that the wisest man is he who "by the experyence of adverse fortune hath byholden and seen the noble Cytes maners and variaunt condycions of the people of many dyverse Regyons . . . dyverse customes Condycyons lawes Acts of sundry nacions."[35] Similarly, in distinguishing between natural histories and human or civil histories, Peter Heylyn observes that

Gilmore, "Freedom and Determinism in Renaissance Historians," *SRen*, 3 (1956), 49–60; and Leonard F. Dean, "Tudor Theories of History Writing," *University of Michigan Contributions in Modern Philosophy*, 1 (1947), esp. 12–13.

32. Guicciardini, *Maxims and Reflections*, B.160.

33. Niccolò Machiavelli, *The Prince*, trans. Edward Dacres, ed. W. E. C. Baynes (London: Alexander Moring, 1929), pp. 113–114.

34. Machiavelli, *The Florentine Historie*, trans. T.[homas] B.[eddingfield], ed. Henry Cust (1905; rpt., New York: AMS Press, 1967), pp. 5, 326.

35. Caxton, Prologue to *Polychronicon*, p. 64.

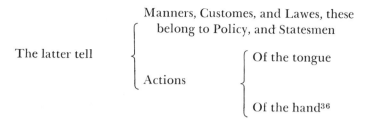

On the other hand, however, neither the decisive relationship of custom to action nor its role in explanation was greatly emphasized by early Renaissance historians. Rather, custom was merely included as one among the many items that the historian recites. "The order of the matter," Polydore Vergil remarks, "requyreth, observaunce of tymes, discripcions of places, the maners, the lives of men, theyr behavoures, purposes, occasions, dedes, saiynges, casualties, achevynges, & finishyng of thynges."[37] Similarly, Erasmus declares that history should include "rites and ceremonies, customs, wonders, institutions, all that is instructive will be pressed into use."[38] Already vulnerable for its lack of a distinctive place among the data of historiography, custom had its importance further diminished by the overriding claims of narrative and moral pattern in exemplary history.

Nevertheless, the early retention of the datum of custom in germinal form prepared the way for its importance in the later theories of historical explanation. In part this elevation was a function of the general shift in the normative perspective that took place in the verbal arts and in the arts of morals, politics, and law. Its special importance for historiography, however, was largely determined by the nexus established between politics and history in Florentine historiography. Remarking on the turmoils that had plagued Florence since 1494, Guicciardini links the power of fortune decisively with the changing shape of public habit over time. The political fortunes of Florence demonstrate, he claims, that it is "important to be born or to live in a time that prizes highly the virtues and qualities in which you excel . . . to be sure, if a man could change his nature to suit the conditions of the times, he would be much less dominated by Fortune. But that is most difficult, and perhaps even impossible." The reason affairs are "constantly being affected by fortuitous circumstances that men could

36. Peter Heylyn, *Microcosmos: Little Description of the Great World* (London, 1629), pp. 16–18.

37. Quoted in Levy, *Tudor Historical Thought*, p. 62.

38. Erasmus, *Concerning the Aim and Method of Education*, p. 144. See also Heinsius, p. 9, and Sypher, p. 358.

neither forsee nor avoid," he claims, is that "from one age to another, not only do words, fashions, and manners change, but—more important —so do the tastes and inclinations of men's minds. This sort of diversity is observable even within the same age among different countries." Accordingly, the power of public custom comes to represent the raw material of political fortune; "the desires and decisions of the people are so unstable," Guicciardini claims, "so much more determined by chance than by reason, that it is senseless for any man to pin his hopes of achieving power on them."[39]

As the embodiment of public habits, values, and expectations, the inarticulate power of custom animates the dialectic of tradition and innovation that is history. Man's attempt to control political fortune by prudently adjusting to pre-existing conditions is roughly analogous to the imposition of form upon matter,[40] and in Machiavelli's view, custom is the matter that resists or enhances attempts at innovation. Consequently, Machiavelli observes, "in States of inheritance, and accustomed to the bloud of their Princes, there are far fewer difficulties to keep them, than in the new." Similarly, when peoples are "of the same Province and the same language . . . it is verie easy to hold them, especially when they are not used to live free . . . it is enough to have extinguished the Princes line who ruled over them: for in other matters, allowing them their ancient conditions, and there not being much difference of matters betwixt them, men ordinarily live quiet enough." Conversely, "when any States are gained in a Province disagreeing in language, manners, and orders, here are the difficulties,"[41] for here the new regime must contend against unfortunate circumstances in the form of public convention. Moreover, so powerful is the influence of convention in shaping history that "institutions and forms should be adapted to the subject, whether it be good or evil, inasmuch as the same form cannot suit two subjects that are essentially different."[42]

History thus came to aid the art of politics by illustrating and explaining the relation of contingency between customary values or public mores and political events and regimes. Accordingly, convention became increasingly important as both a tool and a datum for

39. Guicciardini, *Maxims and Reflections*, C.31, C.30, B.116, C.69, B.156.

40. See J. G. A. Pocock, "Custom and Grace, Form and Matter: An Approach to Machiavelli's Concept of Innovation," in *Machiavelli and the Nature of Political Thought*, ed. Martin Fleischer (New York: Atheneum, 1972), p. 161.

41. Machiavelli, *The Prince*, pp. 4–5, 7, 20.

42. Machiavelli, *The Discourses*, ed. Max Lerner (New York: Modern Library, 1950), 1.18.

historical explanation. In Jean Bodin's *Methodus ad Facilem Histo-riarum Cognitionem* (1572), a treatise well known to English histori-ographers,[43] the broadly inclusive list of historical data recited by the earlier humanists is repeated with a new and practical sense of its importance. The subject of civil history, Bodin claims, is "man leading his life in the midst of society." Consequently, the historian must con-sider as his materials "the obscurity and renown of the race, . . . games and spectacles, . . . glory and infamy, . . . crudity of manners and culture, . . . the financial arts, love and hate, societies and trade."[44]

Such data became particularly essential in the theory of "politic" history. Bacon, for example, traces the influence of historic fortune directly to the configuration of circumstances engendered by human habit. "The mould of a man's fortune," he declares, "is in his own hands . . . if a man look sharply and attentively, he shall see Fortune: for though she be blind, yet she is not invisible."[45] In order to master fortune, men must not only "understand themselves," but also "procure informations of particular touching persons, their natures, their desires and ends, their customs and fashions, their helps and advantages."[46] The chief repository of such information is "the form of writing . . . which Machiavelli most wisely and aptly chose for government; namely, Observations or Discourses upon History and Examples." History is useful because it anatomizes men in the temporal and circumstantial setting of "their principles, fashions, prescribed rules, and the like."[47] Accordingly, history plays an essential part in Bacon's program for "Human Philosophy"; in both *The Advancement of Learning* and *De Augmentis*, Bacon insists upon the consideration of "custom, exer-cise, habit, education." "The opinion of Aristotle," he claims, "seemeth to me a negligent opinion, that of those things which consist by nature nothing can be changed by custom."[48]

43. See Leonard F. Dean, "Bodin's *Methodus* in England before 1625," *SP*, 39 (1942), 160–166.

44. Jean Bodin, *Method for the Easy Comprehension of History*, trans. Beatrice Reynolds (1945; rpt. New York: Norton, 1969), pp. 15, 34; hereafter cited as Bodin, *Methodus*.

45. Bacon, "Of Fortune," in *Works*, VI, 472–473. See Wylie G. Sypher, "Simi-larities between the Scientific and the Historical Revolutions at the End of the Renaissance," *JHI*, 26 (1965), 353–368, and esp. 359.

46. Bacon, *The Advancement of Learning*, bk. 2 in *Works*, III, 461, 456.

47. Bacon, "The Architect of Fortune, or the Knowledge of Advancement in Life," *De Augmentis*, 8.2, in *Works*, V, 56, 60; in *Advancement:* "their principles, rules, observations, and the like," *Works*, III, 456.

48. Bacon, *Advancement of Learning*, in *Works*, III, 349.

This had similarly been the basis of Thomas Blundeville's inclusion of convention as a datum of historiography in his *True order and Methode of wryting and reading Hystories* (1574), an influential redaction of Patrizzi's *della historia* that brought Italian theory to bear in England. Because similar actions have not always had the same results, says Blundeville, "we ought therefore to consider the divers natures of thinges, and the difference of tymes and occasions, and such like accidents, to see if we can possibly find out the cause why men's purposes have taken effect at one tyme, and not at an other."[49] Man's actions, he observes, proceed "by nature, by affection, or by choice or election, and such election springeth either . . . of some passione of the minde, of custome, or els of the discourse of reason" (p. 160). Thus what man chooses for himself apart from his more purely emotional or rational promptings, he chooses as a creature of habit. The historian must therefore consider "the education and nurture" of men, their "exercises, deedes, and speaches, and also the age, and time, wherein every notable act was done" because such factors "breed by custome such a perfect habite in the minde" (p. 160).

Thus the influence of what Bacon called "custom copulate and conjoined and collegiate" became an increasingly important consideration in historical thought. Degory Wheare, first holder of the chair in history at Oxford, officially pronounced that knowledge "of the forgotten Customes . . . is not only necessary for all men, but especially for all those who are Studious of the ancient manners and history."[50] Not only as a measure of the general shift in Renaissance normative perspective, but also as a reflection of the special needs and character of the historical study that this shift precipitated, the shapes and functions of convention became a principal datum in the study of man. This study turned increasingly not only from man's ends to his beginnings in the "set of time," but to the "set of time" itself.

2. The Emergence of Historical Consciousness

In turning the study of man from his ends to his beginnings, Renaissance historical thought liberated the past from its rhetorical role as a repository of examples and made it a repository of norms. In itself, however, this liberation left the character of normative thought essentially unchanged. Although historical reflection shifted the normative

49. Thomas Blundeville, *The true order and Methode of wryting and reading Hystories*, ed. Hugh G. Dick, *HLQ*, 3 (1940), 168; see Dick's introduction, p. 151.

50. Degory Wheare, *The Method and Order of Reading Both civil and Ecclesiastical Histories*, trans. Edmund Bohun (London, 1685), p. 111.

focus from nature to the past, it did not challenge the normative validity of the past or its relevance to the present: history provided norms that differed from philosophic norms only insofar as they were customary rather than natural in character. History was thus brought to bear upon the present merely as an alternative to philosophic reflection. This situation did not change until a growing body of historical research unearthed evidence of substantial historical changes in customary norms, and thus produced conflicting normative interpretations. Such conflicts fostered a sense of discontinuity and skepticism that drastically altered the concept of the past by severing it from the present.

The rapid growth of antiquarian research and legal historiography in sixteenth-century England was thus in origin an essentially normative undertaking. As shown earlier, the "duble name" of custom was the product of a Reformation conflict between two normative theories, one of which claimed to take its prescriptions from Scripture, the other of which claimed to derive them from unwritten custom. In the Catholic view, it was "propre to the heretikes to appeal to the scriptures onely, because they are quickly condemned by tradition, custome, and manner."[1] Protestants attempted to refute this claim on purely doctrinal grounds, maintaining that "custom is of no strength in this case of proving a religion,"[2] but this attempt was increasingly accompanied by an effort to refute the Catholic claim on historical grounds as well. In effect, this amounted very nearly to doctrinal capitulation, and to the extent that custom was accepted as a legitimate form of "testimony," the debate shifted from theological to more purely historical grounds.[3] In this controversy it became the task of history to establish the conformity of religious precepts with the presumably fundamental purity of the primitive church, and to show historically that Roman practices were merely innovations and encrustations upon this pure tradition. John Foxe, the most influential and popular practitioner in this vein, justified his use of history by declaring that "the old acts and histories of ancient time . . . give testimony with us, wherein we have sufficient matter for us to show that the same form, usage, and institution of this our present reformed church, are not the beginning of any new church of our, but the renewing of the old ancient Church

1. John Rastell, quoted in Levy, *Tudor Historical Thought*, p. 107.

2. Thomas Cranmer, *Miscellaneous Writings and Letters*, ed. John Edmund Cox (Cambridge: Parker Society, 1846), pp. 51–52.

3. See Levy, *Tudor Historical Thought*, ch. 3; Joseph H. Preston, "English Church Historians and the Problem of Bias, 1559–1742," *JHI*, 32 (1971), 203–220; and William Haller, *The Elect Nation: The Meaning and Relevance of Foxe's Book of Martyrs* (New York: Harper & Row, 1963), ch. 5.

of Christ."[4] For the same reasons, Matthew Parker and his antiquarian associates attempted to "seeke out the monuments off foremer tymes to knowe the religion of th'ancient fathers and those especiallye which were off the Englishe churche."[5] Because custom was taken as the decisive datum of such research, it was prized for its continuity with the present and its legitimacy as testimony in support of normative discourse.

The historical continuity of custom and tradition was even more strongly emphasized in the preeminently normative art of law. As J. G. A. Pocock has observed, the "European nations attained knowledge of history by reflecting, largely under the stimulus of contemporary political developments and theories, upon the character of their law . . . the historical outlook which arose in each nation was in part the product of its law, and therefore, in turn, of its history."[6] In Chapter II it has already been established that in England the distinction between written and unwritten, or more often, between statutory and common law, became the basis for the elevation of custom to a place of prominence in legal theory. Looking restrospectively to the forms of legal habit that history and experience had established and confirmed, the lawyers inferred through presumptive reasoning the normative validity of these forms for the present. As a form of "second nature," custom merely represented a continuous process of inarticulate adjustment and habitual transmission culminating in the present. Sir John Davies, for example, virtually identified the efforts of the past with the shape of custom in the present:

> a Custome taketh beginning and groweth to perfection in this manner: when a reasonable act once done is found to be good and beneficiall to the people, and agreeable to their nature and disposition, then do they use it and practise it again and again, so by often iteration and multiplication of the act, it obtaineth the force of a Law . . . But a Custome doth never become a Law to bind the people, untill it hath been tried and approved time out of mind.[7]

Thus while the beneficial power of "often iteration" served to shift the search for norms from the philosophic quest for natural laws to a

---

4. John Foxe, *Acts and Monuments,* ed. George Townsend (rpt., New York: AMS Press, 1965), I, 9.

5. John Jocelyn (Parker's secretary), quoted in May McKisack, *Medieval History in the Tudor Age* (Oxford: Clarendon Press, 1971), p. 39; cf. p. 44.

6. Pocock, *Ancient Constitution,* p. 7.

7. Quoted in Pocock, *Ancient Constitution,* p. 33.

retrospective vision of the past, this vision was itself normative in character. In other words, the early legal use of historical discourse merely replaced the uniformity of nature with the continuity of time. According to Sir Edward Coke, the most emphatic spokesman for the role of custom in English legal history, "of every custom there be two essential parts, time and usage; time out of mind and continual and peaceable usage without lawful interruption."[8] This continuity engendered in Coke a profound respect for the sanctity of precedent and tradition, and gave rise to his romanticized and mythical view of the past.

This view was itself, however, a substantial counterbalance to the tradition of philosophic reasoning in the arts of politics and law. As a source of rectitude "fixed and refined by an infinite number of grave and learned men, and by long experience grown to such a perfection," custom, and *ipso facto* historical argument, came to rival the power of individual reason: "no man (out of his own private reason) ought to be wiser than the law, which is the perfection of reason."[9] This elevation of history amounted to an antirational bias; Sir John Dodderidge, for example, a lawyer and original member of the Society of Antiquaries, remarked that he "cannot but think reverently of Antiquity, although I cannot yeeld sufficient reason for their doings therein."[10] Somewhat later, Sir Matthew Hale similarly reacted against the effort of Hobbes to base the art of law on rational principles: "Now if any the most refined Braine under Heaven would goe about to Enquire by Speculation, or by reading Plato or Aristotle . . . to finde out how Landes descend in England . . . he wou'd loose his Labour, and Spend his Notions in vaine, till he acquainted himselfe with the Lawes of England, and the reason is because they are Institutions introduced by the will or Consent of others implicitely by Custome and usage."[11] The law is justified on historical, not rational, grounds, and the judge must "apply the law as it is, and not as it ought to be."[12]

---

8. Sir Edward Coke, *First Institute of the Laws of England*, ed. J. H. Thomas (Philadelphia, 1836), p. 27; see also pp. 5, 17, 22, 27, 29, 48, and the following prefaces to the *Reports* (London, 1826–1827): III, ix, xii, xix; IV, vi; VI, passim; VIII, xix, xxv; IX, xxxiii.

9. Coke, *First Institute*, p. 1; cf. Ferdinand Tönnies, *Custom: An Essay on Social Codes*, trans. A. Farrell Borenstein (New York: The Free Press of Glencoe, 1961), pp. 64–67.

10. Sir John Dodderidge, quoted in McKisack, p. 146.

11. "Reflections by the Lrd. Chief Justice Hale on Mr. Hobbes his Dialogue of the Law," in W. S. Holdsworth, *A History of the English Law* (London: Methuen, 1903–1909), V, 505.

12. Hale, *A History of the Common Law in England*, ed. Charles M. Gray (Chicago: University of Chicago Press, 1971), p. xxxiv.

Paradoxically, however, the nostalgic and prescriptive aims that inspired historical investigation of the "reign or tyranny of custom" also produced techniques, interests, and mental habits that eventually liberated history from its subordinate role as "testimony." This process came about rather slowly in England, partly owing to a lack of accurate historical information, but also owing to lack of a basis for historical comparison. In France, where the French common law coexisted with Roman law, the lawyers and historians were faced immediately and continuously with the task of reconciling two separate legal traditions. By the early sixteenth century, the difficulties encountered in this task gave rise to the recognition that Roman and French law were the products of two distinct traditions. Accordingly, it became the task of the newer *mos Gallicus* to reconstruct the proper social and historical context from which to draw a more fitting interpretation of the law.[13] Treating the law historically rather than systematically, and using philological and antiquarian research almost without regard for its applicability in the present, the French legal scholars "showed an awareness of context and process even before [they] sanctioned the myth of custom . . . their awareness of the unique characteristics of past societies made them the first modern contextualists."[14] In England, the proposed reception of the Roman code had precipitated a retrospective justification of the English law on the basis of its customary longevity, but this conflict remained purely theoretical, and an actual confrontation like the one in France never materialized. Because the fact of historical discontinuity and disparity was not therefore immediately apparent, the myth of custom prevailed and the change in historical thinking had to be effected by the historical evidence itself. In the first place, legal scholarship led increasingly to the discovery of terms and practices remarkably different from those currently in use. The difficulty of interpreting this evidence was created by a vast tract of time standing between the past and present. Commenting on the alien Latin and Anglo-Saxon terms of ancient law, Sir Henry Spelman, for example, complained that

13. See Donald R. Kelly, *"Historia Integra:* François Baudouin and His Conception of History," *JHI,* 25 (1964), 35–57; Kelly, "Budé and the First Historical School of Law," *American Historical Review,* 72 (1967), 807–834; Julian H. Franklin, *Jean Bodin and the Sixteenth-Century Revolution in the Methodology of Law and History* (New York: Columbia University Press, 1963), pp. 11–27 and ch. 3; George Huppert, *The Idea of Perfect History: Historical Erudition and Historical Philosophy in Renaissance Florence* (Urbana: University of Illinois Press, 1970), pp. 40–41, 46, 59–60, 152–156.

14. Fussner, pp. 27–28.

> To tell the Government of England under the Old Saxon
> Laws, seemeth an Utopia to us present; strange and un-
> couth: yet can there be no period assign'd, wherein either
> the frame of those Laws was abolished, or this of ours enter-
> tained; but as the Day and Night creep insensibly, one upon
> the other, so also hath this Alteration grown upon us insen-
> sibly, every age altering something, and no one age seeing
> more. than what themselves were Actors in, nor thinking it
> to have been otherwise than as themselves discover it by the
> present. Like them of China, who never travailing out of
> their own Country, think the World to extend no further.[15]

Often at odds with the immemorial monolith that Coke and other
lawyers tried so hard to mythicize, the historical evidence seemed
to suggest that the relationship between human beings and their
collective practices was in a constant process of change. Hooker, of
course, had already used the English concept of legal custom in conjunction with Aristotelian and Thomistic models of individual and
collective acts in order to arrive at this conclusion. And in moral
philosophy and the verbal arts the mutability of public usage was
already introducing a critical and comparative element into normative
discourse. As perhaps the most conservative and purely prescriptive
type of such discourse, legal philosophy was among the last of the
arts to recognize the dynamic character of its norms. In addition to
its intrinsic conservatism, it was confronted with a particularly deceptive body of evidence. Not only did the English lawyers lack the
obvious basis of comparison that the moral philosophers, rhetoricians,
and French lawyers possessed, but the single tradition with which they
were concerned, as Spelman noted, seemed to be marked by no momentous changes or events. Changing only like "Day and Night . . . insensibly," the English law in its types and functions seemed to be
remarkably continuous with the present. It was, as Sir Matthew Hale
put it, like the Ship of the Argonauts, "the same when it returned
home, as it was when it went out, tho' in that long Voyage it had successive amendments, and scarce came back with any of its former
Materials; and as Titius is the same Man he was 40 years since, tho'
physicians tell us, That in a Tract of seven Years, the Body has scarce
any of the same Material Substance as it had before."[16]

Beneath the deceptive surface of appearances there nevertheless

---

15. Sir Henry Spelman, *Of the Ancient Government of England,* quoted in
Robert L. Schuyler, "The Antiquarians and Sir Henry Spelman," *Proceedings of
the American Philosophical Society,* 101 (1957), 102.

16. Hale, *A History of the Common Law of England,* pp. 39–40.

existed substantial changes. These changes became the serious subject of historical investigation only when the evidence of the past was used in support of conflicting normative interpretations. In response to the increasing prerogatives claimed by the Stuart throne, the lawyers and parliamentarians of the early seventeenth century insisted vehemently on the customary existence of an "ancient constitution." Claiming against the throne that parliamentary rights were not the concessions of a Norman conqueror, but the fundamental corollary of an Anglo-Saxon constitutional monarchy, the legal historians searched deeply into the past in order to show that the Norman conquest had brought no changes in the customary practices of England. As a reaction against the "infamous title of a conquered Nation," and the tyranny of "Norman Lawes and French Guize," the search for Saxon antiquities became a popular quest for the "Teutonick glory and puissance" of a "Teutonick Nation."[17] But in the political turmoils of mid-century, the parliamentary myth of immemorial custom was used to support the views of the Royalists and the House of Lords as well,[18] so that the need for more accurate means of historical interpretation became increasingly apparent.

In response to the particularly vexing problem of misinterpretation, Spelman began to compile his magnificent Anglo-Saxon glossary, the *Archaeologus* (1626). The need to establish the philological context of linguistic usage led Spelman on the further quest for information that would enable him to reconstruct the social and political context of the feudal law. As a result of his research and its continuation by Dugdale, Brady, and others, the study of the past took on increasing respect for the power of custom to change its shape with time. With this redefinition of custom, the legal historiographers became increasingly wary of its uncritical use as "testimony" in support of prescription, and recognized that, as Spelman put it, "when States are departed from their original Constitution, and that Original by tract of time worn out of Memory; the Succeeding Ages viewing what is past by the present, conceive the former to have been like that they live in; and framing thereupon erroneous Propositions, do likewise make thereon erroneous Inferences and Conclusions."[19]

17. See John Hare, *St. Edward's Ghost* (London, 1647), pp. 2, 3, 6; and the pamphlet *Universall Madnesse: or A new merry Litany* (London, 1647), p. 5.

18. See Pocock, *Ancient Constitution*, pp. 149–159, 160–162; see also Philip Styles, "Politics and Historical Research in the Early Seventeenth Century," in *English Historical Scholarship in the Sixteenth and Seventeenth Centuries*, ed. Levi Fox (London: Oxford University Press, 1956), p. 56.

19. Sir Henry Spelman, "Of Parliaments," in *The English Works of Sir Henry Spelman* (London, 1727), p. 57.

While the historical investigation of social and legal custom for prescriptive purposes therefore brought about major changes within the framework of normative discourse itself, it also gave rise to attitudes and interests incompatible with this framework. To the extent that historical research demonstrated the variety and mutability of collective practices over time, preoccupation with the sanctions of the past gave way to emphasis upon the element of change, rather than of continuity, in history. Thus while motivated by prescriptive aims, the growth of antiquarian research also fostered more disinterested concern with knowledge of the past for its own sake.[20] This in turn tended to provide historical knowledge with a distinct epistemological status. Because the historical use of custom as a form of "testimony" involved discovery of a complex setting of contingent times, places, circumstances, causes, and effects, this total setting became the subject of a distinctive type of discourse. Taking as its province a shifting configuration of particulars, historical discourse was increasingly liberated from its subordinate role as "testimony" and allowed far greater claims as an alternative human science.

The foundations for this change were laid in the sometimes lavish accounts of cultural and social customs in the chorographical surveys and county histories of Camden, Carew, Stow, Drayton, and other antiquarians. Camden, for example, prefaced his magnificent county-by-county survey of English antiquities with a lengthy general account of the peoples and history of the island. In the opening chapter of this account, "The First Inhabitants," Camden attempts to sketch the condition of life and manners in pre-Roman Britain, and in the second chapter infers on the basis of linguistic usage that in "habits and customes" the original inhabitants were not Trojans, but Gauls. His task, he claims, "requires that something be added concerning the customs for our Forefathers the Saxons," because "the first Inhabitants of countries had other cares and thoughts withal, than that of transmitting their originals to posterity." Reading the evidence of coins, inscriptions, burrows, Roman structures, churches, monasteries, and charters, Camden attempts to establish the conditions of English life in its various historic stages and locations. From the various layers of evidence Camden infers a complex set of conditions in perpetual change: "it is manifest, that nothing has continued in its primitive state. There's a continual floating in the affairs of mankind. In this vast ark there are daily revolutions: new foundations of cities laid,

---

20. See J. H. Plumb, *The Death of the Past* (Boston: Houghton Mifflin, 1971).

new names given to nations, either by the utter ruin of the former, or by its change into that of a more powerful party."[21]

Among such "daily revolutions" was evidence of changes in the shared values, beliefs, and practices of man. "We stand and behold things afarre-off," John Speed remarks, and

> the like hapeneth in the search and survey, as of all other nations, so of our first *beginnings,* our *antique Customes, behaviours, habits,* & c. the true Circumstances whereof are more difficult to find, in that those things are not onely remote many degrees beyond the kenning of our Eye, (yea so manie Ages from the times wherein we live), but also are shrouded & enwrapped in manifold uncertainties and contrarities, wherewith even those *writers* have perplexed our way, who undertooke to bee both our *Guides* and our *Lights.*[22]

Such cultural changes, which had been for Camden an integral part of historic background, became for Speed essential for the clarification of the changing character of English history.[23] Accompanied with illustrations of Saxon and Norman inhabitants, Speed's researches were intended to underline the differences in "the Manners and Customes of those people."[24]

Together with a growing interest in other contemporary civilizations "discrepant in all nurture,"[25] and in the antiquities of classical and eastern societies,[26] the study of British antiquity began to follow in the steps of other disciplines that had already acknowledged the dynamic character of convention. Manifesting itself in attempts to revivify the Saxon language,[27] in such plays as Fletcher's *Bonduca*

21. William Camden, *Britannia* (1695; rpt., New York: Johnson Reprint Corporation, 1971), pp. xxiv, cxxviii, lii, clxiv.

22. John Speed, *The Historie of Greate Britaine . . . Their Originals, Manners, Habits* (London, 1623), V, 37–38.

23. See Levy, *Tudor Historical Thought,* p. 196.

24. Speed, *The Historie of Great Britaine,* V, 20.

25. John Rolfe, quoted in Louis B. Wright, *The Elizabethans' America* (Cambridge: Harvard University Press, 1966), p. 235; cf. pp. 12, 128–130, 210, 215.

26. See A. Momigliano, "Ancient History and the Antiquarian," in *Studies in Historiography* (London: Weidenfeld and Nicolson, 1966), pp. 1–39; and Karl H. Dannenfelt, "Egypt and Egyptian Antiquities in the Renaissance," *SRen,* 6 (1959), 7–27.

27. See Rosemond Tuve, "Ancients, Moderns, and Saxons," *ELH,* 6 (1939), 165–190, and Richard Foster Jones, *The Triumph of the English Language* (Stanford: Stanford University Press, 1953), chs. 7–8.

(1613) and Speed's *Stonehenge* (1636),[28] and in such collections of anthropological marvels as Casaubon's *Treatise of Use and Custom* (1638), and Boemus's *Manners, Lawes, and Customes of All Nations* (1611), the romantic fascination with cultural diversities became a corollary to study of the past.

Unlike the prescriptive use of the past, this fascination centered on the view that "human history flows mostly from the will of mankind, which ever vacillates and has no objective—nay, rather, each new day new laws, new customes, new institutions, new manners confront us."[29] Such historical diversity and variety, which had so intrigued Montaigne, provided history with a new objective, dictating that in history, as in moral philosophy, "there is nothing more pleasant, more profitable, nor more prayesworthy, than truly . . . to know and understand the situation, lawes, customes, religion, and forme of government in each severall Province of the world."[30] Such knowledge demonstrates, Casaubon claims, that "though some Countries are more constant in their Lawes and customes, than some other are; yet . . . none hath been so constant, where divers things may not be observed, once forbidden and punishable, some; now, legall and lawfull." Accordingly, as the art that mirrors such changes, history comes to claim a special wisdom of its own:

> For since the severall ages of the World differ little one from another, but by those outward markes and recognificences of different rites and Customes: he that knows certainly what hath been the particular estate (if not all:) yet of most ages of the World, wherein they differed one from another, and wherein they agreed; he doth as it were enjoy the memories, of so many yeares, and so many ages past, even as if himselfe had outlived all those yeares, and outlasted all those ages.[31]

This redefinition of historical wisdom helped to undermine the normative value of history, and produced in later Renaissance historians a highly skeptical attitude toward the use of history as "testimony." On the evidence of historical change in social norms, John Hayward, for example, declares that "it is dangerous to frame rules

---

28. See Stuart Piggott, "Antiquarian Thought in the Sixteenth and Seventeenth Centuries," in *English Historical Scholarship in the Sixteenth and Seventeenth Centuries*, ed. Levi Fox (London: Oxford University Press, 1956), p. 103.

29. Bodin, *Methodus*, p. 17; cf. p. 212.

30. Johann Boemus, *The Manners, Lawes, and Customes of All Nations*, trans. Edward Aston (London, 1611), p. 3.

31. Meric Casaubon, *A Treatise of Use and Custome* (London, 1638), pp. 100, 97.

of policy out of countries differing from us both in nature and custome of life and form of government."[32] One reason for this danger, Samuel Daniel claims, is that men entertain "narrow conceits, [and] apprehend not the progresses in the affaires of mankinde; and . . . take all their reason from the example, and *Idea* of the present Customes they see in use."[33] Conversely, as Clarendon, writing "Of the Reverence Due to Antiquity," later remarked, it is a "great disease in the world, too much to adore those who have gone before, and like sheep to tread their steps."[34] Because "forms and circumstances must be different in several climates and regions" (*Essays*, II, 88), we are "liable to be misled in forming our practice or judgement by the rules and measures of antiquity, with reference to the civil and politic actions of our lives" and, similarly, "antiquity will be as blind a guide to us in matters of practice or opinion relative to religions" (II, 78). The briefest survey of European religion, Clarendon explains, demonstrates that there was no point in history when Christianity was not in a constant state of adaptation and change: "the difference of times, the alteration of climates, the nature and humours of nations and people, have introduced many things which were not, and altered other things which were" (II, 91).

Because of these claims of history against the normative use of the past, the theory of historical explanation combined with historical skepticism to produce a highly distinctive mode of discourse. To begin with, the dynamic character of values and beliefs that was increasingly becoming the subject of historiography produced a sense of skepticism inimical to the use of history as "testimony" for unchanging norms. The sheer variety of *doxa* had led many of the ancients to an ahistorical flight from the world of particulars to a philosophic world of universals. In the verbal arts, in the arts of politics and law, and preeminently in the natural sciences, the later Renaissance similarly witnessed a forward-looking flight toward universals that amounted to a repudiation not only of history but of the past as well. At the same time, however, and partly in combination with this novel scientific impulse, the very distinction that led the ancients away from history may be said to have led many Renaissance thinkers toward it. For while the attempt to use the past to justify customary norms had suggested instead that

32. John Hayward, *The Lives of the Three Normans, Kings of England*, in Herschel Baker, *The Later Renaissance in England* (Boston: Houghton Mifflin, 1976), p. 834.

33. Samuel Daniel, *The Collection of the History of England*, in *Works*, ed. Alexander B. Grosart (1896; rpt., New York: Russell and Russell, 1963), IV, 88.

34. Edward Hyde, Earl of Clarendon, "Of the Reverence Due to Antiquity," in *Essays*, ed. James Tanier Clarke (London, 1815), II, 91.

custom was subject to the mutability of historic fortune, the theory of historical explanation provided the further possibility that such changes over time could be explained with reference to the total setting of contingent circumstances. As one writer put it:

> In making judgement of history, and considerately applying it to our present interests, we must specially regard the dispositions of the agents, and diligently remark how they are affected in minde, which is the least deceiving ground of forming opinion: for without this pondering, and knowledge of the qualities of those Nations, which we meet with in reading, a man is unable to make any due comparison between the present particular, and the former example.[35]

In answering to this need, historiography became increasingly concerned with the total setting of events, and with establishing the context in terms of which more useful comparison might be made. Thus while the theories of Machiavelli, Guicciardini, Bacon, and others established a framework of explanation in which a knowledge of customs and contingencies might be used in the present, it took the further development of a sense of the past, of historical relativism, in order for these discoveries to be used in the service of a knowledge of the past. By transforming history from a prescriptive to a descriptive and contextual art, this new sense of the past established the claim of history as a distinctive kind of knowledge, and appointed it with the task of explaining the apparent discontinuity of man's aims and values in light of his natural continuity as an adaptable creature and creator of conventions.

3. "A Genius of Times": The Contexts of Historical Periods

The earliest changes in Renaissance historical thought originated in the critical philosophy of history, in the definition of its aims and methods, its subjects and resources. These changes, however, entailed a transformation of the speculative philosophy of history as well. As historians tended increasingly to focus on customary norms and values in their temporal setting, they began to redefine the concept of the past itself, substituting for the continuity of past with present an awareness of the periodicity of historic time, and especially of the tendency

35. Robert Johnson, *Essaies,* sig. D4v.

of such periods to cohere around shifting configurations or contexts of social values, practices, and beliefs.

This transformation was facilitated by current speculative notions of time. The Renaissance preoccupation with mutability was leading not only to the measurement of time as a commodity, but also to the measurement of historical time in terms of epochs or periods. Periodization had always been a practice of Christian historiographers, who organized time around the cardinal events of salvation history and interpreted this organization in the light of various providential schemes derived from Scripture.[1] Such epochal thinking was decisively transformed, however, by the peculiar self-consciousness of Renaissance thinkers, who modified the epochal division of historical time in order to support a new sense of their own momentous place in history. Thus when Petrarch concluded that he was rediscovering the light of Rome by reversing the "dark" and "light" ages that earlier Christian historiographers had placed before and after the birth of Christ, he was not merely revising an abstract epochal schema; rather, he was redefining the very basis of epochal thought in secular terms.[2] The Renaissance attempt at historical self-definition was therefore not an appeal to timeless order, but an effort to describe human achievement measured against that of other ages and civilizations.[3] History was to be measured not by providential interventions, but by "the dylygence of men."[4]

Respect for the secular integrity of distinct historical epochs was reinforced by the reemergence of the ancient cyclical theory of history.[5] It has been argued with good reason that the cyclical theory resisted the idea of real historical change in its assumption that men and actions

1. See, e.g., C. A. Patrides, *The Phoenix and the Ladder: The Rise and Decline of the Christian View of History* (Berkeley: University of California Press, 1964); and Herschel Baker, *The Race of Time: Three Lectures on Renaissance Historiography* (Toronto: University of Toronto Press, 1967), pp. 56–58.

2. See Theodore Mommsen, "Petrarch's Conception of the 'Dark Ages,'" in *Medieval and Renaissance Studies* (Ithaca: Cornell University Press, 1959); Wallace K. Ferguson, *The Renaissance in Historical Thought* (Boston: Houghton Mifflin, 1948), chs. 1–3; and Ricardo Quinones, *The Renaissance Discovery of Time* (Cambridge: Harvard University Press, 1972), pp. 118–120.

3. See, e.g., Samuel Daniel's efforts to define the Renaissance achievement in historical terms, in *A Defense of Rhyme*, in G. Gregory Smith, II, 369; and in *The Collection of the History of England*, in *Works*, IV, 77.

4. Robert Whittinton, *Vulgaria*, ed. Beatrice White (London: Early English Texts Society, 1932), p. 62.

5. Ably documented by Patrides, passim; for the classical origins of the idea, see J. B. Bury, ch. 1.

always come to the same result,[6] that "man is a creature of the same dimension as he ever was; and how great and eminent soever hee bee, his measure and height is easie to be taken."[7] The "uniformitarianism" to which the cyclical pattern could in some cases lead, however, was offset by another characteristic. The various Christian providential views defined historical epochs in terms of their relation to an abstract linear pattern outside of time itself; the cyclical theory, insofar as it suggested a pattern, was meant to characterize simply the process of historical change itself. LeRoy and Spenser adopted the cyclical pattern in order to show metaphorically that historical periods serve civilization in the same way that physical generation serves nature. For both LeRoy and Spenser, the real changes in the contours of civilization are not cyclical because they are in substance always the same, but because they circumscribe a fundamentally unchanging human nature by satisfying its changing needs in time.[8]

Thus while the cyclical theory could support the continuity of human nature over time, it could also describe real historical change. In the first place, adoption of the cyclical theory entailed rejection of abstract schemas in favor of the actual contours of periods as the basis for historical description. Bodin's defense of the cyclical theory, for example, explicitly involves a refutation of the theories of the Four Monarchies and the Golden Age.[9] Similarly, George Hakewill's *Apology or Declaration of the Power and Providence of God* (1627), takes up concrete historical comparisons at the same time that it abandons the Golden Age as an "idle toy and vain fancy forged by Poets, and taken up by some Historians and believed by the vulgar." Hakewill's use of the cyclical theory is an especially interesting case in point, because his reply to the essentially theological and metaphysical implications of Godfrey Goodman's vision of decline in *The Fall of Man* (1616) entails a conscious rejection of first causes and a movement toward historical explanation. Human reason, Hakewill claims, "by the light

---

6. See Herbert Weisinger, "Ideas of History during the Renaissance," *JHI*, 6 (1945), 415–435.

7. Samuel Daniel, *The First Foure Bookes of the civile wars betweene the two houses of Lancaster and Yorke*, in *Works*, II, 7; see also *The Collection of the History of England*, in *Works*, IV, 86.

8. On the tendency of the cyclical theory to surpass the "Stoic pessimism" that it sometimes implies, see Cecil E. Seronsy, "The Doctrine of Cyclical Recurrence and Some Related Ideas in the Works of Samuel Daniel," *SP*, 54 (1957), 387–407; and Arthur B. Ferguson, "The Historical Thought of Samuel Daniel: A Study in Renaissance Ambivalence," *JHI*, 32 (1971), 185–202.

9. Bodin, *Methodus*, pp. 291, 296.

of nature can rise no higher than ordinarie naturall causes," and on this basis he argues for a mental distinction between the ahistorical macrocosm of first causes and the historical microcosm of second causes. Within this microcosm the apparent decline in human nature is attributable to the second causes of history, which by changing man's setting and practices create the illusion of changes in his nature. "As there is by turnes an entercourse of times," Hakewill explains, "so also of Customes and manners."[10] The cyclical pattern of history demonstrates that while human nature remains unchanged, the proper understanding of this nature requires historical investigation of the setting, and respect for the total context of historical periods, "the age, and time," as Blundeville had put it, "wherein every notable act [is] done."

As a rival model to the schemes of providential history, the cyclical theory therefore encouraged the description of periods as self-defining and self-contained entities, whose pattern of rise and fall, or later, simply beginning and ending, was based upon the contour of history itself. Once historical epochs were in this way regarded as self-contained, it was but a further step to the discovery that they could be not only delineated but also characterized by their own entelechy or entropy. While the cyclical theory suggested analogies with the natural course of human life, the skeptical sense of the past that was emerging from historical research added to this analogy by suggesting that such patterns might differ as widely in character as do individual persons. "Historians have observed," said Thomas May, "a genius of times as well as clymates, as of men."[11] The notion that historical epochs could be characterized by a spirit or "genius" was at least as ancient as Paterculus,[12] and was revived as a corollary to the cyclical theory. Hakewill drew the notion from Bodin in order to refute Goodman on the grounds that "all ages have their proper *genius*, which inclines the mindes of men to certaine studies and courses."[13]

In the later Renaissance, this use of periods for establishing context became an increasingly prominent feature of historical writing. Daniel, for example, promised to divide his *History of England* "into three several Sections, according to the Periods of those Ages that brought

10. George Hakewill, *An Apology or Declaration of the Power and Providence of God in the Commonweal of the World* (London, 1635), pp. 366, 47, 332; see also Victor Harris, *All Cohaerence Gone* (Chicago: University of Chicago Press, 1949), pp. 47, 66, 84.

11. Thomas May, *History of the Long Parliament* (London, 1647), pp. 135–136.

12. Velleius Paterculus, *Compendium of Roman History*, ed. J. S. Watson (New York, 1881), p. 421.

13. Hakewill, *Apology*, p. 39.

forth the most remarkable Changes."[14] While Daniel's framework of
"Sections" or "Periods" is marked by the older criterion of reigns and
cardinal events, it is also intended to convey the differences in the
moral, social, cultural, and political values that motivated actions. As
such, it corrects the error of historians who "take all their reason, from
the example, and *Idea* of the present Customes they see in use." The
Saxon invasion, he observes, was not merely an event, but a cause that
"changed bounds, inhabitants, customes, language" so that "nothing
either of Lawes, Rites, and Customes, came to passe over unto us from
the *Brittaines*." Similarly, the Norman conquest did not simply constitute a change of dynasty, but marked "a time, wherein the State of
England received an alteration of Lawes, Customes, Fashion, manner
of living, writing, new formes of Fights, Fortifications, Buildings, and
generally an innovation in most things." Affecting not only social
values and political institutions, the events of this period changed
artistic values as well, when "after the Norman manner, they build
them goodly Churches, and stately houses of stone, provide better
furnishments, erect Castles, and Towers, in other sort than before."
Moreover, had Daniel extended his *History* beyond the reign of Edward
III and the period covered in the *Civil Wars,* he would, he claims, have
come to describe the Tudor reign not only in terms of its events, but
also as a time distinguished by a unique spirit, "a time not of that
virilitie as the former, but more subtile, and let out into wider notions,
and bolder discovery of what lay hidden before."[15]

The impact of such "contextualism" extended beyond immediate
history, and found increasing application in the study of other periods
as well. With an intense respect for context, Sir Henry's son, John
Spelman, announced his intention in his *Life of Alfred the Great*

> to relate the Carriage of Things in an Age much different
> from the Present, and not particularly enough delivered to
> us: it cannot be less than necessary for the Work it selfe that
> we a little cast our Eye upon the condition of those Times so
> long pass'd: seeing that in a course never so little out of the
> Common tract the Apprehension is very easily misled, unless
> that by the help of some Light it be in some measure recti-
> fy'd. Withal, the Expectation of the Reader would, for his
> own better satisfaction, be somewhat prepared, least, fancy-

14. Daniel, *The Collection of the History of England,* in *Works,* IV, 76, 102–103,
133.

15. Daniel, *Works,* IV, 77. See William Blisset, "Samuel Daniel's Sense of the
Past," *ES,* 38 (1957), 51; and William L. Godshalk, "Daniel's *History*," *JEGP,* 63
(1964), 45–57, and esp. 53–54.

ing to himself another Manner of Frame and Carriage of things than indeed those Times could bear, he reject the knowledge of the Actions than in hand; for that they were not of that Nature, nor managed in that Barbe, that he looked for, and so, unsatisfy'd in his Fancy, loose the benefit his Judgement might otherwise have made in Knowing them.

Accordingly, instead of measuring the achievements of Alfred absolutely against the present, he set them in the context of an already weak national identity under the constant threat of invasion by the Danes. There is as much respect for historical context as neo-classical self-congratulation in his warning that "we must not expect a solemn and steddy manage of Affairs then, as in a full grown state."[16]

Thus the use of history for comparison became increasingly the comparison of contexts as well as of events. Insofar as historical discourse still retained a normative character, it did so by acknowledging, as the moral, political, and verbal arts had come to do, that norms were subject to a variety of contingencies and required elucidation with the aid of critical and comparative procedures. Implicit in this acknowledgement was the recognition that the "defect is always in history, especially when, for want of Discovery of the Reasons and Affections, whereupon the Things and Actions moved, the bare done Deed represents not the Spirit nor Genius that was the Powerfull Agent in them."[17]

4. "A PASSABLE CONTEXTURE": CONVENTION AND THE PRACTICE OF CONTEXTUALISM

The growth in efforts to establish historical context was not a development destined to make the writing of history easier. Indeed, as a result of the problems they encountered in trying to use the past as testimony, the pioneering legal historiographers were among the first to acknowledge the difficulty of constructing the proper context for accurate historical interpretation. Having pointed, in his metaphor of the ship of the Argonauts, to the deceptive appearance of continuity in the process of change in customary norms, Sir Matthew Hale went on to observe that even "if a man could at this Day have the Prospects of all the Laws of the Britains before any Invasion upon them, it

16. John Spelman, *The Life of Alfred the Great*, ed. Thomas Hearne (London, 1709), p. 2.
17. Spelman, *The Life of Alfred the Great*, p. 1.

would yet be impossible to say, which of them were New, and which were Old, and the several Seasons and Periods of Time wherein every Law took its Rise and Original."[1] Not only the intellectual complexity of the problem, but the apparent lack of technical sophistication to address it, gave Nathaniel Brady cause to lament "that for the Lawes, Customes, and Usages of the *Saxons* and *German* People that came hither with them, we must look further than our own Historians, or rest satisfied with a very ordinary, pitiful, and lame account of them."[2]

In addition to the difficulty of securing information, there remained the problem that still faces every historian—the arrangement and exposition of information in such a way as to establish context with due regard for the aims of narrative. William Lambarde had encountered the problem in the sixteenth century and attempted to solve it by placing a separate history of the "lawes, customes, and manners of life" at the conclusion of his narrative of affairs in Kent:

> Although good order mighte have borne the rehersall of the ancient Customes of this Shire, in that generall discourse which we had in the beginning as touching the estate of this whole Countrie, the rather for that it was there shewed by what meanes and policie they were conservyd: yet, least the recitall of the same (being of themselves large and manifold) might have been too great a Parenthesis, or rather an interruption of the Historie, wherein wee were but as newly entred, I thought better to reserve them to this place: to the ende, that both the one and the other, might appeere, without breach, or confusion.[3]

The concept of historical periods, insofar as it provided a temporal framework for the establishment of context, offered a partial solution. "The contexture of our owne Historie" nevertheless plagued even Daniel, for it required "the sowing . . . together" not only of events but also of "the observation of those necessary circumstances, and inferences which the History naturally ministers." Hence "a passable Contexture of the whole History" demands the interweaving of the narrative with an account of the contemporary aims and values, "those

---

1. Sir Matthew Hale, *A History of the Common Law of England*, p. 41.

2. Nathaniel Brady, *The Complete History of England* (London, 1685), p. 41.

3. William Lambarde, *A Perambulation of Kent: Containing the Description, Historie, and Customes of that Shire* (London: Baldwin, Cradock, and Joy, 1826), p. 475.

Reasons of State they had, for what they did in those times."[4] Many early theorists had advised against accounts of circumstance and setting as more fit "for ornament than use," and even Wheare, while insisting upon the importance of "forgotten Customes," recommended their subordination to the narrative in the form of "Domestick Digressions."[5] In response to this problem, Hobbes observed that in the "many excellent and profitable histories" written since Thucydides, "there be inserted very wise discourses, both of manners and of policy. But being discourses inserted, and not of the contexture of the narration, they indeed commend the knowledge of the writer, but not the history itself: the nature whereof is merely narrative." More concerned with such "discourses" for their utility in the present than for their value in establishing historical context, and thus in sympathy with the ancient subordination of history to philosophy, Hobbes declared that they should be submerged within the terms and context of the narrative, so "that the narration itself doth secretly instruct the reader." Even so, however, Hobbes defended the need for background and context, for "without some general notions of these times, many places of [Thucydides'] history are less easy to be understood; as depending upon the knowledge of the original several cities and customs."[6]

Thus, although the growing prominence of convention as a norm in the Renaissance arts allowed increasing claims for the art of history, and while developments in these arts and within historiography itself led to an increasing awareness of the importance of historical context, the theoretical implications of this awareness remained far in advance of actual historiographical achievements. Largely for the reasons that the historians themselves suggested, the consistent practice of contextualism was a decidedly minor current even in the later seventeenth century. Nevertheless, in several areas of historical research—in political and institutional history, in philology, and in the growing interest in cultural history conducted largely under the rubric of geography—the concept of convention was becoming instrumental in the reconstruction of historical context.

In the field of political history, John Selden, for example, urged not only the narration of political events, but also "the careful examination of constitutions and customs, *their received interpretations,* and their force, in the state and age of which any civil disquisition is

4. Daniel, *Works,* IV, 75, 83, 81; for Camden's view of the same problem in his *Annals,* see Fussner, pp. 239–244.

5. Wheare, *The Method and Order of Reading . . . Histories,* p. 111.

6. Hobbes, *Thucydides,* pp. 7, 18, 23–24.

raised."[7] Selden's view reflects not only his traffic with the common law of England, but also the theory of institutional history that was the chief legacy of Bodin's highly influential *Methodus*. Not only had Bodin recommended the study of cultural contexts, but he had relied heavily on Polybius, whom he claimed exemplified the highest qualities of a historian as a man of action whose wide travels and political experience enabled him more readily to "understand the customs of the people and the type of the state." The cosmopolitan outlook of the later Greek historians, and especially of Polybius, Bodin maintained, provided a comparative perspective on "the general institutions of the Romans which the Latins had overlooked."[8]

Indeed, the failure of the ancient and medieval historians in this respect had become a commonplace among the Renaissance theorists. "All historians without exception," Guicciardini complains, "have erred in leaving out of their writings many facts well known to their contemporaries, simply because they presupposed everyone knew them. That is why we lack information on so many points in Roman, Greek, and all other history."[9] Similarly, La Popelinière observes that history should include accounts of "the character, the mores, the customs, and the way of life of the people in question," and thus complains that Thucydides failed to provide "an understanding of the Greek way of life . . . their officers and magistrates, their religion, their laws, their way of life and, in general, the nature of Greek society."[10] Echoing these complaints, Wheare observes that "the Latines neglected as common and well known, their Sacrifices (for instance), Plays, Triumphs, Insigns of Magistrates, and all the Order of the Roman public Government . . . *as if they thought them unchangeable.*"[11] As a response to this shortcoming, Boemus attempts in his compendium to set forth all "memorable lawes, customes, and manners of all nations, and the situation of each severall Countrie, which . . . many other famous Historiographers have confusedly and (as it were) by parts commended unto us in their Commentaries."[12]

As the notable exception to this failure, Polybius' theory of institutional history was adopted by Bodin and others as a corrective.[13] The

7. John Selden, *Titles of Honour,* in *Opera Omnia* (London, 1726), III, 103; my italics.

8. Bodin, *Methodus,* pp. 44, 63; cf. pp. 59–60.

9. Guicciardini, *Maxims and Reflections,* C.143.

10. La Popelinière, quoted in Huppert, pp. 141–143.

11. Wheare, *The Method and Order of Reading . . . Histories,* p. 83; my italics.

12. Johann Boemus, *The Manners, Lawes, and Customes of All Nations,* sig. A.

13. See Beatrice Reynolds, "Shifting Currents in Historical Criticism," *JHI,* 14 (1953), 471–492. Bk. 6, the *locus* of Polybius' theory, was not printed with the early

focus of Polybius upon institutional change originated in his interest in the theory of constitutional types and the dynamics of their repetitive sequence as explained by Plato and refined by Aristotle.[14] In assessing the value of these abstract models, however, Polybius emphasized the need to justify the pattern (*anacyclosis*) with historical explanations (*apodeiktike historia*) of the conditions under which such changes occur.[15] Accordingly, he argued for the historical comparison of institutions; simply to apply Platonic models to actual constitutions would be "to take some statue and compare it with living and breathing men." Thus in attempting to explain the character of the Roman constitution, Polybius used not only Greek political theory, but also a historical account of the "customs and laws *(ethe kai nomoi)*"[16] that were embodied and maintained in institutional forms.

This Polybian interpretation of institutional forms and change in the historical terms of setting, values, and contingent circumstances was the source for Bodin's view that history should explain the institutional peculiarities that characterize different polities,[17] and the basis of Selden's claim that

> the phrases or notions concerning just or unjust, and convenient and inconvenient . . . are often so disproportionate to what they are applied in disquisitions concerning such states as are wholly of another mould or frame, that it cannot be doubted but that if any of those great writers of Greece were now living again, they would in recognizing and fitting their politicks to present use, first inform themselves of the several faces and forms of government, and the constitutions and customes of the present age.[18]

This need to supplement political study with an understanding of institutional history, of the temporal conditions and values that institutions embody and sustain, found its most sensitive application in the

---

Latin translations of the *Histories,* but for the availability of a translation, see J. H. Hexter, "Seyssel, Machiavelli, and Polybius VI: The Mystery of the Missing Translation," *SRen,* 3 (1956), 75–96.

14. See *Republic,* 544C ff., and *Politics,* 1316a ff.; cf. Barker's edition of *Politics,* p. 143n2.

15. Polybius, *The Histories,* 2.37.3, 6.9.10, 6.11.10. See F. W. Walbank, *Polybius* (Berkeley: University of California Press, 1972), pp. 57–140.

16. *The Histories,* 4.47.1–4, 7–10. See also Walbank, pp. 147, 153–154.

17. See Julian H. Franklin, p. 77; and Frank E. Manuel, *Shapes of Philosophical History* (Stanford: Stanford University Press, 1965), p. 55.

18. Selden, *Titles of Honour,* in *Opera Omnia,* III, 104.

efforts of Spelman, Brady, Dugdale, and others to reconstruct the English *feudum*. These efforts brought philology to the aid of institutional history, and thus established context and coherence as the tests of historical truth. The history of such institutions as church tithes, Selden observes, "and not a few other inquiries of subjects too much unknown, fall only under a far more general study; that is, of *Philology*."[19] The link between philology and historical thinking was greatly strengthened by the Reformation debate over the "duble name" of custom, and found expression in the method of historical interpretation applied to Scripture by Erasmus, Colet, and others. This method itself, however, was part of an ever broader revival of rhetorical thought that subjected norms to their social setting. Discourse became an index of changing social contexts; as Erasmus put it in his *Ciceronianus* (1528): "since the whole course of human affairs has been overturned, who today can talk sensibly unless he uses language very different from that of Cicero? Wherever I turn my eyes I see all things changed, I stand before another stage and I behold another play, nay, even a different world."[20] This sense of change provided a "perspective distance" from which civilizations could be viewed as cultural systems "within which all things belonged together."[21] Not only the sense of coherence within historic periods, but also the sense of anachronism between them, led to the establishment of coherence as the test of historic truth.

Beginning with Lorenzo Valla's fifteenth-century exposure of the Donation of Constantine as a forgery, philology increasingly became the servant of historical investigation.[22] The application of philology to institutional history helped to pave the way for such monuments of feudal research as Spelman's *Archaeologus*. William Camden, for example, "having gotten some insight into the old British and Saxon tongues for my assistance . . . towards the discovery of hidden Truth," declared that he "would have the name of every thing to agree with the

19. Selden, *Opera Omnia*, III, 1073; quoted in Levy, *Tudor Historical Thought*, p. 190.

20. Erasmus, *Ciceronianus*, quoted in Myron P. Gilmore, *"Fides et Eruditio:* Erasmus and the Study of History," in *Humanists and Jurists: Six Studies in the Renaissance* (Cambridge: Harvard University Press, 1963), pp. 104–105.

21. Erwin Panofsky, *Renaissance and Renascences in Western Art* (Copenhagen: Russak, 1960), pp. 111–113.

22. See Stephen Toulmin and Jane Goodfield, *The Discovery of Time* (New York: Harper Torchbooks, 1966), pp. 110–113; Arthur B. Ferguson, "Reginald Pecock and the Renaissance Sense of History," *SRen*, 13 (1966), 147–165, and his *The Articulate Citizen in the Renaissance* (Durham: Duke University Press, 1965), pp. 395–396.

thing itself; if it disagree, I give it no admittance."[23] Refining on this method, Selden attempted to eradicate the "intollerable Antichronismes" of Drayton's *Poly-Olbion* on the basis of historical *"Synchronisme* (the best Touchstone in this kind of Triall)."[24] This test of "synchronism" or coherence came increasingly to rely upon not only the historical context of verbal conventions but their place in a wider matrix of social and institutional conventions as well. As Casaubon put it in his *Treatise of Use and Custom:* "the ordinary and surest way generally to find out a counterfeit Authour . . . is by his style, and by an accurate examination of those particular fashions, and customs that he doth either *obiter* or purposely speak of, how well they fit and sute to the time and place that is pretended. Take away these two *criteria* of words and customs, and it will be a hard task for any man to discover and evict the suppositiousness of any writing."[25]

With this recognition that "the times often give great light to the true interpretation,"[26] the test of coherence used in institutional history and philology was extended to include even wider interests in cultural context. In his *View of the State of Ireland* (1596), Spenser invokes "the difference of manners and customs [that] doth follow the difference of nations and people" in order to explain the failure to impose the English common law upon the ancient Brehon law. Such differences constitute a cultural matrix whose coherence is the test of historical truth; it is, says Spenser, from "comparison of times, likewise of manners and customs, affinity of words and names, properties of natures and uses, resemblences of rights and ceremonies, monuments of churches and tombs, and many other like circumstances, I do gather a likelihood of truth, not certainely affirming any thing, but by conferring of times, language, monuments, and such like, I do hunt out a probability of things."[27]

The coherence of historical contexts not only served as a test for "likelihood of truth," but also stood as an object worthy of historical understanding in itself. Just as years and seasons serve to measure physical time, Casaubon claimed, "so varietie of fashions and customs serve unto man for the Civill or politicke distinction of the sev-

23. Camden, Preface, *Britannia* (unpaginated).

24. Selden, "From the Author of the Illustrations," in Drayton's *Poly-Olbion*, in *Works*, ed. J. William Hebel, Kathleen Tillotson, and Bernard Newdigate (Oxford: Shakespeare Head Press, 1931–1941), IV, viii.

25. Casaubon, *A Treatise of Use and Custom*, p. 86.

26. Bacon, *The Advancement of Learning*, in *Works*, III, 330.

27. Spenser, *Works* (London, 1849), pp. 493b, 491a.

erall ages and times of the World" (p. 83). Such contextual "distinctions," Bacon argued, could provide a perspective on the arts as well, for "by tasting [the literary works] here and there and observing their argument, style, and method, the Literary Spirit of each age may be charmed as it were from the dead."[28]

This interest in the total complexion of cultures was undoubtedly stimulated by the expanding importance of geography in the Renaissance world. Not only had the historical thinkers of the Renaissance criticized the ancients for their failure to describe their own cultures, but they had found the ancient historians generally narrow and parochial in outlook.[29] As a remedy to this shortcoming, Bacon, for example, proposed as a branch of civil history, a study "compounded of natural history, in respect of the regions themselves; of history civil, in respect of the habitations, regiments, and manners of the people; and the mathematics in respect of the clymates and configurations toward the heavens."[30] Bacon here recommends as a separate science what the humanists had long recommended as an ancilla to the reading of history.[31] Heylyn had observed that "Geography therefore & History, like the two fire-lights *Castor* & *Pollux,* seene together, crowne our hapines: but parted asunder, menace a shipwracke of our content."[32] Intended originally to illuminate the setting of historic events, geography in historical writing gained importance in proportion with the increasing importance of context. As a reflection of this growth, the antiquarians borrowed from Pliny both the term and framework for the "Chorographicall Description"[33] of their national, county, and local surveys, and they examined laws, customs, artifacts, and monuments in order to produce the fullest possible descriptions of cultures and civilizations.[34] Not assuming until the early eighteenth century its more limited definition as the specialized study of the purely physical fea-

28. Bacon, *Advancement of Learning, Works,* III, 330.

29. See, e.g., Bacon, *New Organon,* in *Works,* IV, 73; cf. Leonard Dean, "Sir Francis Bacon's Theory of Civil History Writing," *ELH,* 8 (1941), 161–183; and Robert R. Crawley, *Unpathed Waters: Studies in the Influence of the Voyagers on Elizabethan Literature* (Princeton: Princeton University Press, 1940), pp. 244–245.

30. Bacon, *Advancement of Learning,* in *Works,* III, 339–340.

31. See, for example, Elyot, *The Boke Named the Governour,* pp. 80–81; Erasmus, *Concerning the Aim and Method of Education,* pp. 143–145; and George B. Parks, *Richard Hakluyt and the English Voyages* (1928; rpt., New York: Frederick Ungar, 1961), pp. 6–7.

32. Heylyn, *Microcosmos,* p. 16.

33. "Delicacies, Chorographicall Description, and Historie, be my subject," Drayton, *Poly-Olbion,* in *Works,* IV, iii; cf. Speed, V, 24; and Lambarde, p. 15.

34. On the geographical precedents for these techniques, see Levy, *Tudor Historical Thought,* p. 140.

tures of a region, geography, or "chorography," in the Renaissance took as its object the description of a total setting, both physical and human, including, as Milton put it, "relations of Manners, Religion, Government and such like, accounted geographical."[35]

In conjunction with historical theory and practice, geography and chorography helped to focus attention upon the setting of human acts and productions, most notably under the pervasive influence of Jean Bodin's *Methodus*. By relating institutional forms and social practice to such factors as linguistic and religious heritage, Bodin further attempted to explain the resulting cultural configurations through the natural influence of climate.[36] Bodin's mathematical and deterministic scheme encountered considerable opposition,[37] and only found its classic formulation in eighteenth-century France in the theories of Montesquieu and Chardin. Even among skeptics, however, and long after it had been rejected by many thinkers, this theory of climatic influence continued to serve as a valuable metaphor for the unique configurations of norms and practices that characterized and sustained a diversity of civilizations and epochs. In its use by thinkers like Dryden, Temple, and Dennis, the theory of "climate," like that of the "genius of times," served to underline the relationships of norms and practices to the character of different civilizations and their different needs in time.[38]

Measured by the standard of the historically minded present, the actual Renaissance achievements in the practice of contextualism were minor; by no single writer was contextualism extensively or consistently practiced. However, the actual history these men wrote was not as important as the attitude with which they came to regard themselves and their relation to their past. As the dominant model of the time, the cyclical theory provided in the single cycle a unit metaphor for the integrity of historical process, and in the repetition of cycles a metaphor for continuity. But unlike the earlier linear framework of the universal historians, the cyclical framework made its final appeal to the plenitude of nature. While man's customs, institutions, and ideals seemed increasingly to rise and pass away, man himself remained, by nature, not only a creature, but a creator of institutions and conven-

35. Milton, *A Brief History of Muscovy*, in *The Prose of John Milton*, ed. J. Max Patrick (New York: Anchor Books, 1967), p. 573.

36. Bodin, *Methodus*, pp. 25, 79–86, 336–337; cf. Wheare, pp. 314 ff.

37. See Huppert, pp. 42–43.

38. See James W. Johnson, "'Of Differing Ages and Climes,'" *JHI*, 21 (1960), 465–480; his *The Foundations of English Neo-Classical Thought* (Princeton: Princeton University Press, 1967), pp. 47–48; and Zera S. Fink, "The Theory of Climatic Influence in Milton," *MLQ*, 2 (1941), 67–80.

tions. As metaphors for this process, Spenser's cantos of *Mutabilitie*, Hakewill's frontispiece, or Hale's ship of the Argonauts all suggest that man remains a child of nature though he inhabits a changing world of his own making.

The implications of these metaphors extend beyond the realm of historiography, however, and find their deepest meanings in the framework of normative debate that preoccupied the Renaissance and helped to redefine the nature, scope, and function of human activity. By placing human acts and products in their temporal setting, historical thought changed the order and study of human things; it shifted the perspective of human philosophy from man's natural ends to the beginnings of his self-created world in time.

V. The Triumph
of Convention

1. "A LATITUDE OF SENSE":
TESTING FOR TRUTH

Until the later sixteenth century, thought about convention did not exceed the limits of the ancient technical tradition or substantially alter it. Rather, the rehabilitation of the arts was a general and widespread search for artistic guidance, rules, and norms that restored the framework to its full potential. As shown earlier, however, this restoration engendered a debate that challenged the possibility of technical order. Thus, when one seventeenth-century writer looked back upon his predecessors, he observed that their quest for "such a guide as they were all bound to follow . . . became a part of the disease for which the cure was intended."[1] In confronting the ideal of natural fitness with the varieties of convention, the normative debate of the sixteenth century brought about the need for what Jonson called a "separation of opinions," a critical effort to determine and judge the grounds on which particular normative claims were made.

The great preoccupation with the nature of truth in the seventeenth century was thus at once an extension and transformation of a sixteenth-century crisis. As Jeremy Taylor explained it, "all men resolved upon this, that though they had not yet hit upon the right, yet some way must be thought upon to reconcile differences in opinion."[2] The result, he claimed, was a "pious endeavor to find out truth." This endeavor was not limited to divines; it was taken up by such giants as Descartes, Hobbes, and Locke and in such forgotten works as Herbert of Cherbury's *De Veritate* (1633), Robert Greville's *The Nature of Truth* (1640), John Wallis' *Truth Tried* (1643), and George Rust's

---

1. Jeremy Taylor, *A Discourse of the Liberty of Prophesying*, in *The Whole Works* (London, 1822), VII, 439, 441.
2. Taylor, *A Discourse of the Liberty of Prophesying*, in *Works*, VII, 440.

Discourse of Truth (1682). It was in part because of the seeming in-compatibility of alternative normative claims that the technical hand-book of the sixteenth century—the *ars* or institute"[3]—became the epis-temological "discourse on method" of the seventeenth, and that the debate about the "duble name" of custom became what Milton called the "wars of truth."[4]

For most seventeenth-century philosophers, the mode of inquiry into truth was not metaphysical, but epistemological; it was essentially an inward turn of mind.[5] This inward focus was a corollary of debate about convention. Just as the growing prominence of convention shifted the normative basis of the arts from their ends in nature to their historical origins in time, so the crisis that this shift engendered turned the search for grounds of certainty to their origins in the mind itself. The result was a novel emphasis on subjective tests of truth. For reasons shortly to be discussed, most seventeenth-century epistemologies parted company with scholastic tradition by referring the test of truth to acts and powers of the mind, to the subjective assent of individuals and to the collective consent of societies. On the one hand, such sub-jective tests involved a tendency to distinguish between universal con-sent and consent limited to particular groups or societies, and thus re-affirmed the objective, logocentric view that distinguished between a universal world order and various social manifestations. On the other hand, the relative degree of validity accorded to the latter created a second dialectic between social consensus and the individual's appre-hensions, so that the varieties of consensus were measured not only against the criterion of universality, but also against the test of clarity and distinctness of individual apprehension. Thus the test of consent at once embraced a dialectic from an older language of legalism and a novel dialectic about the origins of knowledge. The latter became a basic structure of Enlightenment thought—the debate between ra-tionalism, with its emphasis on the *a priori* and the innate powers of mind, and empiricism, with its emphasis on the historical, psychologi-cal, and social origins of knowledge[6]—and, in turn, it furnished a ma-jor argumentative basis for Romanticism.

3. See Thomas M. Greene, "The Flexibility of the Self in Renaissance Litera-ture," in Peter Demetz et al., *The Disciplines of Criticism* (New Haven: Yale Uni-versity Press, 1968), p. 250.

4. Milton, *Areopagitica*, in *Complete Prose Works* (New Haven: Yale University Press, 1959), II, 562.

5. See Basil Willey, *The Seventeenth Century Background* (1935; rpt., New York: Anchor Books, 1953), p. 83.

6. See W. von Leyden, *Seventeenth-Century Metaphysics* (London: Duckworth, 1968), p. 60.

The reasons for the subtle modulations between these older and newer dialectics are apparent in the history of seventeenth-century epistemology itself, in its origins and in the characteristic shape it took. In the first place, the quest for grounds of certainty was in large part a response to normative chaos. In England, at least, theological and political controversy was a major motive and context for epistemological endeavor, though for reasons that will become clear, it did not circumscribe their implications, which were deliberately extended to such fields as morality and science as well. The sixteenth century had witnessed strenuous efforts to reconcile conventional order and practice with the unchanging dictates of faith and reason; Hooker's had been the culminating and most intellectually successful of efforts in this vein. In the early seventeenth century William Laud and his party attempted to build a state church upon the capital of Hooker's theory, but they violated the terms and spirit of the settlement it had been written to defend.[7] Arguing that "unity cannot long continue . . . where uniformity is shut out of the church door,"[8] Laud imposed measures that seemed increasingly inconsistent, arbitrary, and positive. Hooker's reasonable defense of conventional order showed a "distressing tendency to harden into an authoritarian mood," so that one writer complained of what he feared was Laud's "reconciliation with this Babylonish strumpet."[9] Together with the strident and alternative claims of both Catholics and Puritans, Laud's efforts to eradicate dissent seemed to place a barrier between conventional uniformity and an order of true unity. Not surprisingly, such moderates as William Chillingworth, the Cambridge Platonists, and even the Restoration latitudinarians undertook to rehabilitate the truth by appealing in large part to the subjective order of inner light, to the clarity and distinctness of individual assent. Thus, as far as origins are concerned, the habit of opposing convention to universal world order preceded the habit of opposing it to the individual, but this historical priority was a function of a logical apriority. The modern individual could only emerge fully when the concept of convention had exhausted his possibilities of fulfillment in collective order.

This emergence was held in check by the double implications of seventeenth-century epistemology, by its peculiarly transitional character. While the theory of consent was in part an objective theory of

7. See Wilbur K. Jordan, *The Development of Religious Toleration in England* (Cambridge: Harvard University Press, 1932–1940), IV, 266.

8. William Laud, *Works*, IV, 60, quoted in Jordan, II, 134.

9. See Gerald R. Cragg, *Freedom and Authority: A Study of English Thought in the Early Seventeenth Century* (Philadelphia: Westminster Press, 1975), pp. 126, 112.

natural law that reaffirmed the old ideal of collective order, it was also a subjectivist theory that contrasted social consensus to the individual. Most thinkers at once insisted that the test of truth was universal consent *as well as* the clarity and distinctness of assent in the individual mind. If they sometimes failed to distinguish between these grounds of certainty, or habitually slurred over their differences, it is precisely because they occupied a transitional stage between alternative views of man, one of whose accounts of world order was philosophic in the ancient sense, and *ipso facto* normative, where the other was scientific and critical.

In both cases, however, the test of truth was determined by opposition to the lesser and merely relative certainty of limited social consensus. This opposition marked the point of alliance between Neo-Stoic and Baconian nature that, as Thomas Hanzo has shown,[10] was the foundation for the characteristic epistemology of seventeenth-century England. I have already pointed out that the early Neo-Stoic Bacon shared with the scientific Bacon an aversion to the "reign or tyranny of custom," and that his later efforts to reconstruct the foundations of knowledge sought to transcend the arbitrary fictions of merely social consensus. Together with excessive skepticism and excessive credulity, the "common notions" of men, their merely social consent to unexamined premises, formed in Bacon's view one of the three principal impediments of truth.[11] Part of the difficulty, Bacon observed, is the scholastic method, which produces an "intemperance" in the "giving or witholding assent" (*Works,* IV, 68); it relies on commonly accepted notions, proceeds by "Anticipation" rather than by "Interpretation," and thus "commands assent . . . to the proposition, but does not take hold of the thing" (IV, 49). The chief evidence of failure in this method is that it cannot command a universal assent, but merely produces diverse conclusions whose basis is social rather than veridical:

> Formerly there existed among philosophers such great disagreement, and such diversities in the schools themselves; a fact that shows that the road from the senses to the under-

10. Thomas Hanzo, *Latitude and Restoration Criticism* (Copenhagen: Rosenkilde and Bagger, 1961). I am indebted to Hanzo not only for his clarification of the relationship between religion and other modes of thought in the seventeenth century but specifically for the comparison between Bacon and Herbert of Cherbury with which his discussion begins. In points where we cover the same ground, my analysis differs more in its emphasis than in its conclusions.

11. Bacon, *Novum Organum,* in *Works,* ed. James Spedding, Robert Leslie Ellis, and Douglas Demon Heath (New York: Garrett Press, 1968), IV, 65–66, 82.

> standing was not sufficiently laid out . . . And although in
> these times disagreements and diversities of opinion on first
> principles and entire systems are for the most part extin-
> guished, still on parts of philosophy there remain innumer-
> able questions and disputes, so that it plainly appears that
> neither in the systems themselves nor in the modes of dem-
> onstration is there anything certain or sound.   (IV, 76)

One of the causes of such diversity in consensus is the nature of consent itself, which is liable to social contagion; "if the multitude assent and applaud," Bacon warns, "men ought immediately to ex-amine themselves as to what blunder or fault they may have com-mitted" (IV, 77). Nevertheless, Bacon does not abolish the test of consent, but attempts to redefine it: "Upon the point of consent men also are deceived, if the matter be looked into more keenly. For true consent is that which consists in the coincidence of free judgements, after due examination. But the greater number of those who have as-sented to the philosophy of Aristotle have addicted themselves thereto from prejudgement and upon the authority of others; so that it is a following and going along together, rather than consent" (IV, 76).

Bacon's scientific method is intended to command a universal and "true consent" that will be immune to social differences; it "goes far to level men's wits, and leaves but little to individual excellence; be-cause it performs everything by the surest rules and methods" (IV, 109). By drawing a firm line between the universal or "true consent" that is the foundation of knowledge, and the variations of consensus that uphold opinion, Bacon retains a subjective test of truth while in-suring that it is firmly grounded in the universal order. The new con-sent will be a part of the "general consents of things"; it will depend upon the "consents of the senses with their objects" (IV, 242–243), for "we cannot command nature except by obeying her" (IV, 114).

By offering universal consent as the test of truth, Bacon not only ar-rives at grounds for certainty, but distinguishes between orders of truth. Because the mind's consent remains the test of truth, even a merely relative social consensus may serve in such fields as politics and theology, "these things resting on authority, consent, fame and opinion, not on demonstration" (IV, 89). This allows a measure of toleration for areas where opinions differ, even in scientific matters, where con-sensus according to the new method is not universal. "There is," Bacon says, "no reason why the arts which are now in fashion should not continue to supply matter for disputation and ornaments for dis-course, to be employed for the convenience of professors and men of business; to be in short like current coin, which passes among men by consent" (IV, 112). Bacon's contempt and condescension for such "convenience" should not obscure the basic tolerance of opinion that his theory of consent upholds in principle. Having distinguished between universal and relative consent, between certainty and opinion, he is free to tolerate the former where it does not usurp the latter.

Though aimed at scientific interests, Bacon's theory of consent was based on Neo-Stoic grounds that he shared with another pioneering thinker, Edward, Lord Herbert of Cherbury. However different their characteristic aims and methods, both men sought to resolve the conflicting varieties of consensus by appealing to the test of universal consent. While Bacon was disturbed by contention in the scientific community, Lord Herbert addressed himself in *De Veritate* to the unedifying spectacle of political and religious conflict, to "the multitude of sects, divisions, sub-divisions and cross divisions in the schools" that "hopelessly distract the wits of the learned and the consciences of the unlettered."[12] In his "search for truth" (p. 71), Lord Herbert came to rest upon "whatever is universally assented as the truth" (p. 77). Unlike Bacon, however, he found sufficient warrant for this test in the history of normative thought itself, for "while among legal codes differences exist on many points, there is the closest agreement concerning religion or civic and political justice as such. I hold, therefore, that this universal consent is the teaching of Natural Instinct and is essentially due to divine Providence" (p. 117). In deriving his theory of Natural Instinct "from Universal Consent," Lord Herbert concluded that "it ought to be completely trusted *even where no reason for following it can be found*" (p. 77). The proper use of reason was henceforth to be "the process of applying Common Notions as far as it can . . . Common Notions, therefore, are principles which it is not legitimate to dispute; they form that part of knowledge with which we were endowed in the primeval plan of Nature" (p. 127).

In basing his theory of common notions on Stoic epistemology, on what he called "the *koinai ennoiai* of the ancients" (p. 125), Lord Herbert departed in an essential way from scholastic accounts of knowledge, even while he retained much of their machinery. From the Middle Ages through the early Renaissance, most thinkers had insisted that the proper test of truth was the mind's correct conformity with its objects.[13] "In this conformity," Aquinas had argued, "is fulfilled the formal constituent of the true, and this is what *the true* adds

12. Edward, Lord Herbert of Cherbury, *De Veritate*, ed. Meyrick H. Carré (Bristol: J. W. Arrowsmith, 1937), p. 75.

13. See Willey, pp. 83–84.

to being, namely, the conformity or equation of thing and intellect."[14] By way of contrast, the Stoic account of knowledge had posited the test of truth in the act of consent rather than conformity, so that, as Cicero explained, "in every inquiry the unanimity of the races of the world [*consensio omnium gentium*] must be regarded as a law of nature."[15] Where the Stoics had emphasized the objective foundation of universal consent, however, Lord Herbert seized upon the subjective elements of the mind's activity in assent. "Nothing can be true," he says, "at least for intellectual truths, if it does not receive the assent of some faculty, though it may be true in respect of the truth which belongs to the object" (p. 80). Thus "Universal Consent . . . will be found to be the final test of truth" (p. 117), but "if a quicker method is demanded I will give it. Look into your own faculties and you will find God, virtue, and universal eternal truths" (p. 121).

By emphasizing the subjective test of the mind's assent rather than its right and needful conformity with its objects—by coming, as he says, to "measure . . . the entire race by myself" (p. 79)—Lord Herbert substituted for the distinction between truth and error a distinction between certain knowledge and opinion. Because differing opinions are supported by the same power of assent that creates universal consent, differences of opinion on matters where no consensus exists are merely evidence that such matters are not susceptible to final and indubitable resolution. The essential truths, the Common Notions, he explains, comprise "whatever appears the same way in every man . . . As for what remains, there is obviously freedom and a wide diversity of behavior" (pp. 119–120). This epistemological distinction became the basis for a proposed resolution of normative conflict. Men should be advised "to lay aside all fear and irritation and in a calm spirit of sympathy to seek to distinguish what is declared by universal consent from what is not so declared" (p. 118). The only catholic and uniform Church, Herbert declares, "is the doctrine of common notions which comprehends all places and all men" (p. 303). At the same time that the test of universal consent secures the fundamental truth, however, it enables Lord Herbert, like Bacon, to extend a relative measure of validity to differing opinions based on limited social consent, provided they do not conflict with certain truth. The Common Notions do not, in other words, exclude the right of religious societies "to decide all matters which concern external worship or ecclesiastical organization"

14. Thomas Aquinas, *Quaestiones Disputatae de Veritate,* trans. Robert W. Mulligan, S.J. (Chicago: Henry Regnery, 1952), q.1, a.1. (p. 6).

15. Cicero, *Tusculan Disputations,* 1.13.30.

(p. 305), for these are matters relative "to differences of age and country" (p. 289).

In the first half of the seventeenth century, the ever-widening differences of churches and religious sects, and especially their alternative claims in normative matters, inspired a variety of moderate arguments in behalf of religious toleration. No argument, however, was so persuasive and so widespread as the epistemological argument for latitude. It was in part appealing because it placed normative debate on more fundamental grounds, but even more so because the particular notions of assent and consent that it entertained could at once encompass reason and faith, secular and religious truth. If the test of truth were taken as the mind's assent, it could be said that it commanded belief or faith, and hence that all knowledge held to be true was a form of faith. "Faith," John Tillotson declared, "is not opposed to . . . knowledge or opinion."[16] The reason, William Chillingworth explained, is "that as opinion is an assent, so is faith also," and "as opinion, so faith, admits degrees."[17] It was very largely because of their insistence on assent as the test of truth that the seventeenth-century moderates were philosophers even while their subject matter was religion,[18] and that their moral theology was characteristically a natural religion in which, as Nathaniel Culverwell explained in his *Discourse of the Light of Nature,* "Reason and Faith may kisse."[19]

The broadly philosophic spirit of Chillingworth's *Religion of Protestants* (1638), an irenistic work that set the tone for later latitudinarian thought, was thus firmly grounded on the supposition that faith is "nothing else than the understanding's assent" (*Works,* I, 233). Accordingly, as Chillingworth argued, the only religious certainty available to man lies in "a common profession of those articles of faith wherein all consent" (II, 64). On the basis of this common consent, there is sufficient ground for unity; indeed, as he explains, the basic truths on which men agree "amount to many millions (if an exact count were to be taken of them): and, on the other side, those points in variance are in comparison but few, and those not of such a quality, but the error in them may well consist with the belief and obedience

16. John Tillotson, *Works* (London, 1820), IX, 184.

17. William Chillingworth, *The Religion of Protestants a Safe Way to Salvation* (1638), in *Works* (London, 1820), I, 149.

18. See Gerald R. Cragg, *From Puritanism to the Age of Reason* (1950; rpt., Cambridge: Cambridge University Press, 1966), p. 49.

19. Nathaniel Culverwell, *An Elegant and Learned Discourse of the Light of Nature* (1652), ed. Robert A. Greene and Hugh MacCallum (Toronto: University of Toronto Press, 1971), p .13.

of the entire covenant, ratified between God and man" (II, 81). Thus, for Chillingworth, unanimous consent on basic points (which in his view are all embodied in Scripture) is confirmation of their truth and their normative capacity "to end all controversies necessary to be ended. For others that are not so, they will end when the world ends, and that is time enough" (I, 209–210). Chillingworth's willingness to tolerate diversity on such matters is not due to indifference, but to confidence that the same power of assent underlying unanimous consent bestows even a relative and provisional validity on different opinions. Unanimous consent confirms those truths that are impervious to change, but the "variety of circumstance" dictates that on many matters the truth "may be sufficiently declared to one (all things considered), which (all things considered to another) is not sufficiently declared" (I, 376). In such cases, where agreement is not unanimous, opinions may be used as guidance toward the truth, but any final conclusions "are thence-hence deducible, but probably only, not evidently" (I, 161). In order for assent to serve as a test of certainty at all, it must be allowed to operate reliably under limitation. When we consider the strange power of education and prejudice, Chillingworth explains, "we may well imagine that many truths, which in themselves are revealed plainly enough, are yet to such or such a man, prepossessed of contrary opinions, not revealed plainly" (I, 381). To be sure, we observe the difference between certainty and opinion by never giving "a greater assent to the conclusion, than the premises deserve" (I, 316);

> but to overlook the factors that sometimes limit and influence assent would be as reasonable as if you should desire us (according to the fable) to make a coat to fit the moon in all her changes; or to give you a garment that will fit all statues; or to make you a dial to serve all meridians; or to design particularly, what provision will serve an army for a year; whereas there may be an army of ten thousand, there may be one of one hundred thousand.   (I, 376)

Thus the absolute certainty guaranteed by the test of assent where men agree confers a relative measure of validity even in matters where opinions differ. In a crucial passage, Chillingworth very nearly maintains that the assent to truth is as important as the truth itself: "For as I may deny something which you upon your knowledge have affirmed, and yet never disparage your honesty: so I may be undoubtedly certain of God's omniscience, and veracity, and yet doubt of something which he hath revealed; provided, I do not know, nor believe, that he hath revealed it" (I, 157).[20]

Chillingworth's argument was compelling to liberals and moderates alike. It was, for example, just such confidence in the mind's subjective powers that inspired the group of thinkers loosely known as Cambridge Platonists to adopt the test of assent in their epistemological writings, and to use it as an argument in defense of latitude and toleration. For most of these thinkers, as for Chillingworth and Herbert of Cherbury, the final test of truth became "the mind's assent."[21] Most of them, like Culverwell, were careful to observe that truth is essentially objective, that "Reason does not *facere* (make) or *ferre legem* (produce the law), but only *invenire* (discover it)" (p. 65). Nevertheless, they insisted virtually without exception that in all knowing as "in all believing there is an assent,"[22] that for men the measure of the truth is finally and undeniably subjective. Thus the quest for "pure objectivity, the essential element which remains unchanged in all the various forms of the objective, can be achieved and assured only through such subjectivity."[23] For the Platonists, the irreducibly subjective component of knowledge established assent as the test of truth in matters of faith as well as reason, so that, as John Smith put it in *Select Discourses,* "such as Men themselves are, such will God himself seem to be."[24]

Though nurtured by a mystical sensibility, the Platonists' endorsement of assent was deeply rooted in a closely reasoned defense of the mind's subjective contribution to knowledge. To maintain that the mind is "meerly patient," Culverwell argued, "is extremely prejudicial to such a noble Being as the soul of Man is; to which God gave such bright participations of himself" (p. 70). There is "an active sagacity in the Soul," Henry More explained, "an active and *actual Knowledge*" without which man could not "be moulded into an assent to any thing."[25] Indeed, were it not for the activity of mind, there could be no intelligible experience at all; our experience of the world, contended Ralph Cudworth, is "not foreign and adventitious, and mere passive impressions upon the soul from without, but native and domestic to it, or

20. See Herschel Baker, *The Wars of Truth* (Cambridge: Harvard University Press, 1952), p. 226.

21. F. J. Powicke, *The Cambridge Platonists: A Study* (Cambridge: Harvard University Press, 1926), p. 27.

22. Culverwell, p. 139.

23. Ernst Cassirer, *The Platonic Renaissance in England,* trans. James P. Pettigrove (Austin: University of Texas Press, 1953), p. 32.

24. John Smith, *Select Discourses* (London, 1821), p. 5.

25. Henry More, *An Antidote Against Atheism,* in *Philosophical Writings* (London, 1712), pp. 17–20.

actively exerted from the soul itself; no passion being able to make a judgement either of itself or other things."[26] Accordingly, as Cudworth explains in his *Treatise Concerning Eternal and Immutable Morality,* "the criterion of true knowledge is not to be looked for anywhere abroad without our minds, neither in the height above, nor in the depth beneath, but only in our knowledge and conceptions themselves. For the entity of all theoretical truth is nothing else but clear intelligibility, and whatever is clearly conceived is an entity and a truth; but that which is false, divine power itself cannot make it to be clearly and distinctly understood."[27]

The endorsement of assent by the Cambridge Platonists, therefore, originated in a subjectivist bias that they shared with Descartes, whom in certain limited respects they admired and emulated. At the same time, however, their account of truth differed markedly in both the certainty they attributed to universal consent and in the provisional validity they extended to differing opinions. For Descartes, the subjective criterion of clear and distinct apprehension served as the exclusive test of truth against which all manners of consensus were invalid. Unlike the Platonists, Descartes declared that when he "considered the manners of other men," he "found nothing to give me settled convictions." Any search for consensus, he argued, shows that "it is much more custom and example that persuade us of any certain knowledge, and yet in spite of this the voice of the majority does not afford a proof of any value in truths a little difficult to discover, because such truths are more likely to have been discovered by one man than by a nation."[28]

The Platonists could no more subscribe to such extreme subjectivism than they could endorse Descartes' rigid distinction between the realms of mind and body. In their appeal to the logical *a priori* that validates individual assent, they had recourse to the notion of ethical a priority that the Stoa placed in universal consent. The orders of history and collective experience were not to be opposed to individual assent, but to serve as confirmation of it. The power of "judging in a Man," Henry More declared, "is very hard to be called a *private Spirit,* if it judgeth according to the *Universall Sense of humane Na-*

26. Ralph Cudworth, *The True Intellectual System of the Universe* (London, 1845), II, 512.

27. Cudworth, *A Treatise Concerning Eternal and Immutable Morality,* in *The True Intellectual System of the Universe,* III, 635. Subsequent references in the text to the *Treatise* are given by page number only.

28. René Descartes, *Discourse on Method,* in *The Philosophical Works,* trans. Elizabeth S. Haldane and G. R. T. Ross (1911; rpt., Cambridge: Cambridge University Press, 1973), I, 87, 91.

ture, and so as every one judgeth when he is biassed."[29] Truth is thus at
once established on the subjective grounds of individual assent and
on the objective grounds of universal consent. "Whatsoever is clearly
and distinctly perceived in things abstract and universal, by any one
rational being in the whole world," Cudworth maintained, "is not a
private thing, and true to himself only that perceived it; but it is, as
some Stoics have called it, *alethes katholikon,* 'a public, catholic, and
universal truth' " (p. 36). Thus while individual assent remains a valid
test of truth, Culverwell says, "yet there is also a secondary way and
additional way, which contributes no small light to the manifestation
of it: I mean the harmony & joynt consent of Nations" (p. 72).

This appeal to universal consent was an essential confirmation of
the value of history, tradition, and collective experience. Significantly,
the Platonists drew their theory of natural law, not from Suarez, in
whom a scholastic and rationalistic account was currently available, but
from Hugo Grotius, whose account was based on the largely empirical
Stoic theory of *consensus gentium.* The universal law of nature, Grotius
observed, is demonstrable not only from the *a priori* grounds of right
reason, but also from *a posteriori* and empirical grounds of common
consent.[30] Thus Culverwell, for example, quotes Grotius when he observes that the law of nature is confirmed by two tests of truth: "The
proof is *a priori* if it is shown that any thing necessarily agrees or dis-
agrees with a rational and social nature; it is *a posteriori* if it is concluded, not with absolute certainty, but very probably, that it accords
with the natural law which all nations, or at least the more civilized
nations, believe accords with it" (p. 72). Although grounded in the
same subjective power of assent that provides the individual with certainty, the test of universal consent provided an empirical complement
and confirmation of this power. Thus, while insisting on the "clear
and perspicuous" power of individual apprehension, Benjamin Whichcote nevertheless maintained that "general and universal experience,"
along with private reason and Scripture, was "one of the three great
principles of knowledge."[31] "Dry reason," he argued, "is often times
doubted of; but when in conjunction with experience, we then think
we have a double assurance" (*Works,* III, 14). Accordingly, the essential and fundamental "truth of first inscription" (II, 20) is determined
not only by the free "consent of the mind and will" (I, 314), but by

29. Henry More, *An Inquiry into the Mystery of Iniquity* (London, 1664), p. 456.

30. See Hugo Grotius, *De Jure Belli ac Pacis Libri Tres,* trans. Francis W.
Kelsey (1925; rpt., Indianapolis: Bobbs-Merrill, 1962), 1.1.10–12; cf. Introduction, p.
xxxiv. See also Carl J. Friedrich, *The Philosophy of Law in Historical Perspective*
(Chicago: University of Chicago Press, 1963), pp. 65–66.

31. Benjamin Whichcote, *Works* (Aberdeen, 1751), III, 14.

the empirical evidence of history, for it is "such wherein there is universal consent and agreement" (II, 2). The efficacy of individual assent entails, as Whichcote puts it, that "we may take it for granted that the great matters of natural knowledge and faith that have passed thro' so many ages are solid, true, and substantial . . . That which comes down to us thro' the several ages before us, is likely to be sincere and true; because all wits have been employed to search into it" (III, 35).

In appealing to individual assent as well as collective consent, the Platonists, like other latitudinarian thinkers, took an epistemological stance that was, for two related reasons, of great significance in the history of thought about convention. First, their definition of the test of truth placed earlier normative debate on epistemological grounds that embraced what were to become for the Enlightenment alternative grounds of certainty—the order of the individual and the order of society. Significantly, the Platonists opposed the extreme rationalism of Descartes as well as the extreme empiricism of Hobbes, yet their epistemology incorporated some of the most novel elements of both. They managed to uphold the rational apriority of the powers of mind without falling into utter subjectivism, and at the same time to endorse the empirical, *a posteriori*, test of consensus without subscribing to its extremer nominalist implications. Their stance embodied elements of a novel dialectic, but held them in harmonious synthesis by adhering at the same time to an older logocentric order in which the individual and society were bound together. Thus Cudworth could maintain that "true knowledge or science . . . exists nowhere but in the mind itself" (p. 636); but he could also argue that "truths are not multiplied by the diversity of minds that apprehend them; because they are all but ectypal participations of one and the same original or archetypal mind and truth" (p. 71).

By standing midway between older and newer modes of thought, the Platonists could, secondly, survey the problem of normative diversity from the relatively serene standpoint of epistemology. While the subjective test of individual assent confirmed the validity of universal consent, the latter, through appeal to history and experience, could serve as the empirical means of distinguishing between those areas where certainty was absolute and those where certainty was relative to the limitations imposed upon assent by circumstance. The empirical test of consensus showed, as Whichcote argued, that

> there are *majora, insigniora jura,* the greater, the higher, more universal, famous *rights,* and there are also the *inferiora, minutioria, leviora,* the lesser, more particular, and

obscurer rights, that are of more uncertain resolution and
determination. And there is a great difference between these
two sorts upon a two-fold account. There is a great difference in the things themselves, in respect of the matter of
them. And there is a vast difference also in respect of our
evidence and assurance of them. (*Works,* IV, 108).

For Whichcote, as for his colleagues, the differences in "matter" and
"assurance" were intimately related. Universal consent identifies those
truths that are "always the same, in all places, in all times, in all cases,
in respect of all persons, in all seasons, under all dispensations, they
are unalterable, immutable, indispensable, and of perpetual obligation" (IV, 109). In contrast with these certain truths, the history of
religion also shows that there are matters "of more hazardous and uncertain determination; because of change, or variety of circumstance"
(IV, 113). Thus, More explains, the test of universal consent should
"stand for an eternal President, to guide our actions in all like cases,
where circumstances are the same,"[32] but in other cases, he says in
The Apology,

there is a marvelous *Incommensurability* of things in humane affairs; and . . . we may as well expect that the Di-
ameter of a Circle should be symmetrical to the Periphery,
and the Diagonal of a Square to the Side thereof, as that one
thing or one Truth should serve all turns and all occasions.
Nay, though it were in our power to mint Truth as we
please, and to set that stamp and title upon what ever Proposition would serve our turn best, yet we should find that it
would not serve all Emergencies, nor fit all occasions, nor be
exempt from all exceptions.[33]

In thus allowing for the varieties of experience and circumstance, the
Platonists were careful to eschew any skepticism that this allowance
might have seemed to imply. More, for example, was particularly sensitive to the threat of relativism, but argued that an allowance for differences in circumstance was less detrimental to truth than the subjection
of the individual to arbitrary uniformity, for "then he is bound up to
the Religion of his Prince and Nation . . . as if all Religions were

32. More, *Enchiridion Ethicum,* trans. Robert Southwell (1690; rpt., New
York: Facsimile Society, 1930), p. 30.
33. *The Apology of Dr. Henry More,* printed with *An Inquiry into the Mystery
of Iniquity* (London, 1664), p. 544.

alike, and but certain Modes of governing the people" (*Apology*, p. 545). Essentially and consistently, the Platonists' empirical appeal to differences in circumstance reaffirmed their confidence in the mind's reliability. As Cudworth explained, "the intellectual faculties may be made obscure more or less, yet it is not possible they should ever be made false" (p. 636). Among the causes of obscurity, according to Whichcote, there is the "difference in men's outward circumstances" (*Works*, II, 36). Given this difference "it's a matter of high prudence, to know what is fit and comely and convenient, & c." (III, 421). Nevertheless, if the test of assent was to remain reliable at all, it must be supposed to operate with relative certainty within the limits of experience.

In seeking normative guidance, therefore, the individual was to proceed along epistemological lines. In the normative sphere, Whichcote observed, there are "things that are of a mutable and alterable nature, and those things that are immutable and unchangeable" (II, 62). The basis for this distinction, however, is epistemological; the relative validity of norms is "to be proved accordingly, everything in its proportion and capacity," for, as Jeremy Taylor remarked, "some things are demonstrable, and many are probable."[34] While Taylor's deeply Calvinist sensibility distinguished him on many points from the group associated with Cambridge at mid-century,[35] he nevertheless adopted the basic epistemological stance that was the foundation for subsequent latitudinarian thought. On the one hand, he argued from the power of assent ("to what reason cannot consent, in that no being can be supposed," *Works*, XI, 454) that "what is just to one, is so to all, in the like Circumstances" (XI, 419). On the other hand, as he also acknowledged, "men are infinitely influenced by their own acts and relations, by their understandings and proper economy, by their superinduced differences and orders," so that in normative affairs "some reasons are but probable, and some are certain and confessed" (XI, 419, 462). The certainty that distinguishes universal consent from the merely relative probability of differing opinions therefore justifies the argument for latitude on epistemological grounds: "we must come to the notions of things, by deriving them from their proper fountains" (XI, 411).

Because it could at once accommodate certainty and differing opinion, the latitudinarian position was appealing as a reply to dogmatists and skeptics alike. While refuting skepticism by establishing certain

34. Jeremy Taylor, Preface to *Doctor Dubitandem*, in *The Whole Works*, XI, 357.
35. Two of the principal differences were his interpretation of natural law and his skeptical reservations about the mental powers of fallen man. See Robert Hoopes, "Voluntarism in Jeremy Taylor and in the Platonic Tradition," *HLQ*, 13 (1950), 341–354.

truths on which all men agree, it could nevertheless account in reasonable terms for the differences that divide them. Moreover, by extending a relative and provisional validity to differing social values, the position could deny the rigidly authoritarian claims of Catholic dogmatism while yet defending a measure of conventional order against the onslaught of Puritan iconoclasm. Thus while it established certain grounds for religious comprehension, the stance of latitude also involved an appeal to social opinion and probability that was in some degree authoritarian and even potentially Erastian. In granting or withholding his assent, the individual was, as Whichcote said, to "seek the *law of nature,* only among those that live according to nature, and not among those that have abused themselves, by ill use, custom and practice." Nevertheless, where this standard is not clearly established, "custom and usage is to be heeded, for these began by consent, though it does not appear at what time" (II, 62, 66). The basically reliable test of consent on which custom is founded assures that it enjoys a measure of validity in the circumstances where it obtains. The individual mind is to be guided, Taylor says, by "intrinsical and extrinsical" criteria, by "reason . . . and authority" (XII, 33). While never violating its own integrity, the mind may be reliably guided by that authority whose basis is a reasonable consensus: "When it can certainly be told that it is the more common, there the community of the opinion hath the advantage . . . because, where reason is clear and manifest, there we are to go after it, where it is more justly to be presumed" (XII, 97).

This "presumptive" reasoning requires that the reasonable individual pursue the truth by following "Many, before few. Few, before one" (XII, 97). In the context of uncertain matters, Whichcote explains, "it is safe and prudent to see also with other men's eyes. *In multitude of counselors is safety"* (IV, 118). In normative terms, this means that uncertain matters are resolved by reasonable adjustment to circumstance, by "custom and necessity, the usages of society, and the needs of the world" (Taylor, *Works,* XIII, 77). The provisional validity of limited social consensus, More maintained, was evidence enough that "no Institute of the Church, while she keeps within the compass of things indifferent, should . . . excuse a man from joyning in publick Worship with the National Church wherein he lives, and from conforming to her orders" (*Apology,* p. 546). The potentially Erastian implications of this position, however, were held in check by its essentially tolerant epistemological premises. Because it is based on limited consensus, Taylor explains, conventional order is "relative to time and place, to persons and occasions, subject to all changes"; accordingly, it is "but probably collected": while it may be "true or false" in the eyes of God, it can remain to men "but probable" (XIV, 77). Such "probable" status produced a tolerance for the varieties of conventional order at the same time that it supported their provisional value. There was to be "a latitude of sense, interpretation, time and observance"[36] in conventional order because, John Smith declared, "our conversation and demeanour in this world is not, nor can well be, all of a piece" (p. 389).

By encompassing degrees of certainty "ranging from absolute certainty to mere probability,"[37] the latitudinarian test of assent placed the older normative concept of *adiaphora* on new epistemological grounds. Sixteenth-century apologists for the Elizabethan settlement had approached the concept in almost wholly legalistic terms; but even in the early seventeenth century, both lay and religious moderates tended increasingly to argue that controversial beliefs and norms were not subject to certain resolution, and hence were unnecessary to the essential faith. Sir Thomas Browne maintained that "the foundations of religion are already established, and the principles of salvation subscribed unto by all: there remain not many controversies worth a passion";[38] and James Ussher wrote that "still there is but one Foundation, though great Disparity be observed in sundry parts of the Super struction."[39] When coupled with the characteristic epistemology of Platonist and latitudinarian thought, the architectural metaphor of "foundation" and "superstructure" became a popular and influential model for discussing conventional order. Taylor, for example, warned of the dangers in calling "superstructures by the name of fundamental articles";[40] by epistemological definition, matters that do not command universal assent are "not of the foundation of faith, but a remote superstructure" (VII, 442). On the one hand, the architectural metaphor clarified the older normative theory of specification in the natural law, "whose reason and obligation," Taylor explained, "remains unchanged, even when it is made to comply with changing instances" (XII, 273). On the other hand, the metaphor was coextensive with a novel theory of knowledge and truth whose concessions to limitation could explain why, as Edward Stillingfleet put it in *Irenicum,* men

36. Whichcote, *Works*, III, 128.

37. Henry G. Van Leeuwen, *The Problem of Certainty in English Thought, 1630–1690* (The Hague: Martinus Nijhoff, 1963), p. 14.

38. Sir Thomas Browne, *Religio Medici*, in *Selected Writings*, ed. Geoffrey Keynes (Chicago: University of Chicago Press, 1968), p. 71.

39. James Ussher, *A Briefe Declaration of the Universality of the Church of Christ* (1624; rpt., London, 1637), p. 12.

40. Taylor, *A Discourse of the Liberty of Prophesying*, in *The Whole Works*, VII, ccccvi.

"erect a far different fabric upon the very same foundations."[41] The circumstantial factors that limit and shape assent account for the difference between *"jus naturae proprium,* the proper law of nature specific to differing societies," and *"jus naturae obligatium,* the obligatory law of nature" that obtains everywhere *(Irenicum,* p. 62). Thus "churches agreeing in the same faith, often differ in rites and customs" *(Irenicum,* p. xii). In the framework of latitudinarian epistemology, such differences are perfectly reasonable, and "the great matters wherein we are agreed," John Tillotson declared, ought "to be of greater force to unite us, than difference in doubtful opinions, and in little rites and circumstances."[42]

Like the great Platonists who were their teachers, Stillingfleet and Tillotson were gentlemen "of a wide swallow";[43] but as principal architects of the Restoration church, they had the power to establish the theory of social consensus as an official doctrine. As Clarendon observed, the restored king "hoped to provide . . . such a settlement in religion as would prevent any disorder in the state."[44] While such ruthlessly Erastian thinkers as Sir Roger L'Estrange and Samuel Parker insured that any settlement would be politically secure, Stillingfleet, Tillotson, and other moderates spoke for an intellectual settlement based on "those clear truths which are consented to on either side."[45] Tillotson, for example, advised that men should turn from "factious contention about things indifferent, to the serious practice of what is necessary" *(Works,* IV, 296), and Stillingfleet argued that "the only way left for the church's settlement and peace under such variety of apprehensions . . . is to pitch upon such a foundation, if possible to be found out, wherein the different parties retaining their private apprehensions, may yet be agreed to carry on the same work in common" *(Irenicum,* p. 36).

On the one hand, the foundation itself was to consist of "clear and undoubted principles" arrived at through the typically dual tests of their "secret impressions upon the minds of men" and "the common consent and opinion of mankind."[46] As the source of what Locke called

41. Edward Stillingfleet, *Irenicum* (Philadelphia, 1842), p. 34.

42. John Tillotson, *Works* (London, 1760), II, 248.

43. The phrase is Bishop Edward Fowler's (1670), quoted in Cragg, *From Puritanism to the Age of Reason,* p. 63.

44. Clarendon, *Continuation of the History of the Great Rebellion,* quoted in Cragg, *From Puritanism to the Age of Reason,* p. 196.

45. See Cragg, *From Puritanism to the Age of Reason,* p. 27.

46. Tillotson, *Works,* IV, 305, 282, 288.

"the common principles of religion,"[47] these were to provide the grounds for comprehension. On the other hand, the ideal of comprehension was to be circumscribed by an official superstructure that enjoyed the relative and provisional validity extended to social opinion and practice in seventeenth-century epistemology. Where earlier thinkers had argued for a tolerance of diversity, however, the Restoration apologists used similar logic to defend the imposition of conventional order. Because, by earlier logic, opinions and practices were upheld by a limited certainty in the social and temporal circumstances where they obtained, then in matters not immediately or universally apparent, it was argued, men ought to "comply with the church in which they were born and baptized."[48] Matters of ceremony and policy were to be "left to the prudence of every particular church to agree upon."[49] Thus while seeking comprehension, the Restoration apologists reimposed the normative concept of conventional order upon the epistemology of latitude, and thereby reinstated the language of legalism that had always lain beneath its surface.

The return to legalism, however, involved a major transformation of normative thought, for the new defense of conventional order rested on a theory of consensus that was essentially tolerant and epistemologically relativist. In the first place, the epistemological test of provisional and probable consent replaced the normative ideal of natural authority as the proper sanction for conventional order. This produced a greater awareness of the social origins of convention and a more deeply skeptical sense of its limited validity and its capacity for change and variety. In normative debate, Tillotson observed, men were not "to expect a greater evidence for things than they are capable of." Because conventional norms were, as Taylor said, based only on "human authority and probability," they were "no otherwise to be required but as they are obtained and found out, that is, morally, and fallibly, and humanly" (*Works,* VIII, 98, 231).

In the second place, by basing their defense of conventional order on the epistemological sanction of consent, the Restoration apologists helped to insure the emergence of a new dialectic, in which the inner light of individualism replaced universal world order as the test against which social norms were to be measured. As a response to Puritan individualism, the Restoration settlement was less concerned with

47. John Locke, *Reflections upon the Roman Commonwealth,* quoted in H. R. Foxe Bourne, *The Life of John Locke* (London, 1876), p. 149.

48. Tillotson, *Works,* II, 251.

49. Stillingfleet, *Irenicum,* p. 36.

reconciling convention to natural order than with reconciling it with individual apprehensions; the search was for a balance in which men would refrain "from rigidly imposing indifferent customs on the one side; or from contumacy of opposing mere indifferences on the other" (*Irenicum,* p. 90). While the combined powers of church and state did in part continue to attempt "rigid impositions," they did so on the basis of a theory of consensus that broadened as the century progressed and that increasingly took note of changing social needs and expectations.

Thus where the Act of Uniformity (1662) literally commanded every subject to "declare his unfeigned assent and consent" to the revised order of worship, the Act of Toleration (1689) interpreted the consentual basis of convention more broadly by declaring that no imposition of uniformity should "be construed to extend to any person or persons dissenting from the Church of England."[50] The accommodations of 1689 brought about not simply a religious reconciliation, but also a political settlement that sought, as Locke said, to "make good" the new king's "title in the consent of the people."[51] Like the latitudinarians, Locke drew upon the theory of consent in order to argue that "that which begins and actually constitutes any political society is nothing but the consent of any number of freemen capable of a majority to unite and incorporate into such a society."[52] Significantly, the conventionalist dialectic of Locke's theory was not designed to insure the continuity of natural order so much as it was to secure the rights of the individual. Implicitly, the Convention Parliament of 1689 marked the point at which popular consent, partly in line with Locke's theory, replaced divine or natural authority as the acceptable basis of sovereignty. The repudiation of earlier monarchical theories "too easily entertain'd among us" entailed that "every Nation" has "a Liberty of framing to themselves such a Constitution as may be most useful and agreeable."[53] Constitutional thought had for two centuries been an increasingly important strain in English political philosophy; but it was in the later seventeenth century, when under the pressure of events it coalesced with the epistemological theory of consent, with the devel-

50. See Henry Gee and William J. Hardy, *Documents Illustrative of English Church History* (London: Macmillan, 1896), pp. 604, 655.

51. Locke, Preface to *Two Treatises of Government,* ed. Thomas I. Cook (New York: Hafner, 1966), p. 3.

52. Locke, *The Second Treatise of Civil Government,* in Cook, p. 170.

53. Samuel Masters(?), *The Case of Allegiance in our Present Circumstances Consider'd, In a Letter from a Minister in the City to a Minister in the Country* (London, 1689), pp. 3, 8.

oping principles of legal historiography, and with the recently postu-
lated social contract, that constitutionalism began to foster an organic
yet conventionalist state, "a tacit Agreement between the *King* and
Subjects to observe such common Usages and Practices, as by an immemorial Prescription are become the *Common-Law* of our Government."[54]

The theory of consent encompassed major revision in both theology
and politics because it was essentially an epistemological construct: as
an account of human powers and limitations, it provided a potential
substitute for the logocentric framework that had been the center of
technical order. Both practically and theoretically, it was an attractive
alternative, for it allowed for different apprehensions and normative
diversity while retaining the possibility of rational certainty and moral
rectitude. Not surprisingly, its tolerant and nondogmatic implications
answered to the needs of germinating scientific inquiry as well as to
those of normative revision, and just as it had served the Restoration
settlement, so the theory of consent became an official tenet of the new
scientific establishment—the Royal Society. Many of the Society's principal architects—John Wilkins, Thomas Sprat, and Joseph Glanvill,
for example—were influential latitudinarian divines, and they enjoyed
the virtually unqualified support of such latitudinarians as Cudworth,
Stillingfleet, and Tillotson. The basis of their association was a common theory of knowledge intended to provide "a *via media* between
skepticism and dogmatism."[55]

In their outline of scientific method, therefore, the members of the
Royal Society followed "the way of those Great Men, the Lord Bacon
and Des-Cartes" by subjecting accepted interpretations to radical
doubt; the task of science was not to pore over "the Writings and
Opinions of Philosophers, but to seek Truth in the Great Book of
Nature."[56] In keeping with the Neo-Stoic and Baconian bias that lay
at its foundation, the scientific search for nature required a repudiation of merely conventional wisdom. Glanvill complained that "we
judg all things by . . . Anticipations: and condemn, or applaud them,
as they differ, or agree, with our first Opinions. 'Tis on this account
that almost every Country censures the Laws, Customs, and Doctrines

54. Masters, *The Case of Allegiance,* p. 9.

55. Barbara J. Shapiro, "Latitudinarianism and Science in Seventeenth-Century
England," in *The Intellectual Revolution of the Seventeenth Century,* ed. Charles
Webster (London: Routledge & Kegan Paul, 1974), p. 309.

56. Joseph Glanvill, "Of Scepticism and Certainty," in *Essays on Several Important Subjects,* ed. Richard H. Popkin (New York: Johnson Reprint Co., 1970),
p. 44.

of every other . . . we suck in the opinions of our Clime and Country, as we do the common Air, without thought, or choice."[57] This skepticism was offset, however, as it was for Bacon, by the possibility of unanimous rather than conflicting consent. The search for postulations "commanding a sudden assent," or to which "our Assent is universal and indubitable," became an especially efficacious test of truth, because it underlined the pious reciprocity in which "the belief of our Reason is an Exercise of Faith; and Faith an Act of Reason."[58] Thus like their latitudinarian counterparts, who sought to reconstruct religion on universal consent, the Restoration scientists sought to build a scientific edifice upon "such Principles lodged in our minds, that we cannot but assent to . . . they are universal, and believ'd by all Mankind; every one knows, every one useth them: For though they do not lie in the minds of all Men in the formality of such Propositions, yet they are *implicitly* there; and in the force and power of them every Man reasons, and acts also."[59]

As in religious thought, this epistemological stance provided grounds for potential certainty while at the same time undermining dogmatism by conceding to the limitations placed on certainty where assent is not universal. Thus, while they questioned assumptions resting on merely supine authority, the scientists placed such confidence in assent as to extend a hypothetical and provisional validity to differing opinions, and like their Platonist forebears, they were in some respects exceedingly credulous. Unanimous consent was the goal of science as it was of religion, but the limits of certainty, Wilkins declared, made it "utterly impossible . . . that we should always agree in the same apprehension of things."[60] Thus, in order to support its vision of a progressive approach toward certain truth, the Royal Society sought to establish the proper atmosphere of "modest, tentative rationality"[61] in which opinions could contend as hypotheses. In doing so, they conceded to an irreducibly social component at the root of scientific impulse.

The fruits of this concession appear in several aspects of the Royal Society's method. In the first place, because assent was the explicit test of truth, "the indifferent seeker of Truth," as Wilkins said, was "to assent unto that Truth which upon deliberation shall seem most

57. Glanvill, "Against Confidence in Philosophy and Matters of Speculation," in *Essays on Several Important Subjects,* p. 24.

58. Glanvill, "The Agreement of Reason and Religion," in *Essays on Several Important Subjects,* pp. 5, 21; and "Of Scepticism and Certainty," p. 48.

59. Glanvill, "Of Scepticism and Certainty," p. 50.

60. Wilkins, *Sermons Preached on Several Occasions,* p. 414.

61. Shapiro, p. 316.

probable," or, as Glanvill put it, to "proportion the degree of his Assent, to the degree of Evidence."[62] On the one hand, the innate powers of reason and calculation suggested that certain kinds of mathematical knowledge might be "demonstrated invincibly."[63] On the other hand, the evidence of differing opinions suggested that in most matters only a limited and relative certainty was possible. Thus the prudent apportioning of assent was to be circumscribed by several social considerations. First, because every opinion enjoyed a measure of assent, men were, in the most rationally convincing terms, "to propose their Opinions as *Hypotheses,* that *may probably* be true accounts, without peremptorily affirming that *they are.*"[64] Second, such hypotheses were limited by their reliance on report and testimony. While optical instruments and other devices were leading to increased emphasis on precise personal observation, the scientists continued to maintain that testimony and common experience were a reliable form of evidence. In the religious sphere, Taylor had argued that appeal to the logical place of testimony "is not less an act of reason, because it uses another topic" (*Works,* XI, 442), and the scientists, crediting the test of consent, took much the same position. Wilkins, for example, admitted the testimony of Greek and Roman philosophers on grounds that it was generally accepted as true, and Boyle pointed out that the astronomical theories of Descartes were forced to rely upon the reports of others.[65] Finally, all of these factors contributed to the Society's officially skeptical stance of "probabilism," which Dryden defined as "a doubtful academical assent, or rather an inclination to assent to probability."[66] Based on the ancient skeptical Academy of Carneades, this stance found support in Aristotle's theory of the dialectical syllogism as explained in the logics of Thomas Spencer (1628), Robert Sanderson (1640), Gerard Vossius (1668), and Port-Royal (1661).[67] In adopting the theory, the Royal Society acknowledged the limitations of the very test of truth on which it was founded. By appealing to subjective grounds of assent whose goal was universal consent, its founders extended a measure of validity to differing forms of social assent, and outlined a course

62. John Wilkins, *Mathematical and Philosophical Works,* quoted in Shapiro, p. 313; Glanvill, "Of Scepticism and Certainty," p. 47.

63. Robert Hooke, quoted in Shapiro, p. 313.

64. Glanvill, "Of Scepticism and Certainty," p. 44.

65. See Van Leeuwen, pp. 66, 103.

66. John Dryden, "The Life of Plutarch," in *The Works of John Dryden,* ed. H. T. Swedenberg (Berkeley: University of California Press, 1971), XVII, 249.

67. See Hoyt Trowbridge, "The Place of Rules in Dryden's Criticism," in *Essential Articles for the Study of John Dryden,* ed. H. T. Swedenberg (Hamden, Ct.: Archon Books, 1966), pp. 128–129.

of inquiry that was not conventionalist in the nominalist terms that Hobbes proposed, but that was in other ways irreducibly social. As Barbara Shapiro has observed, the thinkers of the later seventeenth century hoped that "science and a moderate, latitudinarian, natural religion might serve as the twin pillars supporting an intellectual life in which the calm, friendly and practical pursuit of truth and goodness could replace abstract debate and ideologically motivated strife."[68] The tolerant and hypothetical status that scientists granted to differing opinions was thus grounded in a vision of truth that also sanctioned normative diversity in religion, politics, and law, and placed increasing emphasis on the role of convention in the lives of men. While this vision emerged in part from an ancient conflict, it laid the foundations for a new one, in which rationalism and empiricism competed as scientifically alternative accounts of man and his works. Both alternatives sought to replace the normative framework, in whose terms they were originally concealed, by subjecting the language of legalism to scientific scrutiny. The epistemological emphasis of the latitudinarians thus reflects the extent to which their "endeavour to find out truth" was coextensive with an old normative dilemma and novel scientific concerns. Their epistemology, in other words, was addressed to an ancient conflict; the terms in which they sought to resolve this conflict, however, laid out new lines of inquiry. Where the normative framework had sought to adjust the claims of nature and society as sources of artistic prescription, the scientific framework weighed the powers of the individual mind against the powers of the environment as alternative descriptions of artistic behavior. Technical debate had given rise to modes of thought that would eventually replace it.

2. REAL AND MENTAL THEATER: THE COMPLEX OF CLASSICISM

In the century roughly spanned by Goethe's lifetime (1749–1832), the classical theory of the arts, and especially the arts of speech, underwent a decisive change. The technical framework that had prevailed for two millennia gave way to psychological, historical, comparative, and biographical methods that served a growing awareness "that for an aesthetic appreciation of a work of art, its relation to the mind of man was fundamental."[1] Historians have rightly understood this trans-

---

68. Shapiro, p. 316. For a different account of the same phenomenon, see Christopher Hill, " 'Reason' and 'Reasonableness,' " in *Change and Continuity in Seventeenth-Century England* (Cambridge: Harvard University Press, 1975), pp. 103–123.

1. J. W. H. Atkins, *English Literary Criticism: Seventeenth and Eighteenth Centuries* (London: Methuen, 1951), p. 374.

formation as one of the origins of modernity. But by assessing this transformation from a standpoint that presumes the superiority of modern theory and method, many historians have imposed upon it terms that obscure the historical context in which it occurred.[2] Though modern modes of inquiry are quite properly defined in opposition to older normative or prescriptive modes, they arose from within and as part of an ancient normative framework inclusive of a variety of emphases. The conflicts engendered by these different emphases forced many seventeenth-century thinkers to turn from normative to epistemological endeavors. The novel modes of inquiry through which these thinkers anticipated the Enlightenment did not originate in simple opposition to normative thought, but as part of the "separation of opinions" called for by the technical tradition itself.

Ernst Cassirer and W. J. Bate, among others, have helped to rectify this misapprehension by emphasizing the dialectical coherence between affective and prescriptive approaches and by treating the transition from classical to Romantic premises of taste and criticism as a shift between points of emphasis implicit in the structure of Enlightenment thought.[3] Bate demonstrates that in rationalist thought a growing insistence on the need for rule and method was accompanied in the form of British empiricism by a "growing attention to the nature of the reasoning and 'methodizing' faculty itself—a tendency which, by the middle of the eighteenth century, was to culminate in a marked skepticism about both reason and method, and was therefore to furnish an argumentative basis for romanticism" (p. 24). By treating the critical thought of the Enlightenment as a single complex of mutual influences and developments, Bate argues that its historical significance is rightly understood in terms of its structure, for the growth of individualism hinged upon the articulation of rationalist thought into empiricism, associationism, and the "premise of feeling."

Both Bate and Cassirer trace this articulation to the decisive impact of Cartesian mathematicism. Appropriately, they analyze the history of eighteenth-century criticism not in classical terms, but in the decisively different terminology that marks a major difference between the ancient and modern human sciences and their approach to rectitude and fitness in the life of man. This new terminology was demanded by

2. See R. S. Crane's review of Atkins, "On Writing the History of Criticism in England, 1650–1800," in *The Idea of the Humanities and Other Essays Critical and Historical* (Chicago: University of Chicago Press, 1967), II, 163.

3. Ernst Cassirer, *The Philosophy of the Enlightenment*, trans. Fritz C. A. Koelln and James P. Pettigrove (Princeton: Princeton University Press, 1951), ch. 7; and W. J. Bate, *From Classic to Romantic: Premises of Taste in Eighteenth-Century England* (Cambridge: Harvard University Press, 1946).

the very nature of the Enlightenment's reassessment of ancient tradition. At the same time, however, this terminology overshadows many elements of continuity between the ancient and modern traditions, and conceals the extent to which many changes in the human sciences grew out of the ancient tradition itself. Thus while Bate takes some pains to point out elements of continuity, he draws a fairly sharp distinction between rationalist neo-classicism and its humanist antecedent: "Classicism assumed the ideal or universal that comprises the absolute standard of taste may be known by the direct use of man's ethical reason; it was often the contention of neo-classic rationalism that this standard was to be known and achieved by a proper use of methods and of rules" (p. 27). Thus the development of affective, psychological, and historical theories in the eighteenth century is seen as a response to the dichotomy between "reason" and "imaginative or emotional response" fostered by rationalism in the extremer forms of neo-classical criticism.[4]

The decisiveness of the Cartesian movement as a turning point must nonetheless be understood in the light of its continuity with an ongoing reassessment of human knowledge and activity. This is especially true of the practical and productive arts, where the aim to establish and shape human practices and products on the basis of universal norms had always been compromised by their temporal and intersubjective setting, and thus by the need to consider social, historical, and psychological factors. Moreover, the interest in method that Bate attributes to modern rationalism had very largely been an explicit part of the technical tradition since its inception. Indeed, since its early association with *episteme* or *scientia,* the concept of *techne* or *ars* had been understood as a practical or productive habit operating in conjunction with norms specified by right reason. At the same time, the apparent alterations of these norms by circumstance and contingency demanded a reassessment of the status and validity of the norms themselves. The resulting intellectual conflict between nature and convention had thus long preoccupied the technical tradition. Quite apart from the separate impetus of the developing natural sciences, this conflict led directly to the crises in which such thinkers as the latitudinarians turned from normative to epistemological modes of inquiry, and to the even more decisive moment at which Bacon, Hobbes, and Descartes began to redesign the study of man on a scientific basis.

In this respect the early Enlightenment may be taken as a culmina-

---

4. See Bate, *From Classic to Romantic,* pp. 35, 43–44. See also A. N. Whitehead, *Science and the Modern World* (1925; rpt., New York: The Free Press, 1953), pp. 73, 87, 94; and Willey, pp. 92–97.

tion as well as a beginning and its main figures may be understood as inheritors as well as progenitors. While the content of Descartes' philosophy was decisive, its purpose was representative; the alternative empirical, psychological, and historical responses to this new rationalism may be taken as extensions of the ancient rhetorical alternatives to natural and abiding fitness. Indeed, the epistemological conflict between reason and experience in the Enlightenment had its precursor in the rival claims of the ancient philosophic and rhetorical traditions, according to which the test of value was placed alternatively in nature or in changing human expectations. As seen earlier, the great epistemological quest of the seventeenth century—its "endeavor to find out truth"—was at once coextensive with the technical debate it sought to resolve and with a novel debate about the origins of knowledge that it engendered. In the same way, the pan-European classicism of the period 1500–1750 encompassed at one threshold the ancient language of legalism, and at the other a dialectic in which a rationalist insistence on the noumenal grounds of fitness, certainty, and rectitude was balanced by empirical claims for their changing social, historical, and psychological contexts. Moreover, just as epistemology characteristically poised itself ambivalently between logocentric order and individual order as alternatives to the varieties of social and conventional order, so the classical complex with which it was contemporaneous typically offset the empirical order of convention by seeking timelessness in an individual search for universal rule and method that easily became a personal reliance on the "inner light" of sensibility and imagination.

This is why the history of European classicism is so deceptive; though rooted in ancient philosophic and rhetorical alternatives, it embodied impulses equally supportive of both Cartesian rationalism and Shaftesburian sensibility, on the one hand, as well as the Hobbesian empiricism to which both were intrinsically opposed, on the other. Just as ancient philosophers had opposed the norm of nature to the conventionalist bias of rhetoric, so Descartes and Shaftesbury, in their vastly different ways, sought to reinvigorate a logocentric order under pressure from the nominalist and psychological forms of empiricism that threatened to exhaust it. The coalescence of these tensions in the mature form of classicism produced what R. S. Crane has called an "aggregate . . . of a highly complex and ambiguous kind, out of which many critical systems and doctrines could be constructed."[5] The influence of Enlightenment rationalism upon neo-classicism did not so much create a novel problem as it radically intensified an old one.

Thus the novel modes of eighteenth-century literary theory are best

5. Crane, p. 168.

distinguished from their normative forebears when both are understood as opposing thresholds of a coherent critical enterprise. By the
same token, the specific differences that distinguish English classicism
from its French counterpart emerge most clearly in the light of a generic classicism that embodied their characteristically contrary impulses.[6]
Indeed, the edifice of French classicism was itself unsteadied by the
contradictions it sought to contain, and thus a paradigm of technical
conflict in its latter stage. In line with the ancient technical alternatives, the poet was, as Boileau said, formally to "aimer . . . la raison,"
but at the same time rhetorically to "chercher le coeur, l'échauffe et le
rémue."[7] For Boileau, as for Pope, at least, the relation between these
points of emphasis remained fluid, because the poet "plait par la
raison seule."[8] Nevertheless, rational order and rhetorical efficacy
tended in principle to precipitate toward two poles. The first dictated
that

> Unerring Nature, still divinely bright,
> One clear, unchanged, and Universal Light,
> Life, Force, and Beauty, must to all impart,
> At once the Source, and End, and Test of Art.[9]

While surrounded by a Cartesian aura, Pope's metaphoric postula-
tion runs along one main line of a technical tradition that insisted
that "Arts, as well as Sciences, are founded upon Reason, and in both
we are to be guided by the light of nature."[10] Prior to the influence

---

6. See Henri Peyre, *Qu'est-ce que le classicisme?* (Paris: A. G. Nizet, 1965), p. 98.
Most studies of English neo-classicism offer useful distinctions from its French
counterpart, but they have tended to overlook the basic technical dilemma generic
to European classicism. See, for example, the companion studies of Paul Spencer
Wood, "Native Elements in English Neo-Classicism," *MP*, 24 (1926–27), 201–208,
and "The Opposition to Neo-Classicism Between 1660 and 1700," *PMLA*, 42 (1928),
182–197; Donald F. Bond, " 'Distrust' of Imagination in English Neo-Classicism,"
PQ, 14 (1935), 54–69; George Williamson, "The Restoration Revolt against Enthusiasm," *Seventeenth-Century Contexts* (Chicago: University of Chicago Press,
1960), pp. 203–239; Louis I. Bredvold, "The Rise of English Classicism: A Study in
Methodology," *CL*, 2 (1950), 253–268; Edwin Berry Burgum, "The Neoclassical
Period in English Literature: A Psychological Definition," *Sewanee Review*, 52
(1944), 247–265.
    7. Nicolas Boileau, *L'art poétique*, in *The Continental Model*, ed. Scott Elledge
and Donald Schier (Ithaca: Cornell University Press, 1970), I, 37, III, 16.
    8. Boileau, *L'art poétique*, III, 423.
    9. Pope, *An Essay on Criticism*, ll. 70–73, in *The Poems of Alexander Pope*, ed.
John Butt (New Haven: Yale University Press, 1963).
    10. René Le Bossu, *Treatise of the Epick Poem* (London, 1695), p. 1.

of Descartes, Malherbe had declared that "l'art est objet de science," and his pronouncement was reinforced by the Italian neo-Aristotelian influence that consolidated in France by 1630.[11] According to Aristotle, the "maître de la raison,"[12] the arts must find their "basis in reason," where, as Jean Chapelain had claimed, "all things may find their place."[13] Thus, while shored on retrospection, the quest for formal integrity in French classicism was essentially an appeal to the unchanging dictates of reason. "The Rules of the Stage," declared the Abbé d'Aubignac,

> are not founded upon Authority, but upon Reason; they are not so much settled by Example, as by the natural judgement of Mankind; and if we call them the Rules of the Art of the Ancients, 'tis only because they have practis'd them with great regularity, and much to their glory; having first made many Observations upon the Nature of Moral Actions, and upon the Probability of Humane Accidents in this life, and thereby drawing the Pictures after the truth of the Original, and observing all due circumstances, they reduc'd to an Art this kind of Poem.[14]

As had often been the case before, this normative appeal to reason included opposition to rationally insupportable conventions. "Nature and Truth had put a certain value to things," Chapelain argued in attacking the success of Corneille's innovative *Cid* (1637), "which cannot be altered by that which chance or opinion sets up."[15] Similarly, d'Aubignac held that "we are not to make Laws to our selves from Custome and Example, but from Reason."[16] When Thomas Rymer attempted to popularize such thinking in England, he faced particularly stiff opposition from the rehabilitation of custom in historiogra-

11. See René Fromilhague, *Malherbe: technique et création poétique* (Paris: Armand Colin, 1954), pp. 59, 129; J. E. Spingarn, *A History of Literary Criticism in the Renaissance* (1899; rpt., New York: Harcourt Brace & World, 1963), pp. 150–152.

12. Hippolyte-Jules de la Mésnadière's phrase, quoted in René Bray, *La Formation de la doctrine classique en France* (1927; rpt., Paris: A. G. Nizet, 1951), p. 59.

13. *Letter or Discourse by Monsieur Chapelain . . . Conveying his Opinion of the Poem "Adone,"* in *The Continental Model,* p. 9.

14. François Hédelin, Abbé d'Aubignac, *The Whole Art of The Stage* (London, 1684), pp. 22–23.

15. Chapelain, *Les sentimens de l'Académie françoise sur la tragicomédie du Cid,* in Barret Clark, *European Theories of the Drama* (Cincinnati: Stewart and Kidd, 1918), p. 125.

16. d'Aubignac, *The Whole Art of the Stage,* p. 22.

phy and law, and thus argued that "many are apt to mistake use for nature, but a Poet is not an Historiographer, but a Philosopher, he is not to take Nature at the second hand, soyl'd and deform'd as it passes in the customs of the unthinking vulgar."[17]

This sort of opposition to convention created a special problem in view of the intersubjective character of the verbal arts. The test of rational fitness in the verbal arts had always been balanced against their necessary function in a pragmatic setting, a setting in which public habit, taste, and expectation were brought to bear in the shape of conventional norms. In French classicism, as in its predecessors, the rhetorical function of the arts established a set of special ends that brought social pressure to bear upon artistic technique. Indeed, the profound influence of rhetoric was reinforced in France by the prominence of drama, a form that best exemplifies the relation between art and its audience, and whose immediate and crystallized effects have so often made the theater a "battleground of criticism."[18] Because "the only Art of the Theatre" was to "speak to the Heart of the Audience," René Rapin observed, "nothing can be delightful but that which moves the Affections, and which makes Impression on the Soul; little known is that *Rhetorick* which can lay open the Passions by all the natural degrees of their Birth, and Progress."[19] As the art most consonant with the changing passions and expectations of an audience, "l'Art de . . . la Rhétorique" was "absolument nécessaire au Poéte & à l'Orateur." Like the orator, d'Aubignac pointed out, "le Poéte doit bien connoistre toutes les passions, les réssorts qui les font agir, et la manière de les exprimer avec ordre, avec énérgie, et avec jugement."[20]

These rhetorical demands challenged the authority of reason not only because of their emphasis on the audience, but also because, with increasing frequency, the critics ceased to attribute pleasure to the detached contemplation of form and began to seat it in the violent movement of passion. Tragedy, Rapin observed, "labors to move the passions, all whose motions are delightful, because nothing is more sweet to the soul than agitation; it pleases itself in changing the objects

17. Thomas Rymer, *The Tragedies of the Last Age* (1678), in *The Critical Works of Thomas Rymer*, ed. Curt A. Zimansky (New Haven: Yale University Press, 1956), p. 62.

18. E. B. O. Borgerhoff, *The Freedom of French Classicism* (Princeton: Princeton University Press, 1950), pp. 5–6.

19. René Rapin, *Reflections on Aristotle's Treatise of Poetry*, in *The Whole Critical Works* (London, 1716), II, 212–213.

20. De la Mésnadière and d'Aubignac, quoted in A. Donald Sellstrom, "Rhetoric and the Poetics of French Classicism," *French Review*, 34 (1961), 428, 429.

to satisfy the immensity of its desires."[21] This meant that in moving the passions, the poet was to have "a nearer Regard to his own Country, and the Necessities he sees his own Country to be under . . . he makes less use of Reasoning, than of the force of Insinuation; accommodating himself to the particular Customs and Inclinations of his Audience."[22] As the institutional form of public desire and passion, conventional habits, values, and manners became the means best suited to arousing passion. "All passions that are not founded upon Opinions and Customs conformable to those of the Spectators," d'Aubignac declared, "are sure to be cold and of no effect."[23]

The rhetorical emphasis on passion in French classicism, and its corresponding challenge to reason, were intensified by an increasingly acute awareness of the double nature of man himself—an awareness that began with the inward focus of the Reformation and flowered in the introspective studies of Montaigne, Descartes, and Pascal. The psychological emphasis of these thinkers, like that of the English latitudinarians, may be understood as a response to legalism, as an effort to reassess the normative basis of activity in light of human agency itself. Throughout the Renaissance, as noted earlier, the apparent conflict between nature and convention was increasingly interpreted as a conflict arising in the human constitution. Accordingly, efforts to reconcile changing norms with universal dictates found their counterparts in efforts to rehabilitate a deeply divided human nature, to reconcile particular acts of will with the rational powers of mind itself. Just as moderate English thinkers finally sought to rehabilitate the "duble name" of custom by turning from normative debate to the inner sources of knowledge, so the normative edifice of seventeenth-century classicism was animated by a shift in focus from world order to the order of the individual. In other words, the peculiar tensions in the legalism of French classicism were grounded in a deep awareness of the powerful human impulses at stake. If the technical standard of natural fitness was reinforced by an obsession within individual "reason," this standard was correspondingly offset by the intensification of rhetorical technique into a powerful affective emphasis on "passion."

The double focus of French classicism was thus the product of an ambivalence that ran so deep as to divide even the two great religious

21. Rapin, *Reflections on Aristotle's Treatise of Poetry,* in *The Whole Critical Works,* II, 141.
22. Le Bossu, *A Treatise of the Epick Poem,* p. 18.
23. d'Aubignac, *The Whole Art of the Stage,* III, 44.

powers of seventeenth-century France—the Society of Jesus and the Society of Jansenius.[24] Like the Augustinian thinkers of the English reformation, the Jansenists opposed themselves in principle to the efficacy of human will, and so to the ability of human habit to maintain consistently a standard of abiding integrity. Accordingly, they objected to the amelioristic notion of the Jesuits that unchanging principles could be adapted to changing circumstance in the form of flexible tradition, "as if the faith, and tradition, its ally, were not always one and the same at all times and in all places; as if it were the part of the rule to bend in conformity to the subject which it was meant to regulate."[25]

As a spokesman for the Jansenist position, Pascal objected to this Jesuitical *obliquo ductu*, but understood profoundly its attractions to a fallen human condition. "We know," he claimed "that opinions are admitted into the soul through two entrances, which are the chief of its two powers, understanding and will. The more natural entrance is the understanding, for we should never agree to anything but demonstrated truths, but the more usual entrance, although against nature, is the will; for all men whatsoever are almost always led into belief not because a thing is proved, but because it is pleasing."[26] Though ideally reason ought to prevail over the will, the misery of the human condition subjects the will instead to the *puissances trompeuses,* the imagination, self-love, and custom:

> We are as much automatic as intellectual; and hence it comes that the instrument by which conviction is attained is not demonstration alone. How few things are demonstrated! Proofs only convince the mind. Custom is the source of our strongest and most believed proofs. It bends the automaton, which persuades the mind without its thinking about the matter . . . it is custom that makes so many men Christians; custom that makes them Turks, heathens, artisans, soldiers, etc. Finally, we must have recourse to it when once the mind has seen where truth is, in order to quench our thirst, and steep ourselves in that belief, which escapes us at every hour; for always to have truths ready is too much

24. See Paul Bénichou, *Man and Ethics: Studies in French Classicism,* trans. Elizabeth Hughes (New York: Anchor Books, 1971), chs. 3, 5.

25. Pascal, *The Provincial Letters* (Chicago: Encyclopedia Britannica Great Books, 1952), XXXIII, 29. All subsequent references to works of Pascal are references to this volume.

26. Pascal, *On Geometrical Demonstration; Section II, Concerning the Art of Persuasion,* p. 440.

trouble. We must get an easier belief, which is custom,
which, without violence, *without art,* without argument,
makes us believe things and inclines all our powers to this
belief, so that our souls fall naturally into it.[27]

Through its claims upon the passions, the power of public habit made
Pascal "much afraid that nature itself is only a first custom, as custom
is a second nature."[28] While adhering to the ideal of an impossible
integrity, Pascal nevertheless allowed that "no matter what we wish
to persuade of, we must consider the person concerned, whose mind
and heart we know, what principles he admits, what things he loves,
and then observe in the thing in question what relations it has to these
admitted principles or to the objects of delight. So that the art of
persuasion consists as much in knowing how to please as in knowing
how to convince." Thus, despite the dangers of excessively Jesuitical
flexibility, and despite his own preference for "the management of
perfect scientific proofs," as taught at Port-Royal,[29] Pascal acknowledged, with profound awareness of the psychological tensions involved, a need to mediate between the claims of nature and convention.

This acknowledgment—not only in religious thought, but in French
classicism as a whole—points to a bond of continuity between the
normative tradition and later empirical and psychological developments. It also explains why the psychological tensions that lay beneath
French classicism often blurred its legalistic distinctions, and strengthened the interdependency of its terms, so that in each case the poet
was obliged to mediate between the universal claims of nature and the
changing expectations of public convention. Instead of rigidly supporting the claims of nature, "la raison nous apprendra pour règle
générale qu'une chose est belle lorsqu'elle a de la convenance avec sa
propre nature et avec la notre."[30] Because of this interdependency, each
critical distinction in French classicism was essentially equivocal, tending to break down into further distinctions between the dictates of
universal nature and the changing demands of men in time. The
famous distinction between the "bienséances intèrnes" and the "bienséances extèrnes," for example, was an effort to reconcile a fitness "entre

27. Pascal, *Pensées*, 252; cf. Roger Hazelton, *Blaise Pascal: The Genius of His
Thought* (Philadelphia: The Westminster Press, 1974), pp. 83–87; and Patricia
Topliss, *The Rhetoric of Pascal: A Study of His Art of Persuasion in the "Provin-
çales" and the "Pensées"* (Amsterdam: Leicester University Press, 1966), pp. 197–208.

28. Pascal, *Pensées*, 93; cf. 25, 92, 294, 325.

29. Pascal, *On Geometrical Demonstration*, pp. 441–442; cf. *Pensées*, 15–16.

30. Pierre Nicole, *Traité de la vraie et de la fausse beauté*, quoted in Bray, p.
216.

l'objet et sa propre nature" with a fitness "entre l'objet et le subjet, c'est à dire le public."[31] In the theory of drama, this led to an unstable distinction between *action* and *passion,* between the philosophic structure of dramatic action and characters whose appeal to the passions hinged upon their conformity with conventional expectations. In his effort to combine an Aristotelian *mimesis praxeos* with his Horatian role as *imitator . . . vitae morumque,* the poet was, as d'Aubignac said, to "contrive every thing as if there were no Spectators," and yet to portray passions "founded upon Opinions and Custom conformable to those of the Spectators."[32]

Yet even this distinction—between a universal "truth of Action," and its actual "Representation" to an audience—often proved equivocal. In the first place, as Rapin observed, the "fable" was to be "admirable," as well as "probable."[33] Furthermore, even probability, the "reasonable Soul" of epic and drama, tended to be undermined by its mediate situation, so that, as Le Bossu declared, "the principal sort of Probability . . . is the Probability according to the common-received Opinion."[34] According to this test, said d'Aubignac, " 'tis not enough that the Cause of some extraordinary Motion of the Mind be true, but it must also (to be agreeably represented upon the Stage) be reasonable and probable, *according to the receiv'd Opinion* of Mankind."[35]

Here again, reassertion of the formal claims of reason produced further distinctions that betrayed an irreducible conflict at their origins. While conceding to an instrinsically dynamic element of social mediation in formal probability, Chapelain, for example, sought to reinforce the claims of reason by limiting the ideal audience to a rational elite. "We must not say with the crowd," he argued, "that a poem is good merely because it pleases, unless the learned and expert are also pleased. Indeed, it is impossible that there can be pleasure contrary to reason."[36] Such efforts to circumvent the difficulties posed by rhetorical adjustment, however, often gave way, like others, be-

31. Bray, p. 216.

32. d'Aubignac, *The Whole Art of the Stage,* pp. 38–39, 44.

33. Rapin, *Reflections on Aristotle's Treatise of Poetry,* in *The Whole Critical Works,* II, 156.

34. Le Bossu, *A Treatise of the Epick Poem,* p. 135; cf. Bray, pp. 49–50, 206–208, and see Edith G. Kern, *The Influence of Heinsius and Vossius upon French Dramatic Theory* (Baltimore: The Johns Hopkins University Press, 1949), pp. 131–135.

35. d'Aubignac, *The Whole Art of the Stage,* III, 42–43.

36. Chapelain, *Les sentimens de l'Académie françoise sur la tragicomédie du Cid,* in *European Theories of the Drama,* p. 126.

neath empirical needs to move the passions in changing contexts. "Aristotle," said Le Bossu, "was of the Opinion, that a Poet, when his Fable so required, was not so strictly tyed up to the Truths of History, to suit himself to the Capacity of the Learned, as he was to that which might pass for Probable in the Eye of the Vulgar."[37] Despite attempts to shore up reason with social distinctions, "the probable" frequently became, as Rapin observed, "whatever suits with common opinion."[38]

It is in part because of such equivocations that the literature of seventeenth-century France achieved its greatness. As the product of a classicism whose ideals were in precarious balance, it was animated by the contradictory tensions which that classicism sought to contain and which were virtually embodied in its greatest representative, Pierre Corneille. Like his contemporaries, Corneille insisted that artistic values were essentially impervious to time, so that "we should not overstep" the precepts of the ancients.[39] At the same time, however, the passionate nature of man made it "necessary to accommodate oneself to the customs of the audience,"[40] for it is "the prejudice of common opinion which hands over the spectators to us already persuaded."[41] The mixture of rational and empirical impulses in Corneille's thought, like his representative place in the context of French classicism as a whole, underlines the great complexity of a tradition aiming to be at once both for its time and above all time. Though subject to varied emphasis, the interdependency of these two aims framed both methodological thresholds of French classicism—its retrospective debt to normative tradition and its anticipation of the Enlightenment dialectic. Every discussion of fitness in French classicism therefore has a double aspect as it seeks to mediate not only normatively between the timeless and the temporal, but also intellectually between the rationally intuited and the empirically determined. This superimposition or overlap between ancient normative alternatives and modern epistemological alternatives accounts for the ambiguous and complex character of classical French theory—a theory that at its

37. Le Bossu, *A Treatise of the Epick Poem*, p. 136.

38. Rapin, *Reflections on Aristotle's Treatise of Poetry*, in *The Whole Works*, II, 157–158.

39. Pierre Corneille, *Premier discours, de l'utilité et des parties du poème dramatique*, trans. Barret Clark, in *European Theories of the Drama*, p. 140.

40. Corneille, *Deuxième discours, de la tragédie et des moyens de la traiter selon le vraisemblence ou le nécessaire*, trans. Henry Hitch Adams and Baxter Hathaway, in *Dramatic Essays of the Neoclassic Age* (New York: Columbia University Press, 1950), p. 18.

41. Corneille, *Premier discours*, p. 139.

best was neither rationally doctrinaire nor empirically skeptical, but "positively and characteristically both."[42]

Because of the inclusive complexity of French classicism, its rationalistic leanings differed from the empirical emphases of its English counterpart more in degree than in kind. Indeed, the "new wave" of critical activity brought to England from France with the publication of William Davenant's Preface to *Gondibert* (1650) and Hobbes's reply amounted to a wholesale importation of normative alternatives and critical ambivalence. On the one hand, according to French precedent, "by a Method the Muse" was to proceed "through the severall walks of Science" and to seek "Nature in her hidden walks."[43] Hobbes endorsed Davenant's enthusiasm for "Method," "Science," and "Nature," by observing that "the workmanship of Fancy" must be "guided by the Precepts of true Philosophy."[44] On the other hand, their demands for rational integrity were balanced by a concern for rhetorical effect. Like their recent French counterparts, however, Hobbes and Davenant analyzed effect not in the traditional rhetorical terms, but in terms of "passion." For Davenant, as for the French critics, the rhetorical end of moving passion impinged upon the relation between the work itself and the objects that it imitates: "Wise poets think it more worthy to seek out truth in the Passions than to record the truth of the Actions, and practise to describe Mankinde just as we are persuaded or guided by instinct . . . Painters are no more than Historians, when they draw eminent persons, though they terme that drawing to the life; but when . . . they draw Passions, though they terme it but *Story,* then they increase in dignity and become Poets." Davenant's modification of Aristotle was thus essentially a psychological appeal to "the relish" of the reader's "pity, joy, hope, and other Passions."[45] As the object of imitation, the passions reflect the function of poetry, which, as Hobbes declared, is to "please . . . by excitation of the mind."[46]

Not surprisingly, both Hobbes and Davenant discuss the power of poetry to move the passions in terms of its accommodation to and

42. Borgerhoff, p. 237; cf. Hugh M. Davidson, *Audience, Words, and Art: Studies in Seventeenth-Century French Rhetoric* (Columbia: University of Ohio Press, 1965), p. 106.

43. William Davenant, Preface to *Gondibert*, in *Critical Essays of the Seventeenth Century*, ed. J. E. Spingarn (1907; rpt., Bloomington: Indiana University Press, 1968), II, 28; cf. Spingarn's Introduction, I, xxx, and Bate, *From Classic to Romantic*, p. 34.

44. "The Answer of Mr. Hobbes to Sr. Will. D'avenant's Preface before Gondibert," in Spingarn, II, 60; hereafter cited as "Answer."

45. Davenant, Preface to *Gondibert*, in Spingarn, II, 3–4, 11.

46. Hobbes, "Answer," in Spingarn, II, 63.

exploitation of opinion, belief, and other forms of customary value arising in the will. "The Readers," Davenant argued, are "a Poets standing Guest, and require Monarchicall respect."[47] It was no doubt to the heritage of Hobbes and Davenant that Rymer referred when he complained of "a kind of stage-quacks and *Empiricks* in Poetry, who have got Receit to please: and no Collegiate like 'em for purging the Passions."[48] Like their endorsement of "Method" and "Science," the concern of Davenant and Hobbes with "passion" originated with the seventeenth-century reassessment of normative alternatives in terms of human nature itself. This was a task that Hobbes in particular shared with the great continental thinkers, but that simultaneously led him in a different direction, just as its result eventually distinguished Dryden and other English critics from their French counterparts in accounting for rhetorical effect. Their differing points of emphasis were really produced not by the normative alternatives themselves, but by a methodological bifurcation resulting from a scientific reassessment of them. In both England and France, natural fitness and rhetorical accommodation remained in dialectical tension, but the aesthetic implications of this tension differed because in each case they were based on differing accounts of the passions and the nature of mental experience. In other words, while classicism as a whole continued to embrace differing emphases on normative alternatives, these emphases were increasingly distinguished and polarized by a developing conflict between scientifically alternative views of man—views archetypally represented by Descartes and Hobbes.

In its latter stages, at least, the French attempt to circumscribe rhetorical effect with reason was thus reinforced by the Cartesian account of mind generally and passion specifically. For Descartes, the problem of passion arose as a corollary of his effort to reconcile the independence and integrity of mind with its apparent interdependence with the world of body. In order to maintain his definition of the thinking being as a unity, Descartes opposed the scholastic view of appetite or passion as "common" to body and soul, and consequently rejected the "strife we are in the habit of conceiving to exist between the inferior part of the soul, which we call the sensuous, and the superior kind which we call the rational, or as we may say, between the natural appetite and the will . . . For there is within us but one soul, and this soul has not in itself any diversity of parts; the same part that is subject to sense impressions is rational, and all the soul's appetites are

47. Davenant, Preface to *Gondibert*, in Spingarn, II, 24.
48. Rymer, *The Tragedies of the Last Age*, in *The Critical Works*, p. 19; cf. Ben Jonson, *The Returne from Parnassus*, in G. Gregory Smith, II, 402.

acts of will." To overcome this strife, Descartes argued that passions produced in the soul by the "machine" of body are not simply passive receptions but active perceptions. Precisely because the soul consciously "regards" or "entertains" a passion, it may be said to *act* in so doing. Consequently, the perceptive *action* of the mind is identical with its *passions,* or desires, "for it is certain that we cannot desire anything without perceiving *by the same means* that we desire it; and, although in regard to our soul it is an action to desire something, we may also say that it is one of its passions to perceive that it desires."[49]

For Descartes, this reciprocity has two related consequences. First, because willing is also perception, it is preeminently an intellectual activity; "passion" is intellectualized. Second, this has the effect of subsuming bodily activity into a world of mind and placing it under the mind's control. Thus, while passions originating in external sensation cannot be "directly excited or removed by the action of our will, they can be so indirectly by *the representation of things which are usually united to the passions which we desire to have,* and which are contrary to those which we desire to set aside. Thus, in order to excite courage in oneself, and remove fear, it is not sufficient to have the will to do so, but we must apply ourselves to consider the reasons, *the objects or examples which persuade us.*" This persuasive power over passion gives rise to crucial aesthetic implications. Because the mind is able to reflect upon and direct its own passions, "we naturally take pleasure in being moved by all sorts of passions, even by sadness and hatred, when the passions are only caused by the strange adventures we see represented in a theatre." This aesthetic pleasure is a passion raised by the mind's dispassionate contemplation of passion:

> We read strange adventures in a book, or see them repre-
> sented in a theatre, which sometimes excite sadness in us,
> sometimes joy, or love, or hatred, and generally speaking all
> the passions, according to the diversity of the objects which
> are offered to our imagination; but along with them we have
> a pleasure in feeling them excited in us, and this pleasure
> is an intellectual joy which may as easily take its origin from
> sadness as from any of the other passions.[50]

49. Descartes, *The Passions of the Soul,* in *The Philosophical Works of Descartes,* I, xlvii, xix; hereafter cited by page number only. See also Hiram Caton, *The Origin of Subjectivity: An Essay on Descartes* (New Haven: Yale University Press, 1973), p. 188, and Jonathan Rée, *Descartes* (London: Allen Lane, 1974), p. 121.

50. Descartes, *The Passions of the Soul,* pp. xlv, xciv, cxlvii; my italics. See also A. J. Krailsheimer, *Studies in Self-Interest, from Descartes to La Bruyère* (Oxford: Clarendon Press, 1962), pp. 42–43.

The theater thus provides Descartes with a perfect metaphor for the independence of mind contemplating itself at once passionately and dispassionately. In its insistence on the power of passion, and on its ultimate independence of physical events, Descartes' account displays a remarkable consonance with the legal dilemma of French classicism, and especially with its rationalistic solution to the problem of passion.[51] Just as Descartes minimized the influence of body in the play of passion, so Rapin, for example, discounted the importance of sensational action and emphasized instead the mental element when he observed that "it is not the admirable Intrigue, the surprising and wonderful Events, the extraordinary Incidents that make the Beauty of a Tragedy; it is the Discourses when they are natural and passionate."[52] Le Bossu similarly clarified the relation between representation and effect by remarking that " 'tis necessary . . . to avoid the vicious Multiplicity of Fables, where there are too many Stories, too many Fables, too many Actions, the Adventures too much divided and hard to be remember'd, and such Intrigues as one can't easily comprehend. All this distracts the Mind, and requires so much attention, that there is nothing left for the Passions to work upon."[53] For similar reasons, d'Aubignac drew a sharp distinction between two types of drama: "The first consists of Incidents, Intrigues, and new Events, when almost from Act to Act there is some sudden change upon the Stage, which alters the Face of Affairs . . . The second sort of Subjects are those rais'd out of Passions; when out of a small Fund the Poet does ingeniously draw

51. The possibility of direct Cartesian influence in this respect is difficult to demonstrate conclusively. See Emile Krantz, *Essai sur l'esthétique de Descartes* (Paris, 1882), p. 224; and Gustav Lanson, "L'influence de la philosophie Cartésienne sur la littérature française," in *Essais de méthode, de critique, et d'histoire littéraire,* ed. Henri Peyre (Paris: Hachette, 1965), p. 213.

If Descartes' psychological interests may be distinguished from the possible influence of his tenets on reason and method, it may be said that the former *do* represent a slightly more novel aspect of French classicism and possibly a more direct source of influence. Such a distinction is made by Nigel Abercrombie, "Cartesianism and Classicism," *MLR,* 31 (1936), 358–376, and by Brewster Rogerson, "The Art of Painting the Passions," *JHI,* 14 (1953), 68–94. While Krantz attributes the psychological interests of French classicism primarily to the *negative* influence of the utterly and exclusively mechanical concepts of nature after Descartes, and thus again anticipates Whitehead and Bate, Abercrombie and Rogerson emphasize the positive aspects of Descartes' *own* interest in subjectivity. This latter argument is the basis of Dean T. Mace's essay, "Dryden's Dialogue on Drama," *JWCI,* 25 (1962), 87–112, which has stimulated my own thinking about the influence of the philosophy of passion on contemporary criticism.

52. Rapin, *Reflections on Aristotle's Treatise of Poetry,* in *The Whole Works,* II, 213.

53. Le Bossu, *A Treatise of the Epick Poem,* p. 143.

great Sentiments and noble Passions . . . by which the Spectators are ravish'd, and their Soul continually mov'd with some new Impression.[54] In Dryden's *Essay of Dramatic Poesy* (1668), the francophile Lisideius remarks upon the classical French bias toward the latter:

> By pursuing close one argument, which is not cloyed with many turns, the French . . . have leisure to dwell on a subject which deserves it; and to represent the passions (which we have aknowledged to be the poet's work), without being hurried from one thing to another . . . they commonly make but one person considerable in a play; they dwell on him, and his concernments . . . 'Tis a great mistake in us to believe the French present no part of the action on the stage: every alteration or crossing of a design, every new-sprung passion, and turn of it, is a part of the action, and much the noblest, except we conceive nothing to be action till they come to blows; as if the painting of the hero's mind were not more properly the poet's work than the strength of his body.[55]

In addition to its support for passion as both object of imitation and rhetorical end, Descartes' theatrical metaphor also effectively subordinated passion to reason. In Descartes' view, experience, the world of body, produced only irresolution and conflicting passions in different men and in different circumstances, so that the true relation of the passions to goodness could only be resolved intellectually by reason and judgment. In seeking rectitude, the individual was not to rely on pleasure or pain, or even on such passions as joy or love or hate, but upon joy "which *proceeds from knowledge*," love "when the things it constrains us to love are *truly good*," and desire "when it *follows a true knowledge*."[56] Descartes' metaphor of the mental theater once again proves illuminating, for in its contemplative aspect, the mental spectator is also a critic; the work of art "arouses in the soul certain passions

54. d'Aubignac, *The Whole Art of the Stage*, p. 68.

55. John Dryden, *Of Dramatic Poesy: An Essay*, in *Of Dramatic Poesy and Other Critical Essays*, ed. George Watson (New York: Everyman's Library, 1962), I, 48, 49, 52. Hereafter cited as "Watson."

56. Descartes, *The Passions of the Soul*, pp. cxl, cxxxix, cxliv; my italics. This qualification has been judged a failure in Descartes' system that returns him to the language of scholasticism he sought to avoid; see Caton, p. 193.

which are judged and classified, and accepted or rejected by the 'public' within the soul itself."[57]

This interdependency helps to explain why the French critics, despite their rhetorical emphasis on moving the passions, remained so closely attached to rational criteria in the depiction of the passions. What was ideally in Descartes the rational correspondence between the passions and the objects that arouse them was also in French classicism a correspondence between rhetorical and mimetic aims, according to which the passions were properly aroused when moved by fictional passions arising from a natural and probable action. This action was meant to reflect not the power of an unruly and chaotic world of objects over the passions, but the basic harmony between human nature and the natural laws that transcend merely random events. Thus to the dramas of action and passion d'Aubignac added an ideal third, in which "the Incidents grow more pleasing by the Passions which as it were uphold them, and the Passions seem to be renew'd, and spring afresh, by the variety of the unthought of Incidents."[58] The passions, in other words, were to be structured probably and correctly. In a larger sense, all of the French demands for probability, verisimilitude, and regularity were aimed at securing the proper passionate response by firmly grounding passion in the universal laws that govern all men's souls.[59] Despite the unresolved double focus of French classicism, despite its respect for the audience (and perhaps because of it), the rhetorical function remained closely tied to a conceptual center of natural fitness.

In English neo-classicism, by contrast, this rational nexus was often unbalanced by an incipient empiricism that liberated rhetorical effects from universals. Like the nascent rationalism that reinforced French classicism, this empirical bias emerged as a scientific critique of the ancient normative framework, but at the same time, it absorbed the tensions of this framework by restating them in novel terms. Thus, like Descartes, Hobbes turned in his reassessment of man to the theater for a metaphor to clarify mental experience; but where Descartes had

57. Rémy G. Saisselin, *The Rule of Reason and the Ruses of the Heart: A Philosophical Dictionary of French Classical Criticism, Critics, and Aesthetic Issues* (Cleveland: The Press of Case Western Reserve University, 1970), p. 251.

58. d'Aubignac, *The Whole Art of the Stage*, p. 69.

59. In his argument against Cartesian influence, Lanson takes the reverse of the case that I have made here, and maintains that such laws as the three unities did not arise from a particularly Cartesian view of passion, but that the interest in passion was the natural consequence of a prior commitment to the unities themselves, p. 212.

emphasized the rational foundations of dramatic structure, Hobbes insisted on its arbitrary and conventional character:

> In the theater it was understood that the actor himself did not speak, but someone else, for example Agamemnon; nevertheless afterwards he was also understood without his false face, namely being acknowledged as the actor himself rather than the person he had been playing. And, on account of commercial dealings and contracts between men not actually present, such artifices are no less necessary in the state than in the theatre.[60]

The context of civil philosophy, to be sure, distinguishes Hobbes's analogy in purpose from that of Descartes, but the conventionalist tenor of the analogy reflects a difference on an essential point of interest that they shared—the nature of man himself. Hobbes thus repeats the conventionalist argument when he objects to Descartes' definition of reason:

> But what shall we now say, if reasoning chance to be nothing more than the uniting together of names or designations by the word *is?* It will be a consequence of this that reason gives us no conclusion about the nature of things, but only about the terms that designate them, whether, indeed, or not there is a convention (arbitrarily made about their meanings) according to which we join these names together. If this be so, as is possible, reasoning will depend on names, and names on the imagination, and imagination, perchance, as I think, on the motion of corporeal organs.[61]

Hobbes's objection is meant to reform scientific discourse by frankly acknowledging that knowledge is not intuited, but constructed by men on the basis of sensory experience. The world of science is a world of human making and as such is subject to the human constitution.

The nominalistic character of this world, its very arbitrary basis, therefore requires that proper science take account of human will and passion in its making. Although for different reasons, passion comes to occupy, as it had done for Descartes, a central place in Hobbes's phil-

---

60. Hobbes, *De Homine*, in *Man and Citizen*, trans. and ed. Bernard Gert, T. S. K. Scott-Craig, and Charles T. Wood (New York: Anchor Books, 1972), 15.1.

61. Hobbes, *Objections*, 3.4, in *The Philosophical Works of Descartes*, II, 65.

osophy. Indeed, passion is the decisive mark of human nature, ruling even over reason, "for the thoughts, are to the Desires, as Scouts, and Spies, to range abroad and find the way to things Desired . . . to have no Desire, is to be Dead: so to have no Passions, is Dulnesse."[62] In taking will as the central motive power and stimulus for all thought, Hobbes effectively subordinates the power of reason. The very cause of reasoning "is the appetite of them, who, having a conception of the end [desired], have next unto it a conception of the next means to them."[63] The very edifice of science is erected on desire.

Moreover, as the motive power of science, passion also impinges upon the structure of science at its very origin. Thought originates in sensory perception when external motions impinge upon and initiate responsive motions in the perceiving subject. This empirical premise gives rise to nominalistic implications. Man is distinguished from beasts by his ability to maintain, and thus to reason with, the "decaying sense" of his conceptions by setting up "a visible or other sensible mark, the which when he seeth again, may bring to his mind the thought he had when he set it up. A *MARK,* therefore is a sensible object which a man erecteth voluntarily to himself, to the end to remember thereby somewhat past, when the same is objected to his sense again."[64] Such marks, or names, become the means by which man linguistically orders his experience: "Speech or language is the connexion of names constituted by the will of men to stand for the series of conceptions of the things about which we think. Therefore, as a name is to the idea or conception of a thing, so is speech to the discourse of the mind."[65]

Thus despite its sensory origins, rational investigation is a science of names; man understands "his conceptions and thoughts, by the sequell and contexture of the names of things." Accordingly, there is "nothing in the world Universall but Names; for the things named, are every one of them Individuall and Singular."[66] It is only through the logical connection of names that "the consequence found in one particular, comes to be registered and remembered, as an Universall rule;

62. Hobbes, *Leviathan,* ed. C. B. Macpherson (Penguin Books, 1968), 1.8.

63. Hobbes, *The Elements of Law, Natural and Politic,* ed. Ferdinand Tönnies (Cambridge: Cambridge University Press, 1928), p. 101; see also p. 35, and cf. R. L. Brett, "Thomas Hobbes," in *The English Mind: Studies in The English Moralists Presented to Basil Willey,* ed. Hugh Sykes Davies and George Watson (Cambridge: Cambridge University Press, 1964), p. 34.

64. Hobbes, *The Elements of Law,* p. 14.

65. Hobbes, *De Homine,* 10.1.

66. Hobbes, *Leviathan,* 1.2, 4; cf. *Elements of Philosophy . . . Concerning Body,* 1.2.9, and *The Elements of Law,* p. 15.

and discharges our mentall reckoning, of time and place . . . and *makes* that which was found true here and now, to be true in all places and all times."[67]

This suggests that the object of human science is not to lead men toward universal moral truths, but to help them understand their own constructed moral world by showing them the truths about the ways in which it comes to be constructed. In moral science we should "conclude not such things to be without, that are within us . . . That is to say, we cannot from experience conclude, that any thing is to be called just or unjust, true or false, nor any proposition universal whatsoever, except it be from remembrance of the use of names imposed arbitrarily by men."[68] Thus the moral world is a nominal construction; "we ourselves *make* the principles—that is, the causes of justice (namely laws and covenants)—whereby it is known what *justice* or what *equity*, and their opposites *injustice* and *inequality*, are. For before covenants and laws were drawn up, neither justice nor injustice, neither public good nor public evil, was natural among men any more than it was among beasts."[69] Thus moral definitions, unlike those of geometry or the natural sciences, contain a component of evaluation that changes with individuals, time, and place. Indeed, moral thinking is coeval with the origin of thought itself, as individual aversions or attractions contribute to the very conceptualization of experience. Accordingly,

> the names of such things as affect us, that is, which please, and displease us . . . are in the common discourse of men, of inconstant signification. For seeing all names are imposed to signifie our conceptions; and all our affections are but conceptions; when we conceive the same things differently, we can hardly avoyd different naming of them. For though the nature of that we conceive, be the same; yet the diversity of our reception of it, in respect of different constitutions of body, and prejudices of opinion, gives everything a tincture of our different passions . . . For one man calleth *Wisdome,* what another calleth *feare;* and one cruelty, what another justice . . . And therefore such names can never be true grounds of any ratiocination.

The arbitrary character of the world of moral discourse therefore stems from its origins in passion; the traditional moral terms "are ever used

67. Hobbes, *Leviathan,* 1.4.
68. Hobbes, *The Elements of Law,* p. 13.
69. Hobbes, *De Homine,* 10.5; cf. Hobbes's "Introduction" to *Leviathan,* pp. 81–82.

with relation to the person that useth them."[70] Except where arbitrary standards are imposed by the contractual state, there is nothing *"agathon haplos,* that is to say, simply good,"[71] and therefore "good is said to be relative to person, place, and time."[72] The fact that "men measure, not onely other men, but all other things, by themselves,"[73] means that passion and will preside over reason in the world of moral discourse; indeed, passion creates the very intellectual concepts with which such discourse is involved. "So, just as the proverb hath it, 'So many men, so many opinions,' one can also say, 'Many men, many different rules for vice and virtue.' "[74]

Thus the truly scientific study of man places his normative heritage on the nominalist foundations of public language. "The custom and common use of speech" often "representeth not unto us our own conceptions," but we "think them to be true: and the admittance of them is called opinion." In their "ignorance of the signification of speech," men "take the habitual discourse of the tongue for ratiocination," and "rely on the opinion of some other, whom they think wiser than themselves."[75] Although inherited from the conventional "contexture of speech," such customary concepts elicit passionate responses as effectively, and as violently, as concepts arising directly from experience, for "our wills follow our opinions, as our actions follow our wills. In which sense they say truly and properly that say the world is governed by opinion." Because "the passions of man . . . are . . . the beginning of speech," language itself becomes an edifice of opinion, "wherein custom hath so great a power, that the mind suggesteth only the first word, and the others follow habitually, and are not followed by the mind."[76]

Thus passion finds its central place in Hobbes's view of man, not as a Cartesian power uniting the world of body with the world of mind, but as a power arising in body and misdirecting mind with its arbitrary sway. Whereas Descartes insulates the mind by treating passion as a function of mind itself, Hobbes attaches passion, through conventional signs, more concretely to the world of experience. Thus the Cartesian spectator, who contemplates the inner play of passions in the mind, gives way to a Hobbesian spectator moved by illusions stemming from a system of values of his own making: "Imagination

70. Hobbes, *Leviathan,* 1.4, 6.
71. Hobbes, *The Elements of Law,* p. 22.
72. Hobbes, *De Homine,* 11.4.
73. Hobbes, *Leviathan,* 1.2.
74. Hobbes, *De Homine,* 13.8.
75. Hobbes, *The Elements of Law,* pp. 16, 20, 51; cf. *Leviathan,* 1.11.
76. Hobbes, *The Elements of Law,* pp. 48, 18.

. . . is raised in man . . . by words, or other voluntary signs."[77] In contrast to the Cartesian view that universal standards of reason rightly prevail over the passions, Hobbes argues that the passions are moved by the conventional norms that cultural or collective passions have created. This provides a novel philosophic underpinning for an empirical approach to rhetorical fitness, and emphasizes the conventional character of the arts of speech. When art is used rhetorically to

> increase or diminish one another's passions, it is the same thing with persuasion: the difference not being real. For the begetting of opinion and passion is the same act; but whereas in persuasion we aim at getting opinion from passion; here, the end is, to raise passion from opinion. And as in raising an opinion from passion, any premises are good enough to infer the desired conclusion; so, in raising passion from opinion, it is no matter whether the opinion be true or false, or the narration historical or fabulous. For not truth, but image, maketh passion; and a tragedy affecteth no less than a murder, if well-acted.[78]

As a psychological reinterpretation, the power of raising "passion from opinion" resulted from an inward and scientific approach to normative conflict that both Hobbes and Davenant shared with French classicism; but at the same time, it offered an alternative, empirical resolution. In keeping with the Hobbesian interpretation of passion, Davenant redefined rhetorical fitness in psychological terms, by observing that "the weakest part of the people is their mindes." This weakness, he argued, provides the poet with an opportunity: "the Minde can never be constrain'd, though it can be gain'd by perswasion: and since Perswasion is the principle instrument which can bring to fashion the brittle and misshapen mettal of the Minde, none are so fit in aids to this important work as the poets . . . whose operations are as resistless, secret, easie, and subtle as the influence of the Planets."[79] The basis of such "secret" and "subtle" persuasion is psychologically empirical, as Davenant's reinterpretation of Aristotelian "probability" reveals. The goal in composition is not the philosophically whole and probable action, but a psychologically artless art that exploits convention in order "to make great Actions credible": "We may descend to

---

77. Hobbes, *Leviathan*, 1.6, 1.2.

78. Hobbes, *The Elements of Law*, p. 52; see also Clarence D. Thorpe, *The Aesthetic Theory of Thomas Hobbes* (Ann Arbor: University of Michigan Press, 1940), pp. 134, 142.

79. Davenant, Preface to *Gondibert*, pp. 44–45.

compare deceptions in Poesie to those of them that professe dexterity of Hand which resembles Conjuring, and to such we come not with the intention of Lawyers to examine the evidence of Facts, but are content, if we like the carriage of their feign'd motion, to pay for being well deceiv'd."[80] Successful deception comes at the costly price of betraying true magic, for "dexterity of Hand" is no longer circumscribed by nature, but only by the limits of human credulousness. As Hobbes puts it in his "Answer," "beyond the actual works of nature a Poet may go; but beyond the *conceived possibility* of nature, never."[81] For Davenant as for Hobbes, however, this "conceived possibility" changes with time and place; it subordinates nature to conventional belief. This, in turn, liberates the poet from ancient precedent.

Because the poet strives to achieve standards "of worthiness and unworthiness, as they are defined by Opinion," it is, says Davenant, "a deficiency and meanness of minde to stay and depend upon the authority of example." Instead of looking solely to natural principles or to tradition for guidance, the poet should "with wise diligence study the People." The empirical test of prevailing social value determines the proper fitness. "If I be accus'd of Innovation," Davenant declares, "or to have transgressed against the method of the Ancients, I shall think myself secure in beleeving that a Poet who hath wrought with his own instruments out a new design, is no more answerable to Predecessors, than Law-Makers are liable to those old Laws which themselves have repealed."[82]

As in the state, so too in poetry, the laws of the art reflect the changing needs and expectations of their human setting. Indeed, because in the Hobbesian view any public standards of rectitude or goodness are defined by collective passions, the effectiveness of poetry in moving the passions will be a function of its conformity with these standards. Because of its nominalist basis, the affective theory of passion in Hobbes's view of man was quite as significant for modern aesthetics as his theory of imagination. Indeed, even his psychological account of imagination links creativity to its empirical setting, for the Judgment that circumscribes Fancy does not intuit universal norms, but distinguishes "between thing and thing . . . particularly in matter of conversation and businesse; wherein, times, places, and persons are to be discerned."[83] Thus, like the Platonists and latitudinarians who ironically opposed him on so many counts, Hobbes helped to validate convention

80. Davenant, Preface to *Gondibert*, p. 11.
81. Hobbes, "Answer," p. 62; my italics.
82. Davenant, Preface to *Gondibert*, pp. 7, 12, 38, 20.
83. Hobbes, *Leviathan*, 1.8.

as a norm by placing technical debate on epistemologically empirical grounds, and consequently by furnishing an argumentative basis for English neo-classicism in its reassessment of tradition. While theorists in England shared a technical complex with their French counterparts, they diverged from them precisely at the point in this complex where new scientific methods were in embryo. Their points of difference were partly held in check by the resilience of the system and by the mutually comprehensible language of legalism; but at the same time they were aggravated by a scientific disjunction that intensified the classical balance between nature and convention into a conflict between the rival claims of reason and experience.

Accordingly, while English theory in the later seventeenth century remained primarily normative or technical in character, it tended to resolve conflicts by appealing psychologically and empirically to the changing values of society. The so-called School of Taste was not essentially an antinomian development, but, in the manner exemplified by latitudinarian tolerance and Royal Society skepticism, an objection to dogmatic efforts "to give strict rules to things that are not Mathematical."[84] In citing the official Restoration epistemology, the critic Robert Howard appealed to the empirical evidence that "the manner of Stage-Entertainments have differ'd in all Ages," and thus argued, from the relative validity that adheres to convention, that "rules for regulating the Stage" should enjoy a merely hypothetical status; they should, he said, "be submitted to the fancy of others, and bear the name of Propositions, not of Confident Lawes, or Rules made by Demonstration; and then I shall not discommend any Poet that dresses his Play in such a fashion as his fancy best approves, and fairly leave it for others to follow, if it appears to them most convenient."[85]

Embodied in "Propositions" rather than "Confident Lawes," the "convenient" relation between the arts and their temporal setting no longer rested simply on the ancient normative grounds, but also on a scientifically empirical interest in what the virtuoso Walter Charleton called "the Mutation of Mens Ingenies by Passions, Customes, Experience, the goods of Fortune, Opinion of ones self, & c."[86] As the product of an inward turn of mind, this interest was the complement and counterpart to the empirical and restrospective turn of a developing

84. Robert Howard, Preface to *The Great Favourite,* in Spingarn, II, 106.

85. Howard, Preface to *Four New Plays* and to *The Great Favourite,* in Spingarn, II, 98, 106.

86. Walter Charleton, *Of the Different Wits of Men,* in *Two Discourses* (London, 1669), pp. 51–52. The title page explains that the treatise *Of the Different Wits of Men* was written in 1664.

historical consciousness. Together, these developments helped to re-place a logocentric universe with a homocentric order, and conse-quently to shift the study of human endeavor from the philosophic contemplation of its ends to a scientific scrutiny of its origins. Not sur-prisingly, Charleton turned to empirical psychology as well as to his-torical contextualism in order to establish what he believed were the true Danish origins of Stonehenge. By definition, its very monumental character "at once corresponded with the fashion of [the Danes'] An-cestors, and expressed the profuseness of their publick joy." This "pub-lick joy," differs essentially from the "intellectual joy" of Descartes. Moreover, where his contemporaries often argued from the architec-tural metaphor of foundation and superstructure, Charleton argued from the real monumental expression of "publick joy" that in the prod-ucts of civilization there is a great "variety . . . owing not onely to the diversity of Peoples and Nations, that founded, erected, composed them . . . after sundry manners, and with various artifices, each ac-cording to their proper Genius, Belief, Customes, Commodities, and Occasions. So that no wonder, if these (as all other works of Man) are vastly different among themselves." Indeed, so great is the variety of public values, that even the works of "one and the same Nation, in one and the same Country," Charleton went on to say, have "been now and then varied in fashion, magnificence, & c., according to the several vicissitudes of Time, mutations of Religion, and other revolutions of Fate."[87]

In Charleton's passing formulations, a novel set of historical, psycho-logical, and scientific interests begins to coalesce around the concept of convention. This coalesence reflects the extent to which older habits of normative thinking were charged with a new interest in the nature and functioning of conventions themselves. Consequently, though still normative and technical in character, the mature phase of classicism in literary theory approached normative order with an increasingly so-phisticated awareness of the mediate character of verbal art, and hence of the social, historical, and psychological factors that help to shape it. This trend is vividly reflected in the criticism of John Dryden, for whom the concept of convention is a central literary principle, a means through which he can at once adhere to the critical tradition he in-herits and respond to the demands of his time. Dryden wrote more ex-tensively and perceptively of convention than almost any man before his time. It is therefore especially fitting that early in his life Dryden should have paid poetic tribute to Charleton for his recovery of the image of a culture from its public monuments. The monumental char-

87. Charleton, *Chorea Gigantum* (London, 1633), pp. 64, 5.

acter of art, its ability to express "the publick joy," informs both Dryden's theory and practice,[88] and it underscores the prominence of convention as a test of fitness in his thinking and in his critical legacy.

3. "Betwixt Two Ages Cast": Dryden's Criticism

In the prime of his dramatic career, and at the height of his critical influence, Dryden described himself in the Prologue to *Aureng-Zebe* (1676), as a man "betwixt two ages cast / The first of this, and hindmost of the last."[1] The description admirably characterizes Dryden's critical influence, for this "father of English criticism" was also one of the last major theorists to have written about literature from within the pan-European classical and technical traditions. Johnson's description of Dryden "as the writer who first taught us to determine upon principles the merit of composition,"[2] wonderfully seizes the double character of Dryden's criticism in its own double emphasis upon Dryden's critical or empirical evaluation of "merit," and his place within an older normative framework that envisions a binding relationship between "composition" and "principles." From the perspective of our own hindsight, these "principles" seem to have been the appreciative rather than prescriptive criteria of psychological, comparative, and historical investigation. As such, they apply to criticism rather than to composition, to the critic or consumer of art rather than the poet or producer. Thus R. D. Hume, for example, has argued that "Dryden is . . . the key figure in a transition from composition-oriented to appreciation-oriented criticism."[3]

The transitional character of Dryden's criticism, however, is intimately related to his place at the end of the technical tradition, when the growing prominence of convention as an adequate test of fitness

88. On monumental and architectural metaphor in Dryden, see Bernard N. Schilling, *Dryden and the Conservative Myth: A Reading of "Absalom and Achitophel"* (New Haven: Yale University Press, 1961), pp. 73–79, 252–255.

1. Dryden, Prologue to *Aureng-Zebe*, ll. 21–22, in *Of Dramatic Poesy and Other Essays*, ed. George Watson (New York: Everyman's Library, 1962), I, 192; hereafter cited as Watson.

2. Samuel Johnson, *Lives of the Poets*, ed. Arthur Waugh (1952; rpt., London: Oxford University Press, 1968), I, 287.

3. R. D. Hume, *Dryden's Criticism* (Ithaca: Cornell University Press, 1970), pp. 24–25. Hume here follows the line of modern Dryden criticism beginning with George Saintsbury, *A History of English Criticism* (New York: Dodd, Mead, 1911), p. 127. See also E. M. W. Tillyard, "A Note on Dryden's Criticism," in R. F. Jones et al., *The Seventeenth Century* (Stanford: Stanford University Press, 1951), p. 338; and George Watson, *The Literary Critics: A Study of English Descriptive Criticism* (New York: Barnes and Noble, 1964), p. 35.

turned the discussion of natural ends toward a critical analysis of their intersubjective origins and specifications in time. Dryden's efforts to relate artistic norms to their human setting were therefore based upon the increasingly critical, empirical, and historical methods being developed in all the human sciences as a result of challenges to their normative framework. The rhetorical character of Dryden's literary theory arose out of a continuity with Renaissance and classical approaches to art, but led toward empirical, psychological, and historical alternatives to these approaches. It is not only the combination of these alternatives, but their intimate relation to each other and to a much broader historical phenomenon, that accounts for the truly transitional character of Dryden's criticism.

This transitional character is nowhere as evident as in the structure, style, and purpose of the critical essays themselves, whose occasional nature and consequently empirical, pragmatic focus is balanced by an effort to articulate the particular in terms of principle. Dryden's critical writing seldom engaged the large philosophic issues involving the nature of art in relation to scientific knowledge or to other forms of human practice and production, and as a result his writing lacks the broadly philosophic approach taken in encyclopedic surveys of the arts or in the earlier defenses of poetry. With the place and purpose of poetry among the arts secured, he turned instead to the "alternatives of practice."[4] Moreover, Dryden's practical interests were always a function of his self-interest, so that the "hasty" character of the essays was often the product of a more carefully calculated art of self-expression that Dryden claimed to have borrowed from Montaigne.[5] Dryden's tentative and skeptical approach, his concreteness and flexibility, thus reflect a personality engaged with the varieties of literary experience and writing in a genre "not yet developed enough to have clear requirements."[6]

At the same time, however, the apparent novelty of both Dryden's pragmatism and his experimental style owed its impetus to developments in the tradition of classical criticism. As that branch of verbal technique most concerned with the contingent and particular, rhetoric had always fostered a skeptical attitude toward artistic fitness, and had always confronted the writer with the necessity of revision in view of the varieties of circumstance. Moreover, the very terminology of the

4. Earl Miner, "Renaissance Contexts of Dryden's Criticism," *Michigan Quarterly Review*, 12 (1973), 101.

5. See Preface to *Fables*, in Watson, II, 278; cf. Preface to *Sylvae*, Watson, II, 33, and Hume, p. 39.

6. Schilling, p. 93.

art, concerned with obtaining effects in relation to changing social values and expectations, contained implicitly a vocabulary for *explaining* effects in the same terms.[7] The descriptive and tentative character of Dryden's essays is not, therefore, an ad hoc innovation, but a natural offshoot of the technical tradition of theorizing and prescribing within which Dryden wrote.[8] This tradition led a twilight existence in Dryden's "loose epistolary way,"[9] and its characteristic tensions stimulated Dryden's search for a style answering the need for flexible mediation between the poetic and rhetorical terms of technical analysis, between conformity with nature and accommodation to circumstance, between normative continuity and change, and between reason and experience as the powers that determine poetic fitness.

In this respect, Dryden resembled his French contemporaries, though he moved between alternative points of emphasis with considerably greater ease; he often played an English Horace to the French Aristotelians.[10] Where the practical criticism of most French critics aimed to show the conformity of practice with unchanging rules, Dryden was more often concerned to show the flexibility with which principles may be applied in practice. In Dryden's criticism, the relatively greater emphasis upon convention as a test of fitness, and his greater confidence in

7. See Robert Marsh, *Four Dialectical Theories of Poetry* (Chicago: University of Chicago Press, 1965), p. 9.

8. See Watson, *The Literary Critics*, p. 35. Hume similarly remarks upon the prevalence of traditional vocabulary in Dryden's criticism, and refutes John M. Aden's view ("Dryden and the Imagination: The First Phase," *PMLA*, 74 [1959], 28–40) of Dryden's interest in the psychology of imagination by observing that even in his later career Dryden "concerns himself principally with the mechanics of representation itself"; "Dryden on Creation: 'Imagination' in the Later Criticism," *RES*, n.s. 21 (1970), 295–314. John C. Sherwood shows that even in Dryden's most concrete and appreciative criticism, he uses the traditional terms and concepts; "Dryden and the Rules: The Preface to the *Fables*," *JEGP*, 52 (1953), 13–26.

9. Dedication of the *Aeneis*, in *Essays of John Dryden*, ed. W. P. Ker (Oxford: Clarendon Press, 1926), II, 164. Because Watson omits significant portions of the Dedication, I cite the edition of Ker, who prints it in its entirety.

10. See Louis Legouis, "Corneille and Dryden as Dramatic Critics," in *Seventeenth Century Studies Presented to Sir Herbert Grierson*, ed. J. D. Wilson (Oxford: Clarendon Press, 1938), p. 291; and John M. Aden, "Dryden, Corneille, and the *Essay of Dramatic Poesy*," *RES*, n.s. 6 (1955), 147–156. Compared with the general neglect of the *Ars Poetica* by French critics (Bray, pp. 59–61), Dryden's more than sixty quotations are so extensive, that, as A. M. Ellis has observed, "the few lines which Dryden failed to quote are, with one exception, elaborations of those which he used. Thus, if the *Ars Poetica* were lost, it could be largely reconstructed through Dryden's references"; "Dryden and Horace," *PQ*, 4 (1925), 42. For Dryden's own account of his critical debt to Horace, see Watson, I, 243, and II, 30.

the power of convention to offer specific alternatives compatible with generic natural standards, was largely a difference from French classicism in degree; the empirical, descriptive, and critical methods that it generated, however, amounted to a difference in kind.

This difference originated in Dryden's substantial concern for rhetorical effects. Few poets or dramatists have so frequently or at such great length lectured, flattered, cajoled, debated, maligned, and pleaded with their audience. Though Dryden shares Jonson's self-interest and habit of special pleading, he lacks his pompous pedantry; and were it not for his affected aloofness, and more limited focus, Dryden might be said to resemble Shaw in his lifelong engagement with his public. Dryden's conception of the poet's relation to his audience expresses itself in its noblest form as an analogy between the theater and the forum. As "a figure who deals with material of public interest,"[11] the "poet is presum'd to be a kind of lawgiver," whose audience is not "to be cheated into passion, but to be reason'd into truth."[12] In much of Dryden's critical writing, however, the theater holds sway over the forum, and it is the audience that dictates the laws. Rhetorical demands affect not only the poet's livelihood, but also the serious nature of his calling, "for delight is the chief, if not the only end of poesy; instruction can be admitted but in the second place, for poesy only instructs as it delights."[13] As Dryden claims, "to imitate well is a poet's work"; but this mimetic aim must be interpreted in relation to its pragmatic function, "to affect the soul, and excite the passions, and above all, to move admiration." "Reasoning" the audience into "truth" depends in part upon the poet's success in "cheating" them into "passion." Dryden's confession that "my chief endeavours are to delight the world in which I live,"[14] suggests his willingness to accept convention as at least one adequate test of fitness:

> They who have best succeeded on the stage,
> Have still conform'd their genius to their age.[15]

11. Lilian Feder, "John Dryden's Use of Classical Rhetoric," in *Essential Articles for the Study of John Dryden,* ed. H. T. Swedenberg (Hamden, Conn.: Anchor Books, 1966), p. 500.

12. Preface to *Religio Laici,* in *The Poetical Works,* ed. George R. Noyes (1937; rpt., Cambridge: Houghton Mifflin, 1950), p. 162; cf. Philip Harth, *Contexts of Dryden's Thought* (Chicago: University of Chicago Press, 1968), pp. 42–43.

13. *A Defence of an Essay of Dramatic Poesy,* in Watson, I, 113–114; cf. Preface to *An Evening's Love,* in Watson, I, 152; Preface to *All for Love,* in Watson, I, 227; and Preface to *Examen Poeticum,* in Watson, II, 162.

14. *A Defence of an Essay of Dramatic Poesy,* in Watson, I, 114, 116.

15. Epilogue to *The Conquest of Granada,* ll. 1–2, in Watson, I, 167.

Dryden's concern for this type of fitness lends to his criticism its empirical character: "if the coin be good," he observes, "it will pass from one hand to another . . . if the public approves it, the bill passes." This mode of currency suggests that artistic norms arise as habitual articulations of collective desires: "we are naturally prone to imitate what we admire; and frequent acts produce a habit."[16] Accordingly, Dryden's criticism frequently follows the legal tradition of presumptive reasoning, inferring from the present fitness between conventional norms and their social setting an original link between such norms and nature. "Thus I grant you," Dryden maintains, "that the knowledge of nature was the original rule; and that all poets ought to study her, as well as Aristotle and Horace, her interpreters. But then this also undeniably follows, that those things which delight all ages *must have been* an imitation of nature." This presumptive reasoning, however, argues from the present fitness of convention rather than from nature itself; to challenge prevailing norms by appealing "to right reason . . . you must prove only that that ought not to please which has pleased . . . and to be thought knowing, you must first put the fool upon mankind."[17] The ultimate test of fitness therefore lies not with reason but with the empirical foundation of rhetorical success: "Customs are changed," Dryden argues, "and even statutes are silently repealed, when the reason ceases for which they were enacted."[18]

At the same time, however, Dryden's design to be for his time was balanced by his desire to be for all time. "As 'tis my interest to please my audience, so 'tis my ambition to be read." Accordingly, his interest in rhetorical effect was balanced by his concern for truth, "for nothing but truth can long continue; and time is the surest judge of truth."[19] Taking upon himself the role of spokesman for artistic integrity, Dryden tried to mediate between the naturally fitting and the conventionally popular. His frequently affected scorn for his audience reflects a deeper theoretical concern with the value of artistic principle in the face of changing circumstance. "To please the people ought to be the poet's aim," Dryden declares, "because plays are made for their delight; but it does not follow that they are always pleased with good plays, or that the plays which please them are always good."[20]

The *raison d'être* of Dryden's criticism was thus his effort to relate generically abiding standards to the specific conditions of the English

16. Dedication of the *Aeneis,* in Ker, II, 234, 159.

17. *The Author's Apology for Heroic Poetry,* in Watson, I, 200; hereafter cited as *Apology.*

18. Preface to *Fables,* in Watson, II, 288.

19. Preface to *The Spanish Friar,* in Watson, I, 278.

20. *Defence of an Essay of Dramatic Poesy,* in Watson, I, 120.

rhetorical setting. In this respect, his role as critic resembles his view of the poet in relation to the technical tradition. In mediating between formal and rhetorical elements of his art, the poet relies on conventional materials, resources, and assumptions in order to compose in keeping with artistic principle a formal whole which unifies "all things in a beautiful order and harmony, that the whole may be of a piece."[21] This process involves a continual reciprocity in which form is accommodated to special rhetorical requirements, and in which these requirements are in turn subsumed into form. In the same way, Dryden as critic stands midway between unchanging natural precepts and the social milieu in which they take effect. Just as the poet shapes his work in such a way as to suit his audience while maintaining artistic integrity, so the critic aims to shape the audience by educating them to the proper response. Insofar as he addresses himself to the public, Dryden as critic aims to show how "mankind is ever the same, and nothing lost out of nature, though every thing is altered."[22]

This interplay between change and continuity shapes the broader outlines of Dryden's literary theory as well. Because he envisions his audience as an imaginative participant in a dynamic literary process, Dryden interprets the *mimesis* of nature as a function of its pragmatic ends. The aim of imitation is to produce an illusion, "to raise the imagination of the audience, and to persuade them, for the time, that what they behold in the theater is really performed."[23] This aim depends, to some extent, upon adherence to natural probability, because "imagination in a man, or reasonable creature, is supposed to participate of reason."[24] Nevertheless, the criterion of what is rationally probable varies with time and place; it is not simply a philosophic, but also a social principle. It is "varied, according to the language and age in which an author writes. That which would be allowed to a Grecian poet, Martiall tells you, would not be suffered in a Roman. And 'tis evident that the English does more nearly follow the strictness of the latter than the freedoms of the former."[25]

Like Davenant and Hobbes before him, Dryden interprets the art of imitation in relation to the passions, and his view of *mimesis* allows for considerable flexibility. To be sure, "truth is the object of our understanding,"[26] but "human impossibilities are to be received as they are

---

21. *A Parallel Betwixt Poetry and Painting*, in Watson, II, 195.
22. Preface to *Fables*, in Watson, II, 285.
23. *Of Heroic Plays*, in Watson, I, 162.
24. *Defence of an Essay of Dramatic Poesy*, in Watson, I, 126.
25. *Apology*, in Watson, I, 206; cf. p. 204.
26. *A Parallel Betwixt Painting and Poetry*, in Watson, II, 194.

then in faith"; Shakespeare, for example, "then writ as people then believed."[27] This latent nominalism never quite undermines Dryden's serious devotion to nature and reason, but it encourages his willingness at times to accept the empirical test of convention as an adequate measure of fitness. Thus he observed of his success with the heroic play that "the common opinion (*how unjust soever*) has been so much to my advantage that I have reason to be satisfied and to suffer with patience all that can be urged against it."[28] Though this willingness found its strongest expression at the height of Dryden's success as a dramatist in the early seventies, it pervades all of his criticism in varying degree.

It is precisely this capacity for greater or lesser extension, for application in varying degree, which accounts for the central role that the concept of convention plays in Dryden's thought, and for the distinctive flexibility that it bestows upon his criticism. The concept of convention serves him as a middle term, as a principle at once artistic and social in character. It enables him to mediate between prescriptive generality and concrete experience, between the rules and reason as well as between the rules and their effects upon an audience that changes with time. Thus the double emphasis of Dryden's criticism is neither a fundamental inconsistency nor an ontological dualism, but a true "complementarity" arising from the pervasive influence of the concept of convention.[29] The different points of view expressed in Dryden's criticism are therefore not primarily the products of his changing personal fortunes or the reflections of a divided personality;[30] rather, they are informed by consistent reference to a concept allowing for emphasis upon either uniformity or diversity. Moreover, while the occasional

27. Preface to *Albion and Albanius,* in Watson, II, 35; Prologue to *The Tempest,* in Watson, I, 136; cf. the similar pronouncements in Preface to *Tyrannic Love,* in Watson, I, 142; *Of Heroic Plays* (Watson, I, 161); and *Discourse Concerning Satire* (Watson, II, 88–89).

28. *Of Heroic Plays,* in Watson, I, 163.

29. Edward Pechter uses this distinction between "complementarity," and inconsistency, contradiction, or dualism in his admirable study of *Dryden's Classical Theory of Literature* (Cambridge: Cambridge University Press, 1975), p. 12. It is my aim to show that the "complementary" relationship that Pechter describes is due in part to the specific place of the concept of convention in Dryden's thought.

30. The charge of inconsistency in Dryden's criticism has always been a corollary of the view that Dryden's political and religious conversions were motivated by largely self-serving interests, and were inconsistent both with any sets of established principles and with anything that could be called a stable personality. On this basis, William E. Bohn divided Dryden's criticism into five biographical periods, and argued that the positions taken in each period reflect Dryden's personal fortunes, "The Development of John Dryden's Literary Criticism," *PMLA,* 22 (1907), 56–139. The view that Dryden was inconsistent for self-serving reasons still prevails in some quarters; see, e.g., Watson's Introduction, I, xiii.

and practical character of much of Dryden's criticism would seem to militate against any consistent articulation of a formal aesthetic,[31] his empirical emphasis is itself a function of his theoretical understanding of human endeavor as an adjustment through various conventions to unchanging principles. This understanding allows for a wide-ranging empirical focus, and for free expression of personality.

It also accounts for what Dryden called his "natural diffidence and scepticism." The need to mediate between the claims of rational principle and those of rhetorical effect entails that "many a fair precept in poetry is like a seeming demonstration in mathematics: very specious in the diagram, but failing in the mechanic operation."[32] Accordingly, because artistic norms arise out of a dynamic interplay between natural principles and changing human expectations, the sort of reasoning by which Dryden supports these norms, and the degree of validity that he supposes them to possess, vary with the placement of his emphasis. Because norms are never exclusively social or rational, Dryden never completely subscribes to that sort of Pyrrhonism[33] which abandons all standards to a purely conventional relativity, nor to that dogmatic rationalism which supports standards of value on grounds of demonstrative certainty. Rather, he follows the main lines of seventeenth-century epistemology in its distinction between those truths that are on the one hand rationally intuited by all men, clearly and distinctly presented to the mind, or deduced with geometric precision from first principles, and those truths on the other hand whose certainty is relative to the kind and degree of evidence available. While Dryden's view of the status and validity of artistic norms might be described as an expression of "probabilism,"[34] this probabilism varies in degree throughout

31. See, for example, Hume, p. 6; and Watson's Introduction, I, xiii. These positions stem in part from T. S. Eliot's influential view of Dryden as a craftsman par excellence. See "Dryden the Critic, Defender of Sanity," *The Listener*, 5 (1931), 274–276.

32. Preface to *Sylvae*, in Watson, II, 26, 19.

33. The strongest case for Dryden's Pyrrhonism in Louis Bredvold's, *The Intellectual Milieu of John Dryden* (Ann Arbor: University of Michigan Press, 1934). The later studies of Trowbridge, Hooker, Le Clerq, and Harth (all cited below), have all been inspired in part by their efforts to respond to Bredvold's important work. The tradition of Pyrrhonism that Bredvold traces was, as noted earlier, an important force in bringing the concept of convention into prominence in the Renaissance. While Dryden's criticism encompasses much more than Pyrrhonism, it is highly indebted to Pyrrhonism's influence on the technical tradition as a whole.

34. See Hoyt Trowbridge, "The Place of Rules in Dryden's Criticism," in Swedenberg, p. 129. "Probabilism" is the term used by Trowbridge to describe Dryden's debt to the modified skepticism of Glanvill, Boyle, Watts, and the Royal Society. Trowbridge's effort to connect Dryden with this particular school of skepticism (as dis-

his criticism. Dryden's might also be described as a "middle"[35] position between extreme dogmatism and extreme skepticism, but this position encompasses such a variety of emphases between the extremes
as to make Dryden's view always a matter of degree rather than kind.[36]
Because the ontological status of artistic norms in Dryden's view involves two axes, one between the norms and universal principles, and
one between the norms and their intersubjective setting, Dryden's
view of their epistemological status and validity is always a diagonal
function of the degree of emphasis along these axes. Prescription based
on nature is subject only to the uncertainties of reason itself; but prescription designed to suit the unpredictability of fashion runs a double
risk. Hence, Dryden's view of the norms runs along a continuum ranging from the most probable criterion of nature to the least probable
criterion of public will. This allows Dryden to encompass both the
uniformity of neo-Aristotelian standards and the empirical variety of
poetic practice, to interpret fitness as both natural and conventional.[37]

The technical tradition had always allowed for both of these possibilities, though it often interpreted them as alternatives. Not only
their interanimation in Dryden's criticism, but also the greater extent
to which Dryden often inclines toward the conventional, marked the
decisive point in the technical tradition at which convention ceased to
function normatively, and became instead a term of critical description,
a means of describing the apparent difference in literary practices and

---

tinguished from two others) suffers, however, from the fact that he considers the
status of the rules to involve the efficacy of the theorist's mind only in relation to
nature, and not in relation to the intersubjective setting. Moreover, because he bases
his argument almost exclusively on the famous passage in the *Defence of an Essay*
(Watson, I, 123), he is overly concerned with establishing the *kind* of Dryden's skepticism, and not enough concerned with the various *degrees* in which it appears
throughout Dryden's criticism.

35. See E. N. Hooker, "Dryden and the Atoms of Epicurus," in Swedenberg, p.
239.

36. In addition to Bredvold's efforts to identify Dryden's views as Pyrrhonist, and
Trowbridge's efforts to identify them with the Royal Society's "probabilism," Richard V. Le Clerq argues that Dryden's view follows the probabilism of the New
Academy, "The Academic Nature of the Whole Discourse of *An Essay of Dramatic
Poesy*," *PLL*, 8 (1972), 27–38. More useful than his discussion of Dryden's general
epistemological orientation, however, is Le Clerq's analysis of the Academic *method*
of discourse as used in the *Essay of Dramatic Poesy*. For further discussion of Dryden's skepticism and the Bredvold thesis, see the series of articles by William Emp-
son, Philip Harth, Robert Hume, and Earl Miner in *Essays in Criticism*, 20 (1970),
172–181, 446–450, 492–495; and 21 (1971), 111–115 and 410–411.

37. Next to Pechter, the critic who best emphasizes this flexibility is John C.
Sherwood, "Precept and Practice in Dryden's Criticism," *JEGP*, 68 (1969), 433–434.

traditions in relation to their temporal setting. The indebtedness of the latter approach to the technical tradition is apparent from the beginning of Dryden's critical career, in *An Essay of Dramatic Poesy*, in which Dryden attempts, as he says, to "relate" the diversity of practice in the European dramatic tradition to the claims that each country or generation makes to natural fitness. Accordingly, Dryden's boast "To the Reader," that he writes "to vindicate the honour of our English writers," should be balanced against his more judicious explanation in the Dedication to Buckhurst that he enters into a "war of opinions" much broader in scope, which "has fallen out among writers of all ages."[38] To treat the *Essay* as an ad hoc defense of English practice[39] is to overlook the central philosophic question with which it is more deeply concerned. Only by examining the status and validity of artistic norms in principle could Dryden mediate between the mimetic and pragmatic problems that his essay encompassed; only by accounting in theory for the relation between universal nature and historical circumstance could he mediate between the forces of continuity and change in literary tradition.

Dryden's efforts to mediate between these claims accounts for the structure of the *Essay* itself. Each of the debates—between Ancients and Moderns (Crites and Eugenius), between French and English (Lisideius and Neander), and between the dramatic virtues of unrhymed and rhymed verse (Crites and Neander)—involves a specific issue, but all of them revolve around a central question: To what extent are artistic norms universal, and to what extent may they be adapted to historic circumstance in order to achieve rhetorical effect without abandoning the criterion of nature? Accordingly, the structure of the *Essay* is dialectical; each position and each debate develops and modifies this central question as it appears in the ones preceding.[40] It is less due to Dryden's special pleading than to the philosophic purpose and structure of the *Essay* itself that it begins by positing a standard of universal nature embodied in the priority and authority of the Ancients, and ends as a debate over a convention of versification. This outcome reflects the general movement of the *Essay* as a whole, in which nature is increasingly interpreted as a standard mediated by conventions arising

38. Preface and Dedication to *An Essay of Dramatic Poesy*, in Watson, I, 17, 15.

39. See George Williamson, "The Occasion of *An Essay of Dramatic Poesy*," in *Seventeenth-Century Contexts*, pp. 272–288. See also Mary Thale, "The Framework of *An Essay of Dramatic Poesy*," *PLL*, 8 (1972), 362–369.

40. F. L. Huntley first argued for this type of structure, though to different purpose, in *On Dryden's "Essay of Dramatic Poesy"* (Ann Arbor: University of Michigan Press, 1951), p. 36.

from historic circumstance. This dialectical progression follows a course reversed yet parallel to the dialectical path in French classicism, in which every tension tended to be resolved by efforts to shore up reason and nature. The structure of Dryden's *Essay* therefore mirrors its theme: the standard of nature posited at the outset is increasingly accommodated to suit rhetorical needs.

It is fitting that the series of debates should begin with a comparison between the Ancients and Moderns, for this comparison involves more than a confrontation of minor historical differences; it marks a decisive point of philosophic consequence in the technical tradition, as a debate in principle over the standards, means, and methods that determine man's right life. Dryden understands the debate in this light, and takes seriously its challenge to philosophic principle.[41]

As spokesman for the Ancients, Crites mounts a defense involving two claims on behalf of nature. First, the Ancients derive their authority from their claim to priority in the knowledge of nature: "all those rules by which we practise the drama at this day . . . were delivered to us from the observations which Aristotle made."[42] Second, this knowledge has secured the abiding rational methods for achieving such kinds of natural fitness as "justness and symmetry of the plot," which "is what the logicians do [mean] by their *finis*" (pp. 27, 29). In order to support his defense of rational nature, however, Crites is forced to open the dialectical threshold of the *Essay* by arguing that this standard has been obscured by modern custom. "Every age has a kind of universal genius (p. 26), and the "genius" of the modern age has been hostile to poetry in general; but more important, the changes wrought by convention have made the ancient standard of nature inaccessible. To admire the Ancients "as we ought, we should understand them better than we do. Doubtless many things appear flat to us whose wit *depended on some custom* or story which never came to our knowledge; or perhaps on *some criticism in their language,* which being so long dead, and only remaining in their books, 'tis not possible that they should make us know it perfectly" (pp. 30–31; my italics). This first mention of conventional adjustment in the *Essay* is meant to serve Crites' defense of what he understands to be universal criteria of fitness. It will be the purpose of Eugenius' reply, however, to widen the application of this principle and thereby to undermine Crites' position.

In order to do so, Eugenius must first show that nature remains

---

41. A challenge underestimated by Guy Montgomery in "Dryden and the Battle of the Books," *University of California Publications in English* 14 (1943), 57–72.

42. *An Essay of Dramatic Poesy,* in Watson, I, 27; hereafter cited in the text by page number only.

equally accessible to the Moderns, and this he does by recurring to the idea of progress as Crites had already applied it to the modern sciences. Eugenius extends this notion to the verbal arts, not to assert unquestionable progress in all human endeavor, but merely to maintain that nature remains accessible against the charge of Crites that "nature . . . is not in" modern works:

> We draw not therefore after their [the Ancients'] lines, but those of nature; and having the life before us, besides the experience of all they knew, it is no wonder if we hit some airs and features which they have missed . . . your instance in philosophy makes for me: for if natural causes be now more known than in the time of Aristotle, because more studied, it follows that poetry and other arts may, with the same pains, arrive still nearer to perfection. (p. 32)

The assumption that nature is the test of fitness remains valid. It is *Crites,* not Eugenius, who has put the case for progress in the knowledge of nature, and Crites who has maintained that nature is the test of fitness. *If* both premises are granted, then how can it be that "nature . . . is not in" modern works? The burden of proof rests with Crites. Eugenius neither affirms the superiority of the Moderns, nor applies the equivocal logic (with the ambiguous term "nature") to argue for scientific progress in poetry. Rather, he merely counters Crites' view that the Ancients have exclusive claim to nature.

Accordingly, Eugenius implies that Ancients and Moderns are distinguished by conventions, not by nature. His treatment of ancient faults and modern beauties is designed not to assert the superiority of the Moderns in any absolute sense, but merely to undermine Crites' contention that the "Ancients have been faithful imitators and wise observers of nature." In order to do so, he follows Howard's argument in the Preface to *Four New Plays,* by pointing out the extreme conventionality of subject matter in ancient drama. The ancient plot, he claims, was usually "some tale . . . worn so thread bare by the pens of the epic poets, and even by the tradition itself of the talkative Greeklings (as Ben Jonson calls them) that before it came upon the stage it was already known to all the audience" (p. 34). This conventionality is even more evident in Roman drama; not only did the Romans borrow their plots from the Greeks, but "by the plot you may guess much of the characters of the persons. An old father who would willingly, before he dies, see his son well married; his debauched son, kind in nature to his wench, but miserably in want of money; a servant or slave, who has so much wit to strike in with him, and help to dupe his father; a braggadocchio captain, a parasite, and a lady of pleasure" (p. 35). It is Eugenius' aim in these arguments to modify Crites' claim that the Ancients were "observers of nature" by showing that their observation was filtered through convention, and that the *mimesis* of nature is always qualified by a dynamic element that is relative or historical.

Moreover, this interdependency affects not simply the "contrivance" of drama, but also its "writing" or style. In turning from comparison of "contrivance" to the expression of wit, Eugenius explicitly picks up and widens the application of convention as it had appeared in Crites' argument: "This would lead me to the consideration of their wit, had not Crites given me sufficient warning not to be too bold in my judgment of it; because the languages being dead, and many of the customs and little accidents on which it depends lost to us, we are not competent judges of it" (p. 38). Crites had used the concept of convention to assert that the natural superiority of ancient wit had been obscured by changing social and linguistic conventions. In keeping with his general aim of demonstrating the continuing accessibility of wit to all men, however, Eugenius extends the notion by showing that all good wit depends upon linguistic convention, and that it is accessible to all men who know the convention, for "though I grant that here and there we may miss the application of a proverb or custom, yet a thing will be wit in all languages; and though it may lose something in the translation, yet to him who reads it in the original, 'tis all the same: he has an idea of its excellency, though it cannot pass from his mind into any other expression or words than those in which he finds it" (p. 38). What is here affirmed is that linguistic conventions are mutually exclusive but that for those who are familiar with the conventions, the quality of wit is universal. This slight alteration of Crites' view is highly significant, for at the same time that it acknowledges the universality of wit, it allows for the conventional integrity of linguistic contexts. It is not, as Crites maintains, that one linguistic context is best for the rendering of wit, but that wit is best rendered within the limits of the prevailing conventional context, "for Horace himself was cautious to obtrude a new word upon his readers, and makes custom and common use the best measure of receiving it in our writings" (p. 39). Thus, once again, convention prevails as the dynamic specification of nature in time; it is ultimately the proper observance of convention that produces the illusion of naturalness.

Finally, as if to offer conclusive evidence of the relation of nature to convention, Eugenius returns to further "consideration of the Ancients" with the intriguing remark that though Ovid was less popular or influential than Seneca in antiquity, if he "had lived in our age, or in his own could have writ with our advantages, no man but must have yielded to him" (p. 41). These "advantages" are apparently the concern with passion, love, and romance that characterizes the prevailing literary conventions, which in spirit Ovid had anticipated. "Advantage," however, is not so much a natural superiority as an opportunity provided by convention; what Ovid really lacked was a prevailing conventional vehicle that would accommodate his interests to public taste. "Advantage" is primarily an intersubjective, not a natural, product, because "the private concernment of every person, is soothed by seeing its own image in a public entertainment" (p. 42). Dryden here briefly exploits, as he will later develop more fully, Lisideius' opening "description" of the drama as a "just and lively image of human nature" (p. 25). Because the aim of imitation is not the Aristotelian representation of an action, but the presentation of an "image of human nature," Dryden has built into his "description" a provision for interpreting *mimesis* in social rather than philosophic terms. Because the audience is moved by "seeing its own image in a public entertainment," the audience functions as an object of imitation, and the imitation of "nature" will therefore be adjusted to conventional demands.

The articulation of this relationship ends the first debate by causing Crites grudgingly to modify his position, allowing that nature finds various expression in conventional "modes":

> Eugenius and I are never like to have the question decided betwixt us; for he maintains the Moderns have acquired a new perfection in writing, I can only grant they have altered the mode of it. Homer described his heroes men of great appetite, lovers of beef broiled upon coals, and good fellows; contrary to the practice of the French romances, whose heroes neither eat, nor drink, nor sleep for love . . . So in their love-scenes . . . the Ancients were more hearty, we more talkative: they writ love as it was then the mode to make it; and I will grant thus much to Eugenius, that perhaps one of their poets, had he lived in our age *si foret hoc nostrum fato delapsus in aevum* (as Horace says of Lucilius), he had altered many things; not that they were not as natural as before, but that he might accommodate himself to the age that he lived in. (p. 43)

"At this point," Dryden reports, *"the moderation of Crites,* as it was pleasing to all the company, so put an end to that dispute; which Eugenius, who seemed to have the better of the argument, would urge no further" (p. 43; my italics). The fact that Eugenius has "the better of the argument," while at the same time Crites refuses to concede any superiority to the Moderns, suggests that the purpose of the debate has not been ultimately to arrive at a judgment of innate superiority on either side. To say that "Dryden ranges himself on the side of the Moderns by giving Eugenius the last word"[43] is not only to misunderstand the nature of the debate, but to misread the *Essay*. It is not in fact Eugenius, but Crites, who speaks last. "We are not," he observes, "to conclude anything rashly against those great men, but preserve to them the dignity of masters, and give that honour to their memories part of which we expect may be paid to us in future times" (p. 43). The *moderation*, not the capitulation, of Crites marks the end of the debate, whose purpose has been to broaden Crites' concept of nature in such a way as to allow for a dynamic interplay between nature and its conventional manifestations. Crites has arrived at the view not that the Moderns are superior, but at precisely the adjustment in his concept of principles that the debate has been designed to bring about. Because of the accommodating power of convention, both Ancients and Moderns follow nature, but by different means. This much Crites reluctantly concedes.

The dialectical "moderation" of natural fitness by convention continues in the second dialogue. Just as the concept of nature originally posited by Crites had been modified by the "progressivist" argument of Eugenius, so Lisideius' extension of that argument into a rigidly neo-Aristotelian concept of natural fitness is in turn modified by Neander. Lisideius follows the cue of Eugenius by interpreting historical change as a teleological process of refinement approaching natural perfection. This perfection, he argues, manifests itself in the regular application of those rules which "of all nations the French have best observed" (p. 44). By rationally deriving "effects from causes," the French "render all events in the play more natural" (pp. 48, 55). Having served its purpose as an argumentative device, however, this hypothetical case for rationalistic progress must now be further modified to show that different literary traditions may follow nature on their own conventional terms. Neander thus begins his reply by conceding to the greater

43. Watson, I, 43n5. Pechter more acutely observes that "Crites bases his reference upon the relation between the artifact and nature, Eugenius on the relation between the artifact and its audience; Crites approves of unity of action as a just imitation, Eugenius approves of a various action as pleasing," p. 45. Accordingly, he concludes that the debate supports neither Ancients nor Moderns conclusively: "One tends to feel that the mimetic and pragmatic questions are finally too interdependent for such rigorous separation, a feeling for which there is ample evidence throughout the rest of Dryden's criticism . . . Eugenius doesn't defeat Crites, doesn't contradict his premises, only adds to them, develops them by subtle shifts of emphasis," p. 46.

regularity of French drama, but at the same time, he attempts to broaden the meaning of natural fitness beyond formal "regularity," so as to accommodate the English dramatic tradition to nature as well. In order to do so, he immediately returns to the opening "description" of drama by observing that "the lively imitation of nature being the definition of a play, those which best fulfill that law ought to be esteemed superior to others" (p. 56).

Neander builds his case on two aspects of this "description." First, by altering the original "just and lively image" to a "lively imitation of nature," he emphasizes the "lively" pragmatic relationship between *mimesis* and its effects rather than the "just" relationship between *mimesis* and nature. In keeping with this emphasis upon effects, Neander therefore interprets *mimesis* as a dynamic process of mediation in time. Second, he returns to the original "image of human nature, representing its passions and humours," in order to suggest that the objects of imitation are not, as Lisideius has maintained, Aristotelian "causes and effects," but men in time. Thus, he observes, " 'Tis true, those beauties of the French poesy are such as will raise perfection higher where it is, but are not sufficient to give it where it is not: they are indeed the beauties of a statue, but not of a man, because not animated with *the soul of poesy, which is imitation of humours and passions*" (p. 56). In making "imitation of humours and passions" the "soul of poesy," Dryden offers an explicit alternative to natural fitness as interpreted in Lisideius' neo-Aristotelian emphasis on plot, which Aristotle had maintained "is the first principle and as it were the soul of tragedy." Moreover, as the objects of imitation, "humours and passions" further support the "lively" or rhetorical aims of *mimesis,* and thus further reinforce Dryden's connection of *mimesis* to a changing temporal dimension, in keeping with Eugenius' earlier assertion that the audience delights in "seeing its own image in a public entertainment." Thus the *mimesis* of "humours and passions" supports the pragmatic function of "liveliness," by presenting the audience with its own image.

In keeping with this pragmatic relationship, Neander counters Lisideius' appeal to abstract reason with an appeal to experience, quoted almost verbatim from Corneille: " 'Tis easy for speculative persons to judge severely; but if they would produce to public view ten or twelve pieces of this nature, they would perhaps give *more latitude to the rules* than I have done, when by experience they had known how much we are bound up and constrained by them, and how many beauties of the stage they banished from it" (p. 63; my italics). This empirical approach dictates that the success of *mimesis* is measured in part by its rhetorical effectiveness, that there is a "latitude to the rules." Neander's empiricism does not completely invalidate Lisideius' defense of French dramatic practice, but it does limit its validity to a particular set of rhetorical circumstances. Thus he does not assert the superiority of English tragicomedy over French regular tragedy in any absolute sense; because regularity in France has "grown into a custom," he does not deny "but this may suit well enough with the French; for we, who are a more sullen people, come to be diverted at our plays; they, who are of an airy and gay temper, come thither to make themselves more serious, and this I conceive to be one reason why comedy is more pleasing to us, and tragedies to them" (p. 60).

Such differences in rhetorical setting not only produce preference for one genre over another, but impinge upon the structure of the genres themselves. Neander insists upon the need for structural "justice" as well as mimetic and rhetorical "liveliness," but just as he has subordinated Lisideius' "whole and complete action" to the "humours and passions" as the objects of imitation, so in terms of the rhetorical distinction between invention and disposition, he subordinates the "justice" of form to the "liveliness" of matter. The French, he thus observes, "have performed what was possible on the ground work of the Spanish plays; what was pleasant before they have made regular" (p. 58).

The sequential subordination of formal disposition to mimetic invention in the single work of art, in other words, applies as well to the historical development of generic norms. Thus Neander opens a historical defense of English dramatic tradition in terms of the rhetorical triad of invention, disposition, and elocution. Like the single work of rhetorical composition produced by these procedures, the English dramatic tradition as a whole has shaped itself to suit a particular place and time. In turning to the temporal origins rather than the natural ends of English dramatic tradition, Neander implies an evolving relationship between the shaping of artistic norms and the audience for whom art is intended. "We endeavour," Neander says, "to follow the variety of greatness of characters [i.e., "image of human nature" or invention], which are derived to us from Shakespeare and Fletcher; the copiousness and well knitting of the intrigues [i.e., "whole and complete action" or disposition] we have from Jonson; and for the verse itself [i.e., elocution] we have the English precedents of elder date than any of Corneille's plays" (p. 65). Thus, like the single rhetorical work of art, the integrity of the English dramatic tradition is defined as an evolving adjustment of artistic norms in time. Significantly, this "evolution" is not the hypothetical neo-Aristotelian teleology posited by Eugenius and seized upon by Lisideius, but a rhetorical process of adjustment, defined by its intersubjective origin rather than its natural end. Accordingly, at each stage of this process, the test of fitness is rhetorical success; the achievement of each poet in the tradition arises in conjunction with his immense status and popularity with the audience: Shakespeare was great "in the age wherein he lived"; Jonson's "reputation was at its highest" in "the last king's court"; and the plays of Beaumont and Fletcher "are now the most pleasant and frequent entertainments on the stage" (pp. 68–69). Thus the English dramatic tradition is indebted to an interplay between pragmatic success and formal integrity; it is justified on the basis of its historical evolution, on the presumptive, rather than Aristotelian, rationale that nature is mediated in conventional form.

Neander's adjustment of Lisideius' concept of nature advances the dialectical progression of the *Essay* by further articulating the relationship between natural and conventional norms that is the theme of the *Essay*, and this structural and thematic interplay is completed in the final debate on rhyme.[44] Like the other debates, this one departs from the adjusted view of nature and convention arrived at in the previous debate. The Crites who objects that the use of rhymed verse is "without any reason," no longer appeals to a reason that is impervious to changing circumstance, but to a "presumptive" reason that dictates art is most "natural" when it observes convention:

> The hand will be too visible in [rhyme] against that maxim
> of all professions, *ars est celare artem,* that it is the greatest
> perfection of art to keep itself undiscovered . . . it is in vain
> for you to strive against the people's inclination, the greatest
> part of which are prepossessed so much with those excellent
> plays of Shakespeare, Fletcher, and Ben Jonson (which
> have been written out of rhyme) that except you could bring
> them as were written better in it, and those too by persons
> of equal reputation with them, it will be impossible for you
> to gain your cause with them who will still be judges.
> (p. 78)

Crites has in fact brought his earlier position into line with that articulated earlier by Neander, and acknowledges that successful imita-

---

44. This debate really involves two issues: the theoretical issue of the way and extent to which the imitation of nature is mediated by convention, and the practical issue as to whether in fact rhymed verse enjoys the conventional support that Neander claims it does. Dryden's later reversal of his position on rhymed drama is not a reversal of the theoretical grounds on which Neander defends it in the *Essay,* but simply a practical revision in his view of the amount of acceptance the convention of rhymed verse enjoys. On the theoretical importance of convention as a principle he remains fundamentally consistent.

tion of nature must be adjusted to the expectations of the audience. He therefore demands that Neander justify the propriety of rhyme against the accepted and prevailing convention of blank verse, which best produces the illusion of "nature."

Neander responds to this challenge by placing even greater emphasis upon the role of convention. In the first place, he argues that Crites has minimized the conventiQnality of blank verse. Insofar as they observe "measure," both rhymed and unrhymed verse are equally "unnatural," equally departures from normal speech rhythms. Second, Neander resorts to the presumptive reasoning of Daniel's *Defence of Rhyme* in order to maintain that "rhyme . . . succeeds to all other offices of Greek and Latin verse . . . since the custom of all nations at this day confirms it . . . the universal consent of the most civilized parts of the world ought in this, as it doth in other customs, to include the rest" (p. 84). Most important, however, Neander moves beyond these basically empirical arguments and into a more deeply theoretical defense. Not only is nature mediated by convention, but different conventions specify different aspects of nature. The "natural" effect of rhyme pertains not to "nature" in any general sense, but to "what is nearest the nature of a serious play: this last is indeed the representation of nature, but 'tis nature wrought up to an higher pitch" (p. 87). The conventional verse form for the "serious" epic kind in antiquity, Dryden claims, was hexameter, but because "the genius of every age is different," the modern use of rhyme has come to prevail as the equivalent heroic convention: "the case is the same in our verse as in theirs; rhyme to us being in lieu of quantity to them" (pp. 85, 88). Therefore, he concludes, rhyme is most proper for heroic drama, because "heroic rhyme is nearest nature, as being the noblest kind of modern verse" (p. 87). This proximity to "nature," however, is clearly within the limits of the "nature" specified by the "noblest kind" of epic convention. The convention of rhyme further contributes to the illusion that the heroic dramatist wishes to project: "A play, . . . to be *like nature,* is to be set above it; as statues which are placed on high are made greater than life, that they may descend to the sight in their *just* proportion" (p. 89). In relating *mimesis* to its effect, the simile of the statue states for a final time the interanimation of the two concepts on which the entire essay has been based, and enables Dryden to arrive at the view that "nature" is at least in part an illusion mediated by conformity to convention.

This dynamic relationship between natural and conventional fitness became the foundation and framework for nearly all of Dryden's subsequent efforts to mediate between classical theory and contemporary practice, between continuity and change in the literary tradition, between universal rules and the practical necessity of rhetorical adjustment. Dryden's double focus found expression in what was to become one of his favorite figures—an architectural distinction between "foundation" and "superstructure." Dryden first used this figure in responding to Howard's objection that in efforts to prescribe artistic norms "the great foundation that is laid to build upon is nothing."[45] Dryden answers that " 'tis very plain that he has mistaken the foundation for that which is built upon it, though not immediately; for the direct and immediate consequence is this: if nature be to be imitated, then there is a rule for imitating it rightly; otherwise there may be an end, and no means conducing to it." Nature remains as the foundation of poetry, to which the resources of art stand related as means to an end. While the end remains as a universal certainty, however, the means, precisely because they exist in a temporal and intersubjective dimension, are less certain. Therefore, says Dryden,

> having laid down that nature is to be imitated, and that proposition proving the next, that there *are* means which conduce to the imitating of nature, I dare proceed no further positively; but only have laid down some *opinions* of the Ancients and Moderns, and of my own, as means which they used, and which I thought *probable* for the attaining of that end. Those means are the same which my antagonist calls the foundations . . . he has only made a small mistake of the means conducing to the end for the end itself, and of the superstructure for the foundation.[46]

The architectural metaphor embodies the basic structure of seventeenth-century epistemology in distinguishing between degrees of clarity or certainty, and follows the main line of English latitudinarian and legal thought in its distinctions between things essential and things indifferent, or between nature and its changing customary expressions in time. Dryden does not deny that there might be some best means of reaching natural ends, but acknowledges at the same time that changing circumstances make the status of such means at best provisional and probable. Accordingly, nature is circumscribed by a number of possible "superstructures," each of which leads to nature as means lead to an end.

Dryden used this architectural metaphor as a central term in two of his most theoretical essays, the *Heads of an Answer to Rymer* (writ-

---

45. Robert Howard, Preface to *The Great Favourite*, in Spingarn, II, 108.
46. *A Defence of an Essay of Dramatic Poesy*, in Watson, I, 122–123.

ten c. 1677), and *The Grounds of Criticism in Tragedy* (1679). In principle, both essays extend the inquiry into the status of artistic norms begun in *An Essay of Dramatic Poesy,* and both consistently follow the basic distinction between nature and convention established therein. Thus, in the notes that he composed as "Heads" of an answer to Rymer in the end papers of his copy of *Tragedies of the Last Age,* Dryden begins by conceding to the ideal of natural fitness that supported Rymer's neo-Aristotelianism. Acknowledging that the "model of tragedy" prescribed by Rymer "is excellent and extreme correct," Dryden objected only that "it is not the only model of all tragedy, because it is too circumscribed in plot, characters, etc."[47]

It is thus with a firm emphasis on a center of natural fitness that Dryden sets out to adjust unchanging natural standards to the diversity of literary practice. His strategy is to modify rather than refute the concept of natural fitness.[48] Consequently, he uses his favorite figure in observing that the Aristotelian "fable is not the greatest masterpiece of a tragedy, tho' it be the foundation of it" (p. 211). Dryden builds upon this "foundation" by emphasizing the other "parts" of tragedy, which are invariably subordinated by plot by Rymer and other Aristotelians. "A fable," Dryden maintains, "never so movingly contrived to those ends of . . . pity and terror, will operate nothing on our affections, except the characters, manners, thoughts, and words are suitable" (p. 211). In emphasizing the need for "suitability" in these parts in order rhetorically to "operate . . . on our affections," Dryden returns to the basic strategy of Neander's reply to Lisideius in the *Essay of Dramatic Poesy;* just as Neander had observed that the regularities of "French poesy are such as will raise perfection higher where it is, but are not sufficient to raise it where it is not," so Dryden now remarks that "action only adds grace, vigour, and more life upon the stage; but cannot give it wholly where it is not first" (p. 214). This echo from the *Essay* returns Dryden directly to the crucially important "description"

47. *Heads of an Answer to Rymer,* in Watson, I, 218–219; hereafter cited in the text by page number only.

48. On this basis, F. L. Huntley argues for consistency between the *Heads* and the *Grounds of Criticism,* in *The Unity of John Dryden's Dramatic Criticism: The Preface to "Troilus and Cressida"* (Chicago: University of Chicago Press, 1944), pp. 182–183. Huntley exaggerates Fred G. Walcott's vision of a conflict between the premises of Rymer and Dryden, for Walcott observes that Dryden "chose to conciliate these conflicting motives"; "John Dryden's Answer to Thomas Rymer's *The Tragedies of the Last Age,*" *PQ,* 15 (1936), 201. Watson, who finds Dryden "oddly respectful" in the *Heads* (I, 211), nevertheless most emphatically insists on a basic difference between Dryden's two essays, and maintains that Dryden wrote the *Heads* "for the direct purpose of refuting Aristotle"; "Dryden's First Answer to Rymer," *RES,* n.s. 14 (1963), 22.

of drama there advanced. Thus he now observes that "upon a true definition of tragedy, it will be found that its work . . . is to reform manners by *delightful representation of human life* in great persons, by way of dialogue" (p. 213; my italics).

This "definition" not only raises the other "parts" of tragedy, such as character and diction, to equal importance with plot, but it also posits the "reforming of manners," along with the arousal of pity and fear, as an additional end of tragedy. In positing this additional end, however, Dryden follows the basic distinction between foundation and superstructure by elevating the reform of manners to the status of a generic end, to which the different ends of Greek and contemporary drama are subordinate as specific means. Thus he observes that "if then the encouragement of virtue and discouragement of vice be the proper [i.e., final] ends of poetry in tragedy: pity and terror, tho' good means, are not the only" (p. 213). This relationship, in which both Greek and English tragedy satisfy an absolute end by different means, allows Dryden to exploit the importance attached to other "parts" of tragedy in his "definition"; while plot, the imitation of action, best arouses the pity and terror that conduce to the reform of manners, the "delightful representation of human life" as accomplished by the other parts of tragedy will produce "a general concernment for the principal actors . . . by making them appear such in their characters, their words, and actions, *as will interest the audience* in their fortunes" (p. 213; my italics).

This insistence on the "interest" of the audience relates *mimesis,* through the other parts of tragedy, to a historical dimension, and links the modern developments in character and diction to their rhetorical efficacy in time. As the changing "superstructures" of drama, these elements are in turn linked to the persistent issue of passion, for the moderns have added to old foundations "new passions":

> that we may the less wonder why pity and terror are not now the only springs on which our tragedies move, and that Shakespeare may be more excused, Rapin confesses that the French tragedies now run all on the *tendre;* and gives the reason because love is the passion which most predominates *in our souls,* and therefore that the *passions represented* become insipid, unless they are conformable to the thoughts of the audience . . . Amongst us, who have a stronger genius for writing, the operations from the writing are much stronger: for the raising of Shakespeare's passions are more from the excellency of the words and thoughts than the justness of the occasion. (p. 216)

Thus, while the different modern dramatic traditions maintain a natural continuity with the Ancients in satisfying the natural end of improving the lives of men, they do so through means and resources that are for the most part conventional. Dryden defends this contention on unabashedly empirical grounds; Rymer may object that English dramatists have not precisely followed the model of ancient tragedy,

> but experience proves against him that those means which they have used have been successful . . . And one reason of this success is, in my opinion, this, that Shakespeare and Fletcher have written to the genius of the age and nation in which they lived; for tho' nature is the same in all places, and reason too the same, yet the climate, the age, the dispositions of a people to whom a poet writes, may be so different that what pleased the Greeks would not satisfy an English audience. And if they proceeded upon a foundation of truer reason to please the Athenians than Shakespeare and Fletcher to please the English, it only shows that what pleased the Greeks would not satisfy an English audience. (p. 214)

By allowing for "the genius of the age and nation," Dryden seeks to arrive at an aesthetic sufficiently broad to encompass the varieties of ancient and modern drama. Though not strictly "related to a planned structure in Dryden's text,"[49] the concepts of nature and convention, foundation and superstructure, enable Dryden to mediate flexibly between alternative demands without involving himself in "a logical contradiction."[50] These concepts also enable Dryden to harden his distinctions and shift his emphasis toward nature in *The Grounds of Criticism in Tragedy*, while at the same time assuring a basic consistency in his thought.[51] Though Dryden there leans heavily toward the neo-Aristotelian definition of "one entire, great, and probable ac-

49. See Hume, "Dryden's *Heads of an Answer to Rymer:* Notes towards a Hypothetical Revolution," *RES*, n.s. 19 (1968), 379.

50. Hume contends that "Dryden . . . falls prey to what we see as a logical contradiction: he upholds both the rules and the Elizabethans, struggling manfully to comprehend both within a single system"; *Dryden's Criticism*, p. 117. Hume explains this contradiction as a failure to distinguish "between the two types of tragedy"; "Dryden's *Heads of an Answer to Rymer*," p. 381.

51. Watson greatly exaggerates Dryden's inconsistency when he observes that "Dryden's former advocacy is now perverted to a boot-licking reverence for authority which does not even have the merit of honesty, in that it pretends a continuity of praise for the Elizabethans which is quite unreal"; "Dryden's First Answer to Rymer," p. 22.

tion," he maintains a balance by reinvoking his favorite figure of foundation and superstructure. In seeking to know "how far we ought to imitate Shakespeare and Fletcher in their plots," Dryden determines that "we ought to follow them so far as they have copied the excellencies of those who invented and brought to perfection dramatic poetry: those things only excepted which religions, customs of countries, idioms of language, etc., have altered in the superstructures, but not in the foundation of the design." This distinction, however, turns out to allow for considerable change, for "after the plot, which is the foundation of the play, the next thing to which we ought to apply our judgment is the manners, for now the poet comes to work aboveground: the ground-work is indeed that which is most necessary, as that upon which depends the firmness of the whole fabric; yet it strikes not the eye so much as the beauties or imperfections of the manners, the thoughts, and the expressions."[52] Thus, while the four artistic criteria of plot—wholeness, order, magnitude, and probability—apply universally and without regard to historical circumstance, the rest of the "parts" of tragedy—manners or character, thought, and diction—are not universal in character, nor do they merely derive inexorably from the structure of the plot; rather, as "beauties" which "strike the eye" they are parts of that "superstructure," that "lively image of human nature,", which had always comprised that dynamic axis in Dryden's complete conception of *mimesis*. As such, they move the audience by confronting it with its *own* image as formed by "religions, customs of countries, idioms of language, etc." This appeal to the intersubjective character of artistic illusion demonstrates the extent to which Dryden continues to conceive of artistic process as a dynamic interplay between a "foundation" of unchanging values and the conventional "superstructures" through which they are expressed. Though in *The Grounds of Criticism in Tragedy* he places the greater stress upon "foundations," they remain in complementary relationship to a "superstructure" encompassing the varieties of artistic experience.[53]

The fluid relationship between these elements accounts for Dryden's

---

52. *The Grounds of Criticism in Tragedy,* in Watson, I, 243, 246, 247–248.

53. John C. Sherwood in fact maintains that the *Grounds* is "more satisfying as a work of criticism" than the *Essay of Dramatic Poesy* precisely because Dryden now firmly states which rules are universal and which are conventional and therefore clarifies the relationship of precepts to practice, so that there is no longer a "conflict between the rules of art and the works of art"; "Dryden and the Rules: The Preface to *Troilus and Cressida,*" *CL,* 2 (1950), 82. Dryden's clarity of purpose in the *Grounds* does stem from his firmer emphasis upon one part of his complementary theory, but his ability to encompass both precept and practice depends also on the fact that he does not firmly fix boundaries between them, but allows them to remain in solution.

role as the preeminent translator, adapter, and popularizer of his time. Having seen a new London rise on old foundations after the Great Fire, Dryden acknowledged that "the first inventors of any art or science . . . are, in reason, to give laws to it; and according to their model, all after-undertakers are to build."[54] At the same time, however, Dryden also maintained that "we must take the foundation . . . build it up, and . . . make it proper for the English."[55] Since " 'tis the continuance, the new turn . . . which alter the property and make it ours,"[56] the superstructure built on lasting foundations must shape itself in keeping with conventional decorum. Thus, because of the social "difference of taste,"[57] Dryden willingly inclines toward convention as the immediate test of fitness. "For my part," he maintains, "I desire to be tried by the laws of my own country."[58]

In keeping with this basic stance, Dryden as translator sought to define and practice a mode of translation that would compromise between a literal translation, or "metaphrase," which fails to respect the new conventional setting, and a free-wheeling "imitation" whose concessions to contemporary fashion disregard the conventional integrity of the original.[59] In the ideal compromise, "paraphrase" requires a current "knowledge of men and manners,"[60] but at the same time it must be informed by the manners that obtained when the original work was written; because every work bears the mark of its cultural setting, "customs and ceremonies" must be "preserved."[61] In order to mediate between cultural contexts, the translator must, in other words, supplement his rhetorical sophistication with historical insight. In translating Juvenal, Dryden thus observes that

> if sometimes any of us (and 'tis but seldom) make him express the customs and manners of our native country rather than of Rome; 'tis either when there was some kind of analogy betwixt their customs and ours; or when, to make him more easy to vulgar understandings, we give him those man-

54. Preface to *Albion and Albanius,* in Watson, II, 35.

55. Preface to *An Evening's Love,* in Watson, I, 153.

56. Preface to *Don Sebastian,* in Watson, II, 49.

57. Preface to *Examen Poeticum,* in Watson, II, 161.

58. Preface to *All for Love,* in Watson, I, 225; cf. *Of Heroic Plays,* in Watson, I, 165; *Dedication to the Aeneis,* in Ker, II, 157.

59. Preface to *Ovid's Epistles,* in Watson, I, 268; on the sources of Dryden's theory of translation, see Thomas R. Steiner, "Precursors to Dryden: French and English Theories of Translation in the Seventeenth Century," *CLS,* 7 (1970), 50–81.

60. Preface to *Sylvae,* in Watson, II, 20.

61. Preface to *Ovid's Epistles,* in Watson, I, 270.

ners which are more familiar to us. But I defend not this innovation, 'tis enough if I can excuse it. For to speak sincerely, the manners of nations and ages are not to be confounded.[62]

As a transaction between two conventional contexts, translation aims to establish a continuity by flexibly mediating between them. In the course of this process, the concept of convention becomes itself a two-fold critical instrument, for while it functions prescriptively as a norm to guide the translator in writing for his time, it also functions descriptively by enabling him to understand the original author's work as it was shaped by its time. Indeed, in Dryden's view, the entire process of history is a process of "translation" between cultural contexts, a *translatio studii,* a passing on of cultural achievement through accommodation to different settings.

Dryden's interest in the past, like that of his contemporaries, depends upon the continuity of past with present, upon the ability of the past to provide exemplary normative guidance. Accordingly, Dryden's linear view of history as "progress" is always subordinated to the uniformitarian assumptions of the ancient cyclical view of history. The analogy between London and Rome in *MacFlecknoe* and the typological parallel between contemporary politics and sacred history in *Absalom and Achitophel* depend for their impetus on a view of history that interprets "progress" as a process of "translation."[63] Thus the cyclical pattern of history provides the element of continuity that renders "progress" intelligible. History, says Dryden, "helps us to judge of what will happen, by showing us the like revolutions of former times. For Mankind being the same in all ages, agitated by the same passions, and mov'd to action by the same interests, nothing can come to pass, but some like President of the like nature has already been produc'd, so that having the causes before our eyes, we cannot easily be deceived in the effects, if *we have Judgement but to draw the parallel.*"[64]

This emphasis on the exemplary value of history, however, leads Dryden precisely in the direction it had led the Renaissance historiog-

---

62. *A Discourse Concerning Satire,* in Watson, II, 154-155.

63. See Achsah Guibbory, "Dryden's View of History," *PQ,* 52 (1973), 198, and Earl Miner, "Dryden and the Issue of Human Progress," *PQ,* 40 (1961), 121.

64. *The Life of Plutarch,* in *The Works of John Dryden,* ed. H. T. Swedenberg, Jr. (Berkeley: University of California Press, 1971), XVII, 270-271. I use this edition (hereafter cited as Swedenberg) because Watson omits significant portions of the *Life* in his edition.

raphers, for historical comparisons inevitably involve differences as well as similarities. Consequently, the effort to use the continuities of history prescriptively requires a descriptive analysis of the conditions from which norms derive. Each period bears the distinctive mark of human will, and accordingly, Dryden uses the period concept developed by Daniel and others in maintaining that "every age has a kind of universal genius."[65] As in the art of translation, so in all historical understanding we must "have Judgement . . . to draw the parallel," for "the manners of nations and ages are not to be confounded." Just as application of ancient norms in the present must be adjusted to suit convention, so the prescriptive use of the past must be adjusted by a descriptive analysis of the ways in which convention has given shape to past achievements. Every literary achievement is both obliged to the unbroken continuity of nature and uniquely indebted to its own time.[66]

This interdependency shapes Dryden's historical consciousness of literary tradition, where continuity always expresses itself as an evolution of literary forms through an ongoing engagement with changing historical circumstance. Dryden's claim to be writing "in a new method" in his grandest "progress" piece—the *Discourse Concerning the Original and Progress of Satire* (1693)—should therefore be understood in the historical light reflected by the structure of the essay.[67] Not only does Dryden's comparison of ancient satirists follow a prior historical analysis of the "origin, the antiquity, the growth, the change" (p. 95) of satire, but his generic "description" (rather than definition) comes at the end of the essay; it emerges from, and is adjusted to, the earlier historical and comparative parts. While he borrows heavily from such continental theorists as Casaubon, Heinsius, and Dacier, he selects and arranges these materials so as to define satire, not in relation to a fixed and natural hierarchy of genres, but in relation to their origins in social ritual. Like Puttenham,[68] Dryden treats the literary kinds as the formal but social specifications of natural impulses as they arise in time.

Consequently, Dryden maintains that the natural impulse toward invective from which all satire originates was coeval with man's nature

65. *An Essay of Dramatic Poesy*, in Watson, I, 26.

66. See Alan Roper's essay on "The Kingdom of Letters," in *Dryden's Poetic Kingdoms* (New York: Barnes and Noble, 1965), pp. 136–184.

67. *A Discourse Concerning the Original and Progress of Satire*, in Watson, II, 135; hereafter cited by page number only.

68. Though Dryden never quotes Puttenham directly, Johnson implies that Dryden may have been indebted to him, *Lives of the Poets*, I, 287; see also Max Nänny, "John Drydens rhetorische Poetik," *Schweitzer Anglistische Arbeiten*, 49 (1958), 1, 16.

as a social being and found its first expression in the bickering of Adam and Eve. Although, as he observes, "the war amongst the critics" begins at the point of "considering satire as a species of poetry," both those who contend for Greek origins and those who argue for Roman origins are agreed upon a provenance that is ritual and social in character: "Since all poetry had its original from religion, that of the Grecians and Rome had the same beginning. Both were invented at festivals of thanksgiving, and both were prosecuted with mirth and raillery, and rudiments of verse: amongst the Greeks by those who represented satyrs; and amongst the Romans by real clowns" (p. 100). While Dryden rejects the false etymological connection between Roman satire and Greek "satyric" drama, he nevertheless maintains that the Roman origins of satire were no less social in character. Satire was, he says, "in occasions of merriment . . . first practised," and though "rude and barbarous and unpolished . . . *somewhat of this custom was afterwards retained*," when Andronicus, Ennius, and Pacuvius began to shape the form in keeping with "the first rudiments of civil conversation" (pp. 106–107). At this stage too, however, public influence came to bear substantially on the form, for "the people . . . ran in crowds to see these new entertainments of Andronicus, as to pieces which were more noble in their kind, and more perfect than their former satires, which for some time they neglected and abandoned . . . But not long afterwards they took them up again, and then they joined them to their comedies" (p. 109). Even at the point where in Dryden's view formal verse satire begins, it begins as a response to public influence, for Ennius, "having considered the genius of the people, and how eagerly they followed the first satires, thought it would be worth his pains to refine upon the project, and to write satires not to be acted in the theater, but read" (p. 110).

In treating the subsequent history of the form from Lucilius to Juvenal, Dryden refuses to follow his critical predecessors in multiplying generic distinctions to account for further developments. Instead, he insists upon the basic continuity of a single form as it passed through changes. In Dryden's view, "the polishing of the Latin tongue, in the succession of times, made the only difference . . . without any change *in the substance* of the poem" (p. 112; my italics).[69] By appealing to the basic continuities in change, Dryden is able in his "new method" of comparing Horace, Juvenal, and Persius to maintain that "the aim and end of our three rivals is the same. But by what methods they have

---

69. The only exception to this general position comes when Dryden treats Varronian or Menippean satire as a wholly different species, "another kind of satire," *Discourse*, p. 113.

prosecuted their intentions is farther to be considered" (p. 122). In part, Dryden explains the different methods in terms of the satirists' different talents and temperaments; but his analysis of temperament is always informed by "the individual satirists' relation to public life, and to the climate, literary or moral, of his age."[70] Different methods, in other words, answer to different needs in a changing surrounding. Persius, for example, differs from Horace and Juvenal not only because the "purity of Latin" was "more corrupted than in the time of Juvenal and Horace" (p. 118),[71] but also because "the fear of his safety under Nero compelled him to . . . darkness in some places." Moreover, Dryden observes that "after so long a time many of his words have been corrupted, and many customs, and stories relating to them, lost to us," because "the knowledge of many things is lost in our modern ages which were of familiar notice to the Ancients" (pp. 118, 121). Implicitly, the proper appreciation of Persius depends upon a historical reconstruction of context.

In the same way, Dryden claims that

> Horace had the disadvantage of the times in which he lived
> . . . they were better for the man, but worse for the satirist
> . . . Horace, as he was a courtier, complied with the interest
> of his master; and, avoiding the lash of greater crimes, con-
> fined himself to the ridiculing of petty vices, and common
> follies . . . though his age was not exempted from the worst
> of villainies, there was no freedom left to reprehend them,
> by reason of the edict [against treasonable writings].   (pp.
> 132, 135)

A similar link with prevailing social values accounts for the different character of Juvenal's satire. Though Dryden errs in his estimate of the relatively prudish Flavian dynasty, he attempts to explain Juvenal's vigor with reference to an imagined setting of prolific vice. "There was," he claims, "more of a need of a Brutus in Domitian's days, to redeem or mend, than of a Horace, if he had been living, to laugh at a fly-catcher" (p. 132). The history of satire is therefore a history of

70. William Frost, "Dryden's Theory and Practice of Satire," in *Dryden's Mind and Art,* ed. Bruce King (Edinburgh: Oliver and Boyd, 1969), p. 193.

71. Dryden's historical error in placing Persius (A.D. 34–62) after Juvenal (A.D. 60–140) is probably due to his desire to account for differences in historical terms. Examining Dryden's *Discourse* "in the light of present day scholarship," Niall Rudd has composed a long and dreary list of Dryden's errors, proving that "Dryden's essay is wrong or misleading on almost every major point"; "Dryden and Horace on Juvenal," *UTQ,* 32 (1963), 155–169.

genius in dialogue with circumstance, a dialogue reflected in the various shapes of satire itself:

> Persius was grave, and particularly opposed his gravity to lewdness, which was the predominant vice in Nero's court at the time when he published his satires, which was before that emperor fell into the excess of cruelty. Horace was a mild admonisher, a Court satirist, fit for the gentle times of Augustus, and more fit for the reasons I have already given. Juvenal was as proper for his times as they for theirs. His was an age which deserved a more severe chastisement.
> (p. 143)

Finally, every writer shapes his work not only to suit historical circumstance, but also as a response to antecedent tradition. Horace, for example, "was a rival to Lucilius, the predecessor, and was resolved to surpass him in his own manner . . . But limiting his desire only to the conquest of Lucilius, he had his ends of his rival who lived before him; but made way for a new conquest over himself by Juvenal, his successor" (p. 131). This treatment of tradition as a dynamic interplay of influence and innovation not only informs Dryden's assessments of his heritage, as in the Preface to the *Fables*,[72] but throughout his career supports his advocacy of change and innovation.[73]

It is only "after so much has been said of satire" historically and comparatively that Dryden arrives at a "description" of satire suffi-

---

72. Preface to *Fables*, in Watson, II, 270–271, 281.

73. Thus Neander had observed of the dramatists of the last age that "not only we shall never equal them, but they could never equal themselves, were they to rise and write again. We acknowledge them our fathers in wit; but they have ruined their estates themselves before they came to their children's hands. There is scarce an humour, a character, or any kind of plot, which they have not blown upon: all comes sullied and wasted to us: and were they to entertain this age, they could not make so plenteous treatments out of such decayed fortunes. This therefore will be a good argument to us either not to write at all, or to attempt some other way"; *An Essay of Dramatic Poesy*, in Watson, I, 85. In this respect, the growing prominence of convention from within the ancient technical tradition appears not only in the Enlightenment conflict between reason and experience, but also in its divorce of authority from priority. At the same time, however, the prominence of this divorce in the Enlightenment should not obscure its classical origins. Immediately after the passage in Paterculus from which Crites borrows his remark that "every age has a kind of universal genius," the Roman historian goes on to remark that "when we once despair of equalling [predecessors], our zeal flags with our hope, ceases to pursue what it cannot attain, and, relinquishing that object . . . turns to something new"; *Compendium of Roman History*, trans. J. S. Watson (New York: Harper, 1881), p. 422.

ciently "common" and "general" to accommodate the historical varieties he has discussed. History, as Dryden implies, militates against generic fixity; any "description" of a genre must be broad because "the
majestic way of Persius and Juvenal was new when they began it, but
'tis old to us; and what poems have not, with time, received an alteration in their fashion? Which alteration . . . is to after times as good a
warrant as the first. Has not Virgil changed the manners of Homer's
heroes in his *AEneis?* . . . Why should we offer to confine our free
spirits to one form, when we cannot so much as confine our bodies to
one fashion of apparel?" (p. 144).

This appeal to fashion marks not only the point at which the concept of convention begins to function as a tool of descriptive and
critical analysis rather than normative prescription, but also the point
at which it begins to work against its origins. It therefore also marks
a decisive point in the history of criticism, in which critical discourse is
no longer addressed to writers, but to readers. It is precisely through
his place within the technical tradition that Dryden is able to transform his rhetorical outlook into a critical and historical one. The growing prominence of convention as a norm leads Dryden to interpret the
artistic process as a transaction between nature and the variety of human circumstance and desire, between natural continuities and historical changes. This in turn requires an assessment of works not only in
relation to their generic forms, intentions, and effects, or to their
antecedent models in tradition, but also in relation to the "Customs
. . . Ceremonies, and the manner of publicke and private living"[74] in
their time, and to the modes of literary influence which these circumstances create, for "great contemporaries whet and cultivate each other;
and mutual borrowing, and commerce, makes the common riches of
learning, as it does of the civil government" (p. 81). Dryden applies
these contextual methods not only in his *Discourse Concerning . . .
Satire,* but also in his efforts to examine Virgil in light of "the conditions of the times in which he lived"; to "compare" Lucian's "style with
the Greek historians, his contemporaries or near his time," and to account for his skepticism as a function "of the age in which he lived";
to examine the shaping influence of Plutarch's education, when "the
custom of those times was very much different from ours"; or to explain
the special prominence and character of literary forms in relation
to their place in historical periods.[75]

---

74. *The Life of Plutarch,* in Swedenberg, XVII, 247.
75. *Dedication of the Aeneis,* in Ker, II, 172; *Life of Lucian,* in *Works,* ed. Sir
Walter Scott and George Saintsbury (London: William Patterson, 1893), XVIII, 70,
75 (because Watson omits significant portions of the *Life,* and because it has not

The challenge presented to the older normative framework by these innovations, as in the other human sciences, reflects the extent to which Dryden, like his contemporaries, attempted to reconcile reason with the varieties of experience. In keeping with his skeptical and practical approach, Dryden turned toward history and psychology as answers to this need. Implicit as one emphasis in the normative framework, and intended in part as means of upholding it, these responses nevertheless became increasingly alternatives to it. Thus in mediating between two aspects of an ancient tradition, Dryden extended himself in such a way as to stand between two ages as well. Having described himself as a man "betwixt two ages cast / The first of this and hindmost of the last," it was most fitting that with his characteristically acute sense of his place in time Dryden should have celebrated the ending of a century in a year that was also the last full year of his life by proclaiming

> 'Tis well an old age is out
> And time to begin a new.[76]

4. "These Broken Ends": Ancients, Moderns, and Modernity

Dryden's distinctive place in history was in part a function of his view of history. This view, which interpreted human achievements through their relation to a changing world of human making, amounted in principle to a redefinition of man—a redefinition that decisively distinguishes the ancient and modern epochs. It is therefore especially significant that Dryden should have begun to articulate his view by trying to resolve the conflicting claims of Ancients and Moderns in the *Essay of Dramatic Poesy*. In Dryden's *Essay*, as in the later seventeenth century generally, the partisans in this debate seemed to be concerned only with establishing which claimant better satisfied a common criterion of natural fitness; the difficulties in resolving the claims of each appeared only to be created by the alternative definitions of nature that each offered. To be sure, each side in the debate was motivated by values that would place any agreement as to fact—if such were possible—completely out of reach. The ancient ideals of literary and civic culture as against the hopes for a new science, a devout veneration of the past as against a complacent dismissal of it, a pervasive pessimism as against an effervescent optimism—all of these

---

yet appeared in the California [Swedenberg] series, I refer to this edition, hereafter cited as Scott and Saintsbury); *Life of Plutarch,* in Swedenberg, XVII, 244; cf. *The Character of Polybius and His Writings,* in Scott and Saintsbury, XVIII, 39.

76. *The Secular Masque,* ll. 95–96, in *The Poetical Works,* p. 902.

played their part in the debate. Insofar as each side cleaved, however, to a central notion of natural perfection—however differently defined—both remained within a fundamental framework of absolute standards. Given these alternative absolutes, the only real question could be, "Which shall be master?" Dryden's decisive modernity, therefore, was not determined by a stand for the Moderns as against the Ancients, or for scientific over philosophic reason; rather it was determined by his large counterclaim, against both definitions of nature, that exclusive of the physical sciences at least, "nature" is available only mediately through the conventional specifications made by men. This counterclaim was no mere pronouncement of historical judgment, but a radically philosophic revision of the ancient view of man. Man's search for his place within a surrounding and sustaining hierarchy of nature, and his effort to perform and produce in keeping with the natural duties, ends, and laws that this hierarchy prescribes, culminated in the contradictory proposition that his place is by nature distinctively human, and that he satisfies his nature by living within a world of his own making. Man, in other words, is by nature both a creature and a creator of habits, laws, and conventions, and is thus in a sense his own creator.

It was this relativism that constituted the truly modern position in the debate, and the one that elicited the most ferocious response from the party of the Ancients. Though Swift frequently satirized the Royal Society, much of his animus was directed instead at the modern relativist approach to human things, and to the implications of the view that human achievement is ephemeral and suited only to the moment in time for which it is intended. Swift's spider is not a scientist, but a creature who inhabits the very world he has spun from his own entrails—he is self-sustaining. The ferocity of Swift and others in this debate suggests that it involved important principles rather than mere preferences, party loyalties, or even habits of thought. Our own view that the quarrel is mainly of "historical interest," that it is "deservedly forgotten,"[1] or even that it has "the interest . . . of all good comedy—potential universality,"[2] is conditioned by our own position in modernity, our own relativism, our own historicism. Though it undoubtedly involved many values, the debate was in large part a decisive expression of and reaction against the growing prominence of the concept of convention. As one thinker has put it, "The question concerning antiquity and modernity is a modern question only in the restricted

1. R. L. Brett, *The Third Earl of Shaftesbury: A Study in Eighteenth-Century Literary Theory* (London: Hutchinson's University Library, 1951), p. 86.

2. W. J. Bate, *The Burden of the Past* (Cambridge: Harvard University Press, 1970), p. 24.

sense, but a timeless question in principle, for the issue between antiquity and modernity is not between epochs but between alternative views of man and his setting."[3]

These were the real alternatives presented to the thinkers of the early Enlightenment under the guise of a conflict between Ancients and Moderns over the franchise of nature. Confronted with the spectacle of two traditions, each defending in the name of reason and nature the special standards derived from its own characteristic aims, some of these thinkers believed they chose not between Ancients and Moderns but in favor of an intellectual principle that could resolve the conflict. This effort not to choose was perhaps the most decisive choice of all, for it was a choice to embarrass the arts, if not reason itself. The arguments of such moderates as Dryden, Saint-Evremond, Dennis, Wotton, and others, were designed to arbitrate between ancient and modern claims by showing that artistic excellence is both indebted and relative to men in time and place. In fact, however, they really undermined the normative tradition by showing the extent to which its aesthetic ideals, supposedly based on universal nature, were actually social in origin. In shifting the discussion of art from its relation to nature to its relationship to men in time, they presented the standard of reason with a special embarrassment, for reason should not have a history like that of societies.[4] The empirical fact of variety in the arts therefore required that if the arts were to be understood rationally at all, it must be through the comparative, critical, historical, and psychological analysis of artistic behavior. These alternatives shaped a new approach to the study of human things; in them "all transcendence," as Cassirer explains, "is precluded from the outset; there can be no logical or metaphysical, only an anthropological, solution."[5] The two major developments in the theory of the arts in eighteenth-century England—the development of literary history and of psychological aesthetics—can thus be understood as rational responses to the challenges posed by relativism. Each of them sought coherent and universal explanations of artistic phenomena in relation to the mind in time, and each of them marked a distinctive difference between the ancient and modern views of man. Thus, while attempting to refute the claims of modern science, the moderates in fact supported the modern scientific analysis of man by insisting on the relativity of nonscientific knowledge, and by subjecting such knowledge to empirical analysis.

3. Joseph Cropsey, Preface to *Ancients and Moderns: Essays on the Tradition of Political Philosophy in Honor of Leo Strauss* (New York: Basic Books, 1964), p. vii.

4. See Cassirer, *The Philosophy of the Enlightenment*, pp. 292–298.

5. Cassirer, *The Philosophy of the Enlightenment*, p. 298.

Ironically, such relativity conflicted with the ideal of nature—however differently defined—upon which the more rigid partisans of both antiquity and modernity based their claims. Notwithstanding their vastly different intentions, both Sir William Temple, a defender of the Ancients, and Charles Pérrault, an advocate for the Moderns, insisted that nature is "still the same . . . toujours la mesme."[6] Though they differed on the methodological means of access to this norm, both assumed the continuity between nature and human endeavor. Moreover, each defended his party on the grounds that the opposite party's knowledge was self-interested, unstable, opinionated, and, in short, merely conventional. "La Poésie est parvenue chez les Modernes à un plus haut dégré de perfection," Pérrault observed, because modern efforts are based on scientific "method," whereas the ancient endeavor relied only "sur l'usage & sur l'éstat des choses de [leur] temps."[7] Temple merely reversed the application of this logic in order to maintain that in contrast to the solid natural foundations of ancient knowledge, modern learning is a "knowledge of the different and contested opinions of men in former ages" and "changes every hundred years."[8] In principle, the real enemy was the specter of conventional relativity, which challenged the claims to reason on both sides.

Dryden had modestly raised this challenge in *The Essay of Dramatic Poesy,* and indeed throughout his work, but always with one eye on the fundamental continuity of art with nature. As another moderate, however, Bernard Fontenelle carried the relativist argument further by suggesting a sharper distinction between art and nature. Though he began, like both Ancients and Moderns, by subscribing to the continuity of nature through time, he quickly turned to a radically Cartesian distinction between knowledge based on universal reason and knowledge tied to a blinded subjectivity. As an instance of the latter, art is imaginative rather than rational, and consequently subject to the historic influences that impinge upon the minds of men. "In every century," Fontenelle declares in *A Digression on the Ancients and the Moderns,* nature "produces men fit to be great but the historical moment does not always let them use their talents. Inundations of barbarians, governments either wholly or generally unfavorable to the

6. Sir William Temple, *An Essay upon the Ancient and Modern Learning,* in *Five Miscellaneous Essays by Sir William Temple,* ed. Samuel Holt Monk (Ann Arbor: University of Michigan Press, 1963), p. 38 (hereafter cited as *Five Essays*); and Charles Pérrault, *Paralèlle des Anciens et des Modernes* (Paris, 1693), I, 402.

7. Pérrault, *Paralèlle des Anciens et des Modernes,* II, 106, 191.

8. Temple, *An Essay upon the Ancient and Modern Learning,* in *Five Essays,* p. 40; and *Some Thoughts upon Reviewing the Essay of Ancient and Modern Learning,* in *Five Essays,* p. 63.

sciences and the arts, prejudices and imaginings which can take end-
lessly different forms . . . often put ignorance and bad taste into the
saddle, and for a long time."[9] Unlike the natural sciences, art is tied to
the "prejudices and imaginings" of human minds, and so is subject to
the forces which shape that mind. "It is obvious," he therefore concludes, "that all the differences, whatever they may be, must be caused
by exterior circumstances, such as the historical moment, the government, and the state of things in general" (p. 360). As a result, the artistic
achievements of different epochs are relative to the different circumstances that prevail in each. Clearly this does not preclude a judgment
of "bad taste," or a preference for modern practice, but it does frankly
acknowledge the social, rather than rational, basis upon which such
judgments rest.

Another skeptical moderate, Charles de Saint-Evremond, substantiated this basis when he argued in "Of the Poems of the Ancients"
that "the differences of Religion, Government, Customs, and Manners,
have introduced so great a change in the world, that we must go, as
it were, upon a new System, to suit with the inclination and genius of
the present age."[10] Saint-Evremond expands upon this rhetorical view
until he makes the much-beleaguered criterion of nature itself a function of changing belief:

> We have other notions of Nature, than the Ancients had.
> The Heavens, that eternal mansion of so many Divinities,
> are nothing else with us, but an immense and fluid space.
> The same Sun shines still upon us; but we assign it another
> course; and instead of hastening to set in the Sea, it goes to
> enlighten another world . . . In short, everything is
> changed, Gods, Nature, Politicks, Manners, Humours, and
> Customs. Now is it not to be supposed, that so many altera-
> tions should not produce a mighty change in our Writings?
> (*Works,* II, 350)

In part, at least, Saint-Evremond understands these "changes" as im-
provements in an absolute sense; with a typically neo-classical note
of self-congratulation, he observes that "we love plain truth; good sense
has gain'd ground upon the illusions of fancy; and nothing satisfies us

9. Bernard Fontenelle, *A Digression on the Ancients and the Moderns* (1688), in
The Continental Model, p. 364.
10. Charles de Saint-Evremond, "Of the Poems of the Ancients," in *The Works
of Monsieur de St. Evremond* (London, 1728), II, 344.

now-a-days, but solid Reason" (II, 344). At the same time, however, this standard is subjected to changing social expectations. While

> there are certain eternal rules, grounded upon good sense, built upon firm and solid Reason, that will always last: yet there are few that bear this Character. Those that relate to . . . Manners, Affairs, and Customs . . . have their certain period and duration. Some die with old age; *ita verborum interit actas:* others perish with their Nation . . . So 'tis plain, there are but very few, that have a right to prevail at all times; and it would be ridiculous to regulate matters wholly new by Laws that are extinct. Poetry would do ill to exact from us, what Religion and Justice do not obtain.
> (II, 351)

Because artistic norms have "changed with things that time hath alter'd" (II, 348), comparisons between Ancients and Moderns must not be made in absolute terms, but should be critically adjusted by "considering the time they liv'd in."[11] Like Fontenelle, Saint-Evremond finds the true character of art, not in its relationship to unchanging natural norms, but in its flexible relationship to the changing "prejudices and imaginings" of the human mind. Man, he says, is "toujours l'homme, mais la nature se varie dans l'homme; et l'Art, qui n'est autre chose qu'une imitation de la nature, se doit varier comme elle."[12]

The effort to avoid a confrontation with antiquity was thus itself a decisive commitment to modernity, for by placing the arts on a conventional basis, it refuted an essential claim that since antiquity had been made on their behalf. The ancient alliance between *episteme* and *techne* was sundered in the interests of modern scientific progress. The new epistemologies developed by latitudinarians and the Royal Society sanctioned this divorce by distinguishing between the certain forms of knowledge and the varieties of opinion in which certainty was relative to circumstance. William Wotton, for example, aligned himself with moderates like Fontenelle and Saint-Evremond when he invoked the new epistemology in order to impose upon the arts and sciences a conceptual distinction between their different sources in convention and nature; the natural sciences, he claimed *in Reflections upon Ancient and Modern Learning,* "are Things which have no De-

11. Saint-Evremond, "Upon Tragedies," in *Works,* II, 156.
12. Saint-Evremond, Letter to Madame la Duchesse de Mazarin, quoted in Quentin M. Hope, *Saint-Evremond: The Honnête Homme as Critic* (Bloomington: Indiana University Press, 1962), p. 61.

pendence on the Opinions of Men for their Truth; they will admit of fixed and undisputed Mediums of Comparison and Judgement: So that, though it may be always debated, who have been the best Orators, or who the best Poets; yet it cannot always be a Matter of Controversie, who have been the greatest Geometers, Arithmeticians, Astronomers, Musicians, Anatomists, Chymists, Botanists, or the like.[13] While the cumulative development of method supports the recent claims of modern science, it fails to apply to the arts, where the "Opinions of Men" provide the rule. Wotton therefore objects that

> Monsieur Perrault takes it for granted, that Cicero was a better Orator than Demosthenes; because, living after him, the World had gone on for above Two Hundred Years, constantly improving, and adding new Observations, necessary to compleat his Art: and so by Consequence, that the Gentlemen of the Academy must out-do Tully, for the same Reasons. This Proposition, which is the Foundation of a great part of his Book, is not very easie to be proved; because Mankind loves Variety in those Things wherein it may be had so much . . . Sometimes the Age will not bear Subjects, upon which an Orator may display his full Force . . . A Thousand Accidents, not discoverable at a distance, may force Men to stretch their Inventions to spoil that Eloquence which, left to it self, would do admirable Things. (pp. 47–48)

At the same time that it refutes Pérrault's scientific absolutism, however, this argument also invalidates the Ancients' appeal to nature. While "some Sciences and Arts, *of a very compounded Nature,* seem really to have been more perfect anciently than they are at present," the "very compounded Nature" of these arts, their intersubjective and temporal character, implies that ancient superiority does not proceed "from a particular force of Genius," but "from the Concurrence of some accidental Circumstances" (Preface; my italics). If such arts have "a fixed foundation in Nature," Wotton asks, "why have we heard of no . . . eminent poets in Peru?" And if they be rationally "attained to by study . . . why not now as well as formerly?" (p. 25).

The answer, Wotton maintains, is that neither nature nor reason outweighs the social character of art, that "compounded Nature" by which it is attached to "the Opinions of Men." Accordingly, the proper assessment of a writer depends upon "a clear Idea of the Way and

13. William Wotton, *Reflections upon Ancient and Modern Learning* (1694), p. 78.

Humour of the Age in which he wrote" (p. 318). In view of their inter-subjective character, the arts should be studied contextually, in order "to see which were proper for their Circumstances, considering what Alterations Time insensibly introduces into the Customs of every Age . . . Mankind raises little, if any thing, any farther than as Customs alter it, from one Age to another" (pp. 13, 16).

By subjecting human acts and products to a changing context, this relativism not only denied the former claims of art; it also subjected them to the critical scrutiny of scientific method. "By reason of the vastly different Circumstances of Times, Places, Persons, Customs, and common received Opinions,"[14] John Dennis explained, the arts could not speak disinterestedly for themselves or for their history. The differences between the Ancients and Moderns, he observes, arise from different historical circumstances, and within the limits "of those different Circumstances, several things which were graceful and decent with them, must seem ridiculous and absurd to us, as several things which wou'd have appear'd highly extravagant to them, must look proper and becoming to us" (*Works*, I, 11). In order to explain these differences in reliably scientific terms, Dennis substitutes for the normative approach an account of art that is at once psychological and historical. Because poetry is distinctively a relationship between art and mind rather than art and nature, its shape is a function of changes in mind through time. In Dennis' view, the greatest psychological effects obtain in a literature that speaks for the power of divinity, and so religious belief exerts the most profound influence in the history of literature. Accordingly, he posits a psychological and historical law to the effect that "in any Age or Country, at whatever Juncture Religion, Language, and Poetical Art, are in greatest force together, at that very Juncture the Poetry of that Country is at its Heighth" (I, 246). In asserting this principle as a universal law, Dennis attempts to transcend historical circumstances in pursuit of absolutes, and thus subjects the arts to scientific scrutiny. For Dennis, as for others, this scrutiny was a necessary corollary to the exhaustion of normative order. In line with the divorce between nature and human practice, and with the correspondingly psychological and nominalistic implications of this divorce, the arts became the inarticulate object of scientific eloquence. Because, as Hobbes had argued, the arts "raise passion from opinion," the proper study of the arts was to be scientifically contextual; as Charles Gildon put it, "there must be a regard had to the Clime, Nature, and Customs of the People; for the Habits of the Mind as well as those of the Body,

14. *The Critical Works of John Dennis,* ed. Edward Niles Hooker (Baltimore: The Johns Hopkins University Press, 1939), I, 60.

are influenc'd by them; and Love and other Passions vary in their Effects as well as Causes, according to each Country and Age.[15]

This appeal to relativism, supposedly designed to compromise between the absolute claims of both Ancients and Moderns, was actually a most decisively modern approach to human things. In defining the modern view of nature as the object of progressive scientific research, the relativists simultaneously denied its relevance to human practice and productions by making a radical distinction between scientific and value-laden norms. As reflections of the changing human mind rather than nature, the latter were ultimately subjected as objects of study to the former. It was therefore not their view of science as such, but its consequences for their view of man that constituted the relativists' greatest threat to the ancient view of things.

This explains why Swift felt less threatened by the new science itself than by the relativism that its redefinition of nature bestowed on human things, and by the correspondingly "critical"—the pedantically philological and contextually historical—study of human practice and productions that this relativism entailed. It is on the modernist grounds of relativism that the mad author of the *Tale of a Tub* pompously proclaims that

> Some things are extremely witty to-day, or fasting, or in this place, or at eight o'clock, or over a bottle, or spoke by Mr. What d'y'call'm, or in a summer's morning: any one of which, by the smallest transposal or misapplication, is utterly annihilate. Thus, wit has its walks and purlieus, out of which it may not stray the breadth of an hair, upon peril of being lost. The moderns have fixed this mercury, and reduced it to the circumstances of time, place, and person. Such a jest there is that will not pass out of Covent-Garden; and such a one, that is nowhere intelligible but at Hyde-Park Corner.[16]

The ephemerality of purely rhetorical wit, responsible only to an always shifting set of circumstances, requires a great proliferation of prefaces, notes, and appendices in order to account for the supposedly vast differences among men; "being extremely solicitous," the author announces,

15. Charles Gildon, "An Essay in Vindication of the Love-Verses of Cowley and Waller, & c.," in *Miscellaneous Letters and Essays* (1694), ed. Arthur Freeman (New York: Garland, 1973), p. 210.

16. Jonathan Swift, *A Tale of a Tub,* in *Gulliver's Travels and Other Writings,* ed. Louis A. Landa (Boston: Houghton Mifflin, 1960), p. 264.

> that every accomplished person who has got into the taste of wit calculated for this present month of August, 1697, should descend to the very bottom of all the sublime throughout this treatise, I hold it fit to lay down this general maxim: whatever reader desires to have a thorough comprehension of an author's thoughts, cannot take a better method, than by putting himself into the circumstances and postures of life, that the writer was in upon every important passage as it flowed from his pen, for this will introduce a parity and strict correspondance of ideas between the reader and the author.   (p. 265)

This absurd parody of the ideal of rhetorical accommodation is integral to Swift's attacks upon the relativism of the modern view. Swift's quarrel with the principles of this view is nowhere more evident than in the fable of the cloaks, in which the rapidly changing fashions of man's outward clothing are made to constitute his essence, so that tailors "daily create men by a kind of manufactory operation" (p. 282). Swift's hatred of inventors and projectors should therefore be understood as an animus not merely toward the new science, but toward the modern view that man defines and invents himself through conventional projections of his changing will.

Indeed, the contemporary semantic shift in the meaning of "invention"—from "finding" to "making"—reflects the basis in principle that divides the ancient and modern views of man, for instead of "finding" his place in the ordered scheme of nature, man "makes" his place as the spider makes his. In satirizing the Lilliputian *Blundrecal* for its maxim "that all true believers shall break their eggs at the *convenient* end,"[17] Swift at once attacks the conceptual root of the modern view and the semantic root of its ennabling principle, convention. Indeed, his choice of the travelogue as the vehicle of parody, with its recitations of "learning, laws, and customs" (p. 45), is part of his satire on modern relativism; the apparent differences among the civilizations encountered by Gulliver are in fact real differences in an absolute sense, so that the Lilliputian disgust with Gulliver, and Gulliver's disgust with the Brobdignagians are a function of their real degree of magnitude and magnanimity. The Lilliputian society, the modern state par excellence in its relativism, is thus measurable by the greater magnanimity of the ancient ideals of Brobdignag.[18] As a puny modern

17. Swift, *Gulliver's Travels,* in Landa, p. 40.
18. See Allan Bloom, "An Outline of Gulliver's Travels," in Cropsey, *Ancients and Moderns,* pp. 242–243.

in the setting of Brobdignag, Gulliver subscribes to relativism, and when accused of lying, he can merely offer the lame excuse that "I had little to say in return, farther than the common answer, that different nations had different customs; for, I confess, I was heartily ashamed" (p. 47).

It is therefore in the light of its implicit relativism that Swift identifies the demon of "criticism" with modernity generally: the hideous philological and historical pedantry of "criticism" is a function of the modern view that convention rules the life of man. As an alternative to the standard of natural continuity, convention had led to changes in the art of historiography and its vision of the past. To the extent that different values prevail at different times, the exemplary uses of the past were increasingly subjected to a "critical" and contextual understanding. Bentley's exposure of Temple's cherished *Epistles of Phalaris* as a fraud, or Wotton's tiresome demands for "critical" philology, were therefore threatening not simply because of their pedantry, but because their pedantry in turn expressed a challenge to the ancient view of normative principles, and to the ancient way of using them.

The Ancients-Moderns debate was thus in part "a dispute over the uses of the past, a quarrel about history."[19] Temple's claims for ancient narrative history, as against Wotton's for the philology of Casaubon and Selden, were not simply conflicting ideals of style, but expressions of different views of man in time. In attacking the ancient narrative historians, Wotton observed that they were admirably eloquent but that they were uncontextual: "all Niceties of Time, and Place, and Person, that might hurt the Flowingness of their Stile, were omitted."[20] In Temple's view, such "vain niceties and captious cavils about words or syllables . . . about antiquated names of persons or places"[21] disrupted not only the flow of style, but the flow of time itself, its continuity with the present, by cutting off its vital normative value and confining it within a limited configuration of circumstances and con-

---

19. Joseph M. Levine, "Ancients, Moderns, and History: The Continuity of English Historical Writing in the Late Seventeenth Century," in *Studies in Change and Revolution: Aspects of English Intellectual History, 1640–1800,* ed. Paul J. Korshin (Menston, Eng.: Scolar Press, 1972), p. 44. Levine rightly points out that the conflicting positions in this quarrel both developed from different points of emphasis in the humanist historical tradition. For further remarks on the philosophical impact of philology, see H. W. Garrod, "Phalaris and Phalarism," in *Seventeenth Century Studies Presented to Sir Herbert Grierson,* ed. J. D. Wilson (Oxford: Clarendon Press, 1938), 360–371.

20. Wotton, *Reflections,* p. 41.

21. Temple, *An Essay upon the Ancient and Modern Learning,* in *Five Essays,* p. 89; cf. p. 62.

ventions. It is precisely upon this disruption that Swift seizes when he repeatedly disrupts his narrative in the *Tale of a Tub* to parody the modern view that there must be "a strict observance after times and fashions." "I have," says his mad critic,

> with much pains and reading, collected out of ancient authors, this short summary of a body of philosophy and divinity, which seems to have been composed by a vein and race of thinking, very different from any other systems, either ancient or modern. And it was not merely to entertain or satisfy the reader's curiosity, but rather to give him light into several circumstances of the following story, that knowing the state of dispositions in an age so much remote, he may the better comprehend those great events which were the issue of them. I advise therefore the courteous reader to peruse with a world of application, again and again, whatever I have written upon this matter. And so leaving these broken ends, I carefully gather up the chief thread of my story and proceed.   (p. 284)

The endless qualifications and digressions required to establish a setting so "very different from any other," do not, however, merely disrupt stylistically the "thread" of narrative; rather they cut the very lifeline of the present to the past, leaving only "broken ends." The flow of narrative is the flow of time itself, the continuity of the present with the past. To limit the relevance of the past to a configuration of outmoded conventions, "tailored" only to obsolete conditions, is to imitate Peter, Martin, and Jack, who "critically" unravel their inheritance and lose sight of their ends. The decisive threat of modernity is not simply stylistic, but philosophic.

It was their recognition of this threat in the guise of moderation that moved Swift and Temple to such fury. The substitution of convention for nature as the ruling force in human activity was in principle more hideous than the specter of modern natural science itself, for it reasserted the Sophistic claim that man is the measure of all things. "His own reason," Temple scoffs,

> is the certain measure of truth, his own knowledge of what is possible in nature; though his mind and thoughts change every seven years . . . nay, though his opinions change every week or every day, yet he is sure, or at least confident, that his present thoughts and conclusions are just and true,

and cannot be deceived: and, among all the miseries to which mankind is born and subjected to the whole course of his life, he has this one felicity to comfort and support him, that in all ages, in all things, every man is always in the right.[22]

Though neither Wotton, Dennis, nor Gildon subscribed to such egotistical individualism, their use of the concept of convention effectively ruled out normative uniformity in the lives of men. In their apparently moderate approach to rectitude, Swift saw a new form of tyranny, the tyranny of fashion. In his radical modernity, based not upon his scientific outlook, but upon his relativism, Swift's mad critic lays claim to "that great and honourable priviledge of being the last writer. I claim an absolute authority in right, as the freshest modern, which gives me a despotic power over all authors before me" (p. 310).

Swift's vision of tyranny proved prophetic of the later phases of the debate. The pretended moderation of Wotton, Dennis, Gildon, and the other Moderns had not only shown that artistic norms change with time, but had also implied the need to readapt such norms to the present. Frequently, however, the distinction between social and natural norms originally implicit in the argument disappeared, and prevailing values came to be identified as the best values, resulting in a "new absolutism."[23] Thus Gildon in his later years composed a rigidly prescriptive work called the *Laws of Poetry* (1721), and Dennis, in *The Grounds of Criticism* (1704) and later works, came to insist increasingly on the natural and innate superiority of modern rules. The modern argument for adaptation, originally intended to combat a strictly progressivist view of the arts, therefore sometimes returned, often arm-in-arm with the Cartesian mathematicism it once had banished, to assert the superiority of the Moderns.[24] Richard Blackmore, for example, pleaded on behalf of his abortive epics by observing that he had written works "such as might bear a Conformity to the Taste of the present Times, and to the Customs, Manners, and establish'd Religion of the Author's Country." Despite his claim to offer a "Mediation" to the Ancients-Moderns dispute, however, Blackmore's view

22. Temple, *Some Thoughts upon Reviewing the Essay of Ancient and Modern Learning*, in *Five Essays*, p. 96; cf. pp. 61–62.

23. Emerson R. Marks, *Relativist and Absolutist: The Early Neoclassical Debate in England* (New Brunswick: Rutgers University Press, 1955), pp. 100–101.

24. See Bate, *The Burden of the Past*, p. 38; Emerson R. Marks, *The Poetics of Reason: English Neoclassical Criticism* (New York: Random House, 1968), p. 44; and John Butt, *The Augustan Age* (New York: Norton, 1966), p. 45.

of adaptation very thinly disguised his real aim "to improve the Art of Poetry."[25]

While such rigidly normative visions of progress and perfection as Blackmore's persisted occasionally throughout the century, however, they did so on the basis of a freedom implicit in the modernist view that art, as a reflection of the public mind, must adapt to its times. Over the objections of Swift, the relativism of the modernist view increasingly prevailed in the development of historical and psychological criticism, both of which were intent upon explaining art in terms of its relationship, not to nature, but to its audience. The concept of convention played a central role in both methods by calling attention to the historical function of social habits and expectations in shaping art, and to the psychological means by which art itself exploits them.

Thomas Blackwell's *Enquiry into the Life and Writers of Homer* (1735) was a decisive playing out of these new roles. Not only did Blackwell's understanding of convention dominate his historical outlook, but it informed his view of the convention-ridden present with a romantic longing for the alien, antique, and primitive. In his search for Homer's greatness, Blackwell turned not to the formal qualities of epic genre, but to the conventions and institutions that "make us what we are . . . a change in any one of them makes an alteration upon us, and taken together we must consider them as the molds that form us into those habits and dispositions which sway our conduct and distinguish our actions."[26] Chief among these influences, he explains, are "The State of a Country where a Person is born and bred; in which I include the common Manners of the Inhabitants, their Constitution civil and religious, with its Causes and Consequences: Their Manners are seen in the Ordinary way of living, as it happens to be polite or barbarous, luxurious or simple. Next, the Manners of the Times, or the prevalent Humours and Passions in vogue: these two are Publick, and have a common effect on the whole generation" (p. 12).

These social influences, Blackwell argues, impinged on Homer's imitation of "nature," for "he took his plain natural Images from Life: he saw Warriors, and Shepherds, and Peasants, such as he drew; and was daily conversant among such People as he intended to represent" (p. 34). Thus although Homer imitates "nature," this is not the ideal

---

25. Richard Blackmore, "An Appendix," in *Essays upon Several Subjects* (1716; rpt., New York: Garland, 1971), pp. 156, 161.

26. Thomas Blackwell, *An Enquiry into the Life and Writings of Homer* (London, 1735), p. 11.

nature of philosophic principle but a function of prevailing social circumstance; Homer's imitation is not a *mimesis praxeos,* but a *speculum consuetudinis,* or, as Dryden had called it, a "lively image of human nature." The empirical character of representation arises as a rhetorical necessity, for in the oral "Situation a Poet wou'd find himself oblig'd, not only to study the Passions of his Hearers while he recited; to observe their Features, watch every Motion of their Eye and Turn of Thought; but to look around him when alone, and lay up store of such Images, as Experience told him wou'd have the strongest Effect" (p. 121).

Thus because of "the Power that Manners, and the Publick Character have over Poetry" (p. 73), Homer's achievement is in part the product of his time. In Blackwell's view, Homer inhabited a civilization midway between the savage and heroic world he describes and the more evolved civilization of the city-states, and was thus able to combine the ideals of each. Not only does Homer's place in time account for his combination of heroic individualism with highly civilized ideals, but in his time "the Greek Language . . . retained a sufficient Quantity of its Original, amazing, metaphorick Tincture" (p. 43). Moreover, Homer's vision of the gods reflects the prevailing beliefs of his time, for "the firm Belief of any Sect makes Men speak and write in the approved Idiom: They introduce it into their Business, allude to it in their Pleasures, and abstain from it in no Part of Life; especially while the Doctrine flourishes, and it appears in Bloom" (p. 52).

But though Homer's poem, like any other, is the product of its time, Blackwell adheres to a hierarchy of values in which the primitive and unaffected, the least convention-ridden, societies are best because they produce the best poems. Homer's is "a Representation of natural and simple Manners: It is irresistable and inchanting; they best show human Wants and Feelings; they give up back the Emotions of an artless Mind" (p. 24). Thus, while the civil virtues of "Peace, Harmony, and good Order" are socially desirable because they "make the happiness of a People," they are at the same time "the Bane of a Poem that subsists by Wonder and Surprize" (p. 27). There is, in other words, in Blackwell's view, an inverse relationship between the state of civilization and the state of poetry: "While a Nation continues simple and sincere, whatever they say has a weight from Truth: Their Sentiments are strong and honest; which always produce fit Words to express them: Their Passions are sound and genuine, not adulterated or disguised, and break out in their own artless Phrase and unaffected Stile" (p. 55). Because civilization is not, in the Aristotelian sense, a fulfillment of nature, but in fact the arbitrary construction of a conventional edifice out of human will, Blackwell laments that in the present highly

conventionalized state of civilization, "we may never be a proper Subject of an Heroic Poem" (p. 28). "State and Form," he complains, "disguise a Man; and Wealth and Luxury disguise Nature . . . and great
Ceremony is at least equally tiresome in a Poem, as in ordinary Conversation" (pp. 24–25). Thus although Blackwell extends the contextual
approach developed in the Ancients-Moderns debate, and argues that
Homer's poem reflects "the Nature of the Times he liv'd in," his primitivism leads to sympathetic endorsement of those times in opposition
to the convention-ridden present.

At the same time, however, Blackwell admits that "the Power of
publick Manners" over art is well-nigh inescapable. Because "nature,"
even in Homeric times, is a function of convention, it is impossible
successfully to imitate the works of one civilization in the context of
another (p. 32). The reason, he explains, is that

> we seem not to be able to master two Sets of Manners, or
> comprehend with facility different ways of Life. Our Com-
> pany, Education, and Circumstances make deep Impressions,
> and form us into a Character, of which we can hardly divest
> ourselves afterwards. The Manners not only of the Age in
> which we live, but of our City and Family stick closely to
> us, and betray us at every turn . . . These we understand,
> and can paint to Perfection; and there is no one so undis-
> cerning as not to see, that we have wonderfully succeeded in
> describing those Parts of modern Life we have undertaken.
> Was there ever a more natural Picture than *The Way of the
> World?* Or can anything in its kind surpass *The Rape of
> the Lock?* The Authors, doubtless, perfectly knew the Life
> and Manners they were painting, and have succeeded ac-
> cordingly. (pp. 33–34)

As the mirror of convention, the *speculum consuetudinis*, the "natural Picture" of poetry is the "painting" of "Life and Manners," and
therefore bears the marks of its time. Even though contemporary art
admirably reflects the social conventions of its milieu, Blackwell's
primitivism takes him in search of the one form of "nature" still available to men—the external nature of the phenomenal world. Thus he
observes in a reference to Thomson's *Seasons* that "the entertaining
Prospects, or rare Productions of a Country . . . *That* is a Subject
still remaining to us if we will quit our Towns, and look upon it: We
find it accordingly, nobly executed by many of the Moderns, and
the most illustrious Instance of it, within these few Years, doing Honour to the British Poetry" (p. 35). It is difficult to assess the many in-

fluences that may have led Blackwell toward this confidence in the powers of external and sentimental nature to rejuvenate poetry, but it is in part a direct outcome of the growing prominence of the concept of convention. This new "nature" is not the intellectual principle that had since antiquity governed the normative approach to human practice and production, to ethics, politics, law, and art. Indeed, it seems to be an alternative to the encroachment upon and exhaustion of this principle by convention. Having been gradually displaced by the arbitrary and shifting sway of convention in the uniform, collective, and normative lives of men, the universal principle of nature reappears in the communion of the individual with nature's phenomenal works. Blackwell clearly envisions this new "nature" as such an alternative, as an escape from the social prison-house when, for the first time in the history of English criticism, he uses not only the concept, but the term "convention" in a sense that borders between the social and the literary. "A Convention of Men of Spirit and Understanding," he observes, "who have the Business of a City or State to manage . . . will naturally produce Speakers and Eloquence," but "the same Men, if they quit their Town and look abroad, will speak of the Objects presented to them by Nature's Face" (pp. 36–37).

As an alternative to the tyranny of "Convention," this individualistic communion with "Nature's Face" stands, along with Blackwell's historical approach, as a decisive anticipation of modernity, and its opposition of the individual to collective order. Blackwell's *Enquiry,* written some thirteen years before Montesquieu's *Esprit des lois* (1748) and before Rousseau had published at all, contributed to Romanticism not only through its influence upon the later Scottish primitivists,[27] but also upon Herder,[28] and through him, upon European Romanticism as a whole. At the same time, Blackwell's view "that every kind of Writing, but especially the Poetick, depends upon the Manners of the Age when it is produced" (pp. 68–69), embodied the historical approach that had come to militate against the normative tradition. Thus, for example, Thomas Warton similarly argued that

27. See, e.g., Hugh Blair, *A Critical Dissertation on the Poems of Ossian* (1763), in Scott Elledge, *Eighteenth-Century Critical Essays* (Ithaca: Cornell University Press, 1961), II, 848; Donald M. Foerster, *Homer in English Criticism: The Historical Approach in the Eighteenth Century* (1947; rpt., Hamden, Conn.: Archon Books, 1969), ch. 4; and Lois Whitney, "English Primitivistic Theories of Epic Origins," *MP*, 21 (1924), 339.

28. See, e.g., Herder's *Reflections on the Philosophy of the History of Mankind,* ed. Frank E. Manuel (Chicago: University of Chicago Press, 1968), p. 175; see also George M. Miller, *The Historical Point of View in English Criticism, 1570–1770* (Heidelberg: C. Winter, 1913): and Foerster, pp. 108–110.

it is absurd to think of judging either Ariosto or Spenser by precepts they did not attend to. We who live in the days of writing by rule are apt to try every composition by those laws which we have been taught to think the sole criterion of excellence . . . In reading the works of a poet who lived in a remote age, it is necessary that we should look back upon the customs and manners which prevailed in that age. We should endeavour to place ourselves in the writer's situation and circumstances.[29]

Blackwell's anticipations of the future, however, were in part a function of his obligations to the past, and especially to the growing prominence of the concept of convention as an alternative to the abiding intellectual standard of nature. Blackwell stood at a crossroads, looking forward in the direction of Wordsworth's Preface, to *The Lyrical Ballads*. But whatever forces beckoned from the future, it was by routes laid out in the course of Renaissance and Enlightenment thought about convention that Blackwell came to the epochal crossroads.

In Blackwell's *Enquiry*, as in the eighteenth century generally, the route of historicism lay parallel to the route of empirical psychology. Hobbes, Dryden, and others, as seen earlier, had developed the theory of rhetorical effects in such a way as to interpret the relation between art and nature as a dynamic function of its relation to the human mind in time. This interpretation was reinforced by the Ancients-Moderns debate, and by the newer epistemologies, which distinguished between the arts and scientific knowledge, and thus subjected the arts to a scientific scrutiny of their historical provenance and their psychological origins in mind. Joseph Addison's distinction in *The Spectator*, 416, between the "primary" and "secondary" imagination, one of the earliest psychological theories in England, was a product of just this divorce between nature and mind in the arts. The "primary" pleasures obtain in the mind's direct contemplation of nature; they differ from the "secondary" pleasures that arise "from that Action of the Mind which compares the Ideas arising from the Original Objects with the Ideas we receive from the Statue, Picture, Description, or Sound that represents them."[30] Though Addison attempts to identify with the "secon-

---

29. Thomas Warton, *Observations on the Faerie Queene* (1754), in Elledge, II, 771–772.

30. Joseph Addison, *The Spectator*, 416, ed. Gregory Smith (1907; rpt., New York: Everyman's Library, 1973), III, 291–292. Subsequent references in the text are to this edition.

dary" pleasures those universal qualities of "beauty," "novelty," and "greatness" that obtain in the mind's "primary" contemplation of nature, the subjective basis of the "secondary" pleasures in "the Action of the Mind" allows that even "the Description of a Dunghill is pleasing to the Imagination, if the Image be represented in our Minds by suitable Expressions" (III, 297).

With the demand for *"suitable* Expressions," however, Addison's psychological theory returns him to the pervasive question of decorum and its equivocal status. It raises the crucial issue of diversity in taste, "how comes it to pass that several Readers, who are all acquainted with the same Language, and know the Meaning of the Words they read, should nevertheless have a different relish of the same Descriptions" (III, 293). "This different Taste," he concludes, "must either proceed from the Perfection of Imagination in one more than in another, or from the *different Ideas* that several Readers affix to the same Words" (III, 293).

Though in his series *The Pleasures of Imagination* Addison never specifically addressed the question of what causes different readers to "affix" different Ideas to the same words, in a later *Spectator* (447), Addison mentioned "Custom" as a possible cause due to its "wonderful Efficacy in making every thing pleasant to us" (III, 378). "The Mind," he says, "grows fond of those actions she is accustomed to, and is drawn with Reluctancy from those Paths in which she has been used to walk" (III, 379).

Addison here drew upon John Locke's psychological theory of the association of ideas, added to the fourth edition (1700) of the *Essay Concerning Human Understanding.*[31] Locke explained that some of our ideas "have a *natural* correspondance and connexion one with another: it is the office and excellency of our reason to trace these, and hold them together in that union and correspondance which is founded in their peculiar beings." At the same time, however, there is "another connexion of ideas owing wholly to *chance* or *custom.*"[32] Not only does the customary association of ideas often dominate the "habits of thinking in the understanding," but it virtually constitutes the world of value: "to this, perhaps, might be justly attributed most of the sympathies and antipathies observable in men, which work as strongly, and produce as regular effects as if they were natural; and are therefore called so, though they at first had no other original but the accidental connexion of two ideas, which either the strength of the first impres-

---

31. See Bate, *From Classic to Romantic,* p. 98.

32. John Locke, *An Essay Concerning Human Understanding,* ed. Alexander Campbell Fraser (1894; rpt., New York: Dover Publications, 1959), 2.33.5.

sion, or future indulgence so united, that they always afterwards keep company together in that man's mind" (2.33.7). Such customary associations prevail not only in the lives of individuals, but in the lives of societies as they shape the individual: "That which thus captivates their reasons, and leads men of sincerity blindfold from common sense, will, when examined, be found to be . . . some independent ideas, of no alliance to one another . . . by education, custom, and the constant din of their party, so coupled in their mind that they always appear there together; and they can no more separate them in their thought than if they were but one idea, and they operate as if they were so" (2.32.18).

Thus the association of ideas provides a psychological explanation for the differences of opinion and conventional norms in societies. Locke's theory follows the general distinction in seventeenth-century epistemology between rational certainty and conventional projections of will. For Addison, as for Locke, the association of ideas accounts only for irrational and arbitrary departures from the rational connection of ideas, which is not properly association at all. In the course of the eighteenth century, however, the association of ideas was expanded to include not simply customary connections of ideas, but their rational connection in terms of the "real affinity" of cause and effect, or resemblance.[33] Although such rational associations continued to be distinguished from merely customary ones, both the empirical character of the theory itself, as well as its continuing account of customary associations, led increasingly to the notion that the standard of "nature" in art is a function of habits formed by association in the mind.[34]

This notion did not go unopposed. Shaftesbury's combination of Platonic idealism and psychological intuitionism, for example, was designed to reassert the uniform criterion of nature in the face of the diversity seemingly supported by the empirical association of ideas. "Things are stubborn," he declared in *Characteristics,* "and will not be as we fancy them or as the fashion varies, but as they stand in Nature."[35] Significantly, however, this reassertion of nature is not so much addressed to normative conflict as to the subsequent epistemological debate that this conflict created. Shaftesbury's naturalism, in other words, is not simply a normative opposition to convention; it is an epistemologically rationalist attack upon empiricism. Nature is not

33. See, e.g., David Hume, *A Treatise of Human Nature,* ed. L. A. Selby-Brigge (Oxford: Clarendon Press, 1964), I, iv.

34. See Martin Kallich, *The Association of Ideas and Critical Theory in Eighteenth-Century England* (The Hague: Mouton, 1970), pp. 46–50.

35. Shaftesbury, *Characteristics,* ed. John M. Robertson (1900; rpt., Gloucester, Mass.: Peter Smith, 1963), I, 228.

a collective legal order, but a Platonic correspondence between the individual mind and the ideal "which fashions even minds themselves, contains in itself all the beauties fashioned by those minds, and is consequently the principal source and fountain of all beauty" (II, 133). Accordingly, Shaftesbury opposes the empirical view of rhetorical judgment on intensely individualistic rather than logocentric grounds: "one would expect it of our writers that if they had real ability they should draw the world to them, and not meanly suit themselves to the world in its weak state" (I, 171–172).

As developed from Shaftesbury's theory of innate sense, the individualistic ideals of sensibility and intuition became a vital critical alternative, but always in a dialectical tension with the theory of convention implied by the empirical association of ideas. Shaftesbury's disciple Hutcheson, for example, argued from a theory of aesthetic intuition that "custom could never have made us imagine any beauty in objects." Nevertheless, he found himself confronted by the empirical diversity of taste, and was forced to turn to Locke for an explanation; "the association of ideas," he observed, "is one great cause of the apparent diversity of fancies in the sense of beauty, as well as in the external senses, and often makes men have an aversion to objects of beauty and a liking to others void of it."[36]

Because of its ability to account for the seeming diversity of taste, the theory of association gained increasing prominence through the century, and lent an increasingly sociological interpretation to the psychological relationship between art and its audience. "The doctrine of association," one anonymous writer explained, "enables us to account for order, beauty, parental affection, love of virtue, and the like, without presupposing . . . a certain innate moral sense as necessary to solve the principal actions of human life." "National virtues and vices" as well as the "contrary sentiments and perceptions of them in different ages and countries," he went on to say, differ "according as men's associations have been different . . . To this is owing almost that infinite variety of tastes so observable in the world . . . Which contrariety of opinion is a demonstrative proof that beauty is nothing positive and independent, but wholly arbitrary and relative to our perceiving faculty; which faculty likewise is *of our own creating*.[37]

The customary basis of the association of ideas thus supported the

---

36. Francis Hutcheson, *An Enquiry into the Original of our Ideas of Beauty and Virtue*, in Elledge, II, 374, 371.

37. *An Enquiry into the Origin of Human Appetites and Affections*, in *Metaphysical Tracts by English Philosophers of the Eighteenth Century*, ed. Samuel Parr (London: Edward Lumley, 1837), pp. 114, 86, 117.

increasingly current redefinition of man as his own creator and as the inhabitant of a world of his own making. This redefinition required a further shift in critical focus from the relation between art and nature to the relation between art and mind. As David Hume explained in his essay *Of the Standard of Taste* (1757):

> a thousand different sentiments, excited by the same object, are all right; because no sentiment represents what is really in the object. It only marks a certain conformity or relation between the object and the organs or faculties of the mind; and if that conformity did not really exist, the sentiment could never possibly have being. Beauty is no quality in things themselves: it exists merely in the mind which contemplates them; and each mind perceives a different beauty.[38]

This does not mean that there can be no true standards of beauty; indeed, Hume says, "some particular forms or qualities, from the original structure of the internal fabric are calculated to please, and others to displease" (p. 9). But because these "forms or qualities" are a function of mind rather than philosophic principles, they can be neither "fixed by reasonings *a priori*, or . . . esteemed abstract conclusions of the understanding, from comparing those habitudes and relations of ideas, which are eternal and immutable. Their foundation is the same with that of all the practical sciences, experience" (p. 7). This experiential basis shifts Hume's attention to "the relation of the spectator to the work of art."[39] In order to arrive at the proper empirical judgment, the spectator must himself be capable of a range and intensity of emotional response; he must, says Hume, possess "a perfect serenity of mind, a recollection of thought, a due attention to the object; if any of these circumstances be wanting, our experiment will be unable to judge" (p. 8). This empirical responsiveness further requires a freedom from the customary "prejudice" that makes us "more pleased . . . with pictures and characters that resemble objects which are found in our own age and country, than with those which describe a different set of customs" (p. 20). Any work of art, Hume explains,

---

38. David Hume, *Of the Standard of Taste and Other Essays*, ed. John W. Lenz (New York: Bobbs-Merrill, 1965), p. 6.

39. Ralph Cohen, "David Hume's Experimental Method and the Theory of Taste," *ELH*, 25 (1958), 274.

in order to produce its due effect on the mind, must be surveyed from a certain point of view, and cannot be relished by persons whose situation, real or imaginary, is not conformable to that which is required by the performance. An orator addresses himself to a particular audience, and must have a regard to their particular genius, interests, opinions, passions, and prejudices . . . A critic of a different age or nation, who should peruse this discourse, must have this circumstance in his eye, and must place himself in the same situation as the audience, in order to form a true judgement of the oration.   (p. 15)

This divestiture of customary habit enhances not only the empirical experience of particulars, but the experience of generality as well. We "ascertain" the relation between "the form and the sentiment," Hume points out, "from the durable admiration which attends those works which have survived all the caprices of mode and fallacy, all the mistakes of envy" (p. 9). Like the test of individual experience, however, this test of generality is established by the relationship between the mind and art; it establishes standards retrospectively and empirically. It is nothing but a "general observation, concerning what has been universally found to please and in all ages" (p. 7).

In the later eighteenth century, the commonplace appeal to "general nature" was essentially an empirical test of fitness, and thus conceded an irreducible social element in art. Samuel Johnson, for example, sought to "distinguish nature from custom, or that which is established because it is right, from that which is right only because it is established"; and accordingly, he insisted on the difference between "transient fashions or temporary opinions," and the lasting truths of "general nature."[40] Nevertheless, this "general nature" was to be determined by neither reason nor intuition, but by the empirical test of long and widespread appeal: "to works not raised upon principles demonstrative and scientifick, but appealing wholly to observation and experience, no other test can be applied than length of duration and continuance of esteem."[41]

This empirical quest for the most general and common values was the only solution David Hartley could find to counteract the prevalence of conventional prejudice:

40. Samuel Johnson, *The Rambler*, 156, ed. W. J. Bate, *The Yale Edition of the Works of Samuel Johnson* (New Haven: Yale University Press, 1968), V, 70; and *Preface to Shakespeare,* ed. Arthur Sherbo, in *The Yale Edition,* VII, 62.

41. Johnson, *Preface to Shakespeare,* in *Works,* VII, 59–60.

as the various Figures used in Speaking and Writing have
great Influences over each other, alter, and are much altered,
as to their Relative Energy, by our Passions, Customs, Opinions, Education, & c. there can be no fixed Standard for
determining what is Beauty here, or what is the Degree of it
. . . Yet, since Mankind have a general Resemblence to each
other, both in their internal Make, and external circumstances, there will be some general Agreements about these
Things common to all Mankind. The Agreement will also
become perpetually greater, as the Persons under Consideration are supposed to agree more in their Genius, Studies,
external Circumstances, etc. Hence may be seen, in part,
the Foundations of the general Agreements observable in
Critics.[42]

The test of general nature is thus a function of its social durability.
Nature is always immediate in the works of man, and appears only in
those common and lasting qualities they share. Beauty is the most
general form of nature, Sir Joshua Reynolds observed, because it is
the most common: "so that though habit and custom cannot be said
to be the cause of beauty, it is certainly the cause of our liking it; and
I have no doubt that if we were more used to deformity than beauty,
deformity would then lose the idea annexed to it, and take that of
beauty—as if the whole world should agree that *yes* and *no* should
change their meaning: *yes* would then deny, and *no* would affirm."
This power of habit, Reynolds observes, accounts for the diversity of
taste: "custom makes, in a certain sense, white black, and black white
. . . It is almost absurd to say that Beauty is possessed of attractive
powers which irresistably seize the corresponding mind with love and
admiration, since that argument is equally conclusive in favour of
the white and the black philosophers."[43] In order for a man to determine "how far we are influenced by custom and habit, and what is
fixed in the nature of things,"[44] Reynolds observes, "he must divest
himself of all prejudices in favour of his age or country; he must disregard all local and temporary ornaments, and look only on *those general habits* which are everywhere and always the same." Nature is
available only in the mediate form of "habits," and critical discrimina-

42. David Hartley, *Observations on Man* (1749), ed. Theodore L. Huguelet
(Gainesville, Fla.: Scholar's Facsimiles and Reprints, 1966), I, 430.

43. Sir Joshua Reynolds, *The Idler*, 82, in Elledge, II, 835–836.

44. Reynolds, *Discourse Seven*, in *Discourses on Art*, ed. Robert J. Wark (New
York: Collier Books, 1966), p. 120.

tion involves "separating modern fashions from the habits of nature."[45] This task, in turn, is rendered difficult by the "slender means of determining, to which of the different customs of different ages or countries we ought to give the preference, since they seem to be all equally removed from nature." In seeking a solution to this dilemma, Reynolds turns to the empirical test of generality, to those associations and practices most common in the lives of men: "We are creatures of prejudice; we neither can nor ought to eradicate it; we must only regulate it by reason; which kind of regulation is indeed little more than obliging the lesser, the local and temporary prejudices, to give way to those which are more durable and lasting."[46]

"Here," said William Blake, "is a great deal to Prove that All Truth is Prejudice." Though the sources, motives, ideals, and instruments of Romantic thought have a vast and complex history of their own, one point contributing to its self-definition was its opposition to the prevailing notion that nature was mediated or circumscribed by social norms. As Blake complained, "the Enquiry in England is not whether a Man has Talents & Genius, but whether he is Passive & Polite & a Virtuous Ass & obedient to Noblemen's Opinions in Art & Science."[47] Blackwell's use of the concept of convention to establish historical context had created in his mind a primitivistic longing for a state of nature free of the baneful influence of convention. Similarly, Shaftesbury and Hutcheson had turned to the innate and individual powers of imagination as an alternative to the tyranny of custom and association over the mind of man. In his Preface to the *Lyrical Ballads,* Wordsworth combined these primitivistic and psychological alternatives in order to arrive at a concept of nature unmediated by convention and based not upon the *consensus gentium,* but upon the individual *ingenium.* While this new ideal of nature derived its own positive and characteristic impetus from a number of influences, both classical and modern, as well as from the unique desires and insights of the Romantic poets themselves, it was in part defined by its opposition to the concept of convention, by its power, as Coleridge put it, of "awakening the mind's attention from the lethargy of custom."[48]

In Wordsworth's view, both the choice of primitive subjects and the "colouring of imagination"—the two eighteenth-century alternatives to the tyranny of convention—were designed to produce "a class of

45. Reynolds, *Discourse Three,* p. 49.

46. Reynolds, *Discourse Seven,* pp. 122, 124.

47. William Blake, *Annotations to Sir Joshua Reynold's Discourses,* in *Complete Writings,* ed. Geoffrey Keynes (London: Oxford University Press, 1966), pp. 475, 453.

48. Coleridge, *Biographia Literaria,* ed. John Shawcross (1907; rpt., Oxford: Oxford University Press, 1962), II, 6.

Poetry . . . well adapted to interest mankind permanently."[49] Words-worth's conscious effort to achieve this end, "in spite of difference of soil and climate, of language and manners, of laws and customs" (p. 81), was clearly informed, however, by an understanding of the ways in which convention prevents such universality by interposing different norms between men and nature. Accordingly, his analysis of the present state of literature in the Preface to the *Lyrical Ballads* used the two characteristically modern methods—historical and psychological—that had developed in the eighteenth century as responses to the displacement and near exhaustion of nature by convention. "To give a full account of the present state of public taste in this country," Wordsworth explains, could not be accomplished "without pointing out, in what manner language and the human mind act and re-act on each other, and without retracing the revolutions, not of literature alone, but likewise of society itself" (p. 70). It is in the light of these interanimations between language and mind, literature and society, that Wordsworth finds himself restricted by history, tradition, and social expectations:

> It is to be supposed, that by the act of writing in verse an Author makes a formal engagement that he will gratify certain known habits of association; that he not only thus apprizes the Reader that certain classes of ideas and expressions will be found in his book, but that others will be carefully excluded. This exponent or symbol held forth by metrical language must in different eras of literature have excited very different expectations: for example, in the age of Catullus, Terence and Lucretius, and that of Statius or Claudian; and in our own country, in the age of Donne and Cowley, or Dryden, or Pope. I will not take upon me to determine the exact import of the promise which by the act of writing in verse an Author, in the present day, makes to his Reader; but I am certain, it will appear to many persons that I have not fulfilled the terms of an engagement thus voluntarily contracted. (p. 70)

Wordsworth's breach of contract involved not only his abandonment of such conventions as personification or poetic diction, but also his efforts in principle to achieve a vision of nature unmediated by convention, in which "the passions of men are incorporated with the

49. Wordsworth, Preface to *Lyrical Ballads*, in *Wordsworth's Literary Criticism*, ed. W. J. B. Owen (London: Routledge and Kegan Paul, 1974), p. 69.

beautiful and permanent forms of nature" (p. 71). Among the many motives for this breach of contract must be counted the conspicuous exhaustion of nature by the concept of convention and the consequent alienation of the individual from collective order. Wordsworth's was an inward and upward reaching for new absolutes in the face of a tradition that had all but turned its back upon them.

Index

Acron, Helenius, 49, 180, 193
Addison, Joseph, 338–339, 340
Adiaphora, 86–90, 257
Aenisidemus, 42
Agricola, Rudolf, 142
Agrippa, Cornelius, 119–120, 123, 128, 129, 131
Alain de Lille, 54, 140n
Allegory, 167–172, 175
Ancients and Moderns debate, 297–308, 321–334, 336
Anglican Church. See Church of England
Aquinas, Saint Thomas, 59–60, 91, 93, 110, 169, 246–247
Ariosto, Ludovico, 196–197
Aristotle: on art, 31–34, 36; on habit, 31; on prudence, 31–32; the universal in, 32, 35, 49; on *mimesis*, 33–34, 37, 46, 178–179; on plot, 34–35, 46; on probability, 35; on fitness, 36, 46. Works: *Ethics*, 31–32; *Physics*, 32; *Metaphysics*, 32–33; *Poetics*, 33–36, 153, 179–180
Art: ancient definitions of, 9, 26–30, 31–34; Renaissance definitions of, 15–19. See also Technical tradition
Arts, classification of. See Classification of arts
Ascham, Roger: on art, 20; on imitation, 22–23; on genres, 148–150; on rhyme, 150–151; on literary history, 154; on history, 210. Works: *The Scolemaster*, 148–154; *Toxophilus*, 62–64, 69
Assent (as test of truth), 242, 243–244, 247, 249–252. See also Consent, Individualism

Association of ideas, 339–344. See also Empiricism and psychology
Atkins, J. W. H., 264–265
Atomism, 41–42
Augustine, Saint: *Confessions*, 54; *De Ordine*, 55; *De Doctrina Christiana*, 55; *The City of God*, 75, 77–79; *De Libero Arbitrio*, 168

Bacon, Sir Francis, 134–136, 170–171, 208, 214–215, 226, 237–238, 244–246
Baldwin, William, 110, 111
Bate, W. J., 265–268
Bede, Saint, 169
Bentley, Richard, 331
Blackmore, Richard, 333–334
Blackwell, Thomas, 4, 334–338
Blake, William, 345
Blundeville, Thomas, 215, 229
Boccaccio, Giovanni, 60, 169, 206
Bodin, Jean, 214, 224, 228, 234–235, 239
Boemus, Johann, 224, 234
Boethius, 54, 142
Boileau, Nicolas, 268
Bolton, Edmund, 210
Bonaventure, Saint, 168
Book of Common Prayer, 87
Bracton, Henry de, 99
Brady, Nathaniel, 221, 232, 236
Braithwaite, Richard, 206–207
Browne, Sir Thomas, 168, 257
Bruni, Leonardo, 62
Bryskett, Lodowick, 110, 111, 112

Calvin, John, 75, 78–79
Camden, William, 222–223, 236–237
Campion, Thomas, 199
Carew, Richard, 222
Carneades, 42

Cartwright, Thomas, 195
Casaubon, Isaac, 316, 331
Casaubon, Meric, 224, 237–238
Cassiodorus Senator, 55–56, 57
Cassirer, Ernst, 265–268, 323
Castelvetro, Lodovico, 20–21
Castiglione, Baldassare, 22, 113–116,
    177, 188
Caxton, William, 206, 211
Ceremony, religious, 74–75, 87–88, 90,
    256–258
Chapelain, Jean, 269, 274
Chapman, George, 170
Charleton, Walter, 288–290
Charron, Pierre, 208–209
Chaucer, Geoffrey, 157, 171
Chillingworth, William, 243, 248–250
Church of England: political character
    of, 80, 89–90, 243, 257; establishment
    of, 86; and Elizabethan Settlement,
    87–89, 257; defense of, 89–90; in
    Restoration, 258–261
Cicero, 39, 49, 91; and fitness, 44–45.
    Works: Orator, 40, 44, 45, 46, 61, 205;
    Brutus, 40; De Oratore, 40, 44, 45, 46,
    62–64, 205; De Legibus, 52, 76–77,
    205; De Republica, 76–77, 168; De
    Officiis, 112–113; Topics, 142; Tus-
    culan Disputations, 247
Cinthio, Giraldi, 196–197
Clarendon, Earl of. See Hyde, Edward
Classicism, 10, 13, 264–268, 275–276, 277,
    288–289
Classification of arts, 55, 107, 139–141,
    205–206 (see also Encyclopedic
    tradition)
Coke, Sir Edward, 218, 220
Coleridge, Samuel Taylor, 4, 6, 9, 345
Colet, John, 72–74, 82, 236
Commonplaces. See Logic
Commonwealth, 105–106; see also Law
    and society
Community, Christian, 75, 77–79, 84–
    85; see also Primitive constitution
Concord, 82, 84–86
Consensus, 12–13, 81, 85, 96, 104–106,
    252, 254–255, 260–261; see also Con-
    sent, Epistemology
Consent (as test of truth), 242, 243–
    246, 248–249, 252; see also Consensus,
    Epistemology

Convenience, 11, 116, 157, 165, 190, 255
Convention, Mode of, 42, 120; see also
    Sextus Empiricus
Convention Parliament, 260
Cooper, Anthony Ashley, Third Earl
    of Shaftesbury, 267, 340–341
Corneille, Pierre, 269, 275
Cornwallis, William, 134–135
Coterie, critical significance of, 170–173
Courtesy, literature of, 112–118, 177
Cox, Leonard, 142, 143
Crane, R. S., 4–5, 265n, 267
Cranmer, Thomas, 71, 216
Croce, Benedetto, 4, 6
Cudworth, Ralph, 250–251, 252, 253,
    255, 261
Culverwell, Nathaniel, 248, 250, 252
Cynicism, 76–77

Dacier, André, 316
Daniel, Book of, 131
Daniel, Samuel, 122, 129, 203. Works:
    A Defense of Rhyme: experience in,
    21; style in, 64–65; rhyme in, 199–202;
    literary tradition in, 200–202; plural-
    ism in, 201; Musophilus, 127–128; A
    Collection of the History of England,
    225, 229–230, 232–233; The Civil
    Wars, 228, 230
Dante, 62, 155
D'Aubignac. See Hédelin, François
Davenant, William, 276–277, 286–287
Davies, Sir John, 217
Day, Angel, 144
De Baïf, Antoine, 172
Decorum: in behavior, 112–114, 118,
    157 (see also Courtesy, literature of);
    literary, 137–139, 142, 145, 148, 157,
    176, 180; bienséances in French
    classicism, 272–275. See also Fitness
Della Casa, Giovanni, 115–116
Dennis, John, 239, 323, 328, 333
Descartes, René, 8, 13, 241, 251, 253,
    265–269, 271, 277; Passions of the
    Soul, 277–281, 285
Dodderidge, Sir John, 218
Donne, John, 189–190, 193; Biathanatos,
    123, 125; Metempsychosis, 123; Satyre
    III, 125–126; Sermons, 126
Drayton, Michael, 222, 237, 238

Dryden, John, 13, 239; probabilism of, 263, 297–298, 309; on passion, 280; critical stance of, 289–297, 308–309; on *mimesis*, 295, 303, 305–307, 310–313; skepticism of, 297–298; on tradition, 306–307, 319–320; on translation, 314–315; on history, 315–321. Works: *Essay of Dramatic Poesy*, 299–308, 310, 321–323, 324; *Heads of an Answer to Rymer*, 309–312; *Grounds of Criticism in Tragedy*, 309, 312–314; *MacFlecknoe*, 315; *Absalom and Achitophel*, 315; *Discourse Concerning . . . Satire*, 316–319, 320; *Preface to Fables*, 319

Du Bellay, Guillaume, 154, 155–156
Dugdale, Sir William, 221, 236
Du Vair, Guillaume, 134–135
Dyer, Sir Edward, 173

Ecclesiastes, Book of, 121, 154
Elizabethan Settlement. *See* Church of England
Elyot, Sir Thomas, 208
Empiricism: Renaissance emphasis on, 20–22, 124–125, 126; in Enlightenment, 242, 253, 264–268; in French classicism, 275; and psychology, 277–290 passim; and historiography, 323–326, 328–329, 337
Encyclopedic tradition, 55–57, 59
Epistemology, 12, 241–274 passim, 277–290 passim; prominence of in seventeenth century, 241–243; and latitude, 248, 253–255; and Royal Society, 261–264; and Enlightenment, 264; and classicism, 264–290 passim
Erasmus, Desiderius, 23, 88–89; on concord, 82–83. Works: *Paraclesis*, 73–74; *Enchiridion*, 74–75; *Colloquies*, 112; *De Ratione Studii*, 207, 212; *Ciceronianus*, 236
Ethos, 46; and *mimesis*, 48–49, 191–193, 274, 303–307, 310–313, 334–335 (*see also Mimesis*, Plot)
Euripides, 51

Fideism, 119–122, 123, 133
Figures, stylistic, 145, 157, 163–164
Fisher, John, 83–84

Fitness: ancient definitions of, 29, 36–39, 44–46; in *Utopia*, 138–139. *See also* Decorum
Fletcher, John, 223–224
Fontenelle, Bernard, 324–325, 326
Fortescue, Sir John, 101–103, 104
Foxe, John, 71, 216–217
Fracastoro, Girolamo, 145
Fraunce, Abraham, 148

Gascoigne, George, 141, 164
Genius, 12, 17, 345
Genre: classification of, 148–150, 153, 163, 184–186; disputes over, 196–199
Geoffrey of Vinsauf, 58, 59
Gildon, Charles, 328–329, 333
Glanvill, Joseph, 261–263
Goodman, Godfrey, 228–229
Greville, Fulke, 120–121, 123, 126, 128, 129, 131
Greville, Robert, 241
Grimald, Nicolas, 137–138
Grotius, Hugo, 252
Guarini, Battista, 198
Guazzo, Stephano, 114–117
Guicciardini, Francesco, 208, 210–211, 212, 226, 234

Habit, 31, 59–60, 110–111, 155
Hakewill, George, 228–229, 240
Hale, Sir Matthew, 218, 220, 231–232, 240
Hales, John, 207
Hall, Joseph, 171
Hanzo, Thomas, 244
Harington, Sir John, 170, 183, 196–197
Hartley, David, 343–344
Harvey, Gabriel, 23, 133, 164, 166, 170, 173–175
Hawes, Stephen, 140, 143
Hayward, John, 224–225
Hédelin, François, Abbé d'Aubignac, 269, 270–271, 274, 279–281
Heinsius, Daniel, 206, 316
Henry VIII, 80–84
Heraclitus, 24–25
Herbert, Edward, Lord of Cherbury, 143, 241, 246–248, 250
Herder, Johann Gottfried von, 337
Herodotus, 26
Heron, Haly, 115, 119

Heylyn, Peter, 211–212, 238

Historicism, 5–6, 204, 322

Historiography, 12; and literary tradition, 50–53, 186, 316–321; relation to rhetoric, 52–54, 205; classification of among the arts, 205–206, 209; exemplary, 205–207; "politic," 208–214, 226; and causality, 209–213; and providence, 210, 227; ecclesiastical, 216–217 (*see also* Primitive constitution); legal, 217–222; antiquarian, 222–223; skepticism in, 224–226, 230–231; periodization in, 226–231, 237–238; narration and context in, 232–233, 331–332; of institutions, 233–235; and geography, 233–235, 238–239; and philology, 233, 236–238, 331; and Ancients-Moderns debate, 331–333

Hobbes, Thomas, 13, 218, 241, 253, 264, 266–267, 328. Works: *Thucydides*, 209, 233; *Answer to Davenant*, 276–277, 287; *De Homine*, 282–285; *Leviathan*, 283–287; *Elements of Law*, 283–286

Hoby, Sir Thomas, 156

Hooker, Richard, 90–99, 102–107, 132–133, 186, 220, 243

Horace, 175, 179–180, 182, 190–193, 274, 292n; *Epistle to Augustus*, 51; *Ars Poetica*: view of art in, 37, 46; view of decorum in, 37–39, 46, 50, 53; *mimesis* in, 37; usage in, 38, 49; view of literary tradition in, 49–50; history of poetry in, 50–53

Hoskins, John, 16, 64–65, 148, 168

Howard, Robert, 288–289, 301

Hugo of St. Victor, 56, 57–58, 140; Victorine School, 168

Humanism, Renaissance: rhetoric and philosophy in, 62, 203; and Scripture, 72–74, 236; ethics in, 108–113, 203–204; and education, 109–110, 155; and historiography, 205–207

Hume, David, 342–343

Hutcheson, Francis, 341

Hyde, Edward, Earl of Clarendon, 225, 258

Imitation (of models), 23, 149, 155, 164–165

Individualism: and originality, 3, 8–9; and latitude, 12–13, 242–244, 250–251, 253, 259–260; and technical tradition, 264–268, 271

Intersubjectivity, definition of, 2, 3, 5

Invention, 141–144

Isidore of Seville, 57

Isocrates, 40

Jansenism, 272–273

Javitch, Daniel, 112–113

Jerome, Saint, 54

Jewel, John, 71–72, 88

John of Garland, 58, 59

John of Salisbury, 56, 58, 140

Johnson, Robert, 114, 116–117, 208, 226

Johnson, Samuel, 290, 343

Jonson, Ben: definition of art, 16–20; on experience, 21, 191; and classification of arts, 107, 141, 195; on rhetoric and poetry, 140–141; critical stance of, 189–191, 194–195, 293; view of decorum, 190–191; use of Horace, 191–192; on comedy and manners, 192–193; on usage, 193; view of ancients, 194–195

Lambarde, William, 232

Latimer, Hugh, 86

Latitudinarians, 12–13, 243–264 passim, 309, 326

Laud, William, 243

Law: common law, 85, 96–104, 175, 187, 201, 260–261 (*see also* Historiography, legal); and society, 94–96, 102, 104–105; positive law, 95, 103–104; canon law, 99; *mos gallicus*, 219. See also Natural law

Le Bossu, René, 268, 271, 274–275, 279

Le Caron, Louis, 169

Le Roy, Louis, 130–132, 133, 228

L'Estrange, Sir Roger, 258

Lever, Ralph, 140, 151, 152

Lewin, William, 20

Liberal arts, 55–56

Lipsius, Justus, 134

Locke, John, 241, 258–259, 260, 339–340

Lodge, Thomas, 166–167

Logic: in medieval *artes*, 55, 140; and rhetoric, 140–143; commonplaces in, 142–144, 146–147, 150–158 passim,

175, 180; and poetics, 143; and history, 204–206

Logocentrism, 8, 16, 242

Lovejoy, A. O., 204

Lucian, 43–44, 52

Luther, Martin, 75, 78–79, 80–83

Lydgate, John, 206

Lyly, John, 198–199

Machiavelli, Niccolò, 208, 211, 212, 214, 226

Macrobius, 168–169

Maggi, Vicenzo, 153, 179

Malherbe, François de, 269

Marcus Aurelius, 76

Marston, John, 171

Martianus Capella, 57

Masters, Samuel, 260–261

Matthew of Vendôme, 59

May, Thomas, 229

Melancthon, Philip, 87

Mésnadière, Hippolyte-Jules de la, 269, 270n

Method, 23, 242, 270–277, 324

Milton, John, 135, 239, 242

Mimesis, 33–34, 36–37, 46, 152, 178–180, 274–275, 295–296. *See also* Probability, Verisimilitude

Minturno, Antonio Sebastiano, 18

Mirror for Magistrates, A, 206, 207–208

Montaigne, Michel de, 122–125, 126, 128, 129, 142, 189, 271, 291

Montesquieu, Charles Louis de Secondat de, 239, 337

More, Henry, 250, 251–252, 254, 256

More, Saint Thomas: *Responsio ad Lutherum,* 83–86; *Dialogue Concerning Heresies,* 85; *Utopia,* 108–110, 113, 133, 138–139

Mulcaster, Richard, 20, 67–69, 111

Music and poetry, 171–175

Mutability, 119–122, 123, 129–131

Natural law: and Plato, 27–28, 30; and Stoicism, 75–77, 252; and Roman law, 76–77, 97–99, (*see also* Roman law); influence on Christianity, 77–78; in Hooker, 91–95, 97; and common law, 100–102; in Donne, 123

Neo-Stoicism. *See* Stoicism

New Custom (moral interlude) , 70

Nicole, Pierre, 273

Norden, John, 121, 123, 128, 131

Norm, definition of, 2, 69, 138

Old Testament, 24

Orpheus, 46–47, 166–167, 171, 175

Parker, Matthew, 88, 217

Parker, Samuel, 258

Parmenides, 24–26, 29

Pascal, Blaise, 271–273

Pastoral, 118

Paterculus, Velleius, 229, 319n

Paul, Saint, 78, 82, 88

Peacham, Henry, 146

Pérrault, Charles, 324, 327

Petrarch, Francesco, 62, 150, 164, 206, 227

Philodemus of Gadara, 41, 43, 44, 46

Pico Della Mirandola, Giovanni, 161

Plato, 11, 40; on art, 27–30; on poetry, 28; on rhetoric, 29–30; view of fitness, 29; ethical bias of, 30. Works: *Cratylus,* 26; *Republic,* 26–27; *Statesman,* 27; *Laws,* 27–28; *Ion,* 28–29; *Phaedrus,* 29; *Gorgias,* 29–30

Platonism, Cambridge, 243, 249–264 passim. *See also* Cooper, Anthony Ashley

Pléiade, the, 169, 172

Plentitude, concept of, 128, 130, 228

Plot, 35–36, 46, 311–313. *See also* Ethos, *Mimesis*

Pluralism, 23; moral, 26, 115–116, 122–123; artistic, 45–46, 64–65, 183, 187–188, 201. *See also* Latitudinarians

Pocock, J. G. A., 217

Polybius, 235–236

Pope, Alexander, 3, 268

Popelinière, Launcelot Voisin, Sieur de la, 234

Port-Royal, logic of, 263, 273

Pragmatism, ethical, 30, 108–114

Presumptive reasoning, 11, 99, 102, 256, 294

Primaudaye, Pierre de la, 110, 111

Primitive constitution, 70, 71, 78–80, 87, 89, 216–217. *See also* Scripture

Probabilism: and latitude, 256–258, 259; and science, 262–264; in Dryden, 297–298, 309

Probability, 35, 162, 179, 274–275, 295–296. *See also* Verisimilitude
Prosody, 171–175, 187. *See also* Rhyme, Vernacular
Protagoras, 26
Providence, 84–86, 90, 210, 227
Prudence, 19, 31–32, 45, 92–94, 110–111, 208–210. *See also* Habit, Pragmatism, Presumptive reasoning
Psychology. *See* Empiricism
Puritans, 88–89, 91, 243, 256, 259–260
Puttenham, George, 15, 176, 316; definition of art, 15–21; view of decorum, 145, 175–176, 181–183; on linguistic usage, 157, 181–182; view of allegory, 168–169; on importance of experience, 177–178, 186–187; critical pluralism of, 183, 187–188; view of tradition, 183–184, 187–188; view of genre, 184–186; practice of literary history, 184–188
Pyrrho the Skeptic, 41–42, 43. *See also* Skepticism

Quintilian, 37, 45–46, 48, 141

Rainolde, Richard, 144–145
Raleigh, Sir Walter, 170
Ramus, Peter, 23
Rapin, René, 270–271, 274–275, 279
Rastell, John, 216
Rationalism, 242, 253, 264–268, 275, 277–290 passim, 333, 340–341
Reynolds, Sir Joshua, 344–345
Rhetoric: ancient sources and tradition, 11, 36, 39–41, 51–52, 54, 61; and functions of poetry, 46–48, 52–53, 156; and history, 52–54, 205; and philosophy in Renaissance humanism, 62, 203; and behavior, 112–114 (*see also* Courtesy, literature); and logic, 140–143; and poetics, 140, 142–144, 156, 176; and French classicism, 270–273; and passions, 276–277, 279–281, 286; and practical criticism, 291–293
Rhyme, 22, 150, 199–202, 307–308
Richard of Bury, 60–61
Ridley, Nicholas, 87–88
Robortello, Francesco, 180
Roman law, 76–77, 219
Rousseau, Jean Jacques, 337

Royal Society, 261–264, 297n, 326
Rust, George, 241–242
Rymer, Thomas, 269, 309–310

Saint-Evremond, Charles de, 323, 325–326
St. Germain, Christopher, 100–101, 102
Salutati, Coluccio, 206
Sanderson, Robert, 263
Satire, 171, 316–319
Scripture: purity of, 72, 74; humanist study of, 72–74, 82, 236; *sola scriptura*, 78, 81–82, 86–87
Sébillet, Thomas, 141
Selden, John, 195, 233–235, 236–237, 331
Seneca, 77, 97
Sextus Empiricus, 42–43, 53, 120
Shaftesbury, Third Earl of. *See* Cooper, Anthony Ashley
Shakespeare, William, 16, 18, 118
Shelley, Percy Bysshe, 9
Sherry, Richard, 145
Sidney, Sir Philip: definition of art, 20, 36, 156–160, 175–176, 183; on poesy vs. poetry, 158; on *mimesis*, 158, 161–162; Platonism of, 160–162; Aristotelianism of, 161–162; on probability, 162; on genres, 163; on style, 163–164, 176; on imitation of models, 164–165; view of tradition, 165; and sense of coterie, 165–174 passim; view of allegory, 167; on prosody, 171–174; view of history, 206
Skepticism, 11, 42–43, 203; of New Academy, 40, 43, 263, 298n; Pyrrhonian, 40, 43, 119, 297n (*see also* Pyrrho); Renaissance revival of, 119–120, 122–126; of Royal Society, 261–264, 297n
Smith, John, 250, 257
Smith, Sir Thomas, 105
Sophism, 11, 25–28, 40–42, 53, 203
Sovereignty, political, 96, 103–105
Speed, John, 223–224
Spelman, Sir Henry, 219–220, 221, 236
Spelman, John, 230–231
Spencer, Thomas, 263
Spenser, Edmund, 128, 133, 165–166, 170, 173, 193, 228. Works: *Faerie Queene*, 129, 132; *Two Cantos of Mutabilitie*, 129–130, 132, 242; *Shep-*

heardes Calendar, 171; *View of the State of Ireland,* 237
Sprat, Thomas, 261
Stanyhurst, Richard, 170, 174
Starkey, Thomas, 97–99, 102
Stillingfleet, Edward, 257–259, 260, 261
Stoicism: and rhetoric, 41, 61; natural law in, 75–77, 91, 108–109, 134, 252; Neo-Stoicism, 134–136, 244, 246, 261; test of truth in, 246–247, 251
Stow, John, 222
Structuralism, 6–8
Suarez, Francisco, 252
Swift, Jonathan, 322, 334; *A Tale of a Tub,* 329–330, 332; *Gulliver's Travels,* 330–331

Tacitus, 53–54
Tasso, Torquato, 19–20
Tayler, Edward, 15, 18
Taylor, Jeremy, 241, 255–257, 259, 263
Technical tradition: definition of, 9–10, 15; medieval consolidation of, 54–55; Renaissance definition of, 69–70, 189; impact of historiography on, 239–242; and relation to epistemology, 243–245; and Enlightenment, 264–268, 323, 326
Temple, Sir William, 239, 324, 331–333
Theophrastus, 41, 44
Tillotson, John, 248, 258–259, 261
Tradition: literary, 49–53, 165, 168–175, 184–187, 200–202, 306–307, 316–321, 346; apostolic, 81, 84; legal, 98–104; cultural, 128, 131–132

Usage, linguistic, 38, 48, 156–157. *See also* Vernacular
Ussher, James, 257

Valla, Lorenzo, 62, 236
Vergerio, Paolo, 206
Vergil, Polydore, 212
Verisimilitude, 179–180, 196–199, 274–275, 295–296, 308. *See also* Probability
Vernacular, 150, 154–157, 174–175, 187. *See also* Rhyme, Usage
Vettori, Pietro, 179
Vienne, Philibert de, 117–118
Vives, Juan Luis, 111–112, 207
Vossius, Gerard, 263

Wallis, John, 241
Walton, Izaak, 98
Warton, Thomas, 337–338
Webbe, Joseph, 155, 157
Webbe, William, 21, 173, 174
Wellek, René, 186, 200
Wheare, Degory, 215, 233, 234
Whetstone, George, 143
Whichcote, Benjamin, 252–254, 255, 256
Whitgift, John, 89–90
Whittinton, Robert, 155n, 227
Wilkins, John, 261–263
Wilson, Thomas: *The Arte of Rhetorique,* 16, 21–22, 142, 150, 156–157; *The Rule of Reason,* 146–148, 152
Wordsworth, William, 338, 345–347
Wotton, William, 323, 326–328, 331, 333